Beyond the Color Line

Beyond the Color Line

New Perspectives on Race and Ethnicity in America

Edited by

Abigail Thernstrom *and* Stephan Thernstrom

HOOVER INSTITUTION PRESS
Stanford University   Stanford, California

MANHATTAN INSTITUTE
New York, New York

The Hoover Institution on War, Revolution and Peace,
founded at Stanford University in 1919 by Herbert Hoover,
who went on to become the thirty-first president of
the United States, is an interdisciplinary research center
for advanced study on domestic and international affairs.
The views expressed in its publications are entirely those of
the authors and do not necessarily reflect the views of the staff,
officers, or Board of Overseers of the Hoover Institution.

www.hoover.org

The Manhattan Institute for Policy Research is a think tank
whose mission is to develop and disseminate new ideas that
foster greater economic choice and individual responsibility.

www.manhattan-institute.org

Hoover Institution Press Publication No. 479

First printing, 2002
07   06   05   04   03   02   01   9   8   7   6   5   4   3   2   1

Manufactured in the United States of America
The paper used in this publication meets the minimum requirements
of American National Standard for Information Sciences—Permanence
of Paper for Printed Library Materials, ANSI Z39.48-1984. ⊗

Library of Congress Cataloging-in-Publication Data
Beyond the color line : new perspectives on race and ethnicity in America /
edited by Abigail Thernstrom and Stephan Thernstrom.
      p.   cm.
   Includes bibliographical references and index.
   ISBN 0-8179-9872-1 (alk. paper)
   1. United States—Race relations.   2. United States—Ethnic relations.
3. Minorities—United States—Social conditions.   4. Minorities—Government policy—
United States.   I. Thernstrom, Abigail M., 1936–   II. Thernstrom, Stephan.
E184.A1 B495   2002
305.8'00973—dc21   00-063481

Contents

Foreword

Projects with multiple authors scattered across the country are often arduous and unfulfilling. To the contrary, this project was neither.

There is a reason we engaged in this effort; we wanted to put together, into one volume, the best work being conducted by the highest-quality scholars addressing race and ethnicity issues facing the citizens of the United States. The opportunity for our two institutions to collaborate with experts in the area of race and ethnic relations to produce this book was one we could not pass on; the results proved to be rewarding.

The exemplary work of the twenty-five scholars and writers that constitute *Beyond the Color Line* has made this volume comprehensive and influential. We thank each of them for their time, patience, and outstanding scholarship. In addition, we are especially grateful to the editors, Abigail and Stephan Thernstrom, for their dedication in undertaking and completing this project.

Based on accumulated knowledge, intellectual rigor, reasoned argument, and sound principles, the Hoover Institution and the Manhattan

Institute are dedicated to producing and disseminating sound research with public policy implications.

JOHN RAISIAN   LAWRENCE J. MONE
Director   *President*
Hoover Institution   *Manhattan Institute*

Contributors

DAVID J. ARMOR is a research professor at the Institute of Public Policy, George Mason University. Formerly he was Senior Social Scientist at the Rand Corporation and Associate Professor of Sociology at Harvard University. He is the author of *Forced Justice: School Desegregation and the Law*, and he has testified as an expert in more than thirty school desegregation cases.

MICHAEL BARONE is a columnist at *U.S. News & World Report*. The author of *Our Country: The Shaping of America from Roosevelt to Reagan* (Free Press, 1992), Mr. Barone regularly appears as an analyst and commentator on various television and radio news shows. He is a graduate of Harvard College and Yale Law School.

DOUGLAS J. BESHAROV is a resident scholar at the American Enterprise Institute and director of the AEI's Social and Individual Responsibility Project. He is also a professor at the University of Maryland School of Public Affairs. He is the author of the forthcoming *America's Families: Trends, Explanations and Choices*, and of many other books and articles that have appeared in major magazines and newspapers across the country. Andrew West was a research assistant at AEI.

CLINT BOLICK serves as vice president and director of litigation at the Institute for Justice, which he co-founded in 1991 to engage in constitutional litigation protecting individual liberty and challenging the regulatory welfare state. He leads the nationwide litigation effort to defend school choice programs and to challenge regulatory barriers to entrepreneurship. The *New York Times* described Mr. Bolick as "the maestro of the political right on issues of race . . . increasingly setting the tone and defining the terms of the national debate."

DAVID BRADY is a senior fellow at the Hoover Institution. He is also Bowen H. and Janice Arthur McCoy Professor of Political Science and Leadership Values in the Stanford Graduate School of Business and associate dean and professor of political science in the School of the Humanities and Sciences at Stanford University. His recent publications include *Revolving Gridlock: Politics and Policy from Carter to Clinton* (Westview Press, 1998).

LINDA CHAVEZ is president of the Center for Equal Opportunity, a Washington, D.C.–based think tank devoted to the promotion of color-blind equal opportunity and racial harmony. She has held a number of political positions, among them White House Director of Public Liaison and director of the U.S. Commission on Civil Rights. She is the author of *Out of the Barrio: Toward a New Politics of Hispanic Assimilation* (Basic Books, 1992) and is currently working on her second book.

WILLIAM A. V. CLARK is a professor of geography at the University of California, Los Angeles. His research is focused on the internal changes in U.S. cities, especially in the changes that occur in response to residential mobility and migration. He is author of *The California Cauldron: Immigration and the Fortunes of Local Communities* (Guilford Press, 1998) and *Households and Housing: Choice and Outcomes in the Housing Market* (Rutgers, 1996).

WARD CONNERLY is chairman of the American Civil Rights Institute, a national not-for-profit organization aimed at educating the public about the problems created by racial and gender preferences. A member of the University of California Board of Regents, Mr. Connerly spearheaded the successful fight to end the University's use of race as a factor in admissions. He has since led campaigns against racial preferences in Florida and Texas.

JOHN J. DIIULIO JR. is a senior fellow at the Manhattan Institute. He directs the Jeremiah Project, an initiative of the Manhattan Institute's Center for Civic Innovation. He is also Frederick Fox Leadership Professor at the University of Pennsylvania and senior counsel to Public/Private Ventures.

TAMAR JACOBY is a senior fellow at the Manhattan Institute, who writes extensively on race issues and other subjects. She is the author of *Someone Else's House: America's Unfinished Struggle for Integration* (Free Press, 1998), a book about race relations in three American cities—New York, Atlanta, and Detroit. Ms. Jacoby's articles and book reviews have been published in a variety of periodicals, including the *New York Times*, the *Wall Street Journal*, *Los Angeles Times*, *Washington Post*, the *New Republic*, *New York Review of Books*, *Commentary*, *Dissent*, *City Journal*, and *Times Literary Supplement*.

EVERETT C. LADD, who died in 1999, was director of the Institute for Social Inquiry at the University of Connecticut and executive director and president of the Roper Center for Public Opinion Research. He was also an adjunct scholar of the American Enterprise Institute, as well as a columnist for the *Christian Science Monitor* from 1987 through 1995. Dr. Ladd was the author of seventeen books, most recently *The Ladd Report on Civic America* (Free Press, 1999).

GEORGE R. LA NOUE is a professor of political science in the Policy Sciences Graduate Program at the Univeristy of Maryland Baltimore County. He is also director of the Project on Civil Rights and Public Contracts at the University. Dr. La Noue's Ph.D. was granted by Yale University.

WILLIAM J. LAWRENCE is publisher of the *Native American Press/Ojibwe News,* an independent weekly newspaper that serves Minnesota's Native American community. In 1997, *Press/ON* was nominated for a Pulitzer Prize for editorial writing and service to the community. The April 1999 issue of *Minnesota Monthly* featured an article about Mr. Lawrence entitled "The Man Tribal Leaders Love to Hate." Dr. Lawrence holds a B.A. from Bemidji State University and a J.D. from the University of North Dakota School of Law. He was a commissioned officer in the U.S. Marine Corps serving in Vietnam, and he is an enrolled member of the Red Lake Band of Chippewa Indians.

NELSON LUND is a professor at the School of Law, George Mason University. Before joining the faculty in 1992, he was associate counsel to President George Bush. Mr. Lund has served in the Office of Legal Counsel and the Office of the Solicitor General of the U.S. Department of Justice and as a law clerk to Justice Sandra Day O'Connor and to U.S Court of Appeals Judge Patrick E. Higginbotham.

CHRISTINE H. ROSSELL is a professor of political science at Boston University. Ms. Rossell is the author of four books and many scholarly articles in the areas of school desegregation and bilingual education policy. She has been an expert witness in more than twenty school desegregation and bilingual education cases and has helped design and defend more than a half dozen voluntary "incentive" desegregation plans.

SALLY SATEL is a practicing psychiatrist and lecturer at Yale University School of Medicine. She is staff psychiatrist at the Oasis Clinic in Washington, D.C. In addition to publishing widely in medical journals and the popular press, Dr. Satel is the author of *PCMD: How Political Correctness Is Corrupting Medicine* (Basic Books, 2000).

THOMAS SOWELL is the Rose and Milton Friedman Senior Fellow on Public Policy at the Hoover Institution. He is the author of a nationally syndicated column that appears in over 150 newspapers. Dr. Sowell has written widely on economics, the history of ideas, and social policy. His most recent book is *The Quest for Cosmic Justice* (Free Press, 1999).

SHELBY STEELE is a research fellow at the Hoover Institution. Mr. Steele's most recent book is *A Dream Deferred: The Second Betrayal of Black Freedom in America* (Harper Collins, 1998). He is also author of *The Content of Our Character: A New Vision of Race in America* (HarperCollins, 1990), which won the National Book Critics Circle Award in 1990.

ABIGAIL THERNSTROM is a senior fellow at the Manhattan Institute and coauthor of *America in Black and White: One Nation, Indivisible* (Simon & Schuster, 1997). Her previous book, *Whose Votes Count: Affirmative Action and Minority Voting Rights* (Harvard University Press, 1987), won four academic prizes. She has been a member of the Massachusetts State Board of Education since 1995 and writes frequently for a variety of journals and newspapers, including *New Republic, Commentary,* the *Wall Street Journal,* the *New York Times,* and *Public Interest.*

STEPHAN THERNSTROM is a senior fellow at the Manhattan Institute and Winthrop Professor of History at Harvard University, where he teaches American social history. His most recent book, coauthored with Abigail Thernstrom, is *America in Black and White: One Nation Indivisible* (Simon & Schuster, 1997). He is also the editor of the *Harvard Encyclopedia of American Ethnic Groups* (Harvard University Press, 1980).

MARTIN TROW is emeritus professor at the Goldman School of Public Policy, University of California, Berkeley. He holds a degree as a mechanical engineer from Stevens Institute of Technology and a doctorate in sociology from Columbia University. He has written widely on the sociology of politics and higher education. He is a foreign member of the Royal Swedish Academy of Sciences and was recently awarded the Berkeley Citation for distinguised service to the University of California.

REED UEDA is a professor of history at Tufts University and on the steering group of the Committee on Migration at the Center for International

Studies of MIT. He is author of *Postwar Immigrant America: A Social History* (Bedford Books of St. Martin's Press, 1994), among other books and articles. Dr. Ueda was also research editor for *Harvard Encyclopedia of American Ethnic Groups* (Harvard University Press, 1980).

EUGENE VOLOKH is a professor at the University of California, Los Angeles, School of Law. Before he joined the faculty at UCLA, he clerked for Justice Sandra Day O'Connor and for U.S. Court of Appeals Judge Alex Kozinski. Mr. Volokh teaches free speech law, copyright law, the law of government and religion, and a seminar on firearms regulation law and policy.

FINIS WELCH is a professor of economics and George T. and Gladys H. Abell Professor of Liberal Arts at Texas A&M University. His specialty is in labor economics, on which he has written many articles and papers. Dr. Welch did his doctoral research at the University of Chicago.

JAMES Q. WILSON taught political science at Harvard University from 1961 to 1987, where he was the Shattuck Professor of Government. From 1985 until 1997 he was the James Collins Professor of Management and Public Policy at UCLA. He is the author or coauthor of fourteen books, the most recent of which is *Moral Judgment* (Basic Books, 1997). In addition, he has edited or contributed to books on urban problems, government regulation of business, and the prevention of delinquency among children.

C. ROBERT ZELNICK, a professor of journalism at Boston University, spent twenty-one years with ABC News, including reporting assignments in Moscow and Israel, at the Pentagon, and covering Congress and politics. A former Hoover Institution visiting fellow, he is the author of *Gore: A Political Life* (National Book Network, 1999) and *Backfire: A Reporter's Look at Affirmative Action* (Regnery, 1996).

Introduction

THE AMERICAN RACIAL and ethnic landscape has been fundamentally transformed in recent decades. But public understanding has lagged behind new realities. Our gaze is often fixed on the rearview mirror, and even that view is distorted. A color line seems to bifurcate the nation. Blacks appear as permanent victims; white racism looks ubiquitous. Asian and Hispanic Americans, who together now outnumber blacks, are but a shadowy presence hovering in the background. Their experience as "people of color" is portrayed as little different from that of African Americans.

White racism, of course, was ubiquitous not that long ago. And it has not entirely disappeared. But the past is not the present. We have been moving forward. Much of the territory that now surrounds us is unfamiliar, and yet old notions persist. The ethnic and racial categories themselves—white, black, Asian, and Hispanic—never made much sense and are, in any case, dissolving. Half of native-born Asian Americans are now marrying whites. A third of all Hispanics marry non-Hispanic whites. The black intermarriage rate is slowly creeping up. A generation ago blacks had much less education and much poorer jobs and were much more likely to live in solidly black neighborhoods than they are today. Differences persist, but they now have multiple and complex causes.

America's changing racial and ethnic scene is the central theme of this volume. In essays on topics ranging from religion and immigration to family structure and crime, the authors seek to illuminate where we have been, where we are, and where we are heading. They share a common vision: the color line transcended. One nation, indivisible is still America's unrealized dream.

The Color-Blind Vision

Pessimism is strikingly pervasive in civil rights circles today. In the heyday of the civil rights movement, by contrast, those who fought for racial equality were optimists, and that optimism seemed vindicated by events. With the passage of the Civil Rights Act of 1964 and the Voting Rights Act a year later, the civil rights movement achieved its main political objectives. As Bayard Rustin, a close adviser to the Reverend Martin Luther King Jr., noted at the time, the "legal foundations of racism in America" had been "destroyed" with dizzying speed. The "elaborate legal structure of segregation and discrimination" had "virtually collapsed."[1] Most Americans—not just those directly involved in the movement—celebrated.

Indeed, the 1964 election returns were a smashing victory for civil rights proponents. Barry Goldwater, the Republican candidate for president who opposed the Civil Rights Act, was resoundingly rejected. Democrats gained an additional thirty-seven seats in the House and one more in the Senate, giving them majorities of more than two-thirds in both chambers. It was a partisan imbalance the like of which has not been seen since.

It is no coincidence that in 1965 the United States also abandoned the discriminatory national origins quotas that had governed its immigration law since the 1920s. The notion that only citizens from countries like Great Britain or Germany would make good Americans lost popular support in the increasingly tolerant and cosmopolitan America of the postwar period.

Congress amended the Immigration and Nationality Act to open the doors to prospective immigrants from all countries on an equal basis.

Immigration reform and the two landmark civil rights bills—the most important since Reconstruction—all rested on a central moral principle: it is wrong to judge Americans on the basis of race, color, creed, sex, or national origin. People are individuals with equal rights, not fungible members of groups. The Constitution is "color-blind," John Marshall Harlan had declared in his famous dissent in *Plessy v. Ferguson*, the 1896 Supreme Court decision that upheld "separate but equal" railroad accommodations.[2] It was the message of the civil rights movement from before the Civil War to the 1960s.[3] Dr. King dreamed of the day when Americans would be judged solely by the "content of their character," not by "the color of their skin."[4] President John F. Kennedy invoked this core principle in supporting the passage of a sweeping civil rights bill that would demonstrate the nation's commitment to "the proposition that race has no place in American life or law."[5]

The Reversion to Color-Consciousness

The clarity of this moral vision was lost, however, in the turbulent and chaotic years of the late 1960s. In 1965 President Lyndon B. Johnson took the first step in a radically different direction. "You do not take a person who, for years, has been hobbled by chains and liberate him, bring him up to the starting line in a race and then say, 'you are free to compete with all the others,'" Johnson argued. Opening "the gates of opportunity" would not suffice; racial "equality as a fact and as a result" had to be the nation's goal.[6] Although Johnson did not use the term "affirmative action," his image of blacks as crippled by racism laid the foundation for a generation of racial preferences—race-conscious measures designed to ensure "equality as a fact." Handicapped citizens were entitled to compete under different rules.

The rationale for the racial preferences that came to be embedded in policies involving employment, education, and public contracting was most famously articulated by Supreme Court Justice Harry Blackmun in 1978. "In order to get beyond racism," he said, "we must first take account of race. There is no other way. And in order to treat some persons equally, we must treat them differently. We cannot—we dare not—let the Equal Protection clause perpetuate racial supremacy."[7] It was not clear why policies that were explicitly race conscious were the only alternative to racial supremacy; in the extraordinarily long debates on the 1964 Civil Rights Act, no one ever made Justice Blackmun's argument. The framers of that statute had envisioned aggressive enforcement of its race-neutral antidiscrimination provisions. But by 1978 the vaguely Orwellian notion that it was necessary to treat some persons "differently" in order to treat them "equally" became civil rights orthodoxy.

The Misguided Diagnosis of the Kerner Report

How did race-conscious policies become so accepted by 1978? The answer, in part, is the racial crisis that erupted in the nation's cities within three months of Johnson's June 1965 speech. In August, the Watts neighborhood of Los Angeles exploded in flames, kicking off four "long, hot summers" of looting, burning, and fighting in predominantly black areas of cities across the land.

The riots came to an end in 1968, as suddenly and mysteriously as they appeared, and what caused them is still open to debate. But the explanation offered by President Johnson's Kerner Commission was a sweeping indictment of American society. Indeed, the Commission's central finding became, and remains, conventional wisdom in the civil rights community, academia, and the national media. The 1968 report portrayed America in stark—literally black-and-white—terms. The American drama was a play with only two characters: bigoted whites and victimized blacks. Whites were mostly living in suburban comfort, while blacks were trapped by white prejudice in decaying, dead-end inner-city neighborhoods. Curiously, the report barely mentioned the great civil rights statutes that had already irrevocably changed the status of blacks in both South and North. It portrayed the nation as moving backward, "toward two societies, one black, one white—separate and unequal." The riots were natural and inevitable protests against "the racial attitudes and behavior of white Americans toward black Americans." An "explosive mixture" had accumulated in the cities "since the end of World War II," and it was not surprising that the powder keg had at last detonated. America would be marked by "deepening racial division" and "ultimately, the destruction of basic democratic values" until "white racism" disappeared.[8]

As an analysis of what had triggered the ghetto riots of the mid-1960s, the Kerner report was useless. Increasing inequality could not have been the explanation; by every conceivable measure the status of African Americans had improved. Their average incomes were rising more rapidly than those of whites—no surprise, given how far behind they had been. In years of schooling, occupational status, quality of housing, and life expectancy, the racial gap was narrowing significantly. The political power of blacks was expanding, and they had an array of new legal rights.[9]

Of course, African Americans were still more likely than whites to live in poverty and suffered from higher unemployment rates, but those conditions were just as pervasive in the cities that had not experienced riots. Moreover, the riots ended in 1968. Why? Inner-city neighborhoods had not been transformed, white racism had not suddenly disappeared, and in the few months that elapsed between the Kerner report and the last racial disturbance, the federal government had not begun the program of massive new spending that the Commission had recommended.

Looking Backward:
Liberal Orthodoxy Today

In spite of these and other glaring flaws, the portrait drawn by the Kerner Commission has had a remarkable life. Its findings are frequently cited as equally valid today. For instance, in December 1999 the attorney general of Massachusetts looked at student scores on statewide tests and recalled the Kerner Commission's "pessimistic conclusion that our nation was 'moving towards two societies, one black, one white, separate and unequal.'"[10] Although the Kerner findings were barely mentioned explicitly, the report of the Race Advisory Board appointed by President Clinton and chaired by Dr. John Hope Franklin was a warmed-over version of the Kerner report with updated rhetoric. Its findings were a prime example of what Orlando Patterson has called the "forever racism" mindset.[11]

New demographics compelled the Franklin Commission to acknowledge the large and rapidly growing presence of Asians and Hispanics, though it did so largely by conflating the experience of all "people of color." The United States, it said, is still governed by an oppressive "system of racial hierarchy" in which whites hold all the power and members of "every minority group" face "significant barriers to opportunity." "Racial and ethnic oppression . . . persist." "Racial stereotypes" and "racist concepts" abound, as ugly and primitive as ever; no area of life is free of "subtle biases."[12]

A similarly gloomy and strident note was struck in a recent address by Julian Bond, the chairman of the NAACP. Though he conceded that African Americans had made some advances since the 1960s, he insisted that the Kerner Commission's "indictment of white America" was still sound. "Everywhere we look we see clear racial fault lines that divide America now as much as in the past." Within a few short years of the Kerner report, a "backlash in the discourse over race" had set in, Bond claimed. Its findings were rejected by "a curious mix of whites and a few blacks, academics, journalists and policy makers," engaged in "blame-shifting" and determined to pervert reality. These "new racists," he said, see continuing black-white disparities as the consequence of "family breakdown," a "lack of middle-class values," a paucity of "education and skills," and the "absence of role models." But "these are symptoms. Racism is the cause; its elimination is the cure."[13]

Looking Forward

The two dozen contributors to this volume disagree about many things; they were not chosen because they follow a particular party line on racial and ethnic issues. But they all reject the civil rights orthodoxy expressed by Julian Bond and the Franklin Commission. The Kerner report was a highly imperfect guide to the American picture when it was first released, and by now it is about as reliable as a telephone directory issued thirty years ago. The ritualistic evocation of a color line perpetuated by old and new racists is futile and counterproductive. The drive for racial equality is unfinished business, yet the civil rights community has almost nothing fresh to offer.

What follows is a guide to the new territory shaped by seismic shifts in American society over the past three decades. How are various groups faring economically, both in absolute terms and in relation to each other? What are the social conditions in the new communities of color? What progress have we made in closing the gap in educational outcomes? How is the law changing? How much has the sharp increase in marriages across racial lines blurred the boundaries between groups and diminished the salience of racial identifications? How are shifting attitudes—white, black, Asian, Hispanic, American Indian—reflected in the nation's politics? Are voters crossing racial lines in casting ballots for candidates?

The twenty-five brief essays offered here address these questions and more. The authors are scholars, journalists, and activists who specialize in the areas they write about. Grounded in research and close observation, almost every chapter shatters an old stereotype.

Many of the essays offer either explicit or implicit public policy recommendations. A common theme unites them: new realities require new thinking—a new civil rights agenda. It is undeniable that serious race-related problems persist—most obviously for black Americans. But the causes of those problems entail complexities of which the Kerner Commission never dreamed. White racism does not work as the simple explanation for the relatively poor academic performance of most black students in contexts ranging from affuent suburbia to black-run school districts. Too many black children live in poverty, but almost all are in single-parent households; how can we encourage young women to postpone pregnancy until they are married or well positioned to support a family? The problems of poverty, inadequate education, high unemployment, among others, appear unchanged, but the facade of continuity is deceptive, and old civil rights strategies will not solve today's problems.

This collection is the work of the Citizens' Initiative on Race and Ethnicity (CIRE), formed in April 1998 as an alternative to what many Americans saw as President Clinton's one-sided "dialogue" on questions of color. The Hoover Institution at Stanford University and the Manhattan Institute for Policy Research generously supported the group's work and the research and writing that went into the essays. Lindsay Young, director of communications at the Manhattan Institute, served as the project coordinator, and Richard Sousa of the Hoover Institution guided the publication process. All thirteen CIRE members contributed to the conception and planning of the volume.

CITIZENS' INITIATIVE ON RACE AND ETHNICITY

Clint Bolick, Institute for Justice
Elaine L. Chao, Heritage Foundation
Linda Chavez, Center for Equal Opportunity
Ward Connerly, American Civil Rights Institute
Tamar Jacoby, Manhattan Institute
Barbara J. Ledeen, Independent Women's Forum
Gerald A. Reynolds, Center for New Black Leadership
T. J. Rodgers, Cypress Semiconductor
Shelby Steele, Hoover Institution
Abigail Thernstrom, Manhattan Institute
Stephan Thernstrom, Manhattan Institute
Robert L. Woodson Sr., National Center for Neighborhood Enterprise
C. Robert Zelnick, Hoover Institution

Notes

1. Bayard Rustin, "From Protest to Politics: The Future of the Civil Rights Movement," *Commentary*, February 1965, reprinted in Rustin, *Down the Line: The Collected Writings of Bayard Rustin* (Chicago: Quadrangle Books, 1971), p. 111.

2. 163 U.S. 537 (1896).

3. See Andrew Kull, *The Color-Blind Constitution* (Cambridge, Mass.: Harvard University Press, 1992).

4. Martin Luther King Jr., "I Have a Dream," speech, 1963 March on Washington. Reprinted in James Melvin Washington, ed., *A Testament of Hope: The Essential Writings of Martin Luther King, Jr.* (San Francisco: HarperSanFrancisco, 1986), p. 219.

5. Radio and Television Report to the American People on Civil Rights," June 11, 1963, in *Public Papers of the Presidents of the United States: John F. Kennedy, Containing the Public Messages, Speeches, and Statements of the President, January 1 to November 22, 1963* (Washington, D.C.: U.S. Government Printing Office, 1964), pp. 468–71.

6. Lyndon B. Johnson, "To Fulfill These Rights," address at Howard University, June 4, 1965, reprinted in Lee Rainwater and William L. Yancey, eds., *The Moynihan Report and the Politics of Controversy* (Cambridge, Mass.: MIT Press, 1967), p. 126.

7. *Regents of the Univ. of Calif. v. Bakke*, 438 U.S. 265, 407 (1978).

8. *National Advisory Commission on Civil Disorders* [Kerner Commission] *Report* (New York: Bantam, 1968), pp. 1, 2, 10.

9. The data on black progress in this period are assembled in Stephan Thernstrom and Abigail Thernstrom, *America in Black and White: One Nation, Indivisible* (New York: Simon & Schuster, 1997), chaps. 3–6.

10. Thomas F. Reilly, "Separate and Unequal Education," *Boston Globe*, op-ed, December 11, 1999, p. A19. For other claims that the Kerner Commission's findings were still correct, see Fred R. Harris and Roger W. Wilkins, eds., *Quiet Riots: Race and Poverty in the United States: Twenty Years After the Kerner Report* (New York: Pantheon, 1988); Douglas S. Massey and Nancy Denton, *American Apartheid: Segregation and the Making of the Underclass* (Cambridge, Mass.: Harvard University Press, 1993), p. 211; and Charles Bullard, J. Eugene Grigsby III, and Charles Lee, eds., *Residential Apartheid: The American Legacy* (Los Angeles: UCLA Center for Afro-American Studies, 1994), pp. 1–2.

11. The Patterson phrase is cited in Jim Sleeper, "Al Gore, Racial Moralist," *New Republic*, March 2, 1998, p. 21.

12. President's Initiative on Race Advisory Board, *One America in the 21st Century: Forging A New Future* (Washington, D.C.: U.S. Government Printing Office, 1998), pp. 36, 43–44.

13. Julian Bond, "Hostility to Civil Rights, 'Color Line' Problems to Continue," *Charlestown Gazette*, April 1, 1999, p. 5A.

PART ONE

THE BIG PICTURE

The Demography of Racial and Ethnic Groups

STEPHAN THERNSTROM

THE UNITED STATES has been a racially and ethnically diverse society from its beginnings. But the conventional wisdom these days is that something radically new is happening now—that demographic changes are fundamentally transforming our society in unprecedented ways. Peering into a crystal ball, many observers have claimed that the groups we currently designate as minorities are destined to become the new majority. By the middle of the twenty-first century, they predict, and perhaps even sooner, whites will have been reduced to minority status and "people of color" will have become the majority. This, it is claimed, will have momentous implications for the nation's political, social, and cultural life.

Such is the argument, for example, of Peter Brimelow's *Alien Nation*, a 1995 volume that contended that current population shifts were "so huge and so systematically different from anything that had gone before as to transform—and ultimately, perhaps, even to destroy—the . . . American nation."[1]

Brimelow is a conservative, but many observers on the multicultural left are equally convinced that a profound demographic transformation is under way. They are cheered rather than dismayed by the prospect, however. They welcome the arrival of a minority majority and see it as evidence of the need for immediate action—for more multicultural education in the schools, continued affirmative action and diversity training programs in higher education and the workplace, and an expanded welfare state.

The demographic projections upon which both sides of this debate depend are too flawed to be taken seriously, as I shall argue later. But the general public seems to have got the message—so it would appear, at least, from the results of a 1995 poll that asked Americans to estimate what proportion of the population belonged to various racial or ethnic groups (see Table 1). This survey revealed that whites (that is, non-Hispanic whites, a distinction to be discussed at a later point) thought that the black population was almost twice as large as it was in fact—24 percent in their minds, just 13 percent in reality—and that there were 50 percent more Hispanics and almost three times as many Asians in the country as the Current Population Survey figures revealed there to be. These three minority groups together, whites thought, made up fully half of the total

Table 1   Public Beliefs About the Racial Composition of the
             U.S. Population, 1995

| | *What percent of the population is . . .?* | | | |
| | MINORITY | | | |
Responses by	*Black*	*Hispanic*	*Asian*	*Total*
Non-Hispanic whites	24	15	11	50
Blacks	26	16	12	54
Hispanics	23	21	11	55
Asians	21	15	8	44
Actual 1995 figures	13	10	4	27

SOURCE: Washington Post–Kaiser Family Foundation–Harvard University survey, as given in Richard Morin, "A Distorted Image of Minorities," *Washington Post*, November 8, 1995, p. A1. Survey results are mean figures. The actual 1995 figures are Current Population Survey estimates reported in U.S. Bureau of the Census, *Statistical Abstract of the United States: 1997* (Washington, D.C.: U.S. Government Printing Office, 1997), table 12.

population, when they actually were little more than one quarter. The "minority majority," in the eyes of whites, was not a possibility in the remote future; whites were already on the brink of losing their traditional majority status.[2]

It is tempting to interpret this misconception as evidence of widespread white paranoia. But the delusion was not confined to whites. Indeed, blacks and Hispanics were even more prone than whites to exaggerate their numbers. They also greatly exaggerated the size of other minority groups: minorities together, they believed, were already a distinct majority of the population, constituting 54 or 55 percent of the total. Asians were a little better informed than other groups, but they too greatly overestimated the size not only of their own group but also of other minorities. Whatever their backgrounds, most Americans tended to have similar misconceptions about the racial-ethnic composition of the nation's population.[3]

It has long been claimed that nonwhite people are socially invisible in American society and that the minority presence deserves to be given far more attention than it receives on television, in the press, in classrooms and textbooks. President Clinton's Race Initiative was based on the premise that most white Americans do not pay sufficient attention to their fellow countrymen with skins of a different hue. These polling numbers suggest that the opposite may be closer to the truth: Americans have become so attentive to racial divisions and so obsessed with racial matters that they have developed a badly distorted picture of the shape of their society.

The Arbitrary and Unscientific Character of the Official Racial-Ethnic Categories in Current Use

The survey referred to above employed four crude categories: white, black, Hispanic, and Asian. Why are these the relevant categories for subdividing the population into cultural groups? Why are these few groups singled out for attention, while a great many others with some claim to a distinct identity are not? What about Italian Americans, for example, or Jews? Are divisions among "races" deeper, more fundamental, and more enduring than divisions among "ethnic groups"?

The idea that "race" is a crucial and immutable division of mankind is a product of the primitive social science of the nineteenth century. According to theorists of the day, all the peoples of the world were divided into four distinct races: white or "Caucasian," black or "Negroid," yellow or "Oriental," and red or Indian. White, black, yellow, and red people were profoundly different from each other, as different as robins from sparrows, trout from salmon, rabbits from squirrels. People who belonged to different races were not only distinct physical types; they differed in innate intellectual potential and in cultural development. If they were to mate across racial lines, their offspring would be biological monstrosities.

Since these race theorists were white, it is hardly surprising that they fervently believed that Caucasians were the superior race. Orientals were next in line, with blacks and American Indians at the bottom of the heap. Given this premise, it was only natural that representatives of the "most advanced" race believed that they were entitled to rule over the "lesser breeds."

Such ideas have long been discredited and are now held only by those on the lunatic fringe. Scientists today agree that the genetic differences that distinguish members of supposedly different "races" are small, and that the races have become so intermixed that few people can claim to be of racially "pure" origins. The range of biological variation within any one race is far greater than the average differences among races.

And yet the government of the United States, remarkably, still utilizes these antiquated and pernicious categories in compiling statistical information about the American people. The entry on the black population in the index to the 1997 edition of the *Statistical Abstract of the United States* gives 230 citations to tables that distinguish African Americans from other Americans. Another 140 citations direct the reader to data on "Hispanics," a newly invented quasi-racial category whose origins will be traced below. Asians and Pacific Islanders get 42 references, and American Indians and Alaskan natives 47. If you want to know how many African Americans regularly use the Internet, how many Asians were treated in hospital emergency rooms in the preceding year, how many Hispanics usually eat breakfast, or how many American Indians were arrested for burglary, the answers are all there. The federal government inundates us with data that convey the unmistakable message that Americans of different "races" differ from each other in many important ways.

It is very striking that the American public is not bombarded with similar official statistics on the socioeconomic characteristics of Catholics, Protestants, Jews, and Muslims, and the many denominational subdivisions within those broad categories. Why not? Religious groups in the United States differ, often quite dramatically, in levels of education, income and wealth, SAT scores, unemployment rates, and most other socioeconomic measures. Why shouldn't the public be able to find out if Jews are much wealthier than Presbyterians, on the average, or if Mormons are more likely to attend college than Southern Baptists? The government of the United States has never inquired into the religious affiliations of individual citizens because religion is regarded as a private matter in American society and not the business of government. If such information did become readily available, the effect might be to heighten tensions between people of different faiths, inspiring some to complain that they did not have their "fair share" of federal judgeships or of seats on the boards of large corporations and that others were "overrepresented" in those positions.

If not religion, why race? The racial categories currently used by the federal government derive from discredited racial theories more than a century old, with only minor changes in nomenclature. "Negroid" has given way to "black" or "African American," and "Oriental" has been replaced by "Asian." But the idea that it is meaningful and socially useful to cram us all into one of the four racial boxes constructed by racist thinkers more than a hundred years ago remains unchanged. The previous decennial census, in 1990, still accepted the traditional premise that every American belongs in one and only one of four mutually exclusive racial categories; people of racially mixed ancestry were required to record just one race on the census forms. The Census of 2000 has broken from this tradition and allowed respondents to give more than one answer to the race question, but for purposes of civil rights enforcement the results will be tabulated in the same old crude categories, rendering the change virtually meaningless.[4]

The issue is not confined to the U.S. Census. Nineteenth-century conceptions of race are also alive and well in the official guidelines that govern the statistical information that all federal agencies must gather. The authoritative statement of current practice is the Office of Management and Budget's Directive No. 15, "Race and Ethnic Standards for Federal Statistics and Administrative Reporting," first issued in 1977 and still in effect.[5] Directive 15 declared that the population of the United States was divided into four "races" and two "ethnic" groups and required all agencies of the federal government to compile data using these categories in order to assess the impact of their programs.

The "racial" groups identified in Directive 15 were the usual ones: whites, blacks, Asians and Pacific Islanders, and American Indians and Alaskan Natives. Even though the old idea of a racial hierarchy with whites on top had lost all intellectual respectability, the guidelines set forth in Directive 15 were designed to subvert that hierarchy. The rationale for requiring all governmental agencies to subdivide the population into these particular racial categories was that these nonwhite groups had been the targets of prejudice in the past. (So had many white immigrant groups, of course, but the guidelines made no mention of that.) It was necessary to monitor how the nonwhite races were faring in the present in order to overcome the allegedly lingering remnants of a history of white supremacy. The three minority races were victim groups that had once "suffered discrimination and differential treatment on the basis of their race." As victims, they were—and are—entitled to a variety of special protections and preferential programs not available to whites.

Does it make sense at the end of the twentieth century to identify "races" as defined by nineteenth-century supporters of white supremacy? The authors of Directive 15 were careful to say that "these classifications should not be interpreted as being scientific or anthropological in nature." True enough, but the admission only makes their decision to utilize them more dubious. If these categories are not "scientific" or "anthropological," what are they? Why should the U.S. government distinguish some citizens from others on a basis that is not "scientific" or even "anthropological" (whatever that means) and use those distinctions in allocating public resources?

Perhaps the answer is that the OMB assumed that Americans today habitually draw these crude distinctions in their daily lives, and that recognition of social reality requires the government to do the same. This is a feeble argument. What is the evidence of a societal consensus on precisely these distinctions? Some Americans may see the population as divided into two groups, whites and nonwhites. Some, on the other hand, may make much finer distinctions than these racial categories provide, seeing Japanese Americans as quite different from Korean Americans, for example. It is certainly questionable whether Koreans and Japanese feel a strong sense of kinship and solidarity as "Asians"; there is considerable antipathy between these groups that grows out of the fact that Korea was under Japanese rule for most of the first half of the twentieth century. Immigrants from Ethiopia and Jamaica likewise differ from blacks whose ancestors came to North America as slaves centuries ago, but those differences are obscured when all are thrown together into the black racial category.

Even if it could be shown that these unscientific racial categories did correspond at least moderately well to the way in which the general public perceives the racial landscape, it does not follow that it is wise for the government to insist upon the saliency of race. Justice Harry Blackmun argued two decades ago that "in order to get beyond racism, we must first take account of race. . . . And in order to treat some persons equally, we must treat them differently."[6] But the race-conscious policies that have been pursued in the United States for a generation have plainly not taken us "beyond racism."[7]

President John F. Kennedy was wiser than Justice Blackmun, I believe, when he said that "race has no place in American life or law."[8] To continue to draw racial distinctions in our laws and to compile massive amounts of official statistical data about racial differences among racial groups will not serve to make race less important in "American life." We need not go so far as to bar government from collecting any information whatever about the ethnic composition of the population. But the evidence necessary to monitor the socioeconomic progress of groups and to identify problems can be obtained without pertetuating the dangerous fiction of race. The census currently includes a question about the "ancestry or ethnic origin" of respondents, a concept broad enough to include African Americans, Asian Americans, and all other Americans. The answers to this question will yield information about what are now classified as racial groups without contributing to the fallacy that they are fundamentally different from other groups based on a sense of common origins and peoplehood.

Is Racial Victimization Hereditary?

The rationale for making racial distinctions in official statistics is remedial. Directive 15 rests on the premise that being a member of a particular race that was treated unfairly at some point in the past leaves an indelible imprint on everyone with the same "blood." Is there no statute of limitations for complaints of historical victimization? Does the discrimination experienced by your grandparents, great-grandparents, or even more remote ancestors have any relevance to your life today?

The case for classifying some Americans as belonging to a victim group is, of course, strongest for blacks. Indeed, it is hard to imagine that official racial statistics would still be gathered but for the continuing "American dilemma," the seemingly never ending problem of how black Americans can be integrated into American society. The situation of blacks in the United States is *sui generis*. Although there are many points of resemblance between African Americans and immigrant groups that also encountered prejudice and discrimination, the differences are fundamental. No other group has such a bitter heritage of centuries of enslavement, followed by several decades of disfranchisement and legally enforced separation and subordination in the Jim Crow South and by intense racist hostility in the rest of the country.

Nonetheless, in spite of this unique history, the assumption that blacks today should still be regarded as victims who must be treated "differently" in order to be treated "equally" is mistaken. African Americans made stunning educational and economic advances in the 1940s and 1950s, which made possible the triumph of the civil rights revolution and the passage of the Civil Rights Act of 1964 and the Voting Rights Act of 1965, and since then they have continued to make gains. And white racial attitudes have changed dramatically for the better.[9] Anti-black racism has by no means disappeared altogether, but it is no longer the chief obstacle in the way of further progress by African Americans.

Note, for example, that more than seven out of ten black babies today are born out of wedlock, and that fully 85 percent of black children living in poverty reside with a mother and no father.[10] Suppose that these children had the same mothers and (absent) fathers and lived in the same neighborhoods but had somehow arrived in the world with white skins. If these children were all "white," would their life prospects be notably better? It seems highly doubtful. Or consider the dismal fact that the average black twelfth-grader today reads at the same level as the average white child in the eighth grade and is about as far behind in math, writing, and science.[11] In an economy that increasingly rewards those with strong cognitive skills, this pattern of low educational achievement guarantees that African Americans will be disproportionately concentrated in the least attractive and poorest-paid jobs. Again, if they had the same limited cognitive skills but white skins, it would not improve their job prospects significantly.

With other "racial" groups, the assumption that exposure to discrimination in the past continues to be a major obstacle is even more questionable. During World War II, Japanese American citizens living on the West Coast were presumed to be of questionable loyalty to the United States because of their "blood" ties to Japan, and for that reason they were forced to abandon their homes and businesses and were locked up in relocation camps for the duration of the war. Almost all of them were deprived of their liberty for four years, and many lost valuable property, receiving only partial compensation long after the war had ended. But by 1990 native-born Japanese Americans had median family incomes 47 percent higher than those of whites, and they were 57 percent more likely to have a college degree.[12] Some doubtless still bore psychic scars from their bitter experience half a century before, but that did not prevent the dramatic upward mobility of the group in the postwar years. By 1990 most of those who been locked up because of their race were retired or dead; two-thirds of the Japanese Americans then alive had been born after the relocation camps had been shut down.[13] And yet Japanese American entrepreneurs today are given an edge over whites in the competition for federal contracts (and state and local governmental contracts in many places) because they belong to the Asian "race."

An even more strained historical argument has been made about another Asian group—Chinese Americans—in the recent report of the Advisory Board to the President's Initiative on Race. The report speaks of "the forced labor of Chinese Americans" as part of "a history of legally mandated and socially and economically imposed subordination to white European Americans and their descendants."[14] This is a lurid and tendentious description of the "coolie" system, a form of indentured servitude in which Chinese merchants advanced passage money to America to unskilled workers who then paid off their debt through labor. But even if the coolie system was as bad as the quoted characterization, how is the indentured labor of the Chinese in California in the 1870s relevant to the situation of Chinese Americans in the 1990s? Chinese immigrants did indeed encounter horrendous prejudice in the nineteenth century and after, but the 1990 Census revealed that native-born Chinese Americans were even more successful than the enormously prosperous Japanese Americans, with median family incomes some 58 percent higher than those of whites.[15] But Chinese Americans are nonetheless favored over whites in various public contracting programs on the assumption that their "race" remains a major handicap.

If the connection between the coolie system or the internment camps and the Chinese and Japanese Americans of today is tenuous, it shrinks to the vanishing point when this purported link is extended to all persons of Asian "race." It happens that more than four out of five Asian American adults living in the United States today were born abroad; indeed, almost all the foreign-born have arrived in the past three decades, at a time when anti-Asian prejudice was disappearing and public commitment to equal treatment for all Americans had brought about strong federal legislation to combat racial discrimination.[16] Many of these newly arrived Asians— Koreans, Cambodians, and Vietnamese, for example—are from countries that sent virtually no immigrants to the United States before World War II, so there was no history at all of racism against their ancestors in the United States. The earlier mistreatment of Chinese and Japanese Americans did nothing to dissuade these newcomers from moving to America in search of greater opportunity, nor should it have. It had no bearing whatever on their prospects for a better life in contemporary America.

The Invention of "Hispanics" as a Quasi-Racial Group

In addition to the three groups presumed to be disadvantaged because of their race, Directive 15 added a fourth—"persons of Hispanic origin."[17] When the OMB issued its guidelines in 1977, the number of Mexican Americans in the United States had been growing dramatically, and immigration from Central and South America was also accelerating. Disproportionately large numbers of the newcomers from Latin countries had poorly paid unskilled jobs and family incomes below the poverty line.

Were their economic difficulties due largely to prejudice against them, or were they due to the fact that they had arrived in the United States with little education, limited or no command of English, and few marketable skills? The OMB did not even acknowledge the question. Directive 15 assumed that the depressed economic and social position of Hispanics was mainly the result of racism and that federal agencies accordingly must compile statistics on the group and do as much as possible to assist them.

Another problem with the "Hispanic" concept was the attitude of the so-called Hispanics themselves, most of whom did not regard themselves as members of a nonwhite "race." Although activists from the group insisted that they were "people of color," that was not the perception of most of those they claimed to speak for. People of Hispanic ancestry typically identified themselves as whites on the census and other official forms that included a race question—marriage licenses and birth and death records, for example.[18]

At one point earlier in the century, Mexican Americans were categorized as nonwhite by the census takers, and the results were instructive. In 1930 the Census Bureau departed from its earlier practice of classifying Mexican Americans as white and instead employed a Mexican "race" category. Enumerators were to use it for "all persons born in Mexico, or having parents born in Mexico" who in their judgment were "not definitely white."[19] People of Mexican ancestry were lumped together with blacks, Asians, and American Indians in the reported totals for "nonwhites." After Mexican American organizations and the Mexican government furiously protested the decision to relegate members of the group to the nonwhite category, census officials abandoned the categorization and restored Mexican immigrants and their children to the white column.[20]

This pattern of racial identification continues today also and applies not only to Mexican Americans but also to other Hispanics. Although Latinos tend to have darker skins than the typical American of European ancestry, a large majority—95.7 percent, according to a 1991 Current Population Survey—report themselves to be white.[21] And very few of those who reject the white designation identify with any of the other three races; they think of themselves as being of racially mixed origins, rejecting the Census Bureau's traditional view that everyone belongs in one and only one racial box.

To overcome this awkward difficulty—alleged victims of racism who did not belong to a nonwhite race—the OMB created a new category, "Hispanic." According to Directive 15, Hispanics were frequently the objects of prejudice and "differential treatment," not because of their "race" but because of their "ethnicity." Federal agencies were required to compile data on Hispanics as well as on the three nonwhite races because "ethnicity" for Hispanics was presumed to be the functional equivalent of race for blacks, Asians, and American Indians.

The concept of "ethnicity" had long been an essential analytical tool for understanding American society, but Directive 15 used the term in a novel, indeed bizarre, way. The common understanding of American society was that immigration had played a central role in its development and that many distinct "ethnic groups" had emerged out of the immigration experience and then faded away as later generations became more integrated into the larger society. Being a stranger in a strange land was difficult, and newcomers naturally felt the need to associate with other people who spoke their native tongue, liked similar food, worshiped in the same way, and had similar customs and values. The *Harvard Encyclopedia of American Ethnic Groups* describes more than one hundred such ethnic groups, many of them extinct or close to it by now.[22]

It is thus remarkable that the official guidelines employed by the federal government maintain that there are just *two* ethnic groups in the United States: persons of "Hispanic origin" and those "not of Hispanic origin."[23] Several dozen white ethnic groups with distinct identities were suddenly collapsed into a single group with the awkward label "not of Hispanic origin." All the white ethnic groups had presumably merged into the general population, while Hispanics were taken to be an unassimilable, race-like group that would be as enduring as the "races" that the federal government was so dedicated to enumerating—even though most Hispanics considered themselves, and had always been officially classified as, "white."

Equally dubious was the assumption that the umbrella label "Hispanic" designated a coherent entity with a common historical experience of oppression at the hands of white Americans. What do Mexican Americans, Puerto Ricans, Cubans, Argentineans, Colombians, Venezuelans, Chileans, and more than a dozen other immigrant nationalities from Central or South America really have in common? Not even some variant of the Spanish language as their mother tongue, because the label has been defined to include people who trace their origins to Portugal or Brazil and are Portuguese-speakers. And it includes a variety of Indian peoples whose

home language is not Spanish. Perhaps most remarkably, the rubric includes the descendants of roughly three-quarters of a million immigrants
from Spain or Portugal, although no one could seriously argue they have
encountered more prejudice in the United States than immigrants from
countries like France, Italy, Poland, or Greece. The category Hispanic is
more like the category European than the category Italian or German, and
no scholar considers the dozens of American ethnic groups that derive
from Europe a single ethnic group with a common experience.

A majority of the Americans now designated as Hispanic are Mexican
Americans, and the case for viewing their history as one dominated by
"racism and oppression" cannot withstand critical scrutiny either. The
report of the President's Initiative on Race advances this charge, speaking
of "the conquest and legal oppression of Mexican Americans and other
Hispanics."[24] This is absurdly oversimplified history. The five southwestern
states from New Mexico to California were indeed once part of Mexico
and were annexed to the United States at the end of a war between the two
nations in the 1840s. But only a tiny fraction of the Mexican American
population today can trace their origins to that conquest. A mere 13,000
people born in Mexico were recorded as U.S. residents in the Census of
1850, and they were people who had chosen to remain and live under
American rule following the Mexican War.[25] Mexican Americans did not
become a quantitatively significant element of the U.S. population until
well into the twentieth century. As late as 1910, they were no more than
0.4 percent of the total U.S. population.[26] The real growth of the group was
the result of a huge wave of immigration from Mexico that began during
the World War I decade, an immigration that was basically similar to the
peasant migrations from eastern and southern Europe early in the century.
Another much larger immigration wave from Mexico began in the 1950s
and continues today.

The idea that the lives of Mexican Americans are somehow blighted
by a legacy of "conquest" makes no sense unless one assumes that the
historical memory of having lost territory to the United States a century
and a half ago is somehow carried in the blood of everyone of Mexican

American descent. Immigrants from Mexico who arrived in the twentieth century encountered prejudice, of course, but whether the hostility was any greater than that met with by Italians, Poles, or Jews is questionable. Certainly they were not subjected to "legal oppression" comparable to what blacks experienced in the Jim Crow South.

Because of their strong historical concentration in the Southwest and their traditional employment as farm laborers, Mexican Americans tended to have low incomes and limited opportunities to obtain an education that would facilitate their mobility in the larger society. In recent decades, movement out of rural areas and agricultural occupations has gradually resulted in the growth of a Mexican American middle class, at a pace comparable to that of groups like Italians and Poles earlier in the century. The impressive upward mobility of Mexican Americans has been obscured, however, by the continuing influx of large numbers of relatively uneducated immigrants from Mexico, both legal and illegal, whose lowly status pulls down the average for the group as a whole.[27]

To view American society as divided into four separate, watertight compartments called "races," with a fifth compartment for a "Hispanic" race that is not quite a race, is profoundly misleading. So is the assumption that public policy should be based on the assumption that three of these races and the Hispanic ethnic group have been oppressed and victimized by the white majority for so long that they need preferential treatment in education, employment, and public contracting into the indefinite future.

The Myth of the Impending Minority Majority

The picture of the American people as divided into oppressors and oppressed racial-ethnic groups is an oversimplification and a distortion. The errors it entails are compounded when we attempt to peer into the future and calculate what the racial and ethnic mix of the American population will eventually be. Projections of precisely this kind have attracted considerable public attention, thanks to a credulous press. The cover story in the April 9, 1990, issue of *Time* featured a Census Bureau projection that concluded that the United States would have a "minority-majority" population by the year 2050, Since then, the official estimates have been revised slightly, with the latest indicating that the "minority" population (blacks, Asians, Hispanics, and American Indians) will be a shade less than a majority in 2050—49.7 percent of the population.[28]

Will this in fact happen? Will it matter if it does? The first thing to notice is that demographers have never been much good at prediction. In the 1930s, population experts were unanimous in foreseeing a sharply declining population in the U.S. and other industrial societies. Not one predicted the postwar Baby Boom or the resumption of mass immigration to American shores. In the past half century, instead of declining, the U.S. population has almost doubled. Demographers project future populations on the basis of currently observable patterns of immigration, fertility, and mortality. The more remote the future, the greater the possibility that these variables will change in unanticipated ways.

Indeed, the Census Bureau recognizes some of the uncertainty by issuing a series of different projections of the expected population at various future dates. The projection cited above is based on the "middle series" estimate, which puts the total U.S. population at 394 million in 2050. But the "low series" estimate the bureau makes for that year is just 283 million, and the "high series" estimate is 519 million.[29] The high and low estimates vary from each other by a staggering 236 million. Thus the population half a century from now may be nearly double what it is today (approximately 270 million), but it might instead be a mere 5 percent larger than it is now. If there is such great uncertainty about what the total population will be half a century from now, there must be similar uncertainty about the size of the various racial and ethnic subgroups that make up the total.

Why do these projections vary so enormously? Because they necessarily rest on assumptions about the determinants of population growth that may prove mistaken. For example, they require accurate estimates of the level of immigration to the United States thirty or forty years hence. Obviously, we cannot know that with any reliability because our immigration policy may become far more restrictive than it is now. Laws enacted in the 1920s sharply cut back on the number of new arrivals, and we cannot be sure that a similar anti-immigrant backlash will not again close the door to newcomers from abroad.

Nor can we be at all sure about a second variable that determines how the size of a population changes over time—its fertility patterns. (Changes in mortality rates can also affect population size, but mortality usually does not fluctuate dramatically enough to make a big difference, except in the case of demographic catastrophes like the Great Plague of the fourteenth century.) At the beginning of the twentieth century, a great many Americans of native stock worried about the consequences of their own rapidly declining fertility. Many feared that they were being swamped by huge waves of new immigrants and the large families the new arrivals typically had. Lothrop Stoddard, a leader of the Immigration Restriction League, warned that Anglo-Saxons were committing "race suicide." According to his calculations, after 200 years 1,000 Harvard men would have left only 50 descendants, while 1,000 Romanian immigrants would have produced 100,000![30]

There was nothing wrong with Stoddard's math. The problem lay with his straight-line projection of the fertility differentials of his day 200 years into the future. He failed to comprehend that in the second and third generations Romanian Americans would adjust their fertility patterns to the American norm and would produce many fewer children than did the immigrant generation.[31]

This process of assimilation to the prevailing national fertility norm continues to operate today. Although the current fertility rate of Mexican immigrant women is twice the national average, Mexican American women born in the U.S. have 23 percent fewer children than did their mothers.[32] And Mexican American women who graduate from college have families that are 40 percent smaller than those of their ethnic sisters with less than nine years of schooling.[33] The high average fertility of women of Mexican origin will drop in the future *if* the group does not continue to be replenished by huge numbers of new immigrants and *if* an increasing proportion of Mexican American females go on to college. Both are big ifs, which indicates how difficult it is to make confident predictions about the demographic future.

Stoddard also erred in his implicit assumption that Romanian immigrants and their children would keep marrying with the group, perpetuating the cultural patterns of their country of origin. Quite the opposite happened. Romanians, like most other immigrants, often married non-Romanians, with the probability rising the longer they lived in the United States. Ethnic intermarriage complicates ethnic identification. Are you still a Romanian American if just one of your four grandparents was Romanian? What if two of the four were? The immigrants of the early twentieth century, like their nineteenth-century predecessors, usually chose mates of the same ethnic background, but many of their children and a great many of their grandchildren did not. The population derived from the great waves of European immigration is by now so thoroughly interbred that their ethnic origins are difficult to disentangle and of little consequence.

Assimilation via the "marital melting pot" has also occurred at a rapid pace among the immigrants of the post–World War II era. Recent evidence as to how many Hispanics are marrying non-Hispanics is lacking, but a classic earlier study of Mexican Americans found that 40 percent of those who wed in Los Angeles County in 1963 chose non-Hispanic mates. By the third generation, indeed, members of the group were more likely to marry non-Hispanic whites than persons of Mexican ancestry.[34] The rate may be somewhat lower today because the volume of recent immigration from Mexico has been so high, but it can be expected to climb if and when the influx of newcomers declines. Asian Americans are, if anything, more likely than Mexican Americans to marry outside the group, almost always to whites.[35] In the past three decades, the rate of black-white intermarriage has also risen precipitously, though it started from a very low level.[36]

If intermarriage continues at such high levels, a very large proportion of all Americans in 2050 and even sooner will have some Hispanic, Asian, or African "blood." But it does not follow that all or even most of these individuals will identify more with their one Hispanic, Asian, or black ancestor than with those who were non-Hispanic whites. To believe that nonwhite "blood" or Hispanic "blood" trumps all other identities is simply an extension of the traditional and pernicious "one drop" rule, the notion that "one drop of black blood makes you black." Even in the case of African Americans, the "one drop" rule is no longer unquestioned, as the example of Tiger Woods suggests. And certainly there is no consensus that one drop of Asian, Hispanic, or American Indian blood consigns you to membership in those groups.

The Census Bureau today has more sophisticated techniques for modeling population change than were available to Stoddard, but it has been no more successful than he was at grappling with the reality of ethnic intermarriage, assimilation, and loss of ethnic identity, a reality that fatally confounds all efforts to extrapolate contemporary ethnic divisions into the remote future. Even if the descendants of Romanian Americans and the other "new immigrants" of the early twentieth century who so worried the Immigration Restriction League are now a majority of the population, as Stoddard feared, who could possibly care? By the time that the groups currently classified as "minority" become a majority, if that ever happens, it will be equally irrelevant, because they will no longer be thought of as minorities.

Moreover, if today's immigrants assimilate into the American stream as readily as their predecessors did at the turn of the century, there will not be any minority majority issue. Whatever their origins, they will have joined the American majority, which is determined not by one's bloodlines but by one's commitment to the principles for which this nation stands.

One America in the 21st Century?

Still, assimilation cannot be taken for granted. We cannot reliably predict the shape of the ethnic and racial future of the United States. The historical parallels drawn above may not hold because the melting pot ideal that was once so widely accepted has by now been largely displaced by the competing ideal of multiculturalism, which implies that racial and ethnic divisions are and should be permanent.

The Clinton administration has optimistically labeled the President's Initiative on Race "One America in the 21st Century," and that phrase was used as the title of the final report of the Race Initiative's Advisory Board. Rhetoric about "one America" is good p.r., but in fact the thinking behind the Race Initiative is likely to lead us toward a balkanized future. Chapter 1 of the Advisory Board's 1998 report is supposed to illuminate the "common values and concerns" that Americans "share, regardless of racial background."[37] But only its first section, headed "Americans Share Common Values and Aspirations," makes the point, and it is just one paragraph long and hopelessly vague—no mention at all of common commitment to the Constitution of the United States and to the rule of law, no reference either to the melting pot ideal.

After this perfunctory nod to the notion of common American values, the chapter devotes a full sixteen pages to platitudes such as "dialogue is a tool for finding common ground," "dialogue helps to dispel stereotypes," "the role of religious leaders," "the role of business leaders," "the role of young leaders." The assumption seems to be that genuine national unity cannot be attained unless we all participate in group discussions designed to enhance our "awareness of the history of oppression, conquest, and private and government-sanctioned discrimination and their present-day consequences."[38] We are all enjoined to "commit at least one day each month to thinking about how issues of racial prejudice and privilege might be affecting each person you come into contact with."[39]

Although the report asserts ritualistically that Americans share "common values and concerns," it rejects the idea that a common American culture binds us together. Highlighted in a box is a quotation from a student who said, at a "children's dialogue on race, poverty, and community," "I don't think we need to become one culture. I think we just need to respect the differences of each culture."[40] The simplistic view that the American people belong to five separate cultures, with all but non-Hispanic whites the victims of racial oppression, is hardly a recipe likely to make us "one nation, indivisible."

If the assumptions behind the President's Initiative on Race continue to shape public policy in the decades to come, the aim of "One America" will not be realized. By continuing race-driven policies in the delusion that they will enable us to "get beyond racism," we will only ensure the perpetuation of racial and ethnic divisions far into the future.

Notes

1. Peter Brimelow, *Alien Nation: Common Sense About America's Immigration Disaster* (New York: Simon & Schuster, 1995), p. 1.

2. Lest it be thought that this 1995 poll was an aberration, it should be noted that a 1990 Gallup poll found that white Americans thought that blacks were no less than 32 percent of the population, even further from the mark than the 24 percent estimate of those polled in 1995. Similarly, African Americans in 1990 thought that blacks were 42 percent of the population, 3.5 times as many as there were in fact. See George Gallup Jr. and Frank Newport, "Americans Ignorant of Basic Census Facts," *Gallup Poll Monthly*, no. 294 (March 1990), p. 2.

3. For some perceptive comments on the implications of this survey, see Orlando Patterson, *The Ordeal of Integration: Progress and Resentment in America's "Racial" Crisis* (Washington, D.C.: Civitas/Counterpoint, 1997), pp. 56–60.

4. Although the Office of Management and Budget has ordered that 63 different racial combinations be tabulated, which becomes 126 when you add Hispanics to the mix, it has ruled that in order to assess possible civil rights violations, those fine distinctions are to be ignored. Persons who report themselves a mixture of white and some other race are all to be put in the other racial category, a reversion to the old "one drop rule." See Stephan Thernstrom, "One Drop Still—A Racialist's Census," *National Review*, April 17, 2000.

5. Office of Management and Budget, Statistical Directive No. 15, "Race and Ethnic Standards for Federal Agencies and Administrative Reporting, as Adopted on May 12, 1977," *Federal Register*, v. 43, 19629–19270. The quotations in this and the following two paragraphs are drawn from this document. For an excellent brief analysis of these guidelines, see Peter Skerry, "Many American Dilemmas: The Statistical Politics of Counting by Race and Ethnicity," *Brookings Review*, Summer 1996, pp. 36–39. In October 1997 the OMB announced some revisions in its classification scheme. It subdivided the "Asian and Pacific Islander" category into two: "Asian" and "Native Hawaiian or Other Pacific Islanders," so there are now five officially recognized races.

And it allowed people of mixed race to select more than one racial designation from the list of five.

6. *Regents of the Univ. of Calif. v. Bakke*, 438 U.S. 265, 407 (1978).

7. See Stephan Thernstrom and Abigail Thernstrom, *America in Black and White: One Nation, Indivisible* (New York: Simon & Schuster, 1997), part III, for a critical analysis of racially preferential policies.

8. As quoted in ibid., p. 138.

9. The history of racial segregation and subordination and the struggle against it are traced in ibid., part I. The enormous progress made by blacks since the 1960s and the sharp decline in white prejudice are reviewed in part II and the conclusion to the work.

10. Ibid., pp. 237, 240.

11. The evidence on the racial gap in cognitive skills at age 17 is set forth in ibid., pp. 352–59. Possible explanations for the gap are reviewed in ibid., pp. 359–82.

12. U.S. Bureau of the Census, 1990 Census of the Population, *Asian and Pacific Islanders in the United States*, 1990 CP-3-5 (Washington, D.C.: U.S. Government Printing Office, 1993), tables 3 and 5; U.S. Bureau of the Census, Current Population Reports, P-60-174, *Money Income of Households, Families, and Persons in the United States: 1990* (Washington, D.C.: U.S. Government Printing Office, 1991), table 13; U.S. Bureau of the Census, *Statistical Abstract of the United States: 1991* (Washington, D.C.: U.S. Government Printing Office, 1991), table 43.

13. *Asian and Pacific Islanders*, table 1.

14. President's Initiative on Race Advisory Board Report, *One America in the 21st Century: Forging a New Future* (Washington, D.C.: U.S. Government Printing Office, 1998), pp. 36, 43.

15. *Asian and Pacific Islanders*, table 5; *Money Income of Households*, table 13.

16. *Asian and Pacific Islanders*, table 1.

17. Some precedent for the creation of this category was provided by the 1970 Census, which identified the "Spanish origin or descent" population by asking respondents whether they were Mexican, Puerto Rican, Cuban, Central or South American, or "other Spanish." See A. J. Jaffe, et al., *Spanish Americans in the United States: Changing Demographic Characteristics* (New York: Research Institute for the Study of Man, 1976), pp. 347–48.

18. A March 1991 Current Population Survey found that 95.7 percent of those who identified themselves as of Hispanic origin considered themselves white, 2.2 percent black, 0.4 percent American Indian, and 1.5 percent of "other race"; U.S. Bureau of the Census, Current Population Reports: Special Studies, P23-182, *Exploring Alternative Race-Ethnic Comparison Groups in Current Population Surveys* (Washington, D.C.: U.S. Government Printing Office, 1992), table A. The 1990 Census, by contrast, found that 51.7 percent of Hispanics regarded themselves as white, and 42.7 percent said they

were of "other race." The difference is attributable to the fact that the CPS accepts "other race" as an answer only when respondents say they are unable to choose among the four given to them, whereas the census lists "other race" as an option, and indeed frames the race question in a way that encourages Hispanics to check the "other race" box. For a critique of the census race question, see Stephan Thernstrom, "American Ethnic Statistics," in Donald L. Horowitz and Gerard Noiriel, eds., *Immigrants in Two Democracies: French and American Experience* (New York: New York University Press, 1992), pp. 100, 108.

19. Jaffe, *Spanish Americans*, p. 346.

20. S. Thernstrom, "American Ethnic Statistics," p. 91.

21. U.S. Bureau of the Census, *Exploring Alternative Race-Ethnic Comparison Groups*, table A.

22. Stephan Thernstrom, ed., *Harvard Encyclopedia of American Ethnic Groups* (Cambridge, Mass.: Harvard University Press, 1980).

23. Statistical Directive No. 15, 19629.

24. *One America in the 21st-Century*, p. 36. For more sophisticated and nuanced treatments of this group, see Peter Skerry, *Mexican Americans: The Ambivalent Minority* (New York: Free Press, 1993), and the essays in Walker Connor, ed., *Mexican-Americans in Comparative Perspectives* (Washington, D.C.: Urban Institute Press, 1985).

25. Jaffe, *Spanish Americans*, p. 134.

26. Ibid., pp. 134–35.

27. For impressive evidence of upward mobility by Mexican Americans in Southern California over the 1980–1990 decade, see Dowell Myers, *The Changing Immigrants of Southern California*, research report no. LCRI-95-04R, Lusk Center Research Institute, University of Southern California, Los Angeles, 1995.

28. The latest estimates appear in U.S. Bureau of the Census, *Statistical Abstract of the United States: 1998* (Washington, D.C.: U.S. Government Printing Office, 1998), table 12.

29. Ibid., table 3.

30. Lothrop Stoddard, *The Revolt Against Civilization: The Menace of the Under Men* (New York: Scribner's, 1923), pp. 112–13.

31. Tamara K. Hareven and John Modell, "Family Patterns," in S. Thernstrom, ed., *Harvard Encyclopedia of American Ethnic Groups*, pp. 348–49. The typical Italian immigrant woman recorded on the 1910 Census gave birth to seven children; their American-born daughters produced an average of five; see S. Philip Morgan, Susan Cotts Watkins, and Douglas Ewbank, "Generating Americans: Ethnic Differences in Fertility," in Susan Cotts Watkins, ed., *After Ellis Island: Newcomers and Natives in the 1910 Census* (New York: Russell Sage Foundation, 1994), pp. 94–95.

32. U.S. Bureau of the Census, 1990 Census of the Population, *Persons of Hispanic*

Origin in the United States, 1990 CP-3-3 (Washington, D.C.: U.S. Government Printing Office, 1993), table 1.

33. James A. Sweet and Larry L. Bumpass, *American Families and Households* (New York: Russell Sage Foundation, 1987), p. 135.

34. Leo Grebler, Joan W. Moore, and Ralph C. Guzman, *The Mexican-American People: The Nation's Second Largest Minority* (New York: Free Press, 1970), pp. 408–9.

35. Harry L. Kitano, *Asian Americans: Emerging Minorities* (Englewood Cliffs, N.J.: Prentice-Hall, 1995), pp. 176–80.

36. Some 12.1 percent of the African Americans who married during 1993 had white mates, as compared with 0.7 of those who wed a generation earlier, in 1963; Thernstrom and Thernstrom, *America in Black and White,* p. 526. Although 12 percent may not seem a very high number, it is much higher than the rate of intermarriage between Jews and Gentiles in New York City and between Japanese Americans and whites in Los Angeles County before World War II; ibid., pp. 526, 536.

37. *One America in the 21st Century,* p. 12.

38. Ibid., p. 35.

39. Ibid., p. 102.

40. Ibid., p. 26.

Immigration and Group Relations

REED UEDA

THE UNITED STATES is the prototype of a country built by immigration and assimilation. The blurring of ethnic lines through the process of assimilation has promoted equality of economic opportunity and produced a cultural life open to popular participation and relatively free of constraints imposed by group membership.[1] African Americans are the obvious exception to this pattern, since their ancestors came as slaves, not as "immigrants"—as the word is customarily used—and they are not a subject in this essay.

Those who arrived as newcomers on the American shore were thrown into a "melting pot," almost every scholar once assumed. It was much too simple a notion. Many immigrants joined the mainstream while preserving much of their own ethnic culture. In fact, American liberty has allowed precisely that process of preservation. Freedom and tolerance have permitted religious and cultural minorities who were marginalized or persecuted in their homelands to maintain a distinctive way of life free from fear. The consequence of limited government has been an extraordinarily strong civil society within which groups have organized on their own terms.[2] Widespread assimilation is thus coupled with a vibrant ethnic pluralism. American society resembles a simmering stewpot of gradually blending fragments; no crucible immediately melted newcomers into homogeneous Anglo-conformity.

But collective ethnic identity has never been a self-evident and permanent "given"; it has required much energy to sustain. The loose, open, and eclectic organization of American society has been, at one and the same time, a gift and a mortal enemy, affording spaces for ethnic life yet confounding those who would preserve a cultural inheritance in its more or less original form. In the era of industrialization and urbanization, an immense array of foreign nationalities settled together in rough propinquity, each group exposed to the different habits of new neighbors, and to a consumer-oriented mass culture that eroded their traditions.[3]

In addition, although immigrant communities have not "melted," with each successive generation they have tended to become increasingly American. Over successive generations, social mobility and acculturation produced positive changes in social class, schooling, and participation in public life and affairs. And thus by intergenerational measures of occupational mobility, residential patterns, income, property ownership, and education, members of European and non-European immigrant groups (to varying degrees) came to look much alike.

Furthermore, paradoxically, as newcomers from the Western Hemisphere, Asia, and Africa made American society more culturally and racially pluralistic, the possibilities for assimilation increased. The influx of newcomers produced a greater tolerance of intergroup differences, making the society more absorptive. Thus Poles, for instance, became more willing to shed their Polishness in favor of "the American way." Had the society been less tolerant, groups would have held fast to their ethnic traditions in residential enclaves. As it was, groups underwent a gradual but steady course of cultural transformation. That process began with northern and western Europeans in the nineteenth century; they were followed in the early twentieth century by southern and eastern Europeans, Asians, and immigrants from Western Hemisphere countries. More recently an influx of people from the Third World have followed in their footsteps. These new Americans shaped a creative assimilative process in which they both changed themselves and became part of the whole by changing the whole. The national culture was porous and absorbent, but so were the subcultures arising out of the adaptation of immigrants and their children.[4]

The movement of immigrant groups into the center of national life constituted a creative achievement in the face of imposing challenges and obstacles. The alienated and disempowered multitudes from abroad arduously devised the arts of coexistence with others. They learned to act together with culturally distant—sometimes hostile—natives and other newcomers who had been strangers or antagonists in the countries they left behind. In their new homes in America, the Jews, Poles, Russians, and Germans of Chicago came to accept each other as neighbors and as equals. Immigration was a rigorous school in which new lessons of group cooperation and interdependence had to be learned for the sake of survival.[5]

The new cultural relationships in which immigrants found themselves inevitably attenuated the transplanted forms of homeland culture. Pathways of multigenerational change varied in timing and length, but they all tended to head in the same direction. The English, the Welsh, the Dutch, and the Scots, and to a lesser degree the descendants of Norwegians, Danes, Swedes, and Germans—those whose ancestors were part of the American population since the colonial and early national era—experienced the greatest divergence from homeland cultural legacies. Americans whose forebears came from southern and eastern Europe, Asia, the Caribbean, and Latin America exhibited a stronger tendency to retain distinctive ethnic features. But even for them, the ties and feelings of a homeland-based identity yielded in degrees to the syncretic and eclectic forms of American culture.

Immigrants were often unaware of how far they had departed in habit and custom from the ancestral culture. An American-born Chinese girl in the 1930s described the experience of self-discovery on a visit to China:

I gave up trying to be a Chinese; for as soon as the people in China learned that I was an overseas Chinese, they remarked, "Oh, you are a foreigner." Some asked, "Where did you learn to speak Chinese?" Some thought it remarkable that I spoke Chinese at all. So you see I was quite foreign to China. I wore Chinese clothes and tried to pass as a Chinese, but I could not so I gave up and admitted my foreign birth and education. I lack very much a Chinese background, Chinese culture, and Chinese manners and customs; I have neither their understanding nor their viewpoint nor their patience. Sometimes I was homesick for America. Where I had friends, I felt better.[6]

The inescapable forces of social change made ethnic identity only one part of personal identity. Increasingly, over the generations, individuals were shaped by the jobs they held, the churches they attended, their places of residence, and by their schooling, peer culture, and consumer tastes.[7] In addition, the public forms of Anglo-Saxon society became, for immigrants and their descendants, a cultural lingua franca. For later descendants of European immigrants, ethnicity itself became increasingly thin and symbolic, a matter of personal choice.[8]

Assimilation also meant a very high degree of linguistic unification in twentieth-century America, in spite of a mass immigration that introduced a linguistic diversity greater than that found in any other modern society. In the early twentieth century, several dozen languages were spoken; in the 1990s, the number of foreign languages in use probably rose even higher and certainly included many more non-European languages. But people may know and use both the language of their homeland and English; over time, immigrants who speak Vietnamese at home have nevertheless become absorbed into an English-language culture.

Thus, a study based on the 1990 U.S. Census showed that among all immigrants, the proportion of those who spoke only English or who spoke English very well rose from 36 percent among those who had been in the United States five years or less, to 57 percent among those who had been residents from sixteen to twenty-five years, to 77 percent for those who had been here for forty or more years.[9]

In addition, the numbers of those who primarily used a foreign tongue dwindled sharply by the second generation. The federal Census of 1980 showed that almost all natives (more than four years old) spoke English as their primary language, although many were of immigrant ancestry. Since many recent immigrants arrived well educated and had often studied English, they moved rapidly into the English linguistic mainstream. Even Hispanics, represented by group spokesmen advocating an official policy of bilingualism, have nevertheless made large strides toward English usage. In the 1970s, the majority of American-born Hispanic adults—including three-quarters of Mexicans, four-fifths of Puerto Ricans and Cubans, and nine-tenths of Central or South Americans—used English as their principal or sole language.[10]

The impressive rise in the rate of intermarriage among the descendants of immigrants may have been the trend with the most profound impact, however. The extraordinary degree to which the American population has become defined by mixed ancestry in the late twentieth century is evident in Census data. "Intermarriage [became] so common in the postwar era that by 1980 the vast majority of Americans had relatives, through birth or their own marriage, from at least two different ethnic backgrounds," an expert on American pluralism has noted.[11]

Indeed, well before World War II, social scientists were calling attention to the rise in ethnic intermarriage. The pioneering sociologist of the University of Chicago, Robert E. Park, saw the fusion of races in Hawaii where "new peoples are coming into existence" as a harbinger of the future.[12] On the other hand, a well-known study of religious intermarriage in 1940 found that, yes, Italians were marrying the Irish, but Catholics were choosing Catholic spouses, Jews other Jews, and Protestants, too, were sticking to their own. As Will Herberg was later to put it, the American experience was thus characterized by not one but three melting pots—Jewish, Catholic, and Protestant. Separate processes of melting took place within each of these pots.[13] Fifty years later, however, that picture had changed. By the 1990s, half of Catholics and Jews were marrying outside the faith.[14]

At the end of the twentieth century intermarriage among both religious and ethnic groups of European origin was pervasive.[15] Indeed, by the third or fourth generation intermarriage is frequent, if not the norm, among many European ethnic groups. In 1972, in a special population survey conducted by the Bureau of the Census, 40 percent of white respondents chose not to identify with any specific heritage.[16] In subsequent years, the number of Americans who saw themselves as simply "American" continued to rise. A 1979 Census survey encouraged respondents to choose ethnic ancestries, and yet 13.5 million refused and gave "American" or "United States" as their ancestry; they became the seventh largest "ethnic" group on the government's list.[17]

That survey included members of non-European groups; newcomers from Asia and Latin America also have significant rates of mixed ancestry and intermarriage. In the 1979 poll, 31 percent of Filipinos, 23 percent of Chinese, 22 percent of Japanese, and nearly 22 percent of the Spanish ancestry population claimed multiple ancestry.[18] These rates of intermarriage provoked a heated debate over whether the federal census of 2000 should include a "multiracial" enumeration category for the rising number of offspring of such unions.[19] These high rates of intermarriage led to the decision to allow multiple answers to the race question on the federal census of 2000.

When Asian or Hispanic minorities marry outside their groups, the spouses are usually white. A study of 1990 federal census returns found that, looking at all married couples with an Asian spouse, 27 percent had a white spouse, and 3 percent had a nonwhite or Hispanic. Among married couples with a Hispanic spouse, 29 percent had a non-Hispanic white spouse, while only 2.1 percent had a nonwhite. Nearly a quarter of the 2.0 million children who had at least one Asian parent, and a quarter of the 5.4 million children with at least one Hispanic parent, lived in interracial households with a white parent or stepparent.[20] The rates of mixed ancestry among Asians and Hispanics appear especially impressive when one takes into account group sanctions against exogamy, the operation of laws barring miscegenation that were not completely stricken from state statutes until the 1960s, and the high percentage of recent immigrants who might have been expected to maintain group ties.

These assimilative patterns obviously took time to take hold, and the process was not all sweetness and light. In the immediate wake of the migrations of the twentieth century, ethnic boundaries usually tightened, cultural distances widened, and social divisions deepened. Large numbers of new immigrants strained institutions and public services. In the Progressive era, middle-class natives complained that Italian, Jewish, and Slavic immigrants meant expensive Americanization programs, overcrowded schools, overburdened charity organizations, spreading slums, disease, crime, political corruption, and the propagation of alien cultural values. These disorders were handled by teachers, policemen, physicians, nurses, inspectors, administrators, bureaucrats, and elected officials at a high cost to the public. In post–Cold War America, the same complaints about the burdens of immigration could be heard in updated form. Those concerned about the continuing flood of newcomers talked about the costs of bilingual and multicultural school programs, the spread of barrios, overtaxed hospital and medical facilities, the environmental impact, ethnic favoritism in the form of racial and ethnic preferences, and the spread of non-Western values and customs.[21]

But such doubts and fears ignore much good news. Immigrants have been producers, consumers, and entrepreneurs, and their economic energy has increased the gross national product and made for greater general prosperity. Often self-educated, hard working, and thrifty, they have also brought to their adopted land valuable cultural capital. Immigrants have helped, too, to expand the dimensions of American liberty and democracy. They have insisted on their right to maintain their ethnic heritage, as well as to modify or reject it. And wanting to ensure their own self-determination—their right to make social, cultural, and political choices—they have widened the degrees of freedom for others.[22]

As a corollary, immigrants have demonstrated that American opportunities for the individual could work to overcome notions of group determinism. They have affirmed the principle that personal achievement is the basis of self-worth and have in that way helped to shape and reaffirm a national culture that rewards individual effort and accomplishment. Immigrants and their descendants have proved they are productive workers, trustworthy neighbors, and patriotic citizens, whatever their ethnic origins, thereby making individual behavior, not background, the standard by which most Americans continue to judge others.[23]

Immigrants have also demonstrated the viability of collective organization for mutual progress. Transplanted communities of Chinese, Japanese, Asian Indians, Greeks, Jews, and Lebanese in different parts of the nation employed similar forms of cultural solidarity to promote group economic progress.[24] Networks of kinship and communalism have been the foundation of their ability to build communities. Immigrant ethnic groups have thus exemplified the formation of social capital—that set of social connections and social assets that promote positive collaborative endeavor. They brought with them norms of reciprocity and networks of civic engagement.[25]

Immigrants have furthered the evolution of a society based on achieved status, voluntary identity, and free association. And what ethnic groups developed in common through mutual activity became more important than what made them different. The opportunities of liberal democracy released the innate talents and drive of immigrants. In the twentieth century, immigrants from Europe, Asia, the Middle East, Africa, the Pacific, and the Western Hemisphere all contributed to economic and social progress.

In the final analysis, the vitality of America's assimilative pluralism limited the ability of policy makers and opinion makers to consign immigrants to permanent compartments. Race, especially, proved an inadequate "container" for ethnic Americans whose core identities continued to shift and expand as employment, levels of educational attainment, marriage and other social patterns, consumer tastes, and places of residence changed. In the era of industrialization, European immigrants were once divided into "The Races of Europe," but racial classifications such as "Southern Italians" and "Hebrews" (actually used by federal immigration agencies from the 1890s to the 1940s) became practically meaningless after two or three generations. The classification of the newest global immigrants as disadvantaged racial minorities labeled African, Hispanic, and Asian and Pacific

American suffers from a similar inadequacy; these categories fail to capture the fluid character of an individual's social identity and social status, which makes the dichotomy "people of color" versus "white" much too simplistic.

The historian Donna Gabaccia has noted:

> In American eyes immigrants of Asian, African, or Native American descent become Americans by becoming racial minorities. Recently arriving elite, well-educated immigrants from the third world contemplate this road with much ambivalence. Many prefer to become ethnic Americans—Korean Americans or Jamaican Americans—rather than "blacks" or "Asian Americans."[26]

The capacity for mobility and adaptation possessed by these newest immigrants will, as Gabaccia points out, "fruitfully challenge American assumptions about class and race." As long as immigrant groups have an open society in which to create new patterns, they will resist the petrifaction of ethnic boundaries into racial boundaries.

Over the course of the twentieth century, immigrants increased the power of such assimilative factors as an expansive economy, an absorbent composite culture, a fluid social structure, and a cosmopolitan democracy. And deeply woven patterns of group intermixing immunized the society against ethnic and racial fragmentation. Whether such assimilative patterns can be carried forward into the twenty-first century will depend on the degree of public commitment to America's nationalizing and democratizing traditions. The successful integration of current and future immigrants will require maintaining a framework for ethnicity that encourages assimilative behavior within a democratic, pluralistic context. Ethnic identities have coexisted with acculturation, pluralism with assimilation, and differences with commonality. That is the mix upon which individual opportunity will continue to depend.

Americans who consider themselves liberal and progressive on ethnic questions often embrace the notion that people must belong to separate groups and cultures. And yet the idea that particular groups have a fixed culture and identity has profound consequences for the future of democracy, especially when it is manipulated by the forces of statism and modernization. The idea that culture and identity are possessed by unique groups encourages a political language that homogenizes and reduces individuals into stereotypical collective categories. Even more important, this sort of ethnic reductionism leads to the dangerous position that in the realm of government only a Hispanic legislator, for instance, can adequately represent Hispanic voters; an "Anglo" inevitably speaks only for "Anglo" interests. Similarly, Asians are disfranchised when a Hispanic is elected from the district in which they live. This form of functional representation can bring more group solidarity, but at a cost: the erosion of the freedom of individuals to define themselves and their interests regardless of their social origins—a freedom fundamental to liberal democracy.

The drive to repackage people by labels and categories that can be publicly managed is not a uniquely American phenomenon; it is well known in other countries with historically less democratic polities. The University of Chicago political scientists Susanne and Lloyd Rudolph see similar patterns in the United States and India:

> Which identities become relevant for politics is not predetermined by some primordial ancientness. They are crafted in benign and malignant ways in print and the electronic media, in textbooks and advertising, in India's T.V. megaseries and America's talk shows, in campaign strategies, in all the places and all the ways that self and other, us and them, are represented in an expanding public culture.[27]

In spite of both the media and the state, which invent official groups, a new diversity is forming in the United States in which ethnic particularism is increasingly irrelevant. Deeply rooted universalizing and acculturating forces are at work. As sociologist Orlando Patterson has argued, American culture is not owned by any particular group:

> Once an element of culture becomes generalized under the impact of a universal culture, it loses all specific symbolic value for the group which donated it. It is a foolish Anglo-Saxon who boasts about "his" language today. English is a child that no longer knows its mother, and cares even less

to know her. It has been adapted in a thousand ways to meet the special feelings, moods and experiences of a thousand groups.[28]

"Ethnic WASP culture is no longer the culture of the group of Americans we now call WASP's," Patterson concluded. Jim Sleeper, who noted these insights by Patterson in his book, *The Closest of Strangers*, recalled how a stint teaching in a New York high school showed him that "the Chinese-American students . . . were [not] interested in adopting 'white' culture as much as they were interested in becoming part of the larger 'universal' culture of constitutional democracy and technological development." Immigrant minorities today have a hard time not being affected by assimilation in the globalizing democratic society that America has become.[29]

In a plural society that aims to be democratic, people need to be free to mix and blend with those outside their ethnic group. All change begins at the margins, and the margins are where individuals can make new changes and choices a part of their lives. Without this dimension of personal freedom, group boundaries and identities tighten and become impassable. It is often today's immigrants who truly understand the value of American freedom. The journalist Richard Brookhiser has reported that when a liberal "pol" tried to tell a Pakistani immigrant cabdriver about the error of registering Republican, the "cabbie defended his dislike of ethnic group politics. 'I came here to get away from it,'" he said.[30]

Those who have seized the opportunity to leapfrog ethnic identities have become the agents for a creative, open, and voluntary national life. Because of his transcultural connections, Fiorello LaGuardia, mayor of New York City during the Great Depression, gained legitimacy and popular support from a variety of ethnic interest groups. Historian Arthur Mann provided an unforgettable glimpse of LaGuardia:

> Tammany Hall may have been the first to exploit the vote-getting value of eating gefullte fish with Jews, goulash with Hungarians, sauerbraten with Germans, spaghetti with Italians, and so on indefinitely, but this unorthodox Republican not only dined every bit as shrewdly but also spoke, according to the occasion, in Yiddish, Hungarian, German, Italian, Serbian-Croatian, or plain New York English. Half Jewish and half Italian, born in Greenwich

Village yet raised in Arizona, married first to a Catholic and then to a Lutheran but himself a Mason and an Episcopalian, Fiorello LaGuardia was a Mr. Brotherhood Week all by himself.[31]

In my own explorations as a historian, I once stumbled upon a page from a 1911 federal immigration report that recorded the numbers of Albanians, Bosnians, Herzegovinians, Serbs, and Croatians arriving in the United States. Almost a century later, their descendants have assimilated and learned to coexist as members of one American nation. In their homeland of former Yugoslavia, by contrast, their countrymen reenact a tragic cycle of destructive ethnic conflict and separatism. The historic American conditions of soft and open group boundaries, once symbolized by the melting pot, ensured that, in this country, southeast European minorities would not follow that path.

It is a cliché to say that those who do not learn the lessons of history are doomed to repeat its errors. But we should not forget that an American framework for ethnicity that rests on the opportunity to assimilate in a pluralistic democracy has proved to be highly effective in getting different people to live and act together productively, on terms of equality and freedom.[32] It is an achievement with important and broad implications. In a time of global ethnic strife, the United States more than ever can demonstrate to the world that pluralism works and can work democratically.

Notes

1. See Richard D. Alba, "Assimilation's Quiet Tide," *Public Interest* 119 (spring 1995): 4.

2. Nathan Glazer, *Affirmative Discrimination: Ethnic Inequality and Public Policy* (New York: Basic Books, 1975), pp. 24–26; Donald L. Horowitz, "Immigration and Group Relations," *Immigrants in Two Democracies: French and American Experience* (New York: New York University Press, 1992), pp. 23–25.

3. Olivier Zunz, *The Changing Face of Inequality: Urbanization, Industrial Development, and Immigrants in Detroit, 1880–1920* (Chicago: University of Chicago Press, 1982), chaps. 4, 7; Lizabeth Cohen, *Making a New Deal: Industrial Workers in Chicago, 1919–1939* (Cambridge: Cambridge University Press, 1990), chaps. 1–3; David Ward, *Cities and Immigrants: A Geography of Change in Nineteenth-Century America* (New

York: Oxford University Press, 1971), chaps. 3, 4; Oscar Handlin, *Boston's Immigrants: A Study in Acculturation, 1790–1880*, rev. ed. (Cambridge, Mass.: Harvard University Press, 1969), chaps. 4–6; James R. Barrett, *Work and Community in the Jungle: Chicago's Packinghouse Workers, 1894–1922* (Urbana: University of Illinois Press, 1987), pp. 75–76, 78–79.

4. John Higham, *Send These to Me: Jews and Other Immigrants in Urban America* (New York: Atheneum, 1975), pp. 18–20, 24–28; Sean Wilentz, "Sense and Sensitivity," *New Republic*, October 31, 1994, p. 46.

5. Oscar Handlin and Mary Handlin, *The Dimensions of Liberty* (Cambridge, Mass.: Harvard University Press, 1961), p. 130.

6. William Carlson Smith, *Americans in Process: A Study of Our Citizens of Oriental Ancestry* (Ann Arbor, Mich.: Edwards Brothers, 1937), p. 243.

7. Richard D. Alba, *Ethnic Identity: The Transformation of White America* (New Haven, Conn.: Yale University Press, 1990), pp. 4–15.

8. Mary C. Waters, *Ethnic Options: Choosing Identities in America* (Berkeley: University of California Press, 1990), pp. 147–55.

9. Barry R. Chiswick and Teresa A. Sullivan, "The New Immigrants," in Reynolds Farley, ed., *State of the Union: America in the 1990s*, vol. 2, *Social Trends* (New York: Russell Sage Foundation, 1995), p. 238.

10. Alejandro Portes and Ruben Rumbaut, *Immigrant America: A Portrait* (Berkeley: University of California Press, 1990), tables 28, 31, p. 208.

11. Lawrence H. Fuchs, *The American Kaleidoscope: Race, Ethnicity, and the Civic Culture* (Hanover, N.H.: University Press of New England, 1990), p. 327.

12. Robert E. Park, *Race and Culture* (Glencoe, Ill.: Free Press, 1950), pp. 116, 149, 151, 191–95.

13. Ruby Jo Reeves Kennedy, "Single or Triple Melting Pot? Intermarriage Trends in New Haven, 1870–1940," *American Journal of Sociology* 49 (1944): 331–39; Will Herberg, *Protestant-Catholic-Jew* (Garden City, N.Y.: Doubleday & Co., 1960; 1955), pp. 32–34.

14. In 1990, Richard D. Alba concluded that "the rising tide of intermarriage is also sweeping across religious lines," thus showing that the triple melting pot theory "does not seem to be holding up." *Ethnic Identity*, p. 14.

15. Alba describes "the wide dispersion of ethnically mixed ancestry" as the most profound ethnic change among whites in the twentieth century. Ibid., pp. 15, 310–13.

16. U.S. Bureau of the Census, "Characteristics of the Population by Ethnic Origin: March 1972 and 1971," *Current Population Reports*, P-20, no. 249 (Washington, D. C.: Government Printing Office, 1973); Higham, *Send These to Me*, pp. 9–11.

17. The English, German, Irish, black, Italian, and French were the only larger groups. U.S. Bureau of the Census, *Current Population Reports, Ancestry and Language in the United States: November 1979*, series P-23, no. 116 (Washington, D.C.: U.S.

Government Printing Office, 1982). Examining this data, sociologists Stanley Lieberson and Mary Waters saw the genesis of a "new American ethnic group" whose members did not identify with premigration antecedents; Stanley Lieberson and Mary C. Waters, *From Many Strands: Ethnic and Racial Groups in Contemporary America* (New York: Russell Sage Foundation, 1988), pp. 264–68. See also Harold J. Abramson, *Ethnic Diversity in Catholic America* (New York: Wiley & Sons, 1973), chap. 4.

18. U.S. Bureau of the Census, *Current Population Reports, Ancestry and Language in the United States: November 1979*, p. 7; David A. Hollinger, *Postethnic America: Beyond Multiculturalism* (New York: Basic Books, 1995), pp. 165–66.

19. Michaell S. Teitelbaum and Jay Winter, *A Question of Numbers: High Migration, Low Fertility, and the Politics of National Identity* (New York: Hill & Wang, 1998), p. 171; Stephan Thernstrom, "One Drop Still—A Racialist's Census," *National Review*, April 17, 2000, pp. 35–37.

20. Roderick J. Harrison and Claudette E. Bennett, "Racial and Ethnic Diversity," in Reynolds Farley, ed., *State of the Union: America in the 1990s*, vol. 2, *Social Trends* (New York: Russell Sage Foundation, 1995), pp. 165–67.

21. U.S. Immigration Commission, *Abstracts of Reports*, vol. 1–2 (Washington, D.C.: U.S. Government Printing Office, 1911); Oscar Handlin, *Race and Nationality in American Life* (Boston: Little, Brown, 1957), chap. 5; Peter Brimelow, *Alien Nation: Common Sense About America's Immigration Disaster* (New York: Random House, 1995).

22. See, e.g., Ellen Smith, "Strangers and Sojourners: The Jews of Colonial Boston" and "'Israelites in Boston,' 1840–1880," in Jonathan D. Sarna and Ellen Smith, eds., *The Jews of Boston: Essays on the Occasion of the Centenary (1895–1995) of the Combined Jewish Philanthropies of Greater Boston* (Boston: Combined Jewish Philanthropies of Greater Boston, 1995), pp. 44, 65.

23. David B. Davis, "The Other Zion," *New Republic*, April 12, 1993, pp. 29–36; Francis Fukuyama, "Immigrants and Family Values," *Commentary*, May 1993, pp. 26–32; John F. Kennedy, *A Nation of Immigrants*, rev. ed. (New York: Harper & Row, 1964), pp. 67–68.

24. The argument that cultural capital operates as an independent variable is found in Thomas Sowell, *Migrations and Cultures: A World Perspective* (New York: Basic Books, 1996).

25. On this point, see Robert D. Putnam, *Making Democracy Work: Civic Traditions in Modern Italy* (Princeton, N.J.: Princeton University Press, 1993), pp. 167, 168–71; Robert D. Putnam, "The Strange Disappearance of Civic America," *American Prospect*, winter 1996, pp. 34–48.

26. Donna Gabaccia, *From the Other Side: Women, Gender, and Immigrant Life in the United States, 1820–1990* (Bloomington: Indiana University Press, 1994), p. xvii.

27. Susan Hoeber Rudolph and Lloyd I. Rudolph, "Modern Hate," *New Republic*, March 22, 1993, pp. 24–29.

28. Orlando Patterson, *Ethnic Chauvinism: The Reactionary Impulse* (New York: Stein & Day, 1977), pp. 149–50.

29. Jim Sleeper, *The Closest of Strangers: Liberalism and the Politics of Race in New York* (New York: W. W. Norton, 1990), p. 234.

30. Richard Brookhiser, "Melting Pot or Boiling Pot?" *New York Observer*, May 28, 1990, p. 5.

31. Arthur Mann, *LaGuardia: A Fighter Against His Times* (Chicago: University of Chicago Press, 1959), p. 21.

32. Recent arguments for the benefits of immigrant assimilation are Linda Chavez, *Out of the Barrio: Toward a New Politics of Hispanic Assimilation* (New York: Basic Books, 1992); John J. Miller, *The Unmaking of Americans: How Multiculturalism Has Undermined the Assimilation Ethic* (New York: Free Press, 1998).

What Americans Think About Race and Ethnicity

EVERETT C. LADD

THE UNITED STATES faces two big challenges in ethnic relations: moving to further eradicate the bitter racial legacy that began with
slavery and Jim Crow; and successfully assimilating into an increasingly
diverse American family millions of new immigrants, drawn heavily from
Central and South America, and Asia. Both areas have problems and tensions aplenty. Norman Hill, president of the A. Philip Randolph Institute,
has reminded readers of an inescapable fact of American history—that
African Americans are the only ethnic group that was brought here against
its will "as chattel," and then faced another century of institutionalized
racism, known as Jim Crow.[1] Even the wisest of subsequent policies could
not have swept away this tragic legacy, and U.S. policies on race over the
last half century have often not been the most enlightened. On immigration,
this country's fabled melting pot has achieved extraordinary successes in
making *e pluribus unum* a substantial reality rather than a pious wish. Still,
each major wave of immigration has brought with it conflict between
newcomers and older, established groups. The present wave is no exception.

We know that problems still abound in ethnic relations. What we need to know is how things are trending. How successful is the contemporary United States in reducing ethnic-based animosity—in giving one of the country's oldest groups, African Americans, a surer sense of opportunity and progress, and its own responsibility, and convincing new immigrants that the promise of American life is for them and the future, not a thing of the past?

The Debate over Racial Progress

Events in America's race relations have periodically prompted fear that we are losing ground. In the midst of the civil rights protests of the late 1960s, a presidential commission chaired by Illinois Governor Otto Kerner concluded that the United States was "moving toward two societies, one black, one white."[2] In 1995, following the verdict in the O. J. Simpson case, a bevy of news magazines and commentators concluded that the Commission's prophecy had been realized. A huge literature on American race relations has appeared in recent years, with authors offering sharply divergent interpretations of whether data show a narrowing or a widening of this largest-of-all ethnic divide. Andrew Hacker has forcefully argued the "two societies" thesis; Stephan and Abigail Thernstrom have found great progress in black-white relations and in the status of African Americans—much more than is usually acknowledged.[3]

A Lessening of the Divide

For more than two decades now, my colleagues and I at the Roper Center for Public Opinion Research have been examining survey findings on ethnic relations. These data show unequivocally that both African Americans and their fellow citizens who are called whites see the country's race relations in terms far more complex and ambiguous than "two societies" envision them. As we would expect, given their experience, those who are called blacks are much more inclined than others to emphasize the problems racism has bequeathed. But they now see comity along with conflict, opportunity as well as discrimination, progress together with persisting difficulties. And like others, African Americans find that the problems confronting their communities in the 1990s have roots running far deeper than present discrimination and requiring new solutions. For all the legacy of pain and anger, separation and name-calling, stereotyping and oversimplification, many Americans see race relations today in hues vastly more subtle than black and white. Let us look at the survey record.

The Legacy of the Past

Because they have felt racism as others have not, African Americans remain today more insistent on the assumption of national responsibility for remedies. They are more inclined than any other group to back calls for government efforts at remediation. Asked, for example, whether we are spending "too much, too little, or about the right amount" on assistance to blacks, two-thirds (65 percent) of African Americans told interviewers for the National Opinion Research Center in 1996 that we're spending too little, a position taken by less than one-fifth (17 percent) of whites. A Gallup poll of early 1997 found whites by roughly two to one saying that government should not make any special effort to help minorities because they should help themselves, blacks by a virtually identical two-to-one majority saying that the national government should make every effort to improve the position of blacks and other minorities.

Though a majority of African Americans say that they have never personally been denied a job or promotion because of their race, the proportion who claim that they have (44 percent) is more than three times that of whites (13 percent; survey by ABC News and the *Washington Post*, March 16–19, 1998). It is not surprising, then, that blacks are much more supportive than whites of affirmative action programs designed to give compensatory preference to minorities. Hispanic Americans are more inclined to endorse affirmative action than non-Hispanic whites but are significantly less so than blacks (Fig. 1).

Beyond Victimization

Yet if African Americans more than other groups see the need for special federal remedial efforts, many in the community now reject the view that their problems are primarily white inflicted. Asked in October 1995 in a Yankelovich Partners survey for *Time*/CNN whether they think "the problems that most blacks face are caused primarily by whites," only 30 percent of blacks (and 13 percent of whites) said they are. An NBC News/*Wall Street Journal* poll conducted that same month found only 25 percent of African Americans saying that the most important step in improving race relations involves "white Americans doing more to recognize and reduce racism by whites against blacks."

Perhaps the most dramatic evidence of African Americans' rejecting victimization as a prime or sufficient explanation for their community's problems comes from surveys taken by Yankelovich Partners for *Time* and CNN in September 1997. Along with regular national samples of white and black adults, the survey added special samples of teenagers. These studies show dramatic generational changes, away from historical stereotypes of the respective groups. For example, while a clear majority of black adults

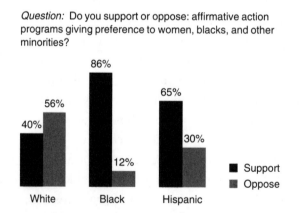

Question: Do you support or oppose: affirmative action programs giving preference to women, blacks, and other minorities?

Fig. 1. Opinions of affirmative action programs; survey by ABC News/ *Washington Post*, August 1–5, 1996.

attribute black Americans having worse jobs, income, and housing (compared with whites) "mainly . . . to discrimination," a solid majority of black teens reject this view (Fig. 2A). This difference seems to result in large part from contrasting generational experiences: whereas a slight majority of adult blacks said they had been victims of racial discrimination, only one black teen in four said he or she had been. Moreover, a large majority of adult blacks think most whites consider blacks inferior, a majority of black teens do not think so.

Important generational shifts are also evident in the white population. A large majority of white adults said that failure to take advantage of

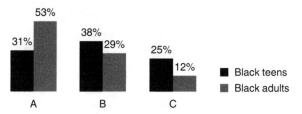

Question: Which of the following statements do you agree with most: (A) Black job applicants have to be better qualified than whites to get a job; (B) Black job applicants have to be as qualified as whites to get a job; (C) Black job applicants can get jobs even when they are less qualified than other applicants?

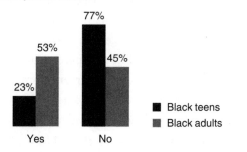

Question: Have you yourself ever been a victim of discrimination because you are black?

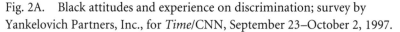

Fig. 2A.   Black attitudes and experience on discrimination; survey by Yankelovich Partners, Inc., for *Time*/CNN, September 23–October 2, 1997.

opportunities is a greater problem for black Americans today than discrimination by whites. Among teens it was reversed: a large plurality of white teenagers called discrimination by whites the greater problem for black Americans (Fig. 2B).

The last chart in Figure 2 (Fig. 2C) confounds expectations about current racial attitudes. All four groups—teens and adults—reject the idea that the problems most black Americans face are caused primarily by whites. Black teenagers are as inclined to this stance as are white adults. White teenagers are more likely than black teenagers to attribute black Americans' problems to whites' prejudice and discrimination. Over half of the black teens think members of their community have worse jobs, income, and so on because "most blacks don't have the motivation or will to pull themselves up out of their poverty"; only 24 percent of white teens take this view.

These extraordinary findings reflect a growing tendency on the part of both groups, especially the young among them, to reject past racial stereotypes and easy, self-serving answers. Both white and black teenagers seem to have moved toward accepting their own group's responsibility for racial problems, rather than dismissing the problems as simply "their fault."

Comity and Opportunity

Few blacks or whites believe that a satisfactory state has been reached in racial comity, but judgments are far from bleak. In a Gallup survey conducted in June 1998, 59 percent of African Americans said that "only a few" of their group dislike whites; 27 percent attributed that stance to "many" African Americans, and only 5 percent to most. The responses were almost identical when whites were asked to assess blacks' feelings toward them. Only 20 percent of black respondents told Gallup interviewers in October 1995 that they believe most white people "want to keep blacks down."

Many blacks see progress and greater opportunity. For example, in a

Question: In your view, which of the following is more of a problem for black Americans today: (A) failure to take advantage of available opportunities, or (B) discrimination by whites?

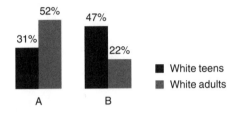

Question: On the average, black Americans have worse jobs, income, and housing than white people. Do you think these differences are . . .

. . . mainly due to discrimination?

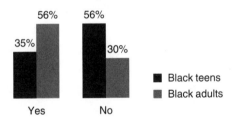

. . . mainly because most blacks don't have the motivation or will power to pull themselves up out of their poverty?

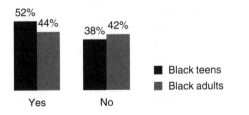

Fig. 2B.   Generational attitude of blacks and whites on questions of discrimination; survey by Yankelovich Partners, Inc., for *Time*/CNN, September 23–October 2, 1997.

survey taken for the *Washington Post* in the summer of 1996, although 45 percent of black respondents said that they have less opportunity than whites to live a middle-class life, 44 percent said they have about the same degree of opportunity, and 6 percent that they have even more. Sixty-five percent of blacks, compared with 63 percent of whites, told interviewers for the National Opinion Research Center in the spring of 1996 that "people like me and my family have a good chance of improving our standard of living."

Integration and Shared Values

What is perhaps most striking in our survey findings is the increase in the proportion of white and blacks alike reporting interaction with members of the other group as friends and neighbors. For example, ABC News and the *Washington Post* have asked whites on a number of occasions since 1981, most recently in 1997, whether they know any African American whom they consider a fairly close personal friend, and the counterpart question (for African Americans) on white friends. We now report many more cross-group friendships than we did a decade ago (Fig. 3). Similarly, surveys taken by the National Opinion Research Center of the

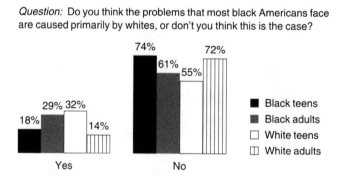

Question: Do you think the problems that most black Americans face are caused primarily by whites, or don't you think this is the case?

Fig. 2C.   White responsibilities—blacks and whites compared; survey by Yankelovich Partners, Inc., for *Time*/CNN, September 23–October 2, 1997.

University of Chicago since the late 1970s show a fairly steady increase in the proportion of whites reporting that they live in neighborhoods with blacks (Fig. 4). The same NORC surveys show a big gain in support for open housing laws—from 37 percent in 1978 supporting legislation that says "a homeowner cannot refuse to sell to someone because of their race or color," to 65 percent backing it in 1996 (Fig. 5).

In a survey taken by Gallup in January and February 1997, only 24 percent of white respondents said they would rather live in a neighborhood with white families only; 61 percent said that if they could find the housing they wanted they would rather live in a neighborhood that had both blacks and whites. In the same study, just 7 percent of blacks opted for a neighborhood exclusively black; 83 percent preferred one that was racially

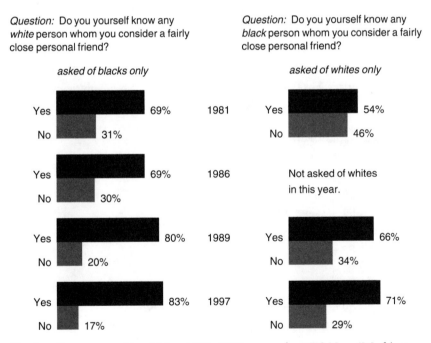

Fig. 3. Cross-group friendships, 1981–1997; survey by ABC News/*Washington Post*, latest that of June 5–8, 1997.

integrated. Such findings need to be viewed cautiously and interpreted carefully. Saying one is committed to integrated housing is now the only acceptable professed norm; some almost certainly opt for it in polls who would not follow it in real life. But professed norms are themselves important. The proportion of Americans living in integrated neighborhoods is on the increase, in fact, and residential integration as a norm has gained substantially.

For all the bitter history of black-white relations in the U.S., the two groups share the same underlying values. There is, then, a real base on which to build better relations. Norman Hill of the A. Philip Randolph Institute finds it remarkable "that blacks, who bear the legacy of slavery, segregation, oppression, exclusion, and the daily indignities of racism are, in many ways, the most resilient archetypal Americans, still holding on to the notion that perseverance and hard work will give them a real shot at opportunity and equality."[4] It is indeed remarkable, though not, I think, surprising. There is broad ideological agreement across the American people on such basic ideals as a distinctive understanding of equality—pegged to opportunity rather than results—and a sense that the American system,

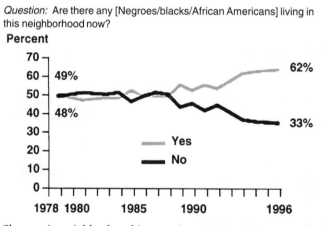

Question: Are there any [Negroes/blacks/African Americans] living in this neighborhood now?

Fig. 4.   Changes in neighborhood integration, 1978–1996; surveys by the National Opinion Research Center-General Social Survey.

for all its faults, does much to extend opportunity. Asked, for example, in a *Los Angeles Times* survey of October 1995 which statement is closer to their opinion, "In the United States today, anyone who works hard enough can make it economically," or "No matter how hard you work you just can't make it economically in this country today," a large majority of blacks took the "anyone can make it" position. The proportion of whites taking that position was higher than that of blacks, but only modestly so.

Immigration and Changing Ethnic Backgrounds

Since its founding, the United States has grappled with vast problems and inequities in black-white relations. But along with this enduring cleavage there has been a series of shifting ethnic group conflicts and accommodations, prompted by succeeding waves of immigration. The

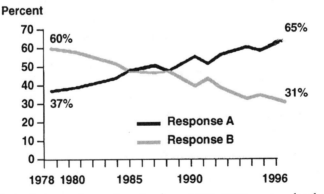

Question: Suppose there is a community-wide vote on the general housing issue. There are two possible laws to vote on. Which law would you vote for? (A) One law says that a homeowner can decide for himself whom to sell his house to, even if he prefers not to sell to [Negroes/blacks/African Americans]. (B) The second law says that a homeowner cannot refuse to sell to someone because of their race or color.

Fig. 5.   Attitudes toward open housing laws, 1978–1996; surveys by the National Opinion Research Center-General Social Survey.

U.S. is highly diverse ethnically, yet for all this heterogeneity, it is a *nation*, not just a collection of separate ethnic groups. It is hardly surprising, given our need to create and maintain a nation on the lines *e pluribus unum* describes, that we have periodically worried about our ability to maintain and indeed enhance "one nation" status.

G. K. Chesterton described the continuing challenge in his brilliant opening chapter of *What I Saw in America*.[5] Chesterton wrote of "the great American experiment; the experiment of a democracy of diverse races which has been compared to a melting pot." This experiment naturally puts great pressure on the vessel: "That metaphor implies that the pot itself is of a certain shape and a certain substance; a pretty solid substance. The melting pot must not melt." How well is the pot holding now, as a new century begins?

After a period of low immigration that followed a vast tightening of American immigration law in the 1920s, legal immigration was again expanded in the 1960s. In recent years, too, substantial numbers of immigrants have entered the country illegally. As a result, the foreign-born population of the U.S. has climbed—from 5.4 percent in 1960 to 9.3 percent in 1996. And, far more than their predecessors, recent immigrants have come from Latin America and from Asia.

Worries about the impact of the new waves of immigration on national unity and values should be greatly tempered by the fact that such concerns have proved ill founded in previous periods, when rates of immigration relative to the base population exceeded those of the present day. They should also be greatly diminished, if not dismissed, by recent survey findings that show newcomers to America committed to its values and confident of their chance to succeed in their adopted home.

In mid-1995, Gallup surveyed a national cross-section of all adult Americans and large samples of immigrants—including "most recent arrivals" who have been in the U.S. ten years or less. The survey found that the immigrants closely resemble the entire adult population on most matters of policy and values. For example, 59 percent of all adults and 59 percent of immigrants (including 57 percent of the most recent arrivals) said national policy should encourage immigrants "to blend into American culture by giving up some important aspects of their own culture." Only 32 percent of all adults and 26 percent of recent immigrants favored encouraging immigrants "to maintain their own culture more strongly." The idea of the U.S. as a melting pot "in which people of different cultures combine into a unified American culture" was endorsed by a full three-quarters of the immigrant population.

The Gallup survey found immigrants even more likely than other Americans to see the country as a land of opportunity: 93 percent of the immigrants surveyed agreed with the statement that "people who work hard to better themselves can get ahead in this country," the position of 85 percent of the entire population. Immigrants overwhelmingly described the reception they received upon arrival as welcoming—by margins of nine to one and better.[6] Looking ahead, three immigrants in every four said they expect their children to have even better economic opportunities in the U.S. than they themselves have had, and that the children will face even less discrimination.

On such matters as the opportunity for themselves and their children to find good jobs, the amount of political freedom, and the chances of being treated fairly under the law, immigrants of all arrival times gave the U.S. extraordinarily positive marks. Seventy-five percent of the immigrants called the U.S. better than their homeland in the amount of political freedom; only 5 percent ranked it lower on this dimension than their place of birth. In two areas, however—feeling safe from crime, and the moral tenor of the society—the U.S. got quite low marks. Only 33 percent said the U.S. was better than their homeland in realizing moral values; 48 percent ranked it lower.

What is most important, we see no signs in the survey findings of a serious split between immigrant newcomers and longer-term residents. States like California and Texas, which have experienced heavy immigration in recent years, certainly have had conflict on issues like bilingual education.

But in all important regards this latest great wave of immigration to the United States resembles the earlier ones. The bulk of the new immigrants seek integration into their new nation and espouse its ideals.

Taking Yes for the Answer

Societies sometimes find themselves inclined to resist good news. Developments in ethnic relations in the United States are now a case in point. It is not hard to see why the extent of the positive trends is resisted. Long-standing tensions and prejudice, especially involving whites and blacks, have been the unhappiest chapter in American historical experience. Stressing the positive now may seem an attempt to gloss over past wrongs and minimize current needs. Against the backdrop of problems as wrenching as those that have surrounded race relations, no analyst wants to be cast in the role of Pollyanna.

Nonetheless, tensions in American ethnic relations have diminished in recent decades. All the groups making up the American mosaic appear more positive and optimistic today than they were when the civil rights revolution began. Set against the standard of where we would like our society to be, the present mix of ethnic group attitudes and relations leaves much ground to be covered. But set against past experience—indeed that of any previous point since the country's founding—today's ethnic relations manifest striking progress.

Notes

1. Norman Hill, "Race in America—Through a Glass, Darkly," *Public Perspective*, February/March 1996, pp. 1–4.

2. National Advisory Commission on Civil Disorders, *Report* (New York: Bantam, 1968), p. 1.

3. Andrew Hacker, *Two Nations: Black and White, Separate, Hostile, Unequal* (New York: Scribner's, 1992); Stephan Thernstrom and Abigail Thernstrom, *America in Black and White: One Nation, Indivisible* (New York: Simon & Schuster, 1997).

4. Hill, p. 3.

5. G. K. Chesterton, *What I Saw in America* (New York: Dodd, Mead & Co., 1922; repr. 1968, Da Capo Press).

6. The survey reported on here was taken by the Gallup organization for CNN and *USA Today*, May 25–June 4, 1995.

Wrestling with Stigma

SHELBY STEELE

I HAVE A WHITE FRIEND who has told me many times that he feels no racial guilt despite the fact that he was raised in the Deep South before the end of segregation. Though he grew up amid the inequality and moral duplicity of segregation, and inevitably benefited from it as a white, he says simply that he did not invent the institution. He experienced it as a fate he was born into. And when segregation was finally challenged in the civil rights era, any solidarity that he felt with other southern whites was grounded more in a sense of pathos than in any resistance to change. So, he says, there is no "objective basis" for racial guilt on his part.

Recently I was surprised to hear the novelist William Styron, a southerner by birth and upbringing, say on television that he, too, felt "no [white] guilt" despite the fact that his grandmother had owned slaves as a girl. And there was something emphatic, even challenging in his pronouncement

This essay was previously published as Part 1 of "Wrestling with Stigma" from *A Dream Deferred: The Second Betrayal of Black Freedom in America*, by Shelby Steele, copyright © 1998 by Shelby Steele. It is reprinted here by permission of HarperCollins Publishers, Inc.

that discouraged questioning. For as long as I can remember, I have heard white Americans of every background make this Pronouncement.

This is certainly understandable. White guilt threatens the credibility of everything whites say and do regarding race. Specifically it threatens them with what I have called ulteriority—the suspicion that their racial stands do not come from their announced motivations but from ulterior ones driven by guilt. We can say, for example, that the white liberal bends over backward because he is motivated by guilt even though he says he is motivated by true concern. Or we can say the anger of the "angry white male" is simply his way of denying guilt. We can use guilt to discredit every position whites take on racial matters. So it is not surprising to hear so many reflexive denials. When people like my friend or Styron do this, they are disclaiming ulterior motives. They want us to accept that they mean exactly what they say.

But I, for one, very rarely do accept this, or at least not without a glimpse past their words to the matter of ulterior motive. This is because there simply is no social issue in American life more driven by ulterior forces than race. One reason for this is that white American motivation in racial matters has gone largely unexamined, except to attribute support for policies like affirmative action to white goodwill and nonsupport to white racism. "White guilt" is almost a generic term referring to any ulterior white motivation. But the degree of ulteriority in American race relations is far too great to be explained entirely by guilt. I think the great unacknowledged event of the civil rights era was that white Americans became a stigmatized group. I also believe that our entire national culture of racial and social reform—the policies, programs, norms, and protocols by which we address race-related problems—has been shaped more by the stigmatization of whites than by any other factor, including the actual needs of blacks.

Ironically, it was the idea of equality that brought stigma to whites. In the civil rights era, when white America finally accepted a legal equality that would extend to different races, it also accepted an idea that shamed it. For three centuries white America had used race to defeat equality. It had indulged in self-serving notions of white supremacy, had transgressed the highest principles of the democracy, and had enforced inequality on others while possessing the ideas to know better. The American racial shame is special in that slavery and segregation were knowing indulgences. The nation's first president had denounced the institution of slavery and freed his own slaves, yet it would take two more centuries for segregation to be outlawed. An evil strung out over the centuries and conducted in a full knowledge of itself.

America's new commitment to equality in the civil rights era brought with it an accountability for all this. What no one could have foreseen was that a great shaming of white Americans and American institutions was a condition of greater racial equality. In a sense the new embrace of equality floated the nation's racial shame, unanchored it, so that it rose to the surface of American life as a truth that the nation would have to answer for. As a result equality in the United States has depended on a vigilance that associates this racial shame with whites and American institutions. This association, of course, is the basis of white stigmatization.

In this way the idea of equality has established a social framework in which white Americans are no longer "universal" people or "Everyman" Americans. Today there is a consciousness that whites are a specific people, a group with a history, a fate, and a stigma like other groups. So far equality has worked by bringing whites down into stigma rather than by lifting lacks and other minorities up out of it. The morality implied in equality stigmatized whites as racist and thus gave them a group identity that they are accountable to in the eyes of others even if they reject its terms. Very often the strongest group identities form in response to stigmatization because stigmas are a kind of fate, a shared and inescapable experience. In any case the history of white racism, the idea of equality, the stigma created by these two things, and the need to wrestle with this stigma as the way back to decency—all this gave white Americans a new post-sixties identity that was not universal. In the way that blacks had been stigmatized as inferior, whites, too, became a group marked by a human incompleteness.

As black Americans know only too well, to be stigmatized is to be drawn into a Sisyphean struggle for redemption from the accusation carried by the stigma. It is also to lose some of one's freedom to the judgment, opinion, or prejudice of others. White Americans now know what it is like to be presumed racist and to have that presumption count as fact against them. What blacks know is that one group's stigma is another group's power. Stigmatized as inferior, blacks were deprived by whites of freedom itself. Now stigmatized as racists, whites can easily be extorted by blacks for countless concessions. So, when a group fights against its stigma, it is also fighting for its freedom from the power of another group.

Being white in America has always meant being free from racial stigma, as if "whiteness" might be defined as simply the absence of stigma. Until recently we never had stigmatizing epithets for whites of any real power. "Honky" hardly compared to the visceral "nigger." (Today the term "racist" is quite effective against whites, but this is a post-sixties phenomenon.) This absence of stigma was always the blessing of being white in the United States, while color, even "one drop," was a stigma in itself that defined all who carried it as alienated "others." In America whites have been the "it," not the "other," so they have always had a rather myopic view of race as essentially a problem of "others."

One of the best-selling books on race during my youth was a book called *Black Like Me* by a white man, John Howard Griffin, who had chemically darkened his skin and traveled the South passing for black. What made the book sensational was that a white man had volunteered for the black stigma, the experience of the alienated other. But it was little more than a novelty book that put off many blacks because its very premise tended to mistake the black stigma for the entire black experience. The reader, whom the narrator presumed to be white, was invited to watch one of his or her own in the land of the "other." And the black "other" was shown to endure little melodramas of man's inhumanity to man at which the "good" white reader could be appropriately aghast. This began an age when white America was invited not to see black life but to be aghast at it. However, the book's greater sin was to suggest that even if whites were morally obligated to support equality, race was still a problem that affected others.

But equality finally gave whites their own racial otherness. The idea of democratic equality—explicitly applied beyond even the boundary of race by the 1964 Civil Rights Bill—showed white Americans as a group to have betrayed the nation's best democratic principles. Even though it was the white embrace of these principles that brought the civil rights victories, it was the need to embrace them in the middle of the twentieth century that proved the white betrayal of them. And this profoundly injured the legitimacy of whites as a group in relation to principles of any kind. They had used race to give themselves license from principle.

Of course, the fact of a group finding a pretext for violating its own principles was hardly new. What is new is for an oppressive group to embrace equality at the expense of its own moral legitimacy so that it has to live with those it once oppressed without the moral authority to enforce the society's best principles. This situation, this fate, comprises the "otherness" of white America today. It is alienating to live with this stigmatic association with shame, and to have lost standing in relation to the principles one was raised to cherish, to watch the institutions of one's society—from the family to the public schools—weaken for want of demanding principles, and to be without the necessary authority to restore them, to lose "universality," to have one's angry former victim define social morality, to feel both a little guilty and falsely accused, to feel pressured toward a fashionable relativism as toward racial decency itself—all this and more has come to whites as an experience of "otherness" that I believe is the unexamined source of U.S. racial policy since the sixties. The idea of racial equality has given a new and unique contour to the white American experience. Perhaps a *White Like Me* is now called for, a book that looks into the world behind the white stigma and reports back to us.

One point such a book would no doubt make is that stigmas are often double binds. The stigma of whites as racists mandates that they redeem the nation from its racist history but then weakens their authority to enforce the very democratic principles that true redemption would require. And this is no small problem, because the United States is no better than its principles. It may be the first country in the world to have principles and ideas for an identity.

The promise of the American democracy was that freedom, and the discipline of principles that supports it, would be the salvation of humanity. This discipline would replace the atavistic power of divine kings and feudalism with a power grounded in reason. Principle would be not only the soul of America but also the basis of its very legitimacy as a nation among nations. The principles of freedom were the case for a new nation.

And yet race is always an atavistic source of power, going back to a primordial source, back to the natural order. Like a divine or natural right, it comes from God or nature and presumes that one's race is free to dominate other races by an authority beyond reason. The white racist believes that God made whites superior so that even a democracy grounded in principle and reason is not obligated to include blacks and other races. Atavistic power always oppresses because it is immune to reason and principle. The great ambition of democracy was precisely to free man from atavistic power through a discipline of principle that would forbid it.

I say all this to make the point that white racism was no small thing. It was a primitivism, a return to atavistic power, and, most important, a flaunting of the precept that America was founded on: that the freedom of man depended on a discipline of fragile and abstract ideas and principles. White racism made America illegitimate by its own terms, not a new nation after all, but an "old world" nation that used God as an excuse for its oppression and exploitation, a pretender to reason and civilization.

So what happens today when a white American leader, even of the stature and popular appeal of a Ronald Reagan, questions affirmative action on grounds of principle? The Reagan administration, famous for its disbelief in racial preferences, refused to challenge these policies because even this extremely popular president lacked the moral authority as a white to enforce the nation's very best principles—advancement by merit, a single standard of excellence, individual rather than group rights, and the rest. Not only have white Americans been stigmatized as betrayers of principle, but also those principles themselves have been stigmatized by their association with white duplicity.

Here were whites exclaiming the sacredness of individual rights while they used the atavism of race to deny those rights to blacks. They celebrated merit as the most egalitarian form of advancement, yet made sure that no amount of merit would enable blacks to advance. Therefore these principles themselves came to be seen as part of the machinery of white supremacy, as instruments of duplicity that whites could use to "exclude" blacks. The terrible effect of this was the demonization of America's best principles as they applied to racial reform.

This situation, I believe, has given post-sixties racial reform its most stunning irony: Because difficult principles are themselves stigmatized as the demonic instruments of racism, white Americans and American institutions have had to betray the nation's best principles in racial reform in order to win back their own moral authority. For some thirty years now white redemption has required setting aside the very discipline of principles that has elsewhere made America great.

If not principles, then what? The answer in a word is deference. Stigmatized as racist, whites and American institutions have no moral authority over the problems they try to solve through race-related reform. They cannot address a problem like inner-city poverty by saying that government assistance will only follow a show of such timeless American principles as self-reliance, hard work, moral responsibility, sacrifice, and initiative—all now stigmatized as demonic principles that "blame the victims" and cruelly deny the helplessness imposed on them by a heritage of oppression. Instead their racial reform must replace principle with deference. It must show white American authority deferring to the nation's racial tragedy out of remorse. And this remorse must be seen to supersede commitment to principles. In fact, any preoccupation with principles can only be read as a failure of remorse. "Caring," "compassion," "feeling," and "empathy" must be seen to displace principles in public policy around race.

But deference should not be read as an abdication of white American authority to black American authority. American institutions do not let blacks, in the name of their oppressive history, walk in the front door and set policy. It is important to remember that these institutions are trying to redeem their authority, not abdicate it. Their motivation is to fend off the stigma that weakens their moral authority. So deference is first of all in the interest of white moral authority, not black uplift. Certainly there may be genuine remorse behind it, but the deference itself serves only the moral authority of American institutions.

And this deference is always a grant of license—relief from the sacrifice, struggle, responsibility, and morality of those demanding principles that healthy communities entirely depend on. And virtually all race-related reform since the sixties has been defined by deference. This reform never raises expectations for blacks with true accountability, never requires that they actually develop as Americans, and absolutely never blames blacks when they don't develop. It always asks less of blacks and exempts them from the expectations, standards, principles, and challenges that are considered demanding but necessary for the development of competence and character in others. Deferential reform—everything from welfare to affirmative action to multiculturalism—is the license to be spared the rigors of development. And at its heart is a faith in an odd sort of magic—that the license that excuses people from development is the best thing for their development.

Nowhere in the ancient or modern world—except in the most banal utopian writing—is there the idea that people will become self-sufficient if they are given a lifetime income that is slightly better than subsistence with no requirement either to work or to educate themselves. Nowhere is there the idea that young girls should be subsidized for having children out of wedlock, with more money for more children. And yet this is precisely the form of welfare that came out of the sixties—welfare as a license not to develop. Out of deference this policy literally set up incentives that all but mandated inner-city inertia, that destroyed the normal human relationship to work and family, and that turned the values of hard work, sacrifice, and delayed gratification into a fool's game.

Deferential policies transform black difficulties into excuses for license.

The deferential policy maker looks at the black teen pregnancy problem with remorse because this is what puts him on the path to redemption. But this same remorse leads him to be satisfied by his own capacity to feel empathy, rather than by the teenage girl's achievement of a higher moral standard. So he sets up a nice center for new mothers at her high school, thereby advertising to other girls that they too will be supported—and therefore licensed—in having babies of their own. Soon this center is full, and in the continuing spirit of remorse, he solicits funds to expand the facility. It was not Joblessness that bred the black underclass; it was thirty-five years of deference.

Deferential policies have also injured the most privileged generation of black Americans in history. Black students from families with incomes above seventy thousand dollars a year score lower on the SAT than white students from families with incomes of less than ten thousand a year. When the University of California was forced to drop race-based affirmative action, a study was done to see if a needs-based policy would bring in a similar number of blacks. What they quickly discovered is that the needs-based approach only brought in more high-achieving but poor whites and Asians. In other words, the top quartile of black American students—often from two-parent families with six-figure incomes and private-school educations—is frequently not competitive with whites and Asians even from lower quartiles. But it is precisely this top quartile of black students that has been most aggressively pursued for the last thirty years with affirmative-action preferences. Infusing the atmosphere of their education from early childhood is not the idea that they will have to steel themselves to face stiff competition but that they will receive a racial preference, that mediocrity will win for them what only excellence wins for others.

Out of deference, elite universities have offered the license not to compete to the most privileged segment of black youth, precisely the segment that has no excuse for not competing. Affirmative action is protectionism for the best and brightest from black America. And because blacks are given spaces they have not won by competition, whites and especially Asians have had to compete all the harder for their spots. So we end up with the effect we always get with deferential reforms: an incentive to black weakness relative to others. Educators who adamantly support affirmative action—the very institutionalization of low expectations—profess confusion about the performance gap between privileged blacks and others. And they profess this confusion even as they make a moral mission of handing out the rewards of excellence for mediocre black performance.

A welfare of license for the poor and an affirmative action of license for the best and brightest—the perfect incentives for inertia in the former and mediocrity in the latter. But this should not be surprising. Because "racial problems" have been a pretext for looking at blacks rather than at whites, we have missed the fact that most racial reforms were conceived as deferential opportunities for whites rather than as developmental opportunities for blacks.

Because deference is a grant of license to set aside demanding principles, it opens the door to the same atavistic powers—race, ethnicity, and gender—that caused oppression in the first place. Again, the United States was founded on the insight that freedom required atavisms to be contained by a discipline of principles. The doctrine that separates church from state is an example. And race, ethnicity, and gender are like religion in that they arise from a different authority than the state. They come from fate, or some would say from God, and so are antithetical to democracy, which comes from an agreement among men to live by a social contract in which no single race can be validated without diminishing all others.

But thirty-some years of deferential social policies that work by relieving us of principle have joined atavisms to the state as valid sources of power. (This also happened recently in Eastern Europe, where the unifying principles of Communism collapsed so that the atavisms of tribe, clan, and religion surged back as valid sources of power and entitlement. War has been the all too frequent result.) A quick look at America's campuses reveals what I have elsewhere called a "new sovereignty," in which each minority carves out a sovereign territory and identity based on the atavisms of race, ethnicity, and gender. And this new atavistic sovereignty supersedes the nation's sovereignty and flaunts its democratic principles. One is a black or a woman before one is an American.

It is no accident that preferential affirmative action became the model for racial and social reform after America's great loss of moral authority in the sixties. Affirmative action is an atavistic model of reform that legalizes the use of atavisms in place of principles right in the middle of a democracy. In this way it mimics the infamous Jim Crow laws that also legalized the atavism of race over democratic principles. In Jim Crow, white supremacy was the motivation; in affirmative action it was deference. The first indulgence in atavisms so wiped out white moral authority that it made the second indulgence inevitable.

To take all this a step further, liberal whites and American institutions also shifted the locus of social virtue itself from principles to atavisms. Since the sixties, social virtuousness has lost its connection to difficult and raceless principles and become little more than a fashionable tolerance for atavisms. Of course tolerance of different races, ethnicities, and genders is virtuous. But moving out of a spirit of deference, white liberals and American institutions have asked that these atavisms be tolerated as legalized currencies of power. This is how the virtue of tolerance becomes a corruption of democratic fairness—you don't merely accept people of different races; you validate their race or ethnicity as a currency of power and entitlement over others.

This is the perversion of social virtue that gave us a multiculturalism that has nothing to do with culture. The goal of America's highly politicized multiculturalism is to create an atavistic form of citizenship—a citizenship of preferential status in which race, ethnicity, and gender are linked to historic victimization to justify entitlements unavailable to other citizens. Culture is a pretext, a cover. The trick of this multiculturalism is to pass off atavisms as if they were culture. So people think they are being "tolerant" of "cultural diversity" when, in fact, they are supporting pure racial power.

In fact multiculturalism actually suppresses America's rich cultural variety, because much actual culture does not mesh with victimization. A troublesome implication of jazz, for example, is that blacks are irrepressible because they created one of the world's great art forms in the midst of oppression. It is images of helplessness that highlight their racial atavism as a source of entitlement. So the black cultural genius for self-invention and improvisation that made jazz possible are not drawn out and celebrated in multiculturalism. Nor are the many other cultural ingenuities—psychological, social, and political—by which blacks managed to live fully human lives despite their hard fate. Culture gets in the way of multiculturalism.

But multiculturalism is the kind of thing that happens when a democracy loses the moral authority to protect the individual citizen as the only inviolate unit of rights. In any society atavisms can only be repressed, never entirely extinguished. They are always waiting for the opportunity to wedge themselves into the life of society under some high-sounding and urgent guise. No one invents the moral mask better than those driven to have their race, ethnicity, or gender bring them a preference over others—whether white segregationists or minority supporters of affirmative action. And when the majority of a society is stigmatized for past betrayal of principles, and when those principles themselves are emblems of duplicity, then primitive atavisms easily present themselves as salvation itself. Multiculturalism masks a bid for pure atavistic power; it is an assault on democracy that Americans entertain because they feel they must. It was conceived not to spread culture but to win some of the territory opened up by the weakened moral authority of American institutions.

PART TWO

PRIVATE LIVES AND PUBLIC POLICIES

Residential Segregation Trends

WILLIAM A. V. CLARK

ETHNIC AND RACIAL SEGREGATION has declined substantially from the 1960s when the Kerner Commission Report suggested that the United States was "moving toward two societies, one black, one white—separate and unequal." Decade by decade, residential integration has increased, and it will probably continue to do so. Of course, this does not mean that segregation has vanished or that housing discrimination has been eliminated, but it does indicate that there has been impressive racial progress in the past three decades.

Seventy years ago, the Chicago school of urban sociology studied the changing residential map of European newcomers who had flooded into cities on the East Coast and in the Middle West. Later, with the influx of African Americans from the South into northern cities, the focus of research shifted to blacks and whites. Today, scholars look beyond black and white, as urban America has become multiethnic and, once again, residential patterns have changed. In fact, two dozen cities now have no majority ethnic or racial group, and the number will grow with continuing immigration.

The changing economic status of members of racial and ethnic groups alters residential patterns, and the evidence from national and selective regional studies indicates that segregation is declining, especially for the more affluent. Yet the residential choices people make inevitably will result in a certain degree of continuing racial and ethnic clustering—a phenomenon that should not be confused with discrimination. For instance, Koreans have gravitated toward certain high-status California suburbs; newly wealthy Asian Indians have chosen to live in certain neighborhoods in Silicon Valley; and Armenians are concentrated in the Glendale region of Los Angeles. Do such patterns suggest unequal residential access? In reality, the residential mosaic is shaped in part by a combination of economic forces and group preferences, and it is simplistic to assume the driving force to be clearly racial animus.

Changing Patterns of Residential Segregation

Residential integration has increased in the past forty years. The changes were slow at first, but the Civil Rights Act of 1964 and subsequent fair housing laws accelerated the process. A standard way of measuring the level of residential segregation is to use what is called the index of dissimilarity, which ranges from a high of 100 (total segregation) to a low of zero (members of racial and ethnic groups randomly distributed). Thus, each census tract (a largish neighborhood of about 4,000 to 6,000 people) in a city with an index of zero would perfectly mirror the racial and ethnic makeup of the larger community.

Table 1 looks at selected cities in the period 1960–1990. In cities in which the minority population is predominantly African American, the index of dissimilarity has dropped from the high 80s to the high 70s; where other minorities are also present, the decline has been considerably greater. Other data from the 1980s confirm this general picture of increased integration, especially in southern and western metropolitan areas with significant new housing construction.[1]

Table 1   Housing Segregation in the Twenty-one Largest Cities with Over 50,000 Blacks

City	INDEX OF DISSIMILARITY [a]			
	1960	1970	1980	1990
Mostly Black Minority				
Chicago	93	93	90	86
Philadelphia	87	84	85	84
Detroit	84	82	84	86
Washington, D.C.	80	79	77	76
Boston	84	84	79	73
Atlanta	89	88	80	81
St. Louis	90	90	76	74
Baltimore	90	89	82	80
Pittsburgh	85	86	79	77
Cleveland	91	90	88	85
Newark	72	76	79	79
Kansas City, Mo.	91	90	83	76
Cincinnati	89	84	79	75
Milwaukee	88	88	81	79
AVERAGES	87	86	82	79
Black and Hispanic				
Los Angeles	82	90	78	66
Houston	94	93	79	66
Dallas	95	96	81	63
Oakland	73	70	71	63
Tampa	94	92	76	65
Miami	98	92	81	74
San Francisco	69	75	65	61
AVERAGES	86	87	76	65

SOURCE: David Armor and William A. V. Clark, "Housing Segregation and School Desegregation," in David Armor, *Forced Justice: School Desegregation and the Law* (New York: Oxford University Press, 1995), p. 128.

[a] For 1960 and 1970 the index is for cities and for whites versus blacks. For 1980 and 1990 the index is for counties and for nonblacks versus blacks.

In Southern California, for example, in many suburban counties outside Los Angeles, indexes of dissimilarity are in the mid-30s. The number of Hispanics, African Americans, and Asians is increasing steadily.[2] Thus, though Orange County may still be viewed as a conservative Republican bastion, by 1990 only a little more than 30 percent of the neighborhoods (census tracts) were over 80 percent non-Hispanic white. Diversity in general had increased dramatically—a picture that squares with the work of scholars who stress the gains brought in recent decades by the drive to reduce discrimination.

The change in the status of blacks is particularly striking. As late as 1970, rich and poor blacks were equally likely to be segregated from white households, but today in Southern California, high-income black households live in highly integrated neighborhoods. Families with incomes less than $10,000 remain in areas with an index of dissimilarity close to 90, but the figure for those with earnings above $60,000 is 40. The civil rights movement is now more than forty years old, and the sustained attack on American racism has paid off.

In 1960 few African Americans lived in suburbia. By 1999 the number of African Americans in the suburbs was about 10.9 million, more than 30 percent of the total black population. Blacks are now about 8 percent of the total population residing in suburbia, and the proportion will continue to increase with rising black incomes. Moreover, increasingly, suburban middle-class blacks are almost indistinguishable from whites with the same education and income.[3]

As the racial gap in family income is further reduced, the level of residential integration will rise. At the same time, it is important to note that the index of dissimilarity is not likely to drop much below 30. Differences in wealth, in neighborhood preferences, and in the structure of urban housing all work to separate members of different racial and ethnic groups.

Residential Patterns

Just why racial and ethnic groups tend to cluster in separate residential areas is a matter of ongoing and contentious debate.[4] Some scholars stress the role of discrimination and argue that income and housing costs play only a minor role in the segregated residential patterns so evident in large metropolitan areas.[5] But there is also a substantial literature that emphasizes not only economic factors but also the choices minorities make—that is, their preference for living with members of their own group (and avoiding others).[6]

The debate over the causes of residential separation is one aspect of the attempt to understand the creation and modification of urban patterns over time. A large literature has documented the role of socioeconomic and family status, as well as ethnic characteristics in defining the ecology of the city.[7] It is certainly possible to identify and classify residential areas within cities on the basis of such variables, and to some degree communities change as the income, ethnicity, and composition of families within them shift. But the intersection between class and race is also important. For instance, white movement out of an inner-city neighborhood that has become heavily African American and often overwhelmingly poor is central to understanding the emergence of black urban concentrations and more affluent, predominantly white suburbs.[8] That classic pattern, however, will continue to change as blacks and Hispanics move up the economic ladder.

Indeed, some new evidence from Southern California suggests that income and education may be more important than previously believed.[9] Well-educated and higher-income black households live in relatively integrated settings—a harbinger of the future in other regions, it would seem (see Fig. 1). Survey data indicate that changing social status, especially that generated by education, has an important effect on the acceptance of "other race" residents in a neighborhood.[10] At the same time, however, low-income households may be experiencing increased segregation, a phenomenon consistent with the pessimism of scholars like Massey and Denton, who write of hypersegregation in many cities.[11]

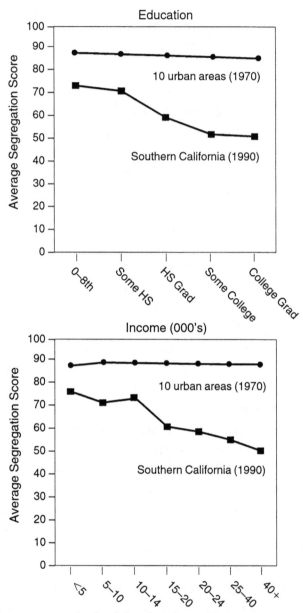

Fig. 1. Average segregation levels by education and income in 1970 and 1990; William A. V. Clark and Julian Wave, "Trends in Residential Integration by Socio-Economic Status in Southern California," *Urban Affairs Quarterly* 32 (1997).

Self-selection and group avoidance have also shaped the residential patterns of European immigrant groups, and that process continues today. Preferences for particular combinations of ethnic neighbors play an important role in the choices families make. But the African American experience has been different from the European. Whites and Asians have a stronger desire than do blacks and Hispanics for neighborhoods of their own race; the ideal mix thus differs for the two groups, and their separate preferences are not so easily reconciled (see Fig. 2). That fact, too, is likely to perpetuate a certain degree of urban residential separation for some time to come.[12]

Diverse preferences, along with group differences in education and income, thus shape the residential landscape, yet some scholars see prejudice as the basic explanation for racial and ethnic clustering.[13] If housing discrimination is indeed still a major force, then changes in the socioeconomic status of blacks—and even in racial attitudes—will not suffice to alter the basic picture. Several studies that have used testers to determine the receptivity of landlords and real estate agents to black families provide evidence that doors are still closed.[14] But surveys that ask households whether they have actually experienced discrimination find relatively few respondents who answer yes. The survey results suggest that the patterns of separation that we see in our cities are more the result of economic differences among groups, and of preferences for living in a neighborhood with people who are similar, than they are of discrimination.[15]

Prospects for Stable
Integrated Neighborhoods

The future of residential integration is bound up with the fundamental demographic changes that are sweeping the nation. The new demography is particularly apparent in California, New York, Florida, Arizona, and Texas—all entry-point states for Hispanic and Asian immigrants. And even though the country is still 75 percent Anglo, several states, including California, as well as some metropolitan areas, already have

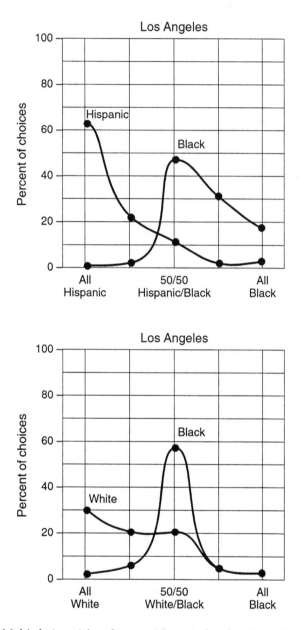

Fig. 2. Multiethnic racial preferences (choices of preferred combinations of neighbors) for Los Angeles and Boston; Multi-City Study of Urban Inequality 1993–1994 (MCSUI).

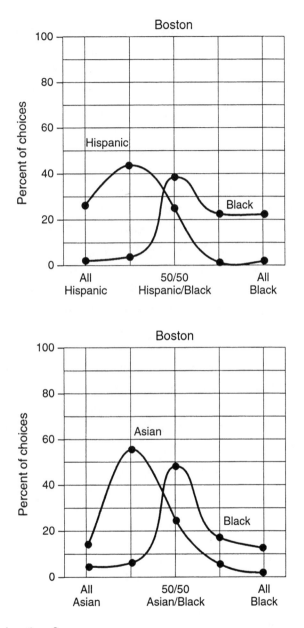

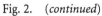

Fig. 2. (*continued*)

populations that are majority minority. Some of the new immigrant groups stick together by choice, and in such a context notions of segregation and separations become increasingly antiquated. In Los Angeles, for example, the index of dissimilarity for Armenians is roughly 90, which means almost total segregation. Several Asian groups (Cambodians, Koreans, Vietnamese, for example) are also residentially concentrated.[16]

There is thus intense clustering for some groups. But, at the same time, old patterns of white flight from incoming African Americans appear to be changing. Overall levels of separation may therefore be declining.[17] On the other hand, stable racially integrated communities are still unusual, and greater integration may simply be the consequence of an influx of white Hispanics rather than of Anglos. Whites and blacks may be living apart, but the arrival of Hispanics has integrated neighborhoods that were formerly overwhelmingly one race—that is, black. The change in the demographic makeup of the nation as a whole, in other words, inevitably has an impact on living patterns.

The two processes—increasing segregation and greater integration—are thus occurring at the same time, although the latter is the stronger (if slower) trend. The future remains unpredictable. As more blacks acquire middle-class status, urban neighborhoods are more and more likely to become a mix of new immigrants and African Americans. But it is also possible that very large scale immigration could undermine the progress made over the past three decades. Moreover, income separates people. The Kerner Report warned against two nations, one black and one white; the real worry may be two societies, one poor and the other affluent—living apart.

Observations and Summary

Pessimists argue that declines in segregation occur only where there are small numbers of African American households, not in the places where most blacks live. And on that basis they conclude that whites want only limited interracial contact. But more affluent and more highly educated black families are clearly welcome in suburban communities, and that fact suggests real change. Will that change be sustained? It will take another decade before we know for certain. Already, however, it is legitimate to ask whether urban concentrations of low-income black households are the result primarily of prejudice or of income constraints.

Notes

1. Reynolds Farley and William Frey, "Changes in the Segregation of Whites from Blacks During the 1980s: Small Steps Toward a More Integrated Society," *American Sociological Review* 59 (1994): 23–45.

2. William A. V. Clark, "Residential Patterns, Avoidance, Assimilation, and Succession," in R. Waldinger and M. Bozorgmehr, eds., *Ethnic Los Angeles* (New York: Russell Sage Foundation, 1996), pp. 109–38.

3. Joel Garreau, *Edge City: Life on the New Frontier* (New York: Anchor Books, 1992); Richard Morrill, "Racial Segregation and Class in a Liberal Metropolis," *Geographical Analysis* 27 (1995): 22–41.

4. William A. V. Clark, "Residential Segregation in American Cities: A Review and Interpretation," *Population Research and Policy Review* 5 (1986): 95–127; William A. V. Clark, "Residential Segregation in American Cities: Common Ground and Differences in Interpretation," *Population Research and Policy Review* 8 (1989): 193–97; George Galster, "Residential Segregation in American Cities: A Contrary Review," *Population Research and Policy Review* 7 (1988): 113–21.

5. Nancy Denton, "The Persistence of Segregation Links Between Residential Segregation and School Segregation," *Minnesota Law Review* 80 (1996): 795–824; John Farley, "Race Still Matters: The Minimal Role of Income and Housing Cost as Causes of Housing Segregation in St. Louis, 1900," *Urban Affairs Review* 3 (1995): 244–54.

6. David Armor and William A. V. Clark, "Housing Segregation and School Desegregation," in David Armor, *Forced Justice: School Desegregation and the Law* (New York: Oxford University Press, 1995), pp. 117–53.

7. Brian Berry and John Kasarda, *Contemporary Urban Ecology* (New York: Macmillan, 1979), provide a review of the ecological background of the urban mosaic.

8. William Frey, "Mover Destination Selectivity and the Changing Suburbanization of Metropolitan Whites and Blacks," *Demography* 22 (1985): 223–43; William J. Wilson, *The Declining Significance of Race: Blacks and Changing American Institutions* (Chicago: University of Chicago Press, 1986).

9. William A. V. Clark and Julian Ware, "Trends in Residential Integration by Socio-Economic Status in Southern California," *Urban Affairs Quarterly* 32 (1997): 825–43.

10. Howard Schuman, Charlotte Steeh, and Lawrence Bobo, *Racial Attitudes in America: Trends and Interpretations* (Cambridge, Mass.: Harvard University Press, 1985).

11. Douglas Massey and Nancy Denton, *American Apartheid* (Cambridge, Mass.: Harvard University Press, 1993).

12. William A. V. Clark, "Residential Preferences and Neighborhood Racial Segregation: A Test of the Schelling Model," *Demography* 28 (1991): 1–19; William A. V. Clark, "Residential Preferences and Residential Choices in a Multi-Ethnic Context," *Demography* 30 (1992): 451–66; Schuman, Steeh, and Bobo, *Racial Attitudes in America: Trends and Interpretations.*

13. George Galster and William Keeney, "Race, Residence, Discrimination and Economic Opportunities," *Urban Affairs Quarterly* 24 (1988): 87–117.

14. See, e.g., John Yinger, *Closed Doors, Opportunities Lost: The Continuing Costs of Housing Discrimination* (New York: Russell Sage Foundation, 1995).

15. Armor and Clark, "Housing Segregation and School Segregation," p. 145.

16. James Allen and Eugene Turner, *The Ethnic Quilt: Population Diversity in Southern California* (California State University, Northridge: Center for Geographical Studies, 1997).

17. Barrett Lee and Peter Wood, "Is Neighborhood Social Succession, Place Specific?" *Demography* 28 (1991): 21–40.

African American Marriage Patterns

DOUGLAS J. BESHAROV AND ANDREW WEST

IN 1968, the Kerner Commission declared that the United States was "moving toward two societies, one black, one white—separate and unequal."[1] Happily, many of the Commission's most distressing predictions have not come true. But with respect to marriage and child rearing, black and white Americans do live in substantially different worlds. Over the past fifty years, for all Americans, marriage rates have declined while divorce rates and out-of-wedlock births have climbed. But the negative changes have been greatest among African Americans.

The Decline of Marriage

NONMARRIAGE

Compared with white women, African American women are 25 percent less likely ever to have been married and about half as likely to be currently married. According to the Census Bureau's Current Population Survey (CPS), in 1998, about 29 percent of African American women aged fifteen and over were married with a spouse present, compared with about 55 percent of white women and 49 percent of Hispanic women.[2] African American women are estimated to spend only half as long as white women married (22 percent vs. 44 percent of their lives).[3]

In the 1950s, after at least seventy years of rough parity, African American marriage rates began to fall behind white rates. In 1950, the percentages of white and African American women (aged fifteen and over) who were currently married were roughly the same, 67 percent and 64 percent, respectively. By 1998, the percentage of currently married white women had dropped by 13 percent to 58 percent. But the drop among African American women was 44 percent to 36 percent—more than three times larger.[4] The declines for males were parallel, 12 percent for white men, 36 percent for African American men.

Among Hispanics, the decline in marriage rates appears to have been less steep, but only because we have no information on Hispanics prior to 1970. From 1970 to 1998, the percentage of currently married Hispanic women dropped 13 percent, from 64 percent to 56 percent (see Fig. 1).[5]

Even more significant has been the sharp divergence in never-married rates. Between 1950 and 1998, the percentage of never-married white women aged fifteen and over rose from 20 percent to 22 percent, a 10 percent rise. But the percentage of never-married African American women about doubled, from 21 percent to 41 percent.[6] For Hispanics, the data begin only in 1970; since then, the percentage of Hispanic never-married women has risen from 24 percent in 1970 to 29 percent in 1998, about a 21 percent rise.[7]

Later marriage among African Americans accounts for only some of this difference. For example, between 1950 and 1998, the percentage of never-married white women aged forty and over actually fell from 9 percent to 5 percent, a 44 percent drop. But the percentage of never-married African American women aged forty and over rose by 200 percent, from 5 percent to 15 percent.[8] (Thus, even adjusting for age at first marriage, marriage rates decline after about 1970 for whites and 1960 for African Americans).[9]

Among Hispanics, there has been almost no change in the percentage of never-married women. In 1970, about 7 percent of women forty and over were never married. By 1998, that figure had risen by only one percentage point.

DIVORCE AND SEPARATION

At the same time that African American women are half as likely to marry as whites, they are more than twice as likely to divorce. Although African American divorce rates have long been higher than those of whites,

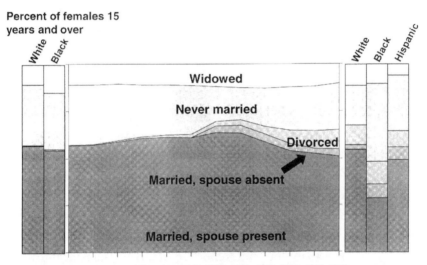

Fig. 1.   Marital trends, 1890–1998. Although the 1890 data have not been analyzed, results from 1910 indicate that about 2 percent of black women classified as widows in that year were actually never-married or divorced. See Samuel H. Preston, Suet Lim, and S. Philip Morgan, "African-American Marriage in 1910: Beneath the Surface of Census Data," *Demography* 29 (February 1992): 1–15. Data for 1890–1990 from decennial census data for those years; data for 1998 from Bureau of the Census, *Marital Status and Living Arrangements: March 1998*, by Terry A. Lugailia (Washington, D.C.: U.S. Government Printing Office, 1999), p. 1, table 1.

they are now more so. For example, in 1890 (the first year for which national census data are available) the number of divorced women per thousand married women was 45 percent higher for African Americans than for whites, 9 vs. 6.[10] These are relatively small numbers, but they suggest that even when families were on the whole much stronger than they are today, African American women were still much more likely to face marital disruption.

These early divorce figures may not be completely accurate, however.[11] Not only was divorce highly stigmatized before the 1960s, making it likely that divorces were underreported in early census years, but also, as E. Franklin Frazier pointed out sixty years ago, "divorces" among rural African Americans were most likely informal agreements (between two married people or two people living together) or the de facto result of long-standing separations.[12] Thus, it is likely that formal divorces among African Americans were much lower, and perhaps much lower than among whites.

Regardless of the reliability of earlier census data, however, the racial difference in divorce is now quite large. By 1998, the African American divorce rate was more than twice as high as the white rate (422 per thousand compared with 190 per thousand). The divorce rate for Hispanic women doubled between 1970, the first year for which data are available, and 1998, from 81 to 171 per thousand (compared with a quadrupling of the African American rate and a tripling of the white rate over the same time period).[13]

Separation is about four times more common among African Americans than among whites and about one and a half times more common than among Hispanics. In 1998, according to CPS data, over 20 percent of married black women aged fifteen and over had an absent spouse, compared with 5 percent of married white women and 13 percent of married Hispanic women of the same ages.[14] Some experts question whether the black separation rate is really this high, speculating that black women consider the breakup of a long-term cohabitation (an informal common-law marriage, if you will) to be a "separation."[15]

NONMARITAL BIRTHS

Along with the weakness of marriage, there has been an increase in nonmarital births, especially among teenagers. Once again, African Americans have experienced the greatest increases, although they have also been responsible for most of the recent decline in both teen births and nonmarital teen births. According to Larry Bumpass and Hsien-Hen Lu, an African American child is three times more likely to be born out of wedlock than a white child and, on average, will spend only six years in a two-parent family, compared with fourteen years for a white child and thirteen years for a Hispanic child.[16]

The proportion of births to unwed mothers has risen steadily since 1950, so that now almost one-third of all American children are born out of wedlock (see Fig. 2). From 1950 to 1997, the proportion of births to unmarried white women (non-Hispanic) increased almost twelvefold, from 2 percent to 22 percent. The African American proportion increased fourfold, from 18 percent to a striking 69 percent. (The African American rate could not have risen much more because it was already so high.) The proportion of births to Hispanic unwed mothers has also increased by 5 percent between 1992 and 1997, rising from 39 percent to 41 percent.[17]

A major factor driving these rates has been the decline in the birthrates for married couples—rather than an explosion of births outside of marriage (Fig. 3). As Thernstrom and Thernstrom point out, "In 1987 the birth rate for married black women actually fell *below the birth rate for unmarried black women*, the first time that has ever happened for any ethnic group."[18] Among white women, the overall fertility rate fell from 102.3 births per thousand women aged fifteen to forty-four in 1950 to 63.9 in 1997. (At the same time, the unwed fertility rate rose from 1.8 to 16.5, in part because there were many fewer marriages.) Had the fertility rate of white married women remained at 102.3 (while the rate for white unwed women rose to 16.5), the proportion of births in 1997 to unwed white mothers would be only 16 percent, not 26 percent.

Similarly, the fertility rate of married African American women fell from 137.3 per thousand in 1950 to 70.7 in 1997 (Fig. 4). Had their fertility rate remained the same, the percentage of African American children born out of wedlock in 1997 would have been 36 percent, not 69 percent.[19] Unfortunately, data for Hispanic out-of-wedlock births are not available for years earlier than 1989, making it impossible to make the equivalent calculation for Hispanics.

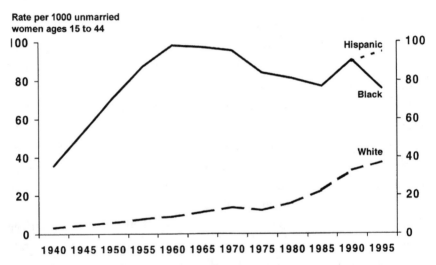

Rate per 1000 unmarried women ages 15 to 44

Fig. 2.   Nonmarital birthrates, 1940–1995, by race. Data on nonmarital birthrates for white and black women 1950–1990 and for Hispanic women in 1980 from Department of Health and Human Services, National Center for Health Statistics, *Births to Unmarried Mothers in the United States, 1980–92,* by Stephanie J. Ventura, Vital and Health Statistics, series 12, no. 53 (Hyattsville, Md.: National Center for Health Statistics, 1995), p. 27, table 1; data on nonmarital birthrates for white, black, and Hispanic women for 1995 from Department of Health and Human Services, National Center for Health Statistics, *Births: Final Data for 1997,* by Stephanie J. Ventura et al., National Vital Statistics Report 47, no. 18 (Hyattsville, Md.: National Center for Health Statistics, 1999), p. 43, table 18.

TEENAGE BIRTHS

Having a baby out of wedlock is difficult enough; having a baby as an unwed teenager is even more difficult. One in five African American babies is born to a teenage mother, about twice the white rate and one and a half times the Hispanic rate. In 1996, about 22 percent of all live births to African Americans were to women under age twenty, compared with just over 10 percent for white women and 13 percent for Hispanic women.[20]

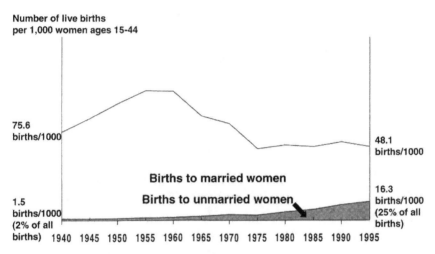

**Number of live births
per 1,000 women ages 15-44**

75.6
births/1000

48.1
births/1000

Births to married women

16.3
births/1000
(25% of all
births)

1.5
births/1000
(2% of all
births)

Births to unmarried women

1940 1945 1950 1955 1960 1965 1970 1975 1980 1985 1990 1995

Fig. 3.   White fertility rates for married and unmarried women, 1940–1995. From authors' calculations based on data from Department of Health and Human Services, National Center for Health Statistics, *Births: Final Data for 1997*, by Stephanie J. Ventura et al., National Vital Statistics Report, vol. 47, no. 18 (Hyattsville, Md.: National Center for Health Statistics, 1999), p. 22, table 1; Department of Health and Human Services, National Center for Health Statistics, *Births to Unmarried Mothers in the United States 1980–92*, by Stephanie J. Ventura, Vital and Health Statistics, series 12, no. 53 (Hyattsville, Md.: National Center for Health Statistics, 1995), p. 35, table 4; data for 1995 taken from Department of Health and Human Services, National Center for Health Statistics, *Report of Final Natality Statistics, 1995*, by Stephanie J. Ventura et al., Monthly Vital Statistics Report, vol. 45, no. 11, supplement (Hyattsville, Md.: National Center for Health Statistics, 1997), p. 40, table 14.

Over the past forty years, the overall teenage birthrate first rose and then declined. Throughout, though, there were sharp racial and ethnic differences. According to the National Center for Health Statistics (NCHS), the birthrate for females aged fifteen to nineteen peaked in 1960, at 79.4 per thousand for whites and 156.1 for African Americans. The rates then declined until 1985 or 1986, when the white rate hit 42.3 and the African American rate 94.1.[21] The rates continued to rise for a few more years and began declining again in 1992 to their 1997 levels of 36 for whites and 91

Fig. 4. Black fertility rates for married and unmarried women, 1940–1995. From authors' calculations based on data from Department of Health and Human Services, National Center for Health Statistics, *Births: Final Data for 1997*, by Stephanie J. Ventura et al., National Vital Statistics Report, vol. 47, no. 18 (Hyattsville, Md.: National Center for Health Statistics, 1999), p. 22, table 1; Department of Health and Human Services, National Center for Health Statistics, *Births to Unmarried Mothers in the United States, 1980–92*, by Stephanie J. Ventura, Vital and Health Statistics, series 12, no. 53 (Hyattsville, Md.: National Center for Health Statistics, 1995), p. 35, table 4; data for 1995 taken from Department of Health and Human Services, National Center for Health Statistics, *Report of Final Natality Statistics, 1995*, by Stephanie J. Ventura et al., Monthly Vital Statistics Report, vol. 45, no. 11, supplement (Hyattsville, Md.: National Center for Health Statistics, 1997), p. 40, table 14.

for African Americans.[22] Among Hispanics, the teen birthrate rose from 100.8 per thousand in 1989 to a 1994 peak of 107.7 per thousand. The birthrate for Hispanic teens has since declined to 97.4 per thousand in 1997.[23]

For those concerned only about too early parenthood, the recent decline in teenage parenthood is good news. But out-of-wedlock birthrates are still at 1975 levels. More important, the decline is largely driven by the sharp drop in teenage marriage (so that there are fewer married couples trying to have a baby). This is, moreover, all teenage births, marital as well as nonmarital. The trend for nonmarital teenage births, as opposed to marital births, is sharply up. Almost all births to black teens are now out of wedlock. As overall births to teenagers were falling, the proportion of out-of-wedlock teenage births continued to rise because teens just don't marry very much any more, but many are still having babies. For African Americans, between 1950 and 1997, the proportion of births to teenage unwed mothers rose from 36 percent to 96 percent, a 166 percent rise. For whites, the rise was steeper, almost twelvefold (because the base was so much lower), 6 percent in 1950 to 71 percent in 1997. The proportion of Hispanic teenage unwed births rose by 71 percent from 1980 to 1997, from 42 percent of all teenage births to 72 percent of all teenage births.[24]

RECENT DECLINES

Recent trends are much more hopeful. For the past few years, nonmarital births have been declining. The rate for whites peaked in 1994 at 28.5 per thousand single women and has declined slightly since then to 27 per thousand. The African American rate has declined more sharply, following a 1989 peak of 90.7. It is now 73.4. The rate for Hispanics reached its zenith in 1994 at 101.2 and has also declined to 91.4.[25] Since 1991, teen births are down 8 percent for whites and 21 percent for African Americans.

Teenage nonmarital births have declined even more, again most significantly for blacks. Nonmarital birthrates for white teenagers peaked in 1994 at 28.1. Since then the rate has declined to 25.9, an 8 percent decline, but this is not a large enough drop to tell us what is happening. The rate for black teens, on the other hand, dropped a substantial 20 percent, from a high of 108.5 in 1991 to 86.4 in 1997. The drop for Hispanics has been only slightly larger than for whites. The rate of nonmarital births to Hispanic teenagers has fallen 9 percent, from a high of 82.6 in 1994 to 75.2 in 1997.[26]

Second-order births are also declining, once again most significantly for African Americans. Data from the NCHS indicate that, in 1992, the second-order or higher birthrate for teens was 15.6 per thousand. In 1997, the rate had fallen by 27 percent to 11.4. In 1992, the rates by race had been 8.3 for white teens, 39.5 for African American teens, and 28 for Hispanic teens. In 1997, the rates had fallen to 6.4, 25, and 23.5, respectively.[27]

A Balanced Perspective

At least since the appearance of Daniel Patrick Moynihan's controversial 1965 report, *The Negro Family: The Case for National Action*, "the plight of the black family" has been the focus of much anxiety and debate. On the one side have been those who think the black family is a "tangle of pathology," to use Moynihan's phrase.[28] On the other side have been those who see the black family as strong and vibrant, emphasizing its "adaptability," to use Belinda Tucker's phrase.[29]

TERMINOLOGY

The disagreement about the state of the black family is partly the result of misunderstanding. The first side tends to use "family breakdown" primarily to mean nonmarriage, divorce, and nonmarital childbearing. The other side tends to use the term "family" more broadly, to include kin networks of parents, grandparents, aunts, uncles, cousins, and so forth, that often help support single mothers and their children and sometimes take them into their own homes. In an attempt to bridge this disagreement, this paper seeks to make a clear distinction between the breakdown of marriage, which it calls "marital breakdown," and the role of extended family structures, which, in all communities, is more important when marriages are weaker.

Without doubt, today's unprecedentedly high rates of divorce and nonmarital childbearing—across all American society and indeed in most other Western nations—should be a matter of grave concern. Marital breakdown harms many of the adults and children involved and, because of its disproportionate impact on African Americans, is a particular tragedy in that community. Public discourse, however, often goes too far in blaming marital breakdown for all the poverty and social dysfunction that afflict the black community. That is an equally terrible mistake because marital breakdown, poverty, and social dysfunction interact. They are, simultaneously, both causes and effects of each other.

MARITAL BREAKDOWN OR POVERTY?

At first glance, marital breakdown has devastating effects on children, and to African American children in particular because so many are born to unwed teenagers. Children born out of wedlock fall substantially below children from intact families on many important measures.[30]

A 1995 report to Congress from the Department of Health and Human Services summarizes:

> Unmarried mothers are less likely to obtain prenatal care and more likely to have a low birthweight baby. Young children in single-mother families tend to have lower scores on verbal and math achievement tests. In middle childhood, children raised by a single parent tend to receive lower grades, have more behavior problems, and have higher rates of chronic health and psychiatric disorders. Among adolescents and young adults, being raised in a single-mother family is associated with elevated risks of teenage childbearing, high school dropout, incarceration, and with being neither employed nor in school.[31]

According to Robert Rector of the Heritage Foundation, data from the National Longitudinal Survey of Youth (NLSY) show that children born out of wedlock to never-married mothers spend 51 percent of their childhood in poverty, compared with only 7 percent of children born to two-parent, married families. Such children spend 71 percent of their childhood receiving some form of welfare (AFDC, Medicaid, food stamps, WIC, or SSI), compared with 12 percent for children born to two-parent, married families.[32] The children of teenaged parents, especially if unmarried, have even more serious problems. For example: "Children of young teen mothers are almost three times as likely to be behind bars at some point in their adolescence or early 20s as are the children of mothers who delayed childbearing."[33]

Although the children in female-headed households tend to do less well on various measures, these are only correlations. Because family poverty and various other characteristics are such important determinants of a child's well-being and life prospects, many children would not have fared well even if their parents had been married or had waited until their twenties to have children.[34]

In recent years, a number of researchers have attempted to disentangle the effects of marital breakdown, poverty, and other personal and contextual factors.[35] Doing so substantially reduces the apparent effects of marital breakdown. For example, when Sara McLanahan and Gary Sandefur analyzed Panel Study of Income Dynamics (PSID) data, they found that young people from single-parent families did substantially worse on a variety of measures:

> Compared with teenagers of who grow up with both parents at home, adolescents who have lived apart from one of their parents during some period of childhood are twice as likely to drop out of high school, twice as likely to have a child before age twenty, and one and a half times as likely to be "idle"—out of school and out of work—in their late teens and early twenties.[36]

Controlling for income cuts these differences in half. The negative effects of growing up in a single-parent family were still large—just not as large as some of our public rhetoric would suggest.[37]

Thus, it is important to maintain a balanced perspective on the con-sequences of "marital breakdown." Although it is an extremely serious problem, it is not the sole determinant of a person's success or happiness. In fact, as other contributors to this volume describe, on many macro indicators of social and economic well-being, African Americans are doing better than ever before. Gaps between whites and African Americans are getting smaller, and in some cases African Americans are making gains relative to whites. Most African Americans—including a majority of those who are unmarried, or divorced, or even born out of wedlock—get up in the morning and go to work or school, like everyone else. Marital break-down makes things worse, not hopeless.

WORLD-WIDE TRENDS

As we have seen, on every measure of marital stability, African Amer-icans do more poorly than whites and Hispanics. The weakness of African American marriages is, however, more accurately viewed as an exacerbated version of the decline in marriage across the entire postindustrial, Western world. Between 1960 to 1986, most Western societies saw divorce rates rise and total birthrates fall while unwed births rose (see Table 1).

The most broadly accepted explanations for marital breakdown are essentially race-blind: greater acceptance of nonmarital sex and unwed parenthood so that young people feel less need to marry, widespread afflu-ence so that it is easier to leave an unhappy marriage, less emotional and economic gain from marriage so that there is less reason to get married, and welfare's marriage penalties that discourage low-income couples from marrying.

African Americans do seem especially vulnerable to these worldwide trends, however. As Figure 5 indicates, nonmarital birthrates vary from a high of 72 percent for American-born African Americans to a low of 4 percent for Korean Americans. What can it be about African Americans—or their more than three centuries living on this continent—that has made them so vulnerable to the forces that weaken families? A number of factors seem to be at work: the devastating effects of slavery and Jim Crow laws on black marriages; endemic poverty, which puts added stress on already weak families; even fewer gains from marriage, especially for women; too early sex that puts young girls at greater risk of unwanted pregnancy; and racial concentration that magnifies the impact of these conditions.[38]

This same set of explanations, with a few modifications, helps explain what is happening to Hispanic marriages, which are often included only as an afterthought in discussions about the family. Although separate data on Hispanic marriages span only the last thirty years, we do have enough information to make some preliminary conclusions.

On most indicators, Hispanic marriages lie somewhere between those of whites and African Americans. This suggests that some of the same factors that affect African Americans, such as endemic poverty, too early

Table 1   Worldwide Marital Weakness, 1960–1986/88

Country	DIVORCE RATE		BIRTHRATE		UNWED BIRTHS (PERCENT)	
	1960	1988	1960	1988	1960	1986
United States	9.4	21.2	3.6	2.1	5.3	23.4
Canada	1.7	12.9	3.8	1.9	4.3	16.9
Austria	5.0		2.7	1.6	13.0	21.0
Denmark	6.0	12.8	2.5	1.6	7.8	43.9
Finland	4.1		2.7	1.7	4.1	15.0
France	2.8	8.5	2.7	2.0	6.1	24.0
Germany	3.4	8.3	2.4	1.4	6.3	9.6
Italy		1.1	2.4	1.4	2.4	5.6
Netherlands	2.2	8.7	3.1	1.7	1.3	8.8
Norway	2.8		2.9	2.0	7.0	24.0
Sweden	4.9	10.7	2.2	1.9	11.3	48.4
United Kingdom	2.2	12.9	2.7	2.0	5.4	21.0

SOURCE: Sheila B. Kamerman, "Gender Role and Family Structure Changes in the Advanced Indus-trialized West: Implications for Social Policy," in Katherine McFate, Roger Lawson, and William Julius Wilson, eds., *Poverty, Inequality, and the Future of Social Policy: Western States in the New World Order* (New York: Russell Sage Foundation, 1995), pp. 231–56.

sex, and residential concentration, also affect Hispanics. At the same time, the different cultural and historical background of Hispanics appears to ameliorate some of the forces that contribute to further marital weakness among African Americans.

The overriding point is simple: The forces that weaken marriage strike *all* families, albeit in different ways for different groups. The sooner we realize this reality, the sooner progress will be made in strengthening all American families, including African American families. This is not a message in black and white, but perhaps it is a message for blacks and whites (and browns).

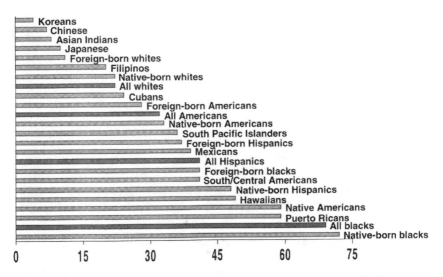

Fig. 5. Nonmarital births by race-ethnicity, 1992–1997. Data for all ethnic groups except Koreans and South Pacific Islanders from Department of Health and Human Services, National Center for Health Statistics, *Births: Final Data for 1997*, pp. 38–39, tables 13 and 14; data for Koreans and South Pacific Islanders from Department of Health and Human Services, National Center for Health Statistics, *Birth Characteristics for Asian or Pacific Islander Subgroups, 1992*, by Joyce A. Martin, Monthly Vital Statistics Report, vol. 43, no. 10, supplement (Hyattsville, Md.: 1995), p. 5, table 4.

Notes

1. The National Advisory Commission on Civil Disorders, *Report of the National Advisory Commission on Civil Disorders* (New York: Bantam, 1968), p. 1.

2. Bureau of the Census, *Marital Status and Living Arrangements: March 1998*, by Terry A. Lugailia (Washington, D.C.: U.S. Government Printing Office, 1999), p. 1, table 1.

3. Andrew J. Cherlin, *Marriage, Divorce, Remarriage*, rev. and enlarged ed. (Cambridge, Mass.: Harvard University Press, 1992), p. 95. A similar estimate for Hispanic women is not available.

4. Data for 1950 from Bureau of the Census, *Census of the Population: 1950*, vol. 1, *General Population Characteristics* (Washington, D.C.: U.S. Government Printing Office, 1952), p. 182, table 104. Data for 1998 from Bureau of the Census, *Marital Status*, p. 1, table 1.

5. Data for 1970 from Bureau of the Census, *1970 Census of the Population*, vol. 1, *General Population Characteristics* (Washington, D.C.: U.S. Government Printing Office, 1972), p. 688, table 216. Data for 1998 from Bureau of the Census, *Marital Status*, p. 1, table 1.

6. Data for 1950 from Bureau of the Census, *Census of the Population: 1950*, p. 182, table 104. Data for 1998 from Bureau of the Census, *Marital Status*, p. 1, table 1.

7. Data for 1970 from Bureau of the Census, *1970 Census*, p. 688, table 216. Data for 1998 from Bureau of the Census, *Marital Status*, p. 1, table 1.

8. Data for 1950 from Bureau of the Census, *Census of the Population: 1950*, p. 182, table 104. Data for 1998 from Bureau of the Census, *Marital Status*, p. 1, table 1.

9. Marriage rates for Hispanic women have been declining since the 1970s, but lacking data before 1970, we cannot determine when marriage rates among Hispanic women began to decline.

10. The divorce rate presented here represents the number of currently divorced women aged fifteen and older per thousand married, spouse-present women. This rate is different from the standard rate used by the National Center for Health Statistics (NCHS), which is equal to the number of divorces decreed in a given year per thousand married women aged fifteen and over. There are three reasons for using the rate presented here. (1) the NCHS divorce rate is not available by race over time; (2) the NCHS rate does not control for the apparent higher rate of separation among African American women; (3) the rate used here, by focusing on divorced women as opposed to the number of divorces, avoids the problems (although admittedly small) created by divorces among interracial marriages. Data for 1890 from Bureau of the Census, *Census Reports: Twelfth Census of the United States, Taken in the Year 1900* (Washington, D.C.: U.S. Government Printing Office, 1901), p. lxxxvii, table 49. Data for 1998 from Bureau of the Census, *Marital Status*, p. 1, table 1.

11. The Census Bureau has recognized the problem in the recording of divorces and has in many cases issued public statements cautioning that the number of divorced persons is underreported. See, e.g., Samuel H. Preston and John McDonald, "The Incidence of Divorce Within Cohorts of American Marriages Contracted Since the Civil War," *Demography* 16 (February 1979): 1–25.

12. E. Franklin Frazier, *The Negro Family in the United States* (Chicago: University of Chicago Press, 1939), chaps. 5 and 18, cited in Samuel H. Preston, Suet Lim, and S. Philip Morgan, "African-American Marriage in 1910: Beneath the Surface of Census Data," *Demography* 29 (February 1992): 10.

13. Data for Hispanics in 1970 from Bureau of the Census, *1970 Census*, p. 688, table 216; data for 1998 from Bureau of the Census, *Marital Status*, p. 1, table 1.

14. Data for 1998 from Bureau of the Census, *Marital Status*, p. 1, table 1.

15. See Preston, Lim, and Morgan for a discussion of how data recorded by the Census Bureau may be inaccurate.

16. Data on likelihood of nonmarital births from Department of Health and Human Services, National Center for Health Statistics, *Births: Final Data for 1997*, by Stephanie J. Ventura et al., National Vital Statistics Report, vol. 47, no. 18 (Hyattsville, Md.: National Center for Health Statistics, 1999), p. 42, table 17. Data on the number of years a child can expect to live with two parents correspond to the number of years between birth and age seventeen a child can expect to live in a home with two parents (either married or cohabiting); from Larry Bumpass and Hsien-Hen Lu, "Trends in Cohabitation and Implications for Children's Family Contexts in the U.S.," working paper, University of Wisconsin–Madison, Center for Demography and Ecology, 1999, p. 36, table 6.

17. Data for 1950 from Department of Health and Human Services, National Center for Health Statistics, *Births to Unmarried Mothers in the United States, 1980–92*, by Stephanie J.Ventura, Vital and Health Statistics, series 12, no. 53 (Hyattsville, Md.: National Center for Health Statistics, 1995), p. 40, table 5. Data for 1997 from Department of Health and Human Services, *Births: Final Data for 1997*, pp. 22, 28, 45, tables 1, 6, and 19.

18. Stephan Thernstrom and Abigail Thernstrom, *America in Black and White: One Nation, Indivisible* (New York: Simon & Schuster, 1997), p. 240; emphasis in original.

19. Authors' calculations based on data from Department of Health and Human Services, *Births: Final Data for 1997*, p. 22, table 1; and Department of Health and Human Services, *Births to Unmarried Mothers*, p. 35, table 4.

20. Department of Health and Human Services, *Births: Final Data for 1997*, p. 39, table 14.

21. Department of Health and Human Services, *Declines in Teenage Birth Rates, 1991–97: National and State Patterns*, by Stephanie J. Ventura, T. J. Mathews, and Sally C. Curtin, National Vital Statistics Report, vol. 47, no. 12 (Hyattsville, Md.: National Center for Health Statistics, 1999), p. 9, table 1.

22. Department of Health and Human Services, *Births: Final Data for 1997*, p. 34, table 9.

23. Department of Health and Human Services, *Declines in Teenage Birth Rates*, p. 10, table 2.

24. Data for 1950 and 1980 from Kristin A. Moore et al., "Data on Teenage Child-bearing in the United States" (prepared by Child Trends, Inc., for the American Enterprise Institute/White House Working Seminar on Integrated Services for Children and Families, Washington, D.C., January 1993), p. 11, table 5. Data for 1997 from Department of Health and Human Services, *Births: Final Data for 1997*, p. 42, table 17.

25. Department of Health and Human Services, *Births: Final Data for 1997*, p. 43, table 18.

26. See note 24.

27. Data for 1992 from Department of Health and Human Services, National Center for Health Statistics, *Advance Report of Final Natality Statistics, 1992*, by Stephanie J. Ventura et al., Monthly Vital Statistics Report, vol. 43, no. 5, suppl. (Hyattsville, Md.: National Center for Health Statistics, 1994), pp. 34, 41, tables 3 and 7. Data for 1997 from Department of Health and Human Services, *Births: Final Data for 1997*, pp. 24, 32, tables 3 and 8.

28. Department of Labor, Office of Planning and Policy Research, *The Negro Family: The Case for National Action*, by Daniel Patrick Moynihan (Washington, D.C.: U.S. Government Printing Office, 1965), p. 75.

29. M. Belinda Tucker, "Family," in *New Directions: African-Americans in a Diversifying Nation*, ed. James S. Jackson (Washington, D.C.: National Policy Association, forthcoming).

30. Sara McLanahan and Gary Sandefur, *Growing Up with a Single Parent: What Hurts, What Helps* (Cambridge, Mass.: Harvard University Press, 1994).

31. Department of Health and Human Services, National Center for Health Statistics, "Nonmarital Childbearing in the United States," executive summary of *Report to Congress on Out-of-Wedlock Childbearing* (Hyattsville, Md.: National Center for Health Statistics, 1995), p. xiii.

32. Robert Rector, data presented at Welfare Reform Seminar Series sponsored by the American Enterprise Institute and the Brookings Institution, Washington, D.C., April 1999).

33. Rebecca A. Maynard, "The Study, the Context, and the Findings in Brief," in *Kids Having Kids: Economic Costs and Social Consequences of Teen Pregnancy*, ed. Rebecca A. Maynard (Washington, D.C.: Urban Institute Press, 1997), p. 16.

34. The impact of poverty is complex, however. As Susan Mayer of the University of Chicago points out: "My review of the research suggests three major conclusions. First, though the effect of parental income is nowhere near as large as many political liberals imagine, neither is it zero, as many political conservatives seem to believe.

Second, though the effect of parental income on any one outcome measure appears to be fairly small, higher income has some effect on most outcomes, so its cumulative impact across all outcomes may be substantial. Third, one reason that parental income is not more important to children's outcomes is probably that government policies have done a lot to ensure that poor children get basic necessities most of the time." *What Money Can't Buy: Family Income and Children's Life Chances* (Cambridge, Mass.: Harvard University Press, 1997), p. 143.

35. The first major work was Arline T. Geronimus and Sanders Korenman, "The Socioeconomic Consequences of Teen Childbearing Reconsidered," *Quarterly Journal of Economics* 107 (November 1992): 1187–1214.

36. There was, for example, a 10 percentage point difference between the high school graduation rates of children from two-parent families and children from single-parent families, 15 percent vs. 25 percent. They also found a 17 percentage point difference in teen birthrates, 14 percent for those from two-parent families compared with 31 percent for young women from single-parent families. There was also a 15 percentage point difference in "idleness" rates for young women. About 26 percent of young women from two-parent families were out of school and out of work, compared with 41 percent of young women from single-parent families. Similarly, 19 percent of young men from two-parent families were idle, compared with 29 percent of young men from single-parent families. McLanahan and Sandefur, *Growing Up with a Single Parent*, pp. 2, 41, 47, 50.

37. Ibid., p. 89, fig. 10.

38. This is not to say that other explanations have not been propounded. But such explanations, such as the existence of extensive kin networks and differing male-female expectations about marriage, do not appear strong enough to account for a substantial share of African American–white differences.

Crime

JAMES Q. WILSON

A CENTRAL PROBLEM—perhaps *the* central problem—in improving the relationship between white and black Americans is the difference in racial crime rates. No matter how innocent or guilty a stranger may be, he carries with him in public the burdens or benefits of his group identity. If you are walking down a street alone at night and you encounter two men in business suits, you are not frightened. If you encounter two teenage boys in blue jeans, you may become a bit nervous. And if you encounter two teenage boys wearing leather jackets and sporting Mohawk haircuts, you will probably be very nervous. You know in advance that the appearance of these six males is no sure guide to their behavior, but given the magnitude of the possible harm—perhaps a sudden assault, possibly a serious injury—you assign a high value to what little you can observe about them. And what you can observe is their group identity.

Estimating the crime rates of racial groups is, of course, difficult because we only know the arrest rate. If police are more (or less) likely to arrest a criminal of a given race, the arrest rate will overstate (or understate) the true crime rate. To examine this problem, researchers have compared the rate at which criminal victims report (in the National Crime Victimization Survey, or NCVS) the racial identity of whoever robbed or assaulted them with the rate at which the police arrest robbers or assaulters of different races. Regardless of whether the victim is black or white, there are no significant differences between victim reports and police arrests. This suggests that, though racism may exist in policing (as in all other aspects of American life), racism cannot explain the overall black arrest rate.[1] The arrest rate, thus, is a reasonably good proxy for the crime rate.

Black men commit murders at a rate about eight times greater than that for white men. This disparity is not new; it has existed for well over a century. When historian Roger Lane studied murder rates in Philadelphia, he found that since 1839 the black rate has been much higher than the white rate.[2] This gap existed long before the invention of television, the wide distribution of hand guns, or access to dangerous drugs (except for alcohol). America is a violent nation. The estimated homicide rate in this country, *excluding* all those committed by blacks, is over three times higher than the homicide rate for the other six major industrial nations.[3] But whatever causes white Americans to kill other people, it causes black Americans to kill others at a much higher rate.

Of course the average African American male is not likely to kill anybody. During the 1980s and early 1990s, fewer than one out of every 2,000 black men would kill a person in any year, and most of their victims were other blacks. Though for young black men homicide is the leading cause of death, the chances of the average white person's being killed by a black are very small. But the chances of being hit by lightning are also very small, and yet we leave high ground during a thunderstorm.

However low the absolute risk, the relative risk—relative, that is, to the chances of being killed by a white—is high, and this fact changes everything. When whites walk down the street, they are more nervous when they encounter a black man than when they encounter a white one. When blacks walk down the street, they are more likely than whites to be stopped and questioned by a police officer. It is important, of course, for whites to know that a chance encounter with a black creates little risk and for police officers to know that they should have more criteria than just skin color to decide who is worth questioning. Many whites and many police officers know this, but in spite of what people know, the racial tension persists. Countless white pedestrians have been worried by the sight of a young black male, and countless innocent black men have had their cars stopped or their walk interrupted by a suspicious cop. White pedestrians may be embarrassed by their own caution; certainly black pedestrians are upset by unwarranted police intrusions.

The differences in the racial rates for property crimes, though smaller than those for violent offenses, are still substantial. The estimated rate at which black men commit burglary is three times higher than it is for white men; for rape, it is five times higher.[4]

The difference between blacks and whites with respect to crime, and especially violent crime, has, I think, done more to impede racial amity than any other factor. Pure racism—that is, a visceral dislike of another person because of his skin color—has always existed. It is less common today than it once was, but it persists and no doubt explains part of our racial standoff. But pure racism once stigmatized other racial minorities who have today largely overcome that burden. When I grew up in California, the Chinese and Japanese were not only physically distinctive, but they were also viewed with deep suspicion by whites. For many decades, Chinese testimony was not accepted in California courts, an Alien Land Law discouraged Asian land purchases, the Chinese Exclusion Act (not repealed until 1943) prevented Chinese immigration, and a Gentlemen's Agreement, signed in 1907, required Japan to cut back sharply on passports issued to Japanese who wished to emigrate to California. When World War II began, the Japanese were sent to relocation camps at great personal cost to them. Yet today Californians of Asian ancestry are viewed by Caucasians with comfort and even pride. In spite of their distinctive physical features, no one crosses the street to avoid a Chinese or Japanese youth. One obvious reason is that they have remarkably low crime rates.

The black murder rate, though it is much higher than the rate for whites or Asians, does not always change in the same way as the white rate.

Between 1976 and 1991, the murder arrest rate for black males aged twenty-five and older fell dramatically even though the murder arrest rate for the nation as a whole did not change at all. Apparently, adult black men were becoming less violent.[5] But in some years, such as 1965 to the early 1970s, the black murder rate increased much faster than the white rate. By the late 1960s the black rate was over eighteen times higher than the white one. Then, beginning around 1975, the black rate declined while the white rate continued to increase, so that the ratio of black arrests to white arrests fell to around six to one. From 1980 until the present, the rate at which adult blacks and whites are arrested for murder dropped more or less steadily. By contrast, the rate at which black and white juveniles are arrested for murder increased sharply from 1985 to the early 1990s, with the white rate almost doubling and the black rate more than tripling. Starting in the mid-1990s, the juvenile rate fell again, almost down to the level it was at in 1985.[6] In short, though the gap sometimes widens and sometimes narrows, white and black homicide rates tend to remain different.

What are we to make of all this? There are four possible responses. One is to deny the facts, but this makes no sense to any objective observer. The high black crime rate cannot be wished away by talk of racism, overarresting, excessive punishment, or whites having allegedly drugged or armed blacks. A second response is to admit the facts and say that people are behaving rationally.[7] Of course whites avoid blacks; of course police officers stop and question blacks. What can you expect? Though it is true that this may be a rational response, it comes at a very high price. Whites are fearful of living amid large numbers of blacks and of sending their children to predominately black schools. Any hope of residential or school integration is dealt a powerful blow by high black crime rates. Moreover, blacks interpret the way they are treated on the streets by white strangers and by police officers as a sign that they can never make much social progress. "No matter what I do, I can never be regarded as innocent," many embittered black men will say. "I cannot hail a cab as easily as a white, and I will be stopped and questioned by the police more than any white. Integration is a joke."

Race matters, and race is unchangeable; hence, race differences that put people at risk pose a difficult burden on almost everyone.

A third strategy, suggested by Professor Randall Kennedy, is to change police practices so that they do not single out blacks for undue attention. He directs our attention to a number of court cases that evaluate the legality of police behavior that uses race as a proxy for dangerousness. In his summary, "Most courts that have confronted the issue have authorized police to use race in making decisions to question, stop, or detain persons so long as doing so is reasonably related to efficient law enforcement and not deployed for purposes of racial harassment."[8] Some state and federal judges have dissented from this view, but it appears to be the leading one. Though in most areas of public policy, the use of a racial test must pass the tough standard of "strict scrutiny," in police investigations a much lower standard is allowed.

To deal with this problem, Kennedy proposes that the courts never, except in extraordinary cases, sustain the use of race as a clue. Because this might lead the police to ignore some forms of suspicious behavior, he suggests spending more money on law enforcement so that it can be an equal burden for whites and blacks. I am not entirely clear, however, how his proposal would work in practice. Should the police question blacks no more often than they now question whites? That raises the question of what, if any, would be the law enforcement losses from abandoning the race proxy. Would there be more crimes? Fewer arrests? Fewer solved crimes? We do not know; as far as I am aware, no information on this subject exists. As an alternative, should the police question whites as often as they now question blacks? How many more police would this require? Is there much chance of hiring them?

If these practical questions are resolved, more principled ones persist. Race is not the only proxy for crime. So also are age and sex, and, like race, neither can be changed by plan. If the courts impose their traditional strict scrutiny test on police questioning of blacks, should they impose a similar test on questioning young men (most of whom, like most blacks, are not offenders)?

Perhaps the courts should adopt a tougher posture on the use of race as a proxy. If a racial distinction is suspect and has to meet the test of strict scrutiny in employment and contracting, there is a case for its meeting that test in police behavior. But producing, by statute or court decision, this outcome will not be easy. And if it can be achieved, it is not obvious that it will change much behavior. Innocent people questioned by the police rarely go to court, and so their complaints would rarely be heard whatever view the courts took. Police practices might change little when the oversight mechanism is so weak. And many police officers can easily find justifications other than race alone to support street stops. ("A crime was reported in the neighborhood." "The black man attempted to flee." "The black man resembled known suspects.") Moreover, restraining police behavior will have little effect, as Kennedy admits, on private behavior. Taxicab drivers may still ignore black customers, and people can still cross the street to avoid young black men. Neither residential nor educational integration will be hastened by tighter rules on police conduct. Schools and neighborhoods will still tend to become overwhelmingly white or black.

The fourth option is to find ways of driving down the high black crime rate. This is a far more difficult task than passing laws, altering court rules, or raising more money to support the police. Though there are programs that help reduce the crime rate of people exposed to them, they have generally been small demonstration programs that as yet have had no significant effect on society as a whole.[9] (This may change if and when the programs become more generally applied.) The rate at which young black men were murdered tripled between 1960 and 1990, and all this in spite of the government's having spent hundreds of billions of dollars on education, welfare, vocational training, food stamps, and crime prevention programs.

It is not hard to think of reasons why many programs have failed to reduce crime. Character is formed by families and reinforced by schools. If, as is the case, families have become weaker and schools less effective, then no one should be surprised that whatever was spent on new schools and social welfare has done little to strengthen character.

Consider families. Though for many years, some sociologists urged us to believe that single-parent families were an "alternative" to two-parent ones, hardly anybody believes that any more. The evidence shows that single-parent families are a major source of misconduct. A federal survey of the families of sixty thousand American children found that at every income level except the highest (over $50,000 a year) and for whites, blacks, and Hispanics, children living with a never-married or a divorced mother were much worse off than those living in two-parent families.[10] A survey of all the leading studies shows that both poverty and living in a single-parent family contribute to children's problems.[11] When William Comanor and Llad Phillips examined data in the National Longitudinal Survey of Youth (NLSY), they found that "the most critical factor affecting the prospect that a male youth will encounter the criminal justice system is the presence of his father in the home."[12] Another look at the NLSY data suggests that African American boys without fathers were 68 percent more likely to be in jail than those with a father. Fatherless Latino boys were nearly three times as likely to be in jail than those with fathers; fatherless white Anglo boys were over four times as likely to be in jail than those with fathers.[13]

These facts suggest that any effort to change a boy's prospects must somehow compensate for an absent father. Many of the crime-prevention programs that have been most rigorously evaluated contain some form of this compensation. Big Brothers–Big Sisters programs equip children with adult mentors, nurse home visitation programs instruct single mothers on how to cope with children, and multisystemic therapy programs try to improve family life. Not all successful programs have these elements, and no one can be certain what it is about any given program that makes it effective.

Compensating for an absent father is no easy task. Some programs, led by a dedicated, highly motivated staff, can make a difference. But whether what such talented staffs do for 100 or 500 children can also be done by ordinary staffs for 100,000 or 500,000 remains to be seen. Scaling up prevention programs so that they reach most of the families that can benefit from them is no easy matter. Happily, some of these efforts are now being tried on a wider scale, and in time we shall learn whether they can be effective on a broad scale.

But the problems that these programs must tackle are not of recent origin. Since the early 1960s there has been a dramatic increase in the number of children living in single-parent families. In 1960 only 6 percent of white children lived with one parent; by 1990 that number had more than tripled. For black Americans, matters are much worse. The proportion of black children living with only one parent rose from about 20 percent in 1960 to 53 percent in 1996. And among black children in single-parent families, those who were living with a mother who had never married rose from less than 10 percent in 1960 to nearly 58 percent in 1996.[14]

In 1965 Senator Daniel Patrick Moynihan pointed out these worrisome trends and suggested that blacks suffered because so many of them were the product of single-parent families. He was immediately attacked for having been wrong on the facts and mistaken in their implications.[15] Many writers said that blacks had had two-parent families until they experienced economic disadvantage, after which their families broke apart. In any event, single-parent families were resilient alternatives to two-parent ones. We now know, however, that these revisionist attacks on the Moynihan view were wrong.

Careful studies of census data now make it clear that at least back to 1880, and perhaps much earlier, black children were more than twice as likely to grow up in a mother-only family than were white children.[16] These differences were not the product of blacks having suddenly moved from farms to cities or from the South to the North, for they existed in both urban and rural locations and in all geographical regions. The differences were universal, but their cause is not well understood. One possibility is that slavery, by denying to blacks the ordinary rites of marriage, destroyed the possibility of family life that had already been powerfully undermined by the African capture and transatlantic shipment of slaves. Another is that in Africa itself nuclear family ties were weak. A third is that the combined effect of slavery and postslavery racism produced this effect.

Whatever the explanation, in the early 1960s differences that had long existed suddenly exploded in magnitude. These new trends affected white as well as black families, though the latter were hardest hit. What caused these trends is a matter of dispute. Some believe the dramatic decline in family unity was the result of the expansion of welfare payments, others that it was caused by the decline in social stigma that attached to out-of-wedlock births, and still others that it was the result of the growing inability of some men, especially black men, to find jobs.

If crime is to a significant degree caused by weak character; if weak character is more likely among the children of unmarried mothers; if there are no fathers who will help raise their children, acquire jobs, and protect their neighborhoods; if boys become young men with no preparation for work; if school achievement is regarded as a sign of having "sold out" to a dominant white culture; if powerful gangs replace weak families—if all these things are true, then the chances of reducing by plan and in the near future the crime rate of low-income blacks are slim. In many cities there are programs, some public, many private, that improve matters for some people. But the possibility that these programs can overcome the immense burdens confronting poor, badly educated, fatherless children is remote.

What, then, is left? Only, I think, broad social and cultural changes as great as those that caused our problem in the first place. Crime is not, happily, the chief feature of African American life today. There has developed, along with a black underclass, a large and growing black working class and a black middle class. Black and white children now complete high school at the same rate. Birthrates among black women, including teenagers, have fallen dramatically. These changes are about what one would expect when the material condition of a people improves. The principles on which these changes have occurred are evident to most of the beneficiaries. They embody three old-fashioned rules: Work hard, get an education, and get married before you have children. These principles are so obvious to so many people that even American professors cannot talk people into ignoring them.

They are principles that most people learn from intuition and experience. They are reinforced by churches and required by life. In the decades ahead, I hope that the reach of these principles will grow and that more and more people learn that the opposite rules—have fun, ignore school, and get sex for free—are, for all but a few entertainers, recipes for disaster. But I also know that there will be reversals. In bad times or when the culture takes an odd spin, fun, drugs, gangs, and sex will appear more attractive.

If my hope is correct, economic growth will stimulate the elemental forces that shape human society to reduce the size and power of any underclass, white or black. In many of our large cities, after all, matters were much worse at the end of the nineteenth century. Life in many parts of Chicago, New York, and San Francisco was dominated by criminal gangs, corrupt police, quick tempers, and floods of alcohol. At night you did not walk in the Five Points area of New York without guards. Crime data are not available in any systematic way for these periods, but the rates were, according to contemporaries, very high. Except for juvenile crime, matters are, I think, much better today.

If they continue to improve, the issue of police "profiling" black persons will slowly disappear. In the long run, I think they will improve, but I confess that my optimism rises and falls with changes in the crime rates. And in the short run, the tension that irritates so many whites and angers so many blacks will persist.

We can do one thing: adopt rules that constrain police freedom to stop and question people based on race alone. We can hope for another: the slow reduction in black crime rates. Doing the first is relatively easy, but it will have little effect. Achieving the second is harder and will take much longer, but it will have a large effect. For the foreseeable future, we must accept small changes with little results and hope for large changes with greater ones.

Notes

1. By estimated crime rate, I mean the racial differences in arrest rates. For nondrug crimes, these arrest rates conform rather closely to the underlying crime rate as shown by Alfred Blumstein, "On the Racial Disproportionality of U.S. Prison Populations,"

Journal of Criminal Law and Criminology 73 (1982): 1259–81, and Blumstein, "Racial Disproportionality of U.S. Prison Populations Revisited," *University of Colorado Law Review* 64 (1993): 743–60.

2. Roger Lane, *Violent Death in the City* (Cambridge, Mass.: Harvard University Press, 1979), p. 113.

3. Randall Kennedy, *Race, Crime, and the Law* (New York: Pantheon, 1997), p. 145.

4. These estimates are from Franklin E. Zimiring and Gordon Hawkins, *Crime Is Not the Problem* (New York: Oxford University Press, 1998), p. 75.

5. Arnold Barnett and Jesse Goranson, "Misapplication Reviews: Good News Is No News?" *Interfaces* 26 (May–June 1996): 35–39.

6. These data were kindly supplied to me by Professor Alfred Blumstein of Carnegie Mellon University.

7. On the concept of "rational discrimination," see Cass R. Sunstein, "Three Civil Rights Fallacies," *California Law Review* 79 (1991): 751–74; Edmund Phelps, "The Statistical Theory of Racism and Sexism," *American Economic Review* 62 (1972): 659–61.

8. Kennedy, *Race, Crime, and the Law*, p. 141.

9. For lucid and scientifically careful summaries of the leading crime prevention strategies, see Delbert S. Elliot, ed., *Blueprints for Violence Prevention* (Boulder: University of Colorado Center for the Study and Prevention of Violence, 1998). As of July 1998, ten effective programs have been described in these reports.

10. Deborah A. Dawson, "Family Structure and Children's Health: United States, 1988," *Vital and Health Statistics*, series 10, no. 178 (June 1991).

11. Sara McLanahan and Gary Sandefur, *Growing Up With a Single Parent: What Hurts, What Helps* (Cambridge, Mass.: Harvard University Press, 1994).

12. William S. Comanor and Llad Phillips, "The Impact of Income and Family Structure on Delinquency," working paper in economics 7-95R, Department of Economics, University of California at Santa Barbara.

13. This analysis of the NLSY data was done for me by Charles Murray (personal communication).

14. *1998 Green Book*, Committee on Ways and Means, U.S. House of Representatives, May 19, 1998, pp. 1252–53.

15. The Moynihan Report, as it was called, was *The Negro Family: The Case for National Action* (Washington, D.C.: U.S. Government Printing Office, 1965). The debate it engendered is analyzed in Lee Rainwater and William L. Yancey, *The Moynihan Report and the Politics of Controversy* (Cambridge, Mass.: MIT Press, 1967).

16. Steven Ruggles, "The Origins of the African-American Family Structure," *American Sociological Review* 59 (1994): 136–51; Ruggles, "The Transformation of American Family Structure," *American Historical Review* 99 (1994): 103–28; S. Philip Morgan et al., "Racial Differences in Household and Family Structure at the Turn of the Century," *American Journal of Sociology* 98 (1993): 798–828.

Health and Medical Care

SALLY SATEL

THE MEDICAL ESTABLISHMENT is strongly supportive of racial preferences in admission to medical school. The most active proponent is the Association of American Medical Colleges; the American Medical Association, the federal Council on Graduate Medical Education, and health philanthropies like the Robert Wood Johnson Foundation advocate racial preferences as well. Their goal is not necessarily to promote diversity for its own sake but to improve the health of minority patients. Support for affirmative action programs has indeed become a test of medical schools' commitment to minority health. "This is not a quota born out of a sense of equity or distribution of justice, but a principle that the best health care may need to be delivered by those that fully understand a cultural tradition," said George Mitchell, the former Senate majority leader and the chairman of the Pew Health Professions Commission.[1]

It is now claimed that a mismatch in race between doctor and patient—especially when the doctor is white and the patient is not—may be enough to trigger subtle, or not so subtle, biases that result in second-rate medical treatment and poorer health. In 1999 the U.S. Civil Rights Commission

informed Congress that "racism continues to infect" the health care system.[2] No less an authoritative voice than the American Medical Association's official newspaper has claimed that "a growing body of research
reports that racial discrepancy in health status can be explained, at least in
part, by racism and discrimination in the health care system itself."[3] This
is why, according to the Reverend Al Sharpton, health will become the
"new civil rights battlefront," a prediction echoed by other black leaders,
including the Reverend Jesse Jackson and NAACP Chairman Julian Bond.[4]

President Clinton himself has spoken of race and health. "Nowhere are
the divisions of race and ethnicity more sharply drawn than in the health
of our own people," he said in a 1998 radio address delivered during Black
History Month. It is indeed true that black Americans have higher infant
mortality rates, more death from cancer, and lower life expectancies than
whites and Asians. But it is far less certain that one of the possible explanations put forth by the president—"discrimination in the delivery of
health care services"—is accurate.[5]

Given the history of systematic racial discrimination and segregation
in the health care system, residual bias seems, at first, plausible. Indeed,
medicine, like other institutions, once practiced overt discrimination. Black
patients were treated on separate and inferior hospital wards—a policy that
persisted among many hospitals in the Deep South until 1968. Black physicians were once routinely barred from joining hospital staffs and medical
societies and started their own institutions to treat other blacks who were
denied adequate care by the white-controlled medical facilities.[6] A particularly frightening episode in medical research was the unethical Tuskegee
Syphilis Study.

Decades later, however, accusations of medical bias still linger. According to Vanessa Northington Gamble, a physician and director of the
Division of Community and Minority Programs at the Association of
American Medical Colleges, "Tuskegee symbolizes for many African-Americans the racism that pervades American institutions, including the medical
profession."[7]

But the known facts suggest other interpretations of race-related differences (or "health disparities"), and I shall present some of them here. This is not to minimize the facts of real discrepancies in access to care, certain medical procedures (even *with* insurance coverage), and in disease rates by race.[8] But I intend to show that they cannot be convincingly traced to bias against minority patients. My second aim is to look critically at one program intended to help close the health gap: racial preferences in medical school admissions.

Do Physicians Treat Minority Patients Differently?

A study in the *New England Journal of Medicine* in 1999 described differences in treatment of lung cancer between black and white patients who were beneficiaries of Medicare insurance.[9] In a careful analysis, Peter B. Bach and his colleagues at Memorial Sloan-Kettering Cancer Center in New York City looked at records of more than 10,000 patients who received diagnoses of operable lung cancer. Seventy-seven percent of the white patients underwent surgery compared with 64 percent of the blacks. Five years after diagnosis, only one-quarter of black patients were still alive compred with one-third of whites.

What accounted for the different rates of surgery? Did doctors not suggest the treatment as often to their black patients, or did these patients more often choose to forgo the recommendation for surgery? Were the black patients more likely to have poor lung function, such as more carbon dioxide buildup, or other problems that would have prohibited surgery or contributed to earlier demise? Details like these would go a long way toward explaining why surgery was never offered and why death rates differed, but those were not the questions that Bach and his colleagues set out to answer.[10] Indeed, the authors specifically said they could not offer an explanation based on the kinds of data they collected.

Other physicians, however, were ready with hypotheses. "Possibly, physicians are treating cancer patients not just based upon their illness and recommended treatment, but on the basis of their race," suggested

Dr. Hugh Stallworth of the American Cancer Society.[11] Dr. Harold Free-man, a surgeon and president of North General Hospital in Harlem, won-dered whether white doctors might have been more scrupulous in getting white patients to accept surgery. "If you [as a doctor] were dealing with somebody who looked exactly like you, would you take another step?" he asked.[12] A more emphatic reaction greeted a report in the *Annals of Emergency Medicine* that found that 74 percent of white patients with fractures received pain medication compared with 57 percent of black patients.[13] "I think it's racism, flat out," said Dr. Lewis Goldfrank, director of emergency services at Bellevue Hospital in New York City.[14]

Responses like these would not surprise John Landsverk of Children's Hospital in San Diego. As he observed: "The usual implication of such disparities [in treatment rates] is that the health care system is biased against persons of the ethnic minority group and that the bias is likely to be found even in professional clinicians' perceptions of clinical problems and [re-ferrals for] clinical procedures."[15] In light of this, Landsverk was especially enthusiastic about a study by a group of doctors at the University of Pittsburgh that found no race-related differences in treatment of children with behavioral problems.[16] Their report appeared in the journal *Medical Care* one month after Bach's study, but it attracted no public attention. It should have; it was "an important non-finding," as Landsverk noted in an accompanying editorial in the same journal. Not only did the Pittsburgh study include a very large sample—almost 15,000 children treated in clinics across the country and Canada—but also, most important, the researchers interviewed the parent and doctor of *every* patient. The results: race and ethnicity of the child had no relationship to clinician patterns in drug prescribing, referral, or diagnosis of behavioral problems. The clinicians also spent slightly *more* time with minority children than with their white counterparts.

This handful of studies is emblematic of the challenges inherent in interpreting health disparities research. First, the vast majority of treatment disparity studies are what scientists call "retrospective." That is, the raw data already exist in hospital records, and researchers use them (in retrospect) when they want to explore a specific question (e.g., are there more visits to emergency rooms on nights with a full moon?). The disadvantage of this approach is that key questions cannot be asked directly of the very people being studied: for example, did subjects in the study want or refuse a specific treatment? Did physicians offer it, and if not, why? Second, as Landsverk's reaction to the University of Pittsburgh study suggests, the *absence* of alleged racial bias does not make news. Consider the following example of a study that made a media splash the first time around.

A Misdiagnosed Case of Physician Bias

We know that black persons generally undergo cardiac catheterization less frequently than whites. Catheterization is a procedure used to discern whether there is blockage in the coronary arteries, the vessels that feed blood to the heart itself, and therefore whether the patient is at risk for a heart attack. The delicate process involves introducing a catheter into an artery in the leg and threading it upward toward the heart. When it reaches the point were the coronary arteries branch off, dye is squirted and the arterial patterns show up on a real-time X-ray. This is generally the first step in determining whether the vessels can be opened wider via a tiny balloon or whether some or all of the vessels must be replaced in a bypass operation.

Struck by the observation that black patients undergo catheterization less often than whites, Dr. Kevin A. Schulman and others at Georgetown University Medical Center wanted to examine how doctors made their decisions to refer patients for the procedure.[17] The researchers recruited 720 general internists at medical conventions and asked them to participate in a study of clinical decision making. The internists were not told that a primary purpose of the study was to explore how the race and sex of the patient might affect those decisions, nor were they told that the researchers expected to find that African Americans (and women) would be referred for cardiac catheterization less frequently than white men.

The doctors watched videotapes of actors wearing dressing gowns and answering questions posed to them by an interviewer who elicited their complaints about chest pain and other relevant medical and personal history, including their insurance status. All the questions asked of the actors and their responses, down to the gestures used to describe the symptoms, were scripted to minimize inconsistencies. Overall, the doctors, who were mostly white, viewed 144 different videotapes, one for every possible combination of race, sex, and age and including differing clinical variables like the nature of the chest pain and the patient's stress test and EKG results.

The physicians were asked whether the patients' complaints appeared to reflect heart disease or another kind of distress, such as indigestion, and to rate the likelihood that the pain was indeed heart-related. As it turned out, all eight groups received similar ratings, leading the authors to assume the doctors would also refer for catheterization at similar rates. Yet, according to Schulman, "women and blacks were significantly less likely to be referred for catheterization than white men." About 9 percent of the white men were not referred versus 15 percent of the women and black patients. If representative of actual clinical outcomes, Schulman said, this would mean that blacks and women "were 40 percent less likely to be referred." Schulman misspoke, however: what it really would have meant was that white men had a 40 percent lower chance of *not* being referred. Quite a difference.

These findings were presented in an article titled, "The Effect of Race and Sex on Physicians' Recommendations for Cardiac Catheterization," published in the *New England Journal of Medicine* in the winter of 1999. In the article Schulman and his associates speculated:

> Our findings that the race and sex of the patient influence the recommendations of physicians independently of other factors may suggest bias on the part of the physicians. However, our study could not assess the form of bias. Bias may represent overt prejudice on the part of physicians, or, more likely, could be the result of subconscious perceptions rather than deliberate actions or thoughts. Subconscious bias occurs when a patient's membership in a target group automatically activates a cultural stereotype in the physician's memory regardless of the level of prejudice the physician has.[18]

The study was a media sensation. On ABC's *World News This Morning*, Juju Chang told viewers: "How your doctor treats your heart may depend on the color of your skin. . . . The bias shows up in the diagnosis and doctors don't even realize it."[19] Peter Jennings predicted that the study would make "political waves" because it showed that "prejudice among doctors causes a gap in the quality of health care between blacks and whites."[20] On *Nightline*, Ted Koppel set up the story like this: "Last night we told you how the town of Jasper, Texas, is coming to terms" with the racially motivated murder of a black man; "Tonight we will focus on [doctors] who would be shocked to learn that what they do routinely fits quite easily into the category of racist behavior."[21] Newspaper headlines echoed the theme: "Cardiac Testing: Study Finds Women, Blacks Are Being Shortchanged," the *Chicago Tribune* said.[22] "Health Care: It's Better If You're White," announced the *Economist*.[23] The articles repeated Schulman's statement that black patients were 40 percent less likely to be referred.

Some of the most intense—indeed, self-flagellating—reactions came from the medical profession itself. An editorial in *The Lancet*, Britain's foremost medical journal, saw the findings as being "as close to a definition of institutionalized racism as doctors and health care providers may dare to get."[24] Aubrey Lewis, a Long Island cardiologist, warned on *Nightline* that "if this [physician bias] continues on, you're looking at literally a decimation of the African-American population."[25]

A Second Sober Look at Schulman's Study

A revelation came six months after the Schulman study appeared when the *New England Journal of Medicine*, the same journal that had printed Schulman's study, published a powerful rebuttal. This analysis was by Lisa M. Schwartz, Steven Woloshin, and M. Gilbert Welch, all physicians at the White River Junction Veterans Administration Hospital in Vermont, who reanalyzed Schulman's data to show that the average referral rates for three of the four groups were in fact the same.[26] White men, white women, and black men were all referred at the rate of 9 in 10; only black women, for unclear reasons, had a lower referral rate, about 8 in 10. Put another way, black women were 87 percent as likely as white women and men of both races to be referred for catheterization. And black men were treated just as aggressively as both white men and white women.

The doctors from White River Junction also expressed dismay at what might be called the statistical sleight-of-hand that supported the Schulman hypothesis of physician referral bias. "The probability of referral for blacks was 7 percent lower. . . . These exaggerations serve only to fuel anger and undermine the trust between physicians and their patients," the White River Junction doctors wrote. They were not alone in expressing concern; the *NEJM* editors published a note in the very same issue regretting that they had not required the authors to use more straightforward statistical measures. "We take responsibility for the media's over-interpretation of [this] article," they admitted.[27]

Even after seeing how his findings had been interpreted by the press and used to goad racial resentments, Schulman would not budge. "Our study will . . . encourage the medical profession to seek ways to eliminate unconscious bias that may influence physicians' clinical decisions," he maintained.[28] Also sticking with Schulman's interpretation was Paul Douglass, a cardiologist at Morehouse School of Medicine. "You can argue with statistics all day," he told *USA Today;* "we have to face the reality of our situation: There is a gender and racial bias."[29] Compared with the tidal wave of coverage triggered by the Schulman study, the article by Schwartz and her colleagues generated a mere trickle of media interest, as noted by columnist John Leo and the media magazine *Brill's Content.*[30]

Alternative Explanations for Differences in Treatment

Accusations of bias make headlines. Less catchy are the mundane but meaningful explanations that are more faithful to the clinical situations that doctors and patients face every day. A judicious approach to the topic has been adopted by the Kaiser Family Foundation. "Even when differences persist, it should be noted that every differential in care is not necessarily a problem," says a 1999 foundation report, "and that the level of care obtained by whites may not be the appropriate standard for comparison."[31]

One reason, for example, that procedure rates differ is that medical problems do not necessarily occur with the same frequency across races. Consider: Uterine fibroid tumors, and thus hysterectomies, are more common in black women than in whites, while osteoporosis-related fractures, and thus hip replacement, are rarer. Limb amputation is more common among black patients because thicker atherosclerosis of the blood vessels in the leg makes it harder to perform limb-saving surgery.[32] African Americans suffer stroke at many times the rate of whites, yet undergo a procedure to unclog arteries in the neck (endarterectomy) only one-fourth as often. Racism? Unlikely. It turns out that whites tend to have their obstructions in the large, superficial carotid arteries of the neck region that are readily accessible to surgery. Blacks tend to have their blockages in the branches of the carotids. These smaller branches run deeper and farther up into the head where the surgeon cannot reach them.[33]

Another consideration is the clinical condition of the patient. Does he have other medical problems that alter the risk-to-benefit ratio of a procedure, making it less favorable? The treatment of heart disease, for example, often needs to be modified in the presence of uncontrolled high blood pressure and diabetes—conditions more typical of black patients with heart disease than of white patients.[34]

Then there is the site of care itself. Some hospitals, for example, simply do not offer certain cardiac procedures. Dr. Lucian L. Leape and his colleagues at the Harvard Medical School found that about one-quarter of all patients needing cardiac procedures failed to get them, in large part because they were admitted to hospitals that did not offer them. Notably, Leape found that failure to undergo procedure occurred at equal rates across all groups of patients—black, white, and Hispanic.[35]

Conversely, under systems of available medical care in the United States (e.g., veterans' affairs medical centers, the military services), some differences in treatment melt away. For example, patients with colorectal and prostate cancer treated in those systems showed no race-related differences in treatment availability, treatment methods, or survival rates. Yet in other instances, even with good health insurance coverage, African American patients may have a lower chance of receiving certain procedures.[36] If money is not an issue in those instances, then the difference in treatment *must* represent bias on the part of the doctors, say those who are quick to charge bias when outcomes differ by race.

As we've seen, this charge makes very lively headlines. But a different interpretation is plausible: that the patients' clinical needs rather than the doctors' personal biases are dictating the care. After all, if not for concern about the patient, why wouldn't physicians perform a reimburseable procedure?

The factors discussed so far are only some of the determinants of whether patients undergo procedures. We must also consider patients' attitudes toward care. For example, what is the nature of a person's belief in his susceptibility to disease, the seriousness with which he perceives disease, and his confidence that treatment will work?[37] Social scientists call this the health belief model. Culturally influenced ideas about illness also play a role in patients' decisions to refuse or delay screening tests and interventions. Fatalistic attitudes toward the value of preventive care and the outcomes of disease as well as magical thinking (e.g., that the devil can cause cancer, that mammography machines cause breast cancer) and the use of folk remedies are more prevalent in minority groups.[38]

Says Lorna G. Canlas, a nurse with an East Harlem clinic that cares for a Latino population, "Most clients I encounter need to be persuaded of the validity and utility of modern medical practices.[39] Other studies have documented a greater aversion to surgery among African American patients compared with whites, even when the white patients' perceptions of current health state, level of education, and age were all taken into account.[40]

A Hasty Allegation of Bias

Kidney transplantation has come under scrutiny of the U.S. Commission on Civil Rights in its 1999 report as a case of "health care inequity," in part because African American patients spend considerably more time on the waiting list for a new kidney than do white patients.[41] This means that they spend more time on the dialysis machine—a thrice-weekly, hours-long process that cleans the blood of toxic products. The ideal treatment is kidney transplantation, but the process is a complicated one. Before a patient can receive a kidney, there must be attempts to "match" the donor with the recipient so that the recipient's immune system does not attack, or "reject," the new kidney. The better the match of biological variables, the better the outcome. According to a report issued by the UNOS Histocompatibility Committee, black recipients wait longer owing to factors such as blood type, sensitization, and some antigens (immune proteins made by the cells).[42]

A technique called antigen matching is used to test for different combinations of six major antigens found on tissues. A perfect six-out-of-six match is the ideal condition for compatibility between donor and recipient. Unfortunately, a complete match is far less common in African American transplant candidates than in whites because they have more possible antigen combinations than whites and some of those antigens are very rare in the general population.

Scientists are still debating the precise physiology of organ rejection and the importance of near-perfect antigen matching. What they do know is that black transplant recipients are more likely to reject their new kidneys. Possible reasons include poor control of hypertension or a more vigorous immune response.[43] Even well-matched transplants can be lost to rejection, suggesting that the standard antigen-matching system may be too simplistic.[44] Clearly, we need a better understanding of transplant immunology so that we can develop new and better medications to prevent rejection.[45]

Meanwhile, if the compatibility is marginal, it is sometimes most practical for the physician to have the patient stay on dialysis longer to wait for a better match. Losing scarce organs to rejection from mismatch actually makes the recipient more likely to reject future kidneys. Also, every rejected kidney means one less donor kidney available to the other people on the waiting list. This is a critical point because donor kidneys are among the nation's scarcest resources. In 1996, for example, more than 70,000 Americans began dialysis for severe renal disease, but only 12,000 received transplants.[46]

Most patients on dialysis, especially black persons, get their organs from donors that are deceased, so called cadaveric donors. Once on the waiting list, how do black patients fare in the allocation of kidneys from cadavers? In 1997 black patients represented one-third of the waiting list for cadaveric kidneys and, as a group, donated 11 percent of all cadaveric kidneys and received 27 percent of them. Thus, more than half of all kidneys received by black transplant recipients came from donors of other races (predominately white). Donation is a gift of life that transcends racial scorekeeping—but it is important to look closely at the numbers when bias in allocation of kidneys is alleged.

Rationale for Affirmative Action in Medical School

Whether the quality of health care for minority patients truly depends upon producing greater numbers of minority physicians is an unresolved empirical question. Nonetheless, proponents of racial preferences in medical school admissions contend that white physicians treat white patients better than minority patients, with whom, it is said, they have difficulty developing a rapport.[47] To be sure, understanding a patient's cultural tradition is important, but need one actually be a product of that tradition to be sufficiently sensitive to a patient? Virtually all the major medical organizations say yes.

Foremost among them is the Association of American Medical Colleges (AAMC).[48] When California and Texas were planning to dismantle racial preferences in 1996, the AAMC formed Health Professionals for Diversity, a coalition of major medical, health, and educational associations, to lobby for the preservation of preferences. By the time Initiative 200, the Washington State referendum to prohibit preferences by race, ethnicity, or gender in public institutions, was on the ballot in 1998, the coalition included fifty-one associations among its membership. According to an association vice president, the true message of race-neutral policy to minority students was: "We don't want you."[49]

Given the relatively small numbers of black, Hispanic, and Native American physicians (3 percent, 5 percent, and less than 1 percent of the nation's medical workforce, respectively), compounded by the declining number of minority applicants in the late 1990s, many feel that medical schools need to rely on racial preferences if they are to boost these numbers in the next few years.[50] (Asian Americans are not considered a minority because they are well represented among practicing physicians: 10 percent versus 4 percent of the general population.)

Racial preferences played a role in raising first-year enrollment to the point where, by 1999, it had reached 8 percent black and about 7 percent Hispanic, though it remains 1 percent Native American.[51] But recruitment has been difficult. In 1995, when racial preferences in medical schools were nearly universal, only about 12 percent of first-year students were black, Hispanic, or Native American. The recruitment challenge was characterized by Robert G. Petersdorf, former president of the AAMC, as follows: "We cannot produce underrepresented minority medical students if there is an insufficient number who are applying to our schools, graduating from college, or even finishing high school with sufficient skills to enable them to survive a premedical course of study."[52] Nonetheless, by 2010 the AAMC hopes to attain racial and ethnic representation among physicians that is in proportion to the general population.

The impact of race-neutral policies in some states will make the 2010 parity goal even more elusive. Within two years after Proposition 209 passed in 1996, there was a 29 percent drop in applications by minorities to six public medical schools in California.[53] This set alarm bells ringing throughout the medical establishment. "There is a national health need for physicians who, after the Tuskegee Syphilis Study, for example, are trusted by large segments of our population," wrote Michael J. Scotti Jr. of the American Medical Association. "It would be deplorable," he went on, "if medical schools were not permitted to consider the needs of patients when determining their criteria for selecting the best qualified applicants."[54] H. Jack Geiger, a professor of public health at the City University of New York, in an essay in the *American Journal of Public Health*, "Ethnic Cleansing in the Groves of Academe," foresaw these "reversals in minority admissions [as] merely the leading edge of a potential public health disaster."[55] A public health disaster? Only if there is nothing more important to Americans about their doctors than race.

Caring Trumps Color

Only a handful of studies have been devoted to the question of whether patients' outcomes are better if they and their doctors are of the same race. Many of these studies were conducted with psychiatric patients, and the majority show that the clinician's race has very little to do with how black and white patients fare in their treatment and recovery.[56]

According to a 1994 Harris poll for the Commonwealth Fund called Health Care Services and Minority Groups, race does not play an especially large role in patients' attitudes about their doctors. When asked to cite the "things that influence your choice of doctor," the physician's "nationality/ race/ethnicity" ranked twelfth out of thirteen possible options; just 5 percent of whites and 12 percent of minorities said it was important. A greater portion of Asians, 28 percent, rated race/ethnicity as important, probably because of language barriers. Even so, over 60 percent of white, black, and Hispanic respondents said they did not consider the doctor's ability to speak their language particularly relevant to their choice of doctor.[57]

For the entire group of 4,000 respondents, factors such as ease of getting an appointment, the convenience of office location, and the doctor's reputation were most influential, cited by about two-thirds of respondents. When respondents who expressed dissatisfaction with their regular doctors were asked for details, only Asians claimed that race or ethnicity was the problem (and the percentage was small, only 8 percent of all Asian respondents). Among the subset of the entire sample who said they "did not feel welcome" at their doctors' offices, a mere 2 percent of African Americans and Hispanics attributed the discomfort to racial/ethnic differences.[58]

The main complaint of almost all groups was "failure to spend enough time with me." And of those who were so dissatisfied that they changed doctors, only 3 percent of Asians and 2 percent of blacks did so on the basis of the physician's race or ethnicity. The most common complaints were "lack of communication," "didn't like him or her," "couldn't diagnose problem," or "didn't trust his or her judgment." Less than one percent of people polled said that they felt limited in their options for care because of racial or ethnic discrimination.

Thus, in this era of managed care's fifteen-minute doctor visit, what much of the research on attitude really tells us is that most patients attach more value to the amount of time they can spend with their doctors than they do to the doctor's race or ethnicity. When patients see a different doctor each time they go to the clinic, as is often the case with municipal clinic patients and those whose HMOs have high turnover, it is even harder to establish comfort and trust.

Academic Performance and Racial Preferences

Acceptance rates for minority students to medical schools have long been higher than rates for white and Asian applicants with similar qualifications, according to the Association of American Medical Colleges. In 1979, for example, a minority student with high grades and board scores had a 90 percent chance of being admitted to medical school, while a white applicant with comparable qualifications had a 62 percent chance. By 1991, the last year for which AAMC has published data, the figures were 90 percent versus 75 percent. And a low-scoring minority applicant had a 30 percent chance of admission, while a similarly low scoring white applicant had a 10 percent chance.

At the University of South Florida College of Medicine, for example, between 1995 and 1997, black applicants with a B+ grade-point average had a roughly 13 percent chance of admission, whereas white and Hispanic applicants with the same grade-point average had only a 4 to 5 percent chance.[59] Even with the passage of Proposition 209 in 1996 in California, minority applicants to some of California's public medical schools were two to almost three times as likely to be admitted as whites and Asians with considerably higher grades.[60]

Notwithstanding the clear race-based advantages in admission to medical schools, the U.S. Commission on Civil Rights charged discrimination, noting a "persistent yet baffling denial of the social, economic, and historical realities depriving our profession of minority physicians."[61] True, many minority students have suffered unfairly in second-rate primary and secondary schools, but medical school seems a risky point in the academic pipeline at which to give an academic break.

Sadly, black and Hispanic applicants, who are favored in medical school admissions, also are overrepresented among students who encounter trouble in medical school. According to the AAMC, they are more likely than other students to repeat their first year or to drop out.[62] Of the medical school class admitted in 1989, over 20 percent of minority students did not graduate four years later, as is typical, with the class of 1993; of white and Asian students in the same class, only 8 percent failed to graduate.[63] In 1996 the picture worsened across the board: 39 percent of minority students were unable to keep pace compared with 15 percent of nonminority students.[64] A 1994 study published in the *Journal of the American Medical Association* found that in 1988 51 percent of black medical students failed Part 1 of the National Medical Boards (taken after the second year of medical school), more than four times the 12 percent rate of white students. (Failure rates for Hispanic students were 34 percent, and for Asians, 16 percent.)[65]

The typical path for students after graduating from medical school is application to residency programs in a chosen specialty. At this level, too, there are different outcomes. "It has been documented consistently over the past decade that a higher proportion of underrepresented minority students failed to obtain first-year residency positions through [the standard process]," wrote Gang Xu of Jefferson Medical College in Philadelphia and colleagues.[66] Moreover, for the period 1996–1999, the yearly dismissal rate for black residents in residency programs (14.4 percent) was almost double that for other groups (7.7 percent).[67] Reasons for dismissal can include persistently unprofessional behavior, chronic absenteeism, and lack of aptitude or interest.

These problems encountered by black and Hispanic medical students are the result of admitting students who are underqualified. When black students were compared with whites who had similar academic credentials, the failure rates were similarly low.[68] A 1987 study by the RAND Corporation found that only about half of black physicians obtained board certification compared with 80 percent of white physicians. Yet African Americans were *more* likely than white physicians to obtain "board certification" in a recognized medical specialty if their grades in college and on the Medical College Admissions Test were strong enough to get them admitted on a competitive basis in the first place.[69]

Though the subject deserves more research, a handful of studies have linked medical school performance with the quality of the physician produced. Robyn Tamblyn of McGill University and colleagues found that licensing examination scores were significant predictors of whether Canadian physicians sought consultations from specialists, prescribed appropriately, and ordered screening mammograms for female patients aged 50–69. Given Canada's universal health insurance, these referral and medicating patterns were unlikely to have been influenced by patients' ability to pay.[70] Another study, among American doctors, found that passing grades on the test to become a specialist (e.g., a cardiac surgeon, a neurologist) and the scores received on the internal medical licensing exam correlated with ratings of performance in practice by fellow doctors.[71]

An Honest Debate

Instituting racial preferences toward the goal of diversity for its own sake or in the spirit of compensation for historical mistreatment are philosophical abstractions for debate in courtrooms, classrooms, and legislatures. But instituting preferences in order to enhance minority health is a practical proposition that can actually be tested using real-world data. Thus far, in my view, the case has yet to be made that improving minority health depends on having more minority doctors.

Racial preferences would seem, for several resons, to be an inefficient way to increase the number of minority doctors—and, thus, minority health. First, simply put, minority representation over the last decade has been fairly stagnant in spite of aggressive admissions policies. Second, minority recruitment has resulted in a two-tiered system of academic standards for admission that has created attendant problems of fairness to other potential medical students and of propelling some students into a career for which they are ill prepared. Third, we lack compelling evidence that same-race (minority) doctor-patient relationships result in better patient outcomes.

No matter who treats our nation's poor and minority patients, we must recognize that they tend to have multiple, chronic medical conditions and are often clinically complicated. They need the best doctors they can get, regardless of race. Not enough doctors choose to work in rural community clinics and poor, inner-city neighborhoods; moreover, in a number of states such as Florida, Illinois, North Dakota, Texas, and New York graduates of foreign medical schools represent one-fourth to one-half of the physician workforce in underserved areas.[72] California has approved legislation requiring its public medical schools to increase the number of training slots for primary-care physicians and to decrease slots for specialists.[73] Other approaches use creative financial incentives (e.g., loan forgiveness, rent rebates, higher pay) to draw young doctors into rural and inner-city communities. We should be capitalizing on these strategies, not lowering standards for admission to medical school.[74] As far as patient preferences are concerned, again it would make more sense to create mechanisms that ensure patient choice than to open the doors of medical schools to unprepared students.

Finally, we must not forget that the physician is part of a larger network of health care providers. For some preventive care (e.g., vaccinations for children and the elderly, prenatal care, routine infant checkups, and blood pressure surveillance), physicians are not even needed. Specially trained nurses can help provide after-hours medical appointments and give basic advice over the telephone; public health nurses or physician assistants cooperating with local churches and community organizations can deliver these services at least as effectively. Inner-city hospitals are now hiring health educators (ideally from within the community) to teach fellow residents about diet and exercise, smoking cessation, and screening for cancer, diabetes, and hypertension. These workers also participate in out-reach efforts to get people into clinics for routine care—an important task because medically indigent people tend to underuse available care, show up in emergency rooms for minor problems, and receive diagnoses for conditions like cancer at an advanced stage.

While well-meaning groups like the AAMC advance the questionable belief that minority health is dependent on minority physicians, evidence points more vigorously toward the virtues of promoting health literacy, the formation of community–health organization partnerships, and the expansion of health coverage to the uninsured. What patients most seem to want is a qualified doctor who will spend unhurried time with them. The racial disparities in health are real, but data do not point convincingly to systematic racial bias as a determinant—nor to the need for racial preferences in medical school admissions as a remedy for health disparities.

Notes

1. Quoted in Laura Meckler, "Panel: Diversify Medical Workforce," Associated Press, December 9, 1998.

2. *The Health Care Challenge: Acknowledging Disparity, Confronting Discrimination, and Ensuring Equality*, vol. 11, *The Role of Federal Civil Rights Enforcement Efforts: A Report of the U.S. Commission on Civil Rights*, September 1999, p. 14.

3. Deborah Shelton, "A Study in Black and White," *American Medical News*, May 1, 2000, p. 22.

4. Curtis L. Taylor, "Mistakes in the Past, Fears in the Present: Wary of System,

Many Blacks Reluctant to Seek Timely Care in the Health Divide Series," *Newsday*, December 4, 1998.

5. *Changing America: Indicators of Social and Economic Well-Being by Race and Hispanic Origin*, prepared by the Council of Economic Advisors for the President's Initiative on Race, published by the National Center for Health Statistics, Centers for Disease Control, 1998.

6. Paul Starr, *The Social Transformation of American Medicine* (New York: Basic Books, 1982).

7. Vanessa Northington Gamble, "A Legacy of Distrust: African-Americans and Medical Research," *American Journal of Preventive Medicine* 9, Suppl. (1993): 35–37.

8. See J. L. Escarce et al., "Racial Difference in the Elderly's Use of Medical Procedures and Diagnostic Tests," *American Journal of Public Health* 83 (1993): 948–54; E. A. Mort, J. S. Weissman, and A. M. Epstein, "Physician Discretion and Racial Variation in the Use of Surgical Procedures," *Archives of Internal Medicine* 154 (1994): 761–67; J. Z. Ayanian et al., "Racial Differences in the Use of Revascularization Procedures After Coronary Angiography," *Journal of the American Medical Association* 269 (1993): 2642–46; Risa B. Burns et al., "Black Women Receive Less Mammography Even with Similar Use of Primary Care," *Annals of Internal Medicine* 125 (1996): 173–82; Jeff Whittle et al., "Do Patients' Preferences Contribute to Racial Differences in Cardiovascular Procedure Use?" *Journal of General Internal Medicine* 12 (1997): 267–73; M. E. Gornick et al., "Effects of Race and Income on Mortality and Use of Services Among Medicare Beneficiaries," *New England Journal of Medicine* 335, no. 11 (1996): 791–99. A particularly elegant study by Johns Hopkins researchers, Daumit et al., found that the gap between better-insured white patients and poorly covered black patients disappeared after the black patients reached age 65 and began receiving health insurance through Medicare: Gail L. Daumit et al., "Use of Cardiovascular Procedures Among Black Persons and White Persons: A Seven-Year Nationwide Study in Patients with Renal Disease, *Annals of Internal Medicine* 130 (1999): 173–82.

9. P. B. Bach et al., "Racial Differences in the Treatment of Early Stage Lung Cancer," *New England Journal of Medicine* 341, no. 16 (1999): 1198–1205.

10. D. E. Campbell and E. R. Greenberg, letter to the editor, ibid., 342, no. 7 (2000): 517.

11. Quoted in Denise Grady, "Not a Simple Case of Health Racism: White Doctors, Black Patients," *New York Times*, October 17, 1999, Weekend p. 1; Denise Grady, "Racial Discrepancy Is Reported in Surgery for Lung Cancer," ibid., October 14, 1999, p. A24.

12. Quoted in Grady, "Not a Simple Case."

13. K. H. Todd et al., "Ethnicity and Analgesic Practice," *Annals of Emergency Medicine* 35 (2000): 11–16.

14. Quoted in Gabrielle Glaser, "In Treating Patients for Pain, A Racial Gap," *New York Times*, December 28, 1999, p. D8.

15. John Landsverk, "Patient Race and Ethnicity in Primary Management of Child Behavior Problems: An Important Non-Finding," *Medical Care* 37, no. 11 (1999): 1089–91.

16. Kelly J. Kelleher et al., "Patient Race and Ethnicity in Primary Care Management of Child Behavior Problems: A Report from PROS and ASPN," ibid., pp. 1092–1104.

17. K. A. Schulman et al., "The Effect of Race and Sex on Physicians' Recommendations for Cardiac Catheterization," *New England Journal of Medicine* 340, no. 8 (1999): 618–26. See also: E. D. Peterson et al., "Racial Variation in the Use of Coronary Revascularization Procedures: Are the Differences Real? Do They Matter?" ibid., 336 (1997): 480–86; M. Laouri et al., "Underuse of Cardiac Procedures: Application of Clinical Method," *Journal of the American College of Cardiologists* 29 (1997): 891–97.

18. Schulman et al., p. 624.

19. "Medical Treatment Based on Color of the Skin: Study Shows Doctors Have Unconscious Bias," *ABC World News This Morning*, February 25, 1999.

20. Peter Jennings, *ABC World News Tonight*, February 24, 1999, as reported in *Health Line*, February 25, 1999, in story "Minority Health: Study Confirms Heart Test Bias."

21. "America in Black and White: Health Care, the Great Divide," *Nightline*, February 24, 1999.

22. "Cardiac Testing: Study Finds Women, Blacks Are Being Shortchanged," *Chicago Tribune*, March 18, 1999, p. C7.

23. *The Economist*, February 27, 1999, pp. 28–29.

24. "Institutionalized Racism in Health Care" (editorial), *The Lancet*, no. 9155 (1999): 765.

25. "America in Black and White: Health Care, the Great Divide," *Nightline*, February 24, 1999.

26. Lisa M. Schwartz, Steven Woloshin, and M. Gilbert Welch, "Misunderstandings About the Effects of Race and Sex on Physicians' Referrals for Cardiac Catheterization," *New England Journal of Medicine* 341, no. 4 (1999): 279–83. Note: average referrals per actor/patients: white male (55 yr.) referred by 91.1% of doctors; white male (70 yr.), 90%; black male (55 yr.), 91.1%; black male (70 yr.), 90%; white female (55 yr.), 92.2%; white female (70 yr.), 88.9%; black female (55 yr.), 84.4%; black female (70 yr.), 73.3%. It is the 70-year-old black female actor/patient, in particular, who garnered the noticeably low rate of referrals. It is not clear why this was so. Because there was only one actor/patient per category, it is possible that this woman was not very convincing in her portrayal of a cardiac patient.

27. Gregory D. Curfman and Jerome P. Kassirer (editors' note), *New England Journal of Medicine* 341, no. 4 (1999): 287.

28. K. A. Schulman, J. A. Berlin, and J. J. Escarce (authors' reply), ibid., p. 286.

29. Quoted in Kathleen Fackelmann, "Does Unequal Treatment Really Have Roots in Racism?" *USA Today*, September 16, 1999, p. 10D.

30. John Leo, "Shocking But Not True," *U.S. News and World Report*, November 22, 1999, p. 18; Jennifer Greenstein, "The Heart of the Matter," *Brill's Content*, October 1999, p. 40.

31. "Key Facts: Race, Ethnicity, and Medical Care," *Henry J. Kaiser Family Foundation*, October 1999.

32. Edward Guadagnoli et al., "The Influence of Race on the Use of Surgical Procedures for Treatment of Peripheral Vascular Disease in the Lower Extremities," *Archives of General Surgery* 130 (1995): 381–86.

33. Ronnie D. Horner, Eugene Z. Oddone, and David B. Matchar, "Theories Explaining Racial Differences in the Utilization of Diagnostic and Therapeutic Procedures for Cerebrovascular Disease," *Milbank Quarterly* 73, no. 3 (1995): 443–62.

34. W. W. O'Neill, "Multivessel Balloon Angioplasty Should Be Abandoned in Diabetic Patients," *Journal of the American College of Cardiology* 31 (1998): 20–22; S. G. Ellis and C. R. Narins, "Problem of Angioplasty in Diabetics," *Circulation* 96 (1997): 1707–10.

35. Lucian L. Leape et al., "Underuse of Cardiac Procedures: Do Women, Ethnic Minorities, and the Uninsured Fail to Receive Needed Revascularization?" *Annals of Internal Medicine* 120 (1999): 183–92.

36. S. A. Optenberg et al., "Race, Treatment, and Long-Term Survival from Prostate Cancer in an Equal-Access Medical Care Delivery System," *Journal of the American Medical Association* 274 (1995): 1599–1605; J. A. Dominitz et al., "Race, Treatment, and Survival Among Colorectal Carcinoma Patients in an Equal-Access Medical System," *Cancer* 82 (1998): 2312–20; W. J. Mayer and W. P. McWhorter, "Black/White Differences in Non-Treatment of Bladder Cancer Patients and Implications for Survival," *American Journal of Public Health* 79 (1989): 772–75.

37. J. A. Harrison, R. D. Mullen, and L. W. Green, "A Meto-Analysis of Studies of the Health Belief Model with Adults," *Health Education Research* 7 (1992): 107–16.

38. B. D. Powe, "Fatalism Among Elderly African Americans: Effects on Colorectal Cancer Screening," *Cancer Nursing* 18, no. 5 (1995): 385–92; C. Maynard et al., "Race and Clinical Decision Making," *American Journal of Public Health* (1986): 1446; P. A. Johnson et al., "Effect of Race on the Presentation and Management of Patients with Acute Chest Pain," *Annals of Internal Medicine* 118 (1993): 593–601; D. R. Lannin et al., "Influence of Socioeconomic and Cultural Factors on Racial Differences in Late-stage Presentation of Breast Cancer," *Journal of the American Medical Association* 279, no. 22 (1998): 1801–7; V. M. Taylor et al., "Mammography Use Among Women Attending an Inner-City Clinic," *Journal of Cancer Education* 13, no. 2 (1998): 96–101.

39. Lorna G. Canlas, "Issues of Health Care Mistrust in East Harlem," *Mount Sinai Journal of Medicine* 66, no. 4 (1999): 257–58.

40. B. J. McNeil, R. Weichselbaum, and S. G. Pauker, "Fallacy of the Five-Year

Survival in Lung Cancer," *New England Journal of Medicine* 299 (1978): 1397–1401; Eugene Z. Oddone et al., "Understanding Racial Variation in the Use of Carotid Endarterectomy: The Role of Aversion to Surgery," *Journal of the National Medical Association* 90 (1998): 25–33.

41. U.S. Commission on Civil Rights, *The Health Care Challenge*, vol. 11 (September 1999), p. 111.

42. UNOS Histocompatibility Committee, *The National Kidney Distribution System: Striving for Equitable Use of a Scarce Resource*, UNOS Update, August 1995.

43. R. H. Kerman et al., "Possible Contribution of Pre-Transplant Immune Responder Status to Renal Allograft Survival Difference of Black Versus White Recipients," *Transplantation* 51 (1991): 338–42; S. Hariharan, T. J. Schroeder, and M. R. Frist, "Effect of Race on Renal Transplant Outcome," *Clinical Transplantation* 7 (1993): 235–9; B. L. Kasiske et al., "The Effect of Race on Access and Outcome in Transplantation," *New England Journal of Medicine* 342 (1991): 302–7.

44. Glenn M. Chertow and Edgar L. Milford, "Poor Graft Survival in African-American Transplant Recipients Cannot be Explained by HLA Mismatching," *Advances in Renal Replacement Therapy* 4 (1997): 40–45.

45. Starting in 1995 new immunosuppressants (drugs that help prevent rejection) became available. This breakthrough may not only improve survival after transplantation for black patients, but it may also obviate the need for tight antigen matching and thus move blacks more quickly up the waiting list. In spite of the tremendous promise of these drugs, the clinical verdict on their success will not be in for several years because it takes at least two years after a transplant to be certain whether a kidney will function over the long term (Clive O. Callender, August 9, 1999, personal communication).

46. Renal Data Systems. USRDS 1998 Annual Report. Bethesda, Md., National Institute of Diabetes, Digestive and Kidney Diseases, April 1998.

47. Joel C. Cantor, Lois Bergeisen, and Laurence C. Baker, "Effect of Intensive Educational Program for Minority College Students and Recent Graduates on the Probability of Acceptance to Medical School," *Journal of the American Medical Association* 280 (1998): 772–76.

48. In 1992 the AAMC introduced an initiative called Project 3000 by 2000 whose goal was to see 3,000 underrepresented minority students enter medical school by the year 2000.

49. Jeffrey Mervis, "Wanted: A Better Way to Boost Numbers of Minority Ph.D.s," *Science* 28 (1998): 1268–70.

50. Randal C. Archibold, "Applications to Medical Schools Decline for Second Straight Year," *New York Times*, September 2, 1999, p. A23; Holcomb B. Noble, "Struggling to Bolster Minorities in Medicine," ibid., September 29, 1998, p. F7.

51. Barbara Barzansky, Harry S. Jonas, and Sylvia I. Etzel, "Educational Programs

in U.S. Medical Schools, 1998–1999," *Journal of the American Medical Association* 282 (1999): 840–46.

52. Robert G. Petersdorf, "Not a Choice, An Obligation," presented at the plenary session of the 102nd meeting of the AAMC, Washington, D.C., November 10, 1991.

53. Kevin Grumbach, Elizabeth Mertz, and Janet Coffman, "Under-Represented Minorities in Medical Education in California," March 1999, California Center for Health Workforce Studies at the University of California, San Francisco (report avail. at ‹http://futurehealth.ucsf.edu›). Nationwide, minority applications dropped 13 percent between 1996 and 1998. In large part, though not exclusively, this was due to the California initiative and to the three states (Texas, Louisiana, and Mississippi) that in the wake of the 1996 Hopwood case no longer considered race as a factor in medical school admission. Even though minority applications again declined between 1998 and 1999, there is no evidence that the pool of potential minority applicants is shrinking. The percentage of black and Hispanic students getting bachelor of science degrees has remained constant, as have those races' percentage of college graduates (personal communication, Ella Cleveland, Division of Community and Minority Programs, January 6, 2000). No one really understands why medical school is relatively unpopular among these students. Perhaps some are discouraged by the high educational debt they will assume or by the loss of physician autonomy in the world of managed care. Interestingly, not all these developments were a result of Proposition 209 and Hopwood. First, across the country, applications from whites have been going down as well; there was a 6 percent drop in all applicants from 1998 to 1999, the third straight year of decline. Second, the decline in minority applicants in California actually started two years before passage of Proposition 209. Third, at California's three *private* medical schools, which were unaffected by the new law, there was also a large drop in minority applications (25 percent) after its passage.

54. Michael J. Scotti Jr., "Medical School Admission Criteria: The Needs of Patients Matter," *Journal of the American Medical Association* 278 (1997): 1196–97.

55. H. Jack Geiger, "Ethnic Cleansing in the Groves of Academe," *American Journal of Public Health* 88 (1998): 1299–1300, quotation on p. 1299.

56. M. J. O'Sullivan et al., "Ethnic Populations: Community Mental Health Services Ten Years Later," *American Journal of Community Psychology* 17 (1989): 17–30; Robert Rosenheck and Catherine L. Seibyl, "Participation and Outcome in a Residential Treatment and Work Therapy Program for Addictive Disorders: The Effects of Race," *American Journal of Psychiatry* 155 (1998): 1029–34; S. Sue et al., "Community Mental Health Services for Ethnic Minorities Groups: A Test of the Cultural Responsiveness Hypothesis," *American Psychologist* 59 (1991): 553–40; R. A. Rosenheck and A. F. Fontana, "Race and Outcome of Treatment for Veterans Suffering From PTSD," *Journal of Traumatic Stress* 9 (1996): 343–51.

57. "Health Care Services and Minority Groups: A Comparative Survey of Whites, African-Americans, Hispanics, and Asian Americans," conducted for the Common-

wealth Fund by Louis Harris and Associates, New York 1994 (study no. 932028), table 1-18, p. 34.

58. Ibid., table 3-27, p. 93.

59. Thomas R. Dye, *Race as an Admissions Factor in Florida's Public Law and Medical Schools* (Tallahassee: Lincoln Center, 1999).

60. ‹http://www.acusd.edu/e_cook/›

61. U.S. Commission on Civil Rights, *The Health Care Challenge*, vol. 11 (September 1999); p. 116.

62. As cited in *Balancing the Scales of Opportunity: Ensuring Racial and Ethnic Diversity in the Health Professions* (Washington D.C.: National Academy Press, 1994), p. 24.

63. H. W. Foster Jr., "Reaching Parity for Minority Medical Students: A Possibility or a Pipe Dream?" *Journal of the National Medical Association* 88 (1996): 17–21.

64. Minority Students in Medical Education: Facts and Figures, IX (Washington, D.C.: AAMC, 1998).

65. Beth Dawson et al., "Performance on the National Board of Medical Examiners Part 1 Examination by Men and Women of Different Race and Ethnicity," *Journal of the American Medical Association* 272 (1994): 674–79.

66. G. Xu et al., "The Relationship Between Race/Ethnicity of Generalist Physicians and Their Care for Underserved Populations," *American Journal of Public Health* 87 (1997): 817–22.

67. Rebecca S. Miller, Marvin R. Dunn, and Thomas Richter, "Graduate Medical Education, 1998–1999: A Closer Look," *Journal of the American Medical Association* 282 (1999): 855–60.

68. Dawson et al., 1994.

69. S. N. Keith, R. M. Bell, and A. P. Williams, "Assessing the Outcome of Affirmative Action in Medical School: A Study of the Class of 1975," RAND Corporation publication no. R-3481-CWF, August 1987.

70. Robyn Tamblyn et al., "Association Between Licensing Examination Scores and Resource Use and Quality of Care in Primary Care Practice," *Journal of the American Medical Association* 280 (1998): 989–96.

71. P. G. Ramsey et al., "Predictive Validity of Certification by the American Board of Internal Medicine," *Annals of Internal Medicine* 110 (1989): 719–26.

72. Leonard D. Baer, Thomas C. Ricketts, Thomas R. Konrad, "International Medical Graduates in Rural, Underserved Areas," *Findings Brief, Cecil G. Sheps Center for Health Services Research*, University of North Carolina, Chapel Hill, May 1998.

73. Jay Greene, "Primary Push," *American Medical News*, March 13, 2000, pp. 10–12.

74. T. P. Weil, "Attracting Qualified Physicians to Underserved Areas," *Physician Executive* 25 (1999): 53–63.

Supporting Black Churches

JOHN J. DIIULIO JR.

UNDER WHAT, IF ANY, conditions can the life prospects of today's black inner-city poor be improved, and how, if at all, can we foster those conditions? My argument in this essay is that supporting black churches and other faith-based grassroots organizations that perform youth and community outreach functions in poor inner-city neighborhoods is a necessary and vital although insufficient condition for repairing the social fabric and restoring economic vitality in truly disadvantaged urban neighborhoods. The case for supporting black churches rests upon a certain constellation of ideas and findings concerning inner-city poverty, religiosity and volunteers, religious faith as a factor in ameliorating social problems, and the extent of church-anchored outreach in black urban neighborhoods.

This essay was previously published under the title "Black Churches and the Inner-City Poor," in Christopher H. Foreman Jr., editor, *The African American Predicament* (Washington, D.C.: Brookings Institution, 1999), pp. 116–40. A shorter version, entitled "Supporting Black Churches: Faith, Outreach, and the Inner-City Poor," appeared in *The Brookings Review*, Spring 1999, pp. 42–45. It is reprinted here by permission of the Brookings Institution.

Black Inner-City Poverty

Recent research by the editors of this book and others has clearly shown that black Americans have progressed economically over the last half century.[1] Even analysts who have emphasized the persistence of black poverty and black-white income gaps have acknowledged that "there have been significant improvements since 1940 in the absolute and relative positions of blacks"; that black Americans represent a trillion-dollar-plus annual market larger than that of "most countries in the world"; that "the majority of working-class and middle-class black families have made some important gains"; and that since "the early 1990s, black family income has risen."[2] But as I have argued elsewhere, unless we propose to do nothing more than continue idle academic or ideological debates, the triumph of overall black economic progress neither can nor should obscure the tragedy of black poverty and joblessness.[3]

Black Americans made substantial economic progress in the 1960s, but each post-1970 recession exacted a disproportionate toll on blacks regardless of family structure; for example, Robert B. Hill estimated that the four recessions between 1970 and 1985 led to a tripling in the jobless rates among blacks in two-parent families as well as among blacks in mother-only households.[4] As the national economy improved in the late 1980s, black men and women still had unemployment rates more than double those of whites. Even after the boom years of the 1990s, 40 percent of black children, concentrated heavily in central city neighborhoods, continued to live in below-the-poverty-line households.[5]

Some analysts deflect such concerns about black inner-city poverty by debating statistical measures of what it means to be poor, or by stressing that intra-group rates of poverty and other social ills among blacks have varied largely according to marital status and other conditions that reflect individual choices. There is, however, no genuine empirical or moral basis for denying that millions of black children, through absolutely no fault of their own, remain economically disadvantaged in neighborhoods where jobs are few and drugs, crime, and failed public schools are common.

Religiosity and Volunteers

How we approach black inner-city poverty is bound to be affected by religious ideals, influences, and institutions. "The United States," observes George Gallup Jr., "is one of the most devout nations of the entire industrialized world, in terms of religious beliefs and practices."[6] Black Americans are in many ways the most religious people in America. Some 82 percent of blacks (versus 67 percent of whites) are church members; 82 percent of blacks (versus 55 percent of whites) say that religion is "very important in their life"; and 86 percent of blacks (versus 60 percent of whites) believe that religion "can answer all or most of today's problems."[7]

As Father Andrew Greely has observed, both "frequency of church attendance and membership in church organizations correlate strongly with voluntary service. People who attend services once a week or more are approximately twice as likely to volunteer as those who attend rarely if ever."[8] The best available data suggest that religious organizations and "relationships related to their religion" are the major forces in mobilizing volunteers in America; even a third of purely secular volunteers (persons who did not volunteer for specifically religious activities) relate their service "to the influence of a relationship based in their religion."[9] Similarly, as Gallup has reported, "Churches and other religious bodies are the major supporters of voluntary services for neighborhoods and communities. Members of a church or synagogue . . . tend to be much more involved in charitable activity, particularly through organized groups."[10]

Faith Factor Findings

But what, if any, social consequences for blacks and other Americans flow from religiosity and faith-based charitable, volunteer, and community-serving work? Is there any scientific evidence to justify the faith of most black Americans that religion can "answer all or most of today's problems"?

James Q. Wilson has succinctly summarized the small but not insignificant body of credible evidence to date: "Religion, independent of social class, reduces deviance."[11] For example, consider the latest research of David B. Larson, the medical research scientist who pioneered the development of research on public health outcomes (physical health, mental health, addictions) that led to new training programs at Harvard and three dozen other medical schools.[12] With criminologist Byron Johnson, Larson has reviewed some 400 juvenile delinquency studies published between 1980 and 1997. They report that "the better the study design and measurement methodology, the greater the likelihood the research will produce statistically significant and beneficial results associated with 'the faith factor.'"[13] In other words, the more scientific the study, the more optimistic are its findings about the extent to which "religion reduces deviance."

This conclusion squares with the results of another major review of the relevant research literature as it pertains to adult criminals: "Our research confirms that the religiosity and crime relationship for adults is neither spurious nor contingent. . . . Religion, as indicated by religious activities, had direct personal effects on adult criminality as measured by a broad range of criminal acts. Further, the relationship held even with the introduction of secular controls."[14] In other words, "religion matters" in reducing adult crime.

Beyond crime and delinquency, in a 1996 synopsis of faith factor research, Patrick Fagan of the Heritage Foundation summarized studies suggesting that religion enhances family stability (the family that prays together is indeed more likely to stay together), improves health, reduces adolescent sexual activities and teenage pregnancies, cuts alcohol and drug abuse, and reinforces other measures of "social stability."[15]

In 1985, Harvard economist Richard Freeman reported that churchgoing, independent of other factors, made young black males from high-poverty neighborhoods substantially more likely to escape poverty, crime, and other social ills.[16] In a forthcoming reanalysis and extension of Freeman's work, Larson and Johnson mine national longitudinal data on urban black youth and find that religion is indeed a powerful predictor of escaping poverty, crime, and other social ills.[17]

Black Church Outreach Tradition

The black church has a unique and uniquely powerful youth and community outreach tradition. The black church's historic role in providing education, social services, and a safe gathering place prefigured its historic role in the civil rights movement.

There are eight major historically black Christian churches: African Methodist Episcopal, African Methodist Episcopal Zion, Christian Methodist Episcopal, Church of God in Christ, National Baptist Convention of America, National Baptist Convention, USA, National Missionary Baptist Convention, and the Progressive National Baptist Convention. There are also scores of independent or quasi-independent black churches and at least nine certified religious training programs operated by accredited seminaries that are directed toward ministry in black churches and black faith communities. Together, the eight major black denominations alone encompass some 65,000 churches and about 20 million members.

Until the 1990s, however, the richly religious lives of black Americans and the black church outreach tradition were given short shrift by both historians and social scientists, and not just by white historians and social scientists. Writing in 1994 in a special double edition of *National Journal of Sociology*, Andrew Billingsley, a dean of black family studies, noted that the subject was largely ignored even by leading black scholars who were keenly aware of "the social significance of the black church," including many who "were actually members of a black church."[18]

An empirically well-grounded perspective on contemporary black church outreach is provided by sociologist Harold Dean Trulear, an ordained black minister who taught for eight years at the New York Theological Seminary, has conducted extensive research on black clergy training, and is presently vice president for research on religion and at-risk youth at Public/Private Ventures in Philadelphia. "When it comes to youth and community outreach in the inner city," Trulear cautions, "not all black urban churches are created equal":

> Naturally, it's in part a function of high resident membership. Inner-city churches with high resident membership cater more to high-risk neighborhood youth than . . . black churches with inner-city addresses but increasingly or predominantly suburbanized or commuting congregations. [The high resident membership black churches] tend to cluster by size and evangelical orientation. . . . It's the small- and medium-sized churches . . . [especially] the so-called . . . blessing stations and specialized youth chapels with their charismatic leader and their small, dedicated staff of adult volunteers [that] . . . do a disproportionate amount of the up-close and personal outreach work with the worst-off inner-city youth."[19]

Surveys of Church-Based Outreach

When it comes to solving urban problems and the plight of the black inner-city poor, black churches cannot do it all (or do it alone), and not all black churches do it. But that reality should not obscure the black church outreach tradition and its many and powerful contemporary manifestations. The pathbreaking research of scholars such as Eric C. Lincoln and Lawrence H. Mamiya, combined with recent systematic research by Trulear and others, should persuade even a dedicated skeptic to take church-based outreach seriously, especially where the black community is concerned.

In a forthcoming study, P/PV's Jeremy White and Mary de Marcellus report on the results of their intensive six-month field exploration of youth-serving ministries in the District of Columbia.[20] They interviewed leaders and volunteers in 129 of the city's faith-based ministries, including on-site visits to 79 churches, faith-based nonprofit organizations, and schools, virtually all led by blacks and serving predominantly black populations. From this research, they concluded that "there is a critical mass of faith-based organizations in Washington, D.C., that work directly and intensively with at-risk youth." The programs fell into "six major categories: after-school or tutoring programs; evangelization; gang violence prevention; youth groups; and mentoring."[21]

None of the programs studied by White and de Marcellus required youth to be the children of a particular church, profess any particular religious beliefs, or agree to eventual "churching" as a condition for receiving services, entering church buildings, or otherwise benefiting from the programs. Also, almost none of the programs, even those that furnished children with material goods such as clothes or books, charged a fee. In the words of one of the outreach ministers quoted on the first page of their report, "The cost of real love is no charge."[22]

The results of a survey of "faith-based service providers in the nation's capital" were published in 1998 by the Urban Institute.[23] The survey found that 95 percent of the congregations performed outreach services. The 226 religious congregations (out of 1,100 surveyed) that responded (67 of them in the District, the rest in Maryland or Virginia) provided a total of over 1,000 community services to over 250,000 individuals in 1996.

In the mid-1990s, a six-city survey of how over 100 randomly selected urban churches (and four synagogues) constructed in 1940 or earlier serve their communities was undertaken by Ram A. Cnnan of the University of Pennsylvania. The survey was commissioned and published by Partners for Sacred Places, a Philadelphia-based national nonprofit organization dedicated to the care and good use of older religious properties.[24] Congregations were surveyed in Philadelphia, New York, Chicago, Indianapolis, Mobile, and the Bay Area (Oakland and San Francisco). Each church surveyed participated in a series of in-depth interviews. Among the Cnnan-Partners survey's key findings were the following: 93 percent of the churches opened their doors to the larger community; on average, each church provided over 5,300 hours of volunteer support to its community programs (the equivalent of two and a half full-time volunteers stationed year-round at the church); on average, each church provided about $140,000 a year in community programs, or about sixteen times what it received from program beneficiaries; on average, each church supported four major programs and provided informal and impromptu services as well; and poor children who were not the sons or daughters of church members or otherwise affiliated with the church benefited from church-supported programs more than any other single group.

The best known and still the most comprehensive survey focusing exclusively on black churches was published in 1990 by Lincoln and Mamiya.[25] In *The Black Church in the African-American Experience*, they reported on the results of surveys encompassing nearly 1,900 ministers and over 2,100 churches. Some 71 percent of black clergy reported that their churches engaged in many community outreach programs, including day care, job search, substance abuse prevention, and food and clothing distribution.[26] Black urban churches, they found, were generally more engaged in outreach than rural ones. Though many urban churches also engaged in quasi-political activities and organizing, few received government money, and most clergy expressed concerns about receiving government money; only about 8 percent of all the churches surveyed received any federal government funds.[27]

A number of site-specific and regional surveys of black churches followed the publication of Lincoln and Mamiya's book. So far, they all have been broadly consistent with the Lincoln-Mamiya survey results on black church outreach. To cite just two examples, in a survey of 150 black churches in Atlanta, Naomi Ward and her colleagues found that 131 of the churches were "actively engaged in extending themselves into the community."[28] And a survey of 635 Northern black churches found that two-thirds of the churches engaged in a wide range of "family-oriented community outreach programs," including mentoring, drug abuse prevention, teenage pregnancy prevention, and other outreach efforts "directed at children and youth."[29]

The data from the Lincoln-Mamiya surveys were reanalyzed in the course of a 1997 study of black theological education certificate programs (Bible institutes, denominational training programs, and seminary non-degree programs). The study was directed by Trulear in collaboration with Tony Carnes and commissioned by the Ford Foundation.[30] Trulear and Carnes compared certain of the Lincoln-Mamiya survey results with data gathered in their own survey of 724 students representing twenty-eight theological certificate programs that focused on serving black students. Three-quarters of those surveyed by Trulear and Carnes reported that their church encouraged them "to be involved in my local community," more than half said relevance to "my community's needs" was of major importance to them in choosing a theological certificate program, and about half were already involved in certain types of charitable community work.[31]

Religious Racial Reconciliation

If black church outreach is so potent, why is it that inner-city poverty, crime, and other problems remain so severe? That is a fair question, but it can easily be turned around: How much worse would things be in Boston and Austin, Philadelphia and Los Angeles, and other cities were it not for largely unsung faith-based youth and community outreach efforts? How much more would government or charitable organizations need to expend, and how many new volunteers would need to be mobilized, in the absence of church-anchored outreach? The answers are "much worse" and "lots."

Citizens who for whatever reasons are nervous about enhanced church-state partnerships should be reassured by the consistent findings that faith-based outreach efforts benefit poor unchurched neighborhood children most of all, and that most outreach ministries receive no government money. If these churches are so willing to support "the least of these," surely they deserve the support of the rest of us—corporations, foundations, and, where appropriate, government agencies.

Persons of all faiths and of no faith should support black church outreach efforts. At a minimum, the black church paramedics of inner-city America's civil society deserve the support of Christian churches, both black and white, both urban and suburban. A genuine dialogue about racial reconciliation among Christians, accompanied by a Christ-centered commitment to help—or to help those who help—the inner-city minority poor, would light the way.

It is morally wrong and socially myopic to turn our heads and harden our hearts to the plight of the black inner-city poor. As Father Richard John Neuhaus has argued, rather than merely exposing "liberal fatuities about remedying the 'root causes' of poverty and crime . . . there must be another way. Just believing that is a prelude to doing something. The something in question is centered in religion that is both motive and means, and extends to public policy tasks that should claim the attention of all Americans."[32] Say amen.

Notes

1. Stephan Thernstrom and Abigail Thernstrom, *America in Black and White: One Nation, Indivisible* (New York: Simon & Schuster, 1997).

2. See: National Research Council, *A Common Destiny: Blacks and American Society* (Washington, D.C.: National Academy Press, 1989), p. 274; Marcus Alexis and Geraldine R. Henderson, "The Economic Base of African-American Communities: A Study of Consumption Patterns," in *National Urban League, The State of Black America 1994* (New York: National Urban League, January 1994), p. 81; Robert B. Hill et al., *Research on the African-American Family: A Holistic Perspective* (Westport, Conn.: Auburn House, 1993), p. 2; Council of Economic Advisors, *Changing America: Indicators of Social and Economic Well-Being by Race and Hispanic Origin* (Washington, D.C.: President's Initiative on Race, September 1998), p. 33.

3. John J. DiIulio Jr., "State of Grace," *National Review*, December 22, 1997, pp. 62–66.

4. Robert B. Hill, "The Black Middle Class: Past, Present, and Future," *National Urban League: The State of Black America 1986* (New York: National Urban League, 1986), pp. 43–64.

5. Council of Economic Advisors, *Changing America*, p. 38.

6. George Gallup Jr., *Emerging Trends, Princeton Research Center* 18 (March 1996): 5. See also Richard Morin, "Keeping the Faith: A Survey Shows the United States Has the Most Churchgoing People in the Developed World," *Washington Post Weekly Edition.*

7. George Gallup Jr., "Religion in America: Will the Vitality of Churches Be the Surprise of the Next Century?" *Public Perspective*, October–November 1995, p. 4.

8. Andrew Greely, "The Other Civic America: Religion and Social Capital," *American Prospect* 32 (May–June 1997): 70

9. Ibid., p. 72.

10. Gallup, "Religion in America," p. 2.

11. James Q. Wilson, "Two Nations," paper delivered as Francis Boyer Lecture, American Enterprise Institute, December 4, 1997, p. 10.

12. See David B. Larson et al., *Scientific Research on Spirituality and Health* (Radnor, Pa.: John M. Templeton Foundation, October 1, 1997).

13. David B. Larson and Byron Johnson, "Systematic Review of Delinquency Research," preliminary draft, 1998, and personal correspondence with Larson, September 1, 1998.

14. T. David Evans et al., "Religion and Crime Reexamined: The Impact of Religion, Secular Controls, and Social Ecology on Adult Criminality," *Criminology* 33, no. 2 (1995): 211–12.

15. Patrick Fagan, "Why Religion Matters: The Impact of Religious Practice on Social Stability," *Heritage Foundation Backgrounder*, no. 164 (January 25, 1996).

16. Richard B. Freeman, "Who Escapes? The Relation of Church-Going and Other Background Factors to the Socio-Economic Performance of Black Male Youths from Inner-City Poverty Tracts," working paper no. 1656, National Bureau of Economic Research, Cambridge, Mass., 1985.

17. David B. Larson and Byron Johnson, "Who Escapes? Revisited," final draft, 1998, and personal correspondence with Larson, September 1, 1998.

18. Andrew Billingsley, "The Social Relevance of the Contemporary Black Church," *National Journal of Sociology* 8, nos. 1 and 2 (summer–winter 1994): 3.

19. Interview with the author, June 1998.

20. Jeremy White and Mary de Marcellus, draft of *Faith-Based Outreach to At-Risk Youth in Washington, D.C.: Report of the Partnership for Research on Religion and At-Risk Youth* (Philadelphia: Public/Private Ventures, forthcoming).

21. Ibid., p. 4, 6.

22. Ibid., p. 1.

23. Tobi Jennifer Printz, *Faith-Based Service Providers in the Nation's Capital: Can They Do More?* (Washington, D.C.: Urban Institute, April 1998).

24. Diane Cohen and A. Robert Jaeger, *Sacred Places at Risk* (Philadelphia: Partners for Sacred Places, 1998).

25. Eric C. Lincoln and Lawrence H. Mamiya, *The Black Church in the African-American Experience* (Durham, N.C.: Duke University Press, 1990).

26. Ibid., p. 151.

27. Ibid., p. 15.

28. Naomi Ward et al., "Black Churches in Atlanta Reach Out to the Community," *National Journal of Sociology* 8, nos. 1 and 2 (summer–winter 1994): 59.

29. Roger H. Rubin et al., "The Black Church and Adolescent Sexuality," ibid., pp. 131, 138.

30. Harold Dean Trulear and Tony Carnes, *A Study of the Social Service Dimension of Theological Education Certificate Programs: The 1997 Theological Certificate Program Survey*, submitted to the Ford Foundation, November 1, 1997.

31. Ibid., pp. 34, 40–41.

32. Richard John Neuhaus, "The Public Square: A Continuing Survey of Religion and Public Life," *First Things* 81 (March 1998): 63–65.

PART THREE

ECONOMICS

Discrimination, Economics, and Culture

THOMAS SOWELL

RACIAL DISCRIMINATION is usually not very discriminating, in the sense in which a wine connoisseur is discriminating in being able to detect subtle differences in tastes, aromas, or vintages. When Marian Anderson was refused permission to sing in Washington's Constitution Hall in 1939, it had nothing to do with her characteristics as a singer or as a person. She was black and that was it. Similarly in baseball, before Jackie Robinson broke the color line in 1947, no one cared what kind or quality of pitcher Satchel Paige was or how powerful a slugger Josh Gibson was. They were black and that was enough to keep them out.

If we are to examine discrimination and its consequences today, we cannot be as indiscriminate as the racists of the past or present. We must make distinctions—first as to some consistent meaning of the word "discrimination" and then in deriving criteria for determining when it applies. We must also distinguish discrimination from other social or cultural factors that produce economic and other differences in outcome for different individuals and groups.

Meanings of Discrimination

To many—perhaps most—Americans, there is racial discrimination when different rules and standards are applied to people who differ by race. To these Americans, there is "a level playing field" when the same rules and the same standards apply to everybody, regardless of race.

As traditional as this meaning of discrimination has been, a radically different conception of discrimination has a strong hold on many in the media and the academic world today, as well as among political and legal elites. For them, differences in "life chances" define discrimination. If a black child does not have the same likelihood as a white child of growing up to become an executive or a scientist, then there is racial discrimination by this definition, even if the same rules and standards are applied to both in schools, the workplace, and everywhere else.

For those with this definition of discrimination, creating "a level playing field" means equalizing probabilities of success. Criteria which operate to prevent this are considered by them to be discriminatory in effect, even if not in intent.

Whatever definition—and accompanying set of policies—one believes in, a serious discussion of racial discrimination or of racial issues in general requires that we lay our cards face up on the table and not hide behind ambiguous and shifting words that render any attempt at dialog futile and ultimately poisonous.

For purposes of our discussion here, the definition of "discrimination" will be the traditional one. Other views behind other definitions will not be dismissed, however, but will in fact be examined closely.

Cause and Effect

Definitions are not chosen out of thin air. Underlying different definitions of racial discrimination are different beliefs about the way the world operates. So long as these beliefs confront each other only as opposing dogmas, there is no resolution other than by trying to shout each other down or prevail by force, whether political or physical.

Many people believe that differences in life chances or differences in socioeconomic results are unusual, suspicious, and probably indicative of biased or malign social processes that operate to the detriment of particular racial and other groups.

While there have certainly been numerous examples of discrimination—in the traditional sense of applying different rules or standards to different groups—in the United States and in other countries around the world, that is very different from claiming the converse, that group differences in prospects or outcomes must derive from this source.

Intergroup differences have been the rule, not the exception, in countries around the world and throughout centuries of history.

Today, one need only turn on a television set and watch a professional basketball game to see that the races are not evenly or randomly represented in this sport and are not in proportion to their representation in the general population of the United States. Racially, the teams do not "look like America."

Although not visible to the naked eye, neither do the beer companies that sponsor this and other athletic events. Most, if not all, of the leading beer-producing companies in the United States were founded by people of German ancestry. So were most of the leading piano manufacturers. Nor is German domination of these two industries limited to the United States.

The kind of demographic over-representation in particular lines of work found among blacks in basketball or Germans in beer brewing and piano-making can also be found among Jews in the apparel industry—not just in contemporary New York but also in the history of medieval Spain, the Ottoman Empire, the Russian Empire, Brazil, Germany, and Chile. At one time, most of the clothing stores in Melbourne were owned by Jews, who have never been as much as one percent of the Australian population.

Most of the people laying cable in Sydney, Australia, are of Irish ancestry. All the billionaires in Thailand and Indonesia are of Chinese ancestry. Four-fifths of the doughnut shops in California are owned by people of Cambodian ancestry. The list goes on and on.

It would be no feat to fill a book with statistical disparities that have nothing to do with discrimination.[1] What would be a real feat would be to get people to realize that correlation is not causation—especially when the numbers fit their preconceptions.

Very often the groups predominating in a particular field have no power to keep others out, except by excelling in the particular activity. Blacks cannot discriminate against whites in basketball, where the franchises are owned by whites. The Chinese minority in Malaysia or Indonesia cannot stop Malaysians or Indonesians from opening businesses, though historically most of the major domestic enterprises in both countries were created by people of Chinese ancestry. Nor could immigrants from India stop either blacks or whites from opening businesses in Kenya, though Indian entrepreneurs were once so predominant in Kenya and other parts of East Africa that the rupee became the predominant currency in that region.

Some statistical disparities are of course caused by discrimination, just as some deaths are caused by cancer. But one cannot infer discrimination from statistics any more than one can infer cancer whenever someone dies. The absence of corroborating evidence of discrimination has forced some into claiming that the discrimination has been so "subtle," "covert," or "unconscious" as to leave no tangible evidence. But this method of arguing—where both the presence and the absence of empirical evidence prove the same thing—would prove anything about anything, anywhere and any time.

Sources of Differences

Perhaps the most sweeping explanation of intergroup differences is that people are innately, genetically different and that these differences permeate everything they do. As Madison Grant put it in his best-selling book *The Passing of the Great Race* in the early twentieth century, "race is everything."

Virtually no one believes that any more and the Nazis revolted the world by showing where such doctrines can lead. However, the innate inferiority doctrine remains important socially and politically because it is an ominous presence in the background of discussions about other immediate practical issues. Much of the tone and substance of what is said today reflects a desire of many whites to escape the charge of racism and of many blacks to escape the charge of inferiority. A whole range of current trends, from cultural relativism to bombastic Afrocentrism, are hard to explain on their own intrinsic merits, without reference to the ominous racial doctrines that they are seeking to exorcise.

Without getting into the IQ controversy that I have dealt with elsewhere,[2] history alone makes it hard to believe in fixed or innate superiority or inferiority among the peoples of the world. A thousand years ago, the Chinese were clearly far more advanced than the Europeans, whether technologically, organizationally, or economically. Equally clearly, that relationship has reversed in recent centuries—without any corresponding changes in the genetic makeup of either the Chinese or the Europeans. Within a much shorter period of time, Eastern European Jews in the United States went from having below-average scores on intelligence tests during the First World War to having above-average scores on such tests within one generation afterward.

The enormous variety of geographic, cultural, demographic, and other variables makes an even, random, or equal distribution of skills, values, and performances virtually impossible. How could mountain peoples be expected to have seafaring skills? How could an industrial revolution have occurred in the Balkans, where there are neither the natural resources required for it nor any economically feasible way of transporting those resources there? How could the indigenous peoples of the Western Hemisphere have transported the large loads that were transported overland for great distances in Europe and Asia, when the Western Hemisphere had no horses, oxen, camels or other comparable beasts of burden?

Add to this great differences in the flora, fauna, climate, disease environments, topography and fertility of land from one region of the world to another, among other variables, and the prospects of equal achievements among peoples whose cultures evolved in very different settings shrinks to the vanishing point, even if every individual in the world had identical genetic endowments at the moment of conception.

Nor are the effects of these environmental factors likely to vanish immediately when people from a given culture in a given environment move to another culture in another environment. Particular skills and general attitudes may follow the same people around the world. Given that Germans were brewing beer in the days of the Roman Empire, there is no reason to be surprised that they continued to brew beer in Milwaukee, St. Louis, Buenos Aires, and Australia's Barossa Valley. Even when two groups begin to acquire skills initially foreign to both, they may do so making different choices and applying themselves to different things. During the decade of the 1960s, the Chinese minority in Malaysia earned more than four hundred engineering degrees, while the Malay majority earned just four. Nor can such differences be reduced to external differences in the immediate environment, for the Malays had preferential access to financial aid for higher education. But they came from a culture very different from that of the Chinese.

Just a superficial glance like this suggests something of the innumerable factors operating against the even or random distribution of peoples in different activities and institutions that is assumed as a baseline for measuring discrimination statistically. In some cases we can trace through history the particular skills that led to the dominance of one group or another in particular industries or occupations. But in other cases we cannot. In no case can we presuppose that the distribution would be random in the absence of discrimination.

Empirical Evidence

If we cannot rely on simple statistical differences, presuppositions, or definitions to determine how much discrimination exists, much less its actual effects on end results, then we must depend on corroborating empirical evidence. How much income difference, for example, is there between blacks and whites with the same objective qualifications? Do these qualifications predict future performances of each group equally or for either group validly? What of cultural bias in these criteria?

If our purpose is to weigh beliefs against facts, rather than simply to generate plausible-sounding propaganda, then we must consider whether the inputs or the output that we are measuring are really the same. Family income data, for example, can be wholly misleading if the families differ in size from group to group and from one time period to another.

American families and households have been declining in size over the years, as parents have fewer children and children are better able to afford their own living quarters in early adulthood. Black families are smaller than white families, due to more breakups of marriage and more failures to get married in the first place. Moreover, higher income families average substantially more people per household.

An individual, however, always means one person, regardless of race or income, so per capita income data can present a very different picture from that deriving from family or household income data. Real income per black household rose only 7 percent from 1967 to 1988, but real income per black person rose 81 percent over the same span. On a household basis, blacks' average income was a lower percentage of whites' average income at the end of this period than at the beginning but, on a per person basis, blacks were earning a significantly higher percentage of what whites were earning in 1988 than in 1967.[3] Needless to say, those who deal in politicized indignation prefer to cite family or household data. But if we are talking about job discrimination, we are talking about what happens to individuals. Employers do not employ households.

As far back as 1969, black males who came from homes where there were newspapers, magazines, and library cards had the same incomes as white males from similar homes and with the same number of years of schooling.[4] In the 1970s, black husband-and-wife families outside the South earned as much as white husband-and-wife families outside the South.[5] By 1981, for the country as a whole, black husband-wife families where both were college educated and both working earned slightly *more* than white families of the same description.[6] By 1989, black, white, and Hispanic males of the same age (29) with the same IQ (100) who worked year-around all averaged between $25,000 and $26,000 in annual income.[7]

In various ways, these data all tell the same story—that similar cultural inputs lead to similar economic outputs across racial lines. Note, however, that these inputs are somewhat more sharply defined here than in most intergroup comparisons, such as all black high school graduates versus all white high school graduates or all blacks with bachelor's degrees or Ph.D.s versus all whites with high school diplomas, bachelor's degrees or Ph.D.s.

On average, the pre-college educations of blacks and whites have never been equal. During the Jim Crow era in the South, blacks did not even go to school as many days in a year as whites, so that a black individual with 9 years of education might have been in school no more days than a white individual with 6 years of education. Even after the numbers of days in school were brought into line, the resources put into the schools were not the same and, after that had been remedied to some extent, large differences in test scores showed that the two groups of students were not learning the same, for whatever reasons.

At both the college and postgraduate levels, black and white degrees do not mean the same. First of all, they differ in the fields in which the students specialize—as do various groups in other countries around the world. Regardless of how much of these differences are due to discriminatory provision of education by government, or to differences in cultural values or other causes, when we are measuring education as an input that contributes to economic output, we are comparing apples and oranges if our comparisons of blacks and whites does not go beyond paper credentials.

In those cases where the statistics permit a finer breakdown that includes qualitative measures, the racial gap shrinks or disappears. We have already seen that with black, white, and Hispanic year-around workers with the same IQs. An earlier (1975) study of black, white, and Asian professors with Ph.D.s from departments of the same quality ranking and with similar numbers of publications showed the blacks generally earning at least as much as the whites and usually more than Asians with the same qualifications.[8]

If our definition of a level playing field is applying the same rules, standards, and rewards, regardless of race, that was approximated years ago. But if our definition is equal prospects of success, then none of these data indicate that, for different proportions of different groups come from homes with library cards or from good quality schools and different proportions of them are in different regions of the IQ distribution. All these are serious social problems but they are not employer discrimination— and talking as if they are only distracts attention from the real causes that need attention.

In many other areas as well, discrimination has been claimed on the basis of statistics which treat people as comparable who are not in fact comparable. For example, the fact that black applicants for mortgage loans are turned down at a higher rate than white applicants has been widely cited as proof of racism among lending institutions. The *Washington Post*, for example, reported that a "racially biased system of home lending exists"[9] and Jesse Jackson called it "criminal activity" that banks "routinely and systematically discriminate against African-Americans and Latinos in making mortgage loans."[10] But the very same data also showed that whites were turned down at a higher rate than Asian Americans.[11] Was that proof of racism against whites, and in favor of Asians? Of course not.

A widely-cited Federal Reserve study of racial disparities in mortgage loan approval rates did not control for net worth, nor take into account the loan applicants' credit histories or their existing debts.[12] Nor was "the adequacy of collateral" included.[13] When a more detailed follow-up study was done for the Boston area by the Federal Reserve Bank of Boston, it was discovered that in fact black and Hispanic applicants for mortgage loans had greater debt burdens, poorer credit histories, sought loans covering a higher percentage of the value of the properties in question, and were also more likely to seek to finance multiple-dwelling units rather than single-family homes.[14] Loan applications for multiple-dwelling units were turned down more often among both white and minority applicants but obviously affect the rejection rate more so among the latter, since they applied more often for loans for such units.[15] Even among those applicants whose loans were approved—and the majority of both minority and white applicants had their loans approved—minority borrowers had incomes only about three-quarters as high as whites and assets worth less than half the value of the assets of the white borrowers.[16]

None of this implies that subjective prejudice has vanished. But a whole field of the economics of discrimination has been created by Nobel Prize-winning economist Gary Becker to show how the translation of subjective prejudice into actual discrimination can be very costly to the discriminator. One need only imagine a basketball franchise owner who refuses to hire blacks to see how financially ruinous it can be.

Nothing is easier than to find statistical disparities between groups. They exist in countries around the world, with and without discrimination, and many of these intergroup disparities in income, education, and other factors are greater than black-white differences in the United States. Merely parading these disparities may be sufficient for political purposes. But, if the purpose is to improve the condition of the less fortunate, then discrimination must be investigated in a more discriminating manner and other causes dealt with when they turn out to be more salient.

None of this means that prejudice and discrimination are things of the past. What it does mean is that their actual socioeconomic effects are an empirical question, not a foregone conclusion. Few would doubt that there has been more prejudice and discrimination against blacks in the United States than in Brazil. Yet black Americans have achieved higher incomes, both absolutely and relative to white incomes, than is the case in Brazil.[17] Discrimination is just one factor among many and cannot be automatically presupposed to be the most powerful factor, however politically convenient that assumption might be.

In practical terms, there is neither unlimited time nor unlimited resources available for dealing with racial issues. In order to maximize the impact of those resources, we must first decide whether our top priority is to smite the wicked or to help the less fortunate.

Implications

No one can be happy when life chances are so radically different among racial or other groups, especially when this means that serious prospects of rising out of poverty may be gone before a child's age reaches double digits. If we mean to improve this situation substantially, then we cannot simply "round up the usual suspects," such as discrimination.

Nor can we let the ghost of Madison Grant or of Adolf Hitler paralyze us from recognizing factors internal to various groups themselves. If Asian children are more likely to catch grief from their parents when they bring home report cards with Bs than black children are when they bring home report cards with Cs, then do not be surprised if Asian youngsters end up with higher grade point averages in school and higher test scores after years of such differences. It would be astonishing if it were otherwise.

Preoccupation with discrimination also distracts from achievements from within the black community, even in the face of racial discrimination. For example, in 1899 there were four academic high schools in Washington—three white and one black. In standardized tests given that year, the black high school scored higher than two of the three white academic high schools. Yet, nearly a century later, it would be considered utopian, by almost anyone, to set as a goal that black high schools score higher on standardized tests than most white high schools in the same city—especially if that city is Washington, D. C.[18] Nor was this a one-time fluke. That same school repeatedly met or exceeded the national average in IQs for decades and sent more of its graduates on to college than most white high schools around the country.[19]

We need not speculate on what can be done or assume that only esoteric programs can succeed. Success has already been achieved in many black schools and in many black families, usually by doing the same kinds of things that have brought success to white or Asian schools and white or Asian families.

A word may be in order about "cultural bias" and the quest for "culture-free" tests. If cultural bias means that a given criterion will not predict either academic success or career success as accurately for one group as for another, then that is a purely empirical proposition that can be and has been tested innumerable times—and it has been found to be wrong innumerable times, not only as regards blacks in the United States but also as regards Indonesians halfway around the world.[20]

As for "culture-free" tests, they would be relevant only in a culture-free society—and there is no such society anywhere. Even the most primitive societies in the world today contain a wealth of skills that an outsider would be hard-pressed to master.

Any success or failure, anywhere in the world, is going to take place in a given culture. We need not question whether blacks can succeed in the current American culture because there is no way to declare impossible what has already happened, often despite considerable opposition. The question is whether increasing the odds of more success can take precedence over the politically more tempting goal of rounding up the usual suspects and sounding the usual rhetoric.

Notes

1. Numerous, documented examples can be found in just two recent books of mine: *Conquests and Cultures* (Basic Books, 1998), pp. 43, 124, 125, 168, 221–222; *Migrations and Cultures* (Basic Books, 1996), pp. 4, 17, 30, 31, 567, 118, 121, 122–123, 126, 130, 135, 152, 154, 157, 158, 162, 164, 167, 176, 177, 179, 182, 193, 196, 201, 211, 212, 213, 215, 224, 226, 251, 258, 264, 265, 275, 277, 278, 289, 290, 297, 298, 300, 305, 306, 310, 313, 314, 318, 320, 323–324, 337, 342, 345, 353–354, 354–355, 355, 356, 358, 363, 366, 372–373. Extending the search for intergroup statistical disparities to the writings of others would of course increase the number of examples exponentially,

even when leaving out those cases where discrimination might be a plausible cause of the disparities.

2. "New Light on Black IQ," *New York Times*, March 27, 1977, pp. 15 ff; "Ability and Biology," *Newsweek*, September 8, 1997, p. 14; *Race and Culture*, chap. 6.

3. Compare U. S. Bureau of the Census, *Current Population Reports*, Series P-60, No. 167, pp. 9, 68.

4. Richard B. Freeman, *Black Elite* (New York: McGraw-Hill, 1976), chap. 4.

5. U. S. Bureau of the Census, *Current Population Reports*, Series P-23, No. 80 (Washington: U. S. Government Printing Office, no date), p. 44.

6. U. S. Bureau of the Census, *Current Population Reports*, Series P-20, No. 366 (Washington: U. S. Government Printing Office, 1981), pp. 182, 184.

7. Richard J. Herrnstein and Charles Murray, *The Bell Curve: Intelligence and Class Structure in American Life* (New York: The Free Press, 1994), p. 323.

8. American Council on Education data are tabulated and presented in Thomas Sowell, "Affirmative Action in Faculty Hiring," *Education: Assumptions versus History* (Stanford: Hoover Institution Press, 1986), pp. 85–87.

9. Joel Glenn Brenner, "A Pattern of Bias in Mortgage Loans," *Washington Post*, June 6, 1993, p. A 1.

10. Jesse Jackson, "Racism is the Bottom Line in Home Loans," *Los Angeles Times*, October 20, 1991, p. B 5.

11. See, for example, Paulette Thomas, "Blacks Can Face a Host of Trying Conditions in Getting Mortgages," *Wall Street Journal*, November 30, 1992, p. A 8.

12. Paulette Thomas, "Behind the Figures: Federal Reserve Detail Pervasive Racial Gap in Mortgage Lending," *Wall Street Journal*, March 31, 1992, p. A 1.

13. Glenn B. Canner, "Expanded HMDA Data on Residential Lending: One Year Late," *Federal Reserve Bulletin*, November 1992, p. 801.

14. Alicia H. Munnell, *Mortgage Lending in Boston: Interpreting HMDA Data*, Working Paper No. 92-7, October 1992, Federal Reserve Bank of Boston, pp. 2, 24, 25.

15. Ibid., p. 25.

16. Ibid., p. 24. Some further problems of the study are discussed in Peter Brimelow and Leslie Spencer, "The Hidden Clue, *Forbes*, January 4, 1993, p. 48.

17. See data and sources in Thomas Sowell, *Conquests and Cultures: An International History* (New York: Basic Books, 1998), p. 168.

18. Henry S. Robinson, "The M Street High School, 1891–1916," *Records of the Columbia Historical Society of Washington, D. C.*, Vol. LI (1984), p. 122.

19. The M Street School was subsequently renamed Dunbar High School. Its history

has been sketched in Thomas Sowell, "Black Excellence: The Case of Dunbar High School," *The Public Interest*, Spring 1974, pp. 3–21. See also Mary Gibson Hundley, *The Dunbar Story* (New York: Vantage Press, 1965).

20. Numerous studies can be found cited in Thomas Sowell, *Conquests and Cultures*, p. 474 (footnote 99).

Half Full or Half Empty?
The Changing Economic Status
of African Americans, 1967–1996

FINIS WELCH

WE HEAR SO MUCH about crime, drugs, school dropouts, low-quality schools, low wages, unemployment, teen pregnancy, children in single-parent homes, etc., among African Americans that it is hard to imagine that things are getting better. And, even if they are, the part of us that demands social justice wonders whether a sorry past excuses a sorry present. But every student of change understands that lasting improvement occurs slowly and that anyone with an eye to the future needs to examine the past. Half full is half empty, but half full and filling is better than half empty and emptying.

This essay offers a brief history of change in the labor market status of African Americans over the past three decades. Beginning with the good news, I examine trends in wages, education, occupations, and industry. Although I conclude on a pessimistic note concerning employment, I believe the gains have been so impressive that they deserve much greater recognition and appreciation than they have generally received.

Most of the numbers reported here are calculated from the March Annual Demographic Supplement to the Current Population Survey

(CPS), 1968–1997. The Survey is collected by the U.S. Census Bureau for the Bureau of Labor Statistics and usually includes responses for individuals in 50,000–60,000 households. The wage and employment levels are for the year preceding each Survey, so the analysis spans the thirty years 1967–1996.

Growing Inequality in the Structure of Wages

The past three decades have brought remarkable changes in the structure of wages. Wage gaps have widened in the aggregate as well as in several narrowly focused dimensions. In particular, the wages of those with more education have increased sharply in comparison with wages of those with less.

Table 1 describes educational differentials in weekly wages for black and white men. Look first at the figures in the bottom panel of the table. During the first five-year period, 1967–1971, young white male college graduates earned 40.5 percent more on average than white males with no more than a high school diploma. The corresponding differential for black men was 51.9 percent. The higher premium for black college graduates, it is important to note, was a recent development. At the time of the 1960 U.S. Census, schooling paid black men far less than it paid white men. But since the mid-1960s, the economic incentives for staying in school as long as possible have been pretty much the same for blacks and whites. That does not mean that African American men had the same average earnings as whites; as we shall see shortly, that was far from the case. But the advantage that blacks with a lot of schooling had over their brethren with little schooling was actually a little greater than it was for whites.

Over the past thirty years, Table 1 reveals, the rewards of being well educated have grown strikingly. The differentials of the 1990s are far greater than in the 1960s. This is true whether we examine the wage disadvantage experienced by high school dropouts (shown in the top panel of Table 1), the advantage those with some college (the center panel) had over high

Table 1   Percentage Differences in Average Weekly Wages Between Men with the Indicated Levels of Education and Wages of High School Graduates Less than 10 Years Out of School

Years	White	Black
	HIGH SCHOOL DROPOUT	
1967–71	−18.1	−20.8
1972–76	−21.6	−26.2
1977–81	−22.7	−25.9
1982–86	−26.9	−28.8
1987–91	−26.8	−29.6
1992–96	−30.1	−27.4
	SOME COLLEGE	
1967–71	19.2	22.0
1972–76	19.8	19.4
1977–81	18.7	25.6
1982–86	27.5	33.2
1987–91	33.5	38.9
1992–96	35.0	50.8
	COLLEGE GRADUATES	
1967–71	40.5	51.9
1972–76	41.7	45.5
1977–81	40.3	57.1
1982–86	63.3	86.5
1987–91	83.2	83.9
1992–96	96.1	97.4

NOTE: Wages are imputed for those who did not work 40+ weeks or 35+ hours. The imputation includes the usual demographic factors—age, race, education—as well as weeks worked and usual hours per week (bottom coded at 35). To preserve dispersion, the imputation also includes a randomly selected empirical residual from the full-time/full-year sample used to generate the fitted values. College graduates include those with postgraduate education. The wage used for college graduates is a fixed-weight average of the average for those with exactly 16 years of schooling and the average for those with more.

school graduates, or the advantage enjoyed by college graduates (bottom panel). After a brief and slight decline in the mid-to-late 1970s, the college wage premium for men has continued to grow and is now at the highest level at any time in the entire postwar period. In their first decade out of school, young male college graduates currently earn roughly twice as much as high school graduates, a premium almost double that of three decades earlier, and one as great for blacks as for whites.

While the wages of college graduates were rising relative to those of high school graduates, the wages of high school dropouts were falling relative to those of high school graduates. Again, there are no major racial differences in the pattern. Education is paying ever larger dividends in the labor market.

These figures are averages. A more refined way of looking at recent trends in wage inequality is provided in Table 2. In the years 1967–1971, white men at the 90th centile (at the bottom of the top tenth of the wage distribution, that is) earned 3.38 times as much per week as white men at the 10th centile (at the top of the bottom tenth of the distribution). Black men near the top of the earnings distribution had an even bigger advantage

Table 2   Ratios of Weekly Wages, 90th Percentile/10th Percentile
             (Ratios are measured relative to the 1967 value, 3.38,
             for white men)

| | MEN | | WOMEN | |
Years	White	Black	White	Black
1967–71	1.00	1.16	0.99	1.51
1972–76	1.13	1.17	0.96	1.10
1977–81	1.29	1.28	0.96	0.99
1982–86	1.56	1.53	1.09	1.06
1987–91	1.61	1.62	1.21	1.17
1992–96	1.75	1.72	1.30	1.24

NOTE: As in Table 1, wages are imputed for those men not full-time/full-year. However, observations for women are restricted to full-time/full-year. The centile location is 100n/(N+1). The average for centiles 5.5 − 14.5 is the first decile wage; the average for centiles 85.5 − 94.5 is the ninth decile wage.

over those close to the bottom than the 3.38 figure for whites; the wage difference between black males at the 10th and 90th centiles was 16 percent higher than it was for whites.

What has changed since the 1960s? The phenomenal growth in wage inequality among men over the next three decades is the most important trend visible in Table 2. By the 1990s, the spread between the 10th and the 90th centiles was approximately 75 percent greater than it had been 25–30 years earlier for both white and black men.

This increase in the dispersion of wages means that wages that were below the mean were falling relative to the mean, while wages above the mean were rising relative to the mean; the lower the wage, the greater the relative decline, and the higher the wage, the greater the relative increase. If the increased dispersion of wages shown in Table 2 was equally the result of rising real wages for those at the top and falling real wages for those at the bottom—probably not far from the truth—it would mean that the purchasing power of the 90th centile wage increased 37.5 percent, while the 10th centile wage fell 37.5 percent between the late 1960s and the mid-1990s.

The trend toward increased inequality was much less pronounced for female workers. The increase in wage dispersion was 30 percent for white women, well under half of that for men of both races. Among black women, somewhat puzzlingly, inequality was at its greatest at the beginning of the period studied, in 1967–1971.[1] It then fell to the same level as that for white women and grew thereafter at the same slow pace as among white women.

Racial Differences in Wages

In an earlier paper, James P. Smith and I compared the wage position of black men relative to white men using the 1940–1980 decennial U.S. Censuses. Comparing ratios of average wages, we found remarkable progress for black men during the 1940s, followed by a distinct slowing in the 1950s. In the 1960s, the wages of black men again increased substantially more than those of whites.

What has happened since? In the 1970s, 1980s, and 1990s, the sharp growth in wage dispersion would lead us to expect that the black/white ratio of average wages would fall because wages were becoming more disperse and the average wage of blacks was below that of whites. This gloomy scenario has not come about. Black males have not fallen further behind whites; they have made further gains, though not large ones. And black women have improved their economic position quite spectacularly.

Table 3 sets forth the evidence on median wages indexed to 1967 values for white men (i.e., the 1967 average wage for them is 100.0). For white men, the 1967–1971 average of 106.1 had fallen to 92.9 by 1992–1996. This represents a 12.4 percent drop in real wages over this thirty-year period.[2]

The 1967–1971 median wage earned by black men was 71.5 percent of that of white males in 1967, and it fell to 66.1 percent for the most recent interval, a decline of 7.6 percent. Over the three decades, the median wages of black and white men moved on approximate parallel paths. Both were declining somewhat, though the drop was a bit less for black men than for white men.

The picture for women, white and black, is much brighter. Instead of

Table 3   Median Weekly Wages of Full-Time Year-Round Workers
               (Wages are PCE deflated and measured relative to 1967 values
               for white men)

	MEN		WOMEN	
Years	*White*	*Black*	*White*	*Black*
1967–71	106.1	71.5	58.9	46.6
1972–76	109.2	76.0	63.3	56.7
1977–81	104.6	73.0	63.9	60.4
1982–86	98.4	65.1	67.7	63.5
1987–91	97.6	66.6	71.0	65.7
1992–96	92.9	66.1	72.8	65.5

NOTE: Wages are imputed for men who were not full-time (usual hours less than 35 per week) or full-year (less than 40 weeks worked). Observations for women are restricted to those who were full-time/full-year.

declining or remaining stagnant, the median wage of black women compared with that of white males in 1967 increased by a remarkable 40.6 percent over the next three decades. For white women, the gain over the same period was a healthy 23.6 percent.

These are significant facts, but no single measure of black/white wage differentials ("the" gap) is adequate. Table 4 uses an alternative, more complex method for comparing wages of black men and black and white women to the wages of white men. Table 4 is divided into four panels. Panel A compares wages of all black men with those of white men. In panel B, the wages of black men are matched to those of white men of the same age and education. Panels C and D compare black women and white women, respectively, with white men.

The top row of each of panel gives as a reference the position of white men in their own wage distribution. If, for example, we assign each man a wage centile, analogous to a test score percentile, then because there would be equal numbers at each centile from 0 to 100, the average would be 50. The next three measures provide, respectively, population percentages exceeding the three wage quartiles, the 25th, 50th, and 75th centiles. In the referenced distribution, 75 percent of white men have wages above the first quartile simply because that defines the first quartile. Similarly, 50 percent exceed the median or second quartile, and 25 percent exceed the third quartile.

The first point of comparison is the average centile location of the wages of other groups in the wage distribution of white men. In 1967–1971, the average centile location of black men in the distribution of white men's wages was 27.2. That means that if we were to select a number of white men at random for comparison with an equal number of randomly selected black men in those years, the black man has the higher wage in only 27.2 percent of the pairs. Conversely, in 72.8 percent of the pairs the white man would come out on top.

Things have changed modestly for the better in the years since. The probability of being the higher-paid worker increased for black men from

Table 4   Comparisons with Weekly Wages of White Men: Centile Averages and Percentages Exceeding Indicated Quartiles in the Wage Distribution of White Men

| | | QUARTILE | | |
Years	Average centile	First	Second	Third
A. ALL BLACK MEN, UNCORRECTED FOR AGE AND EDUCATION				
Reference	50.0	75.0	50.0	25.0
1967–71	27.2	41.8	19.7	7.0
1972–76	30.4	48.1	22.7	7.3
1977–81	33.3	52.8	26.4	8.9
1982–86	33.3	53.0	25.8	8.9
1987–91	34.7	54.9	28.4	10.4
1992–96	36.5	58.0	30.8	11.3
B. ALL BLACK MEN, MATCHED ON AGE AND EDUCATION				
Reference	50.0	75.0	50.0	25.0
1967–71	31.4	47.6	24.9	10.2
1972–76	34.5	53.8	28.1	11.1
1977–81	36.5	57.5	30.6	11.4
1982–86	35.8	57.0	28.6	10.5
1987–91	37.2	58.4	31.4	12.5
1992–96	38.8	59.8	34.3	14.2
C. FULL-TIME/YEAR-ROUND BLACK WOMEN				
Reference	50.0	75.0	50.0	25.0
1967–71	11.9	15.1	4.7	0.7
1972–76	18.0	26.0	7.3	1.6
1977–81	24.0	38.5	11.9	2.4
1982–86	30.4	51.7	18.2	3.8
1987–91	32.2	54.4	22.2	5.0
1992–96	35.2	60.2	26.4	7.5
D. FULL-TIME/YEAR-ROUND WHITE WOMEN				
Reference	50.0	75.0	50.0	25.0
1967–71	17.7	23.8	7.9	2.2
1972–76	21.6	31.9	10.1	2.5
1977–81	26.1	42.7	13.5	3.3
1982–86	33.2	56.7	22.2	5.6
1987–91	35.8	59.9	27.6	8.1
1992–96	39.5	66.7	33.1	10.9

NOTE: The reference line shows corresponding comparisons of white men with themselves.

27.2 percent to 36.5 percent by 1992–1996. This was a gain of more than a third during a comparatively short period.

In addition to the average centile, the table provides three other measures, showing, respectively, the percentages of each group whose wages exceed the three quartiles of the reference, white men's wage distribution. Among black men in the initial 1967–1971 period, 41.8 percent had wages in excess of the first-quartile wage for white men. Thus, a substantial majority of black men (100.0 − 41.8 = 58.2 percent) had wages no higher than those of white males in the bottom quarter. Only 19.7 percent of black men had wages above the median (which is the second quartile) for white men, and a mere 7.0 percent had wages in the top quarter of the white male distribution.

Over the following three decades, black men made impressive progress. The proportion with wages in the lowest one-fourth of the white men's distribution fell from 58 percent to 42 percent. The fraction of black men with wages above the median for white men jumped from 19.7 percent to 30.8 percent, an increase of more than 50 percent. The proportion of black men whose wages put them in the top quarter of the white male distribution rose by 61 percent, from 7.0 to 11.3 percent.

Panel B of Table 4 refines the comparison by considering black and white men of the same age and education. The first point to notice is that the convergence of black and white wages within the age-education matched populations suggests that the gains just noted are not exclusively a matter of blacks "catching up" in the amount of schooling they acquired. They remain even after the effects of education on wages are removed from consideration. By 1992–1996, controlling for age and education made little difference to the results, suggesting that the gains resulting from the increase in schooling received by the average black male worker have been largely exhausted.

The matched age-education comparisons continue to reveal large black/white differences in male wages. We can look to the past and be proud of the obvious gains that have been achieved. With respect to racial differences in wages, the United States of today bears only scant resemblance to the U.S. portrayed in Gunnar Myrdal's 1944 classic, *An American Dilemma*. But in spite of enormous progress, the existing differentials among men are so large that it is inconceivable that we have achieved anything approximating full equality of opportunity.

If the economic progress made by black men in postwar America can be considered rapid, then the gains for women revealed in the two lower panels of Table 4 can only be described as spectacular. The proportion of African American women with wages in the top quartile has multiplied tenfold in only thirty years (the figure jumped from 0.7 to 7.5)! The average black woman worker was at the 12th centile of the white male distribution just a generation ago; now she is at the 35th centile. Equally striking, just 15.1 percent of working black women had wages above the bottom quartile for white males; by the mid-1990s, fully six out of ten were above that line. In the late 1960s, African American women were far behind not only white men but also black men in the wage competition. By now they have narrowed the gap between them and white men, and have just about caught up with African American men; their average centile in the 1990s was 35.2, only trivially different from the 36.5 for black men.

White women have also moved upward very rapidly. The rate of increase has been a little slower than the spectacular gains of their black sisters, but they started out ahead of them and are still a little ahead in wages. The differences are small, however, and would be smaller still if the higher average educational levels of white women were taken into account.[3]

Educational and Occupational Progress

The advances that black men and women (especially the latter) have made toward parity in wages would not have been possible had they not made strong gains in education. Table 5 shows how full-time school enrollment rates for young men and women aged 16–24 have changed in recent decades. The enrollment data show smooth upward trends for black men and women and for white women as well, with all three groups narrowing or eliminating the large gap between them and white men that existed at the end of the 1960s. White men aged 16–24 were then considerably more likely than members of the other three groups to be attending school full time. Three decades later, the school enrollment rate for white men was one point lower than it had been a generation earlier. The rate for black men rose by 5 points in the period, that for white women by 8.3 points, and that for black women by a striking 11.1 points. By this measure, only black men are now significantly behind white men, and the gap between the two groups has been cut in half.

Table 6 shows the percentages of college and professional degrees that

Table 5   Changes, 1967–1971 to 1992–1996, in the Representation of Black Men, Black Women, and White Women

| | Percentages representation in the white men weeks wage distribution | | | |
| | QUARTILE | | | |
Group/period	First	Second	Third	Fourth
A. ALL BLACK MEN, UNCORRECTED FOR AGE AND EDUCATION				
1992–96	42.0	27.2	19.5	11.3
1967–71	58.2	22.1	12.7	7.0
Change	−16.2	5.1	6.8	4.3
B. ALL BLACK MEN, MATCHED ON AGE AND EDUCATION				
1992–96	40.2	25.5	20.1	14.2
1967–71	52.4	22.7	14.7	10.2
Change	−12.2	2.8	5.4	4.0
C. FULL-TIME/YEAR-ROUND BLACK WOMEN				
1992–96	39.8	33.8	18.9	37.5
1967–71	84.9	10.4	4.0	0.7
Change	−45.1	23.4	14.9	6.8
D. FULL-TIME/YEAR-ROUND WHITE WOMEN				
1992–96	33.3	33.6	22.2	10.9
1967–71	76.2	15.9	5.7	2.2
Change	−42.9	17.7	16.5	8.7

SOURCE: Table 4.

were awarded to African American men and women in the most recent
year (1995–1996) and the earliest year that such data are available (1975–
1976), and also examines the gender balance among both black and white
degree recipients.

In each category, from associates (i.e., two-year college degrees) to
Ph.D.s and degrees from professional schools (law, medicine, business,
architecture, etc.), the proportion of African Americans rose in almost
every category over this period of a little less than two decades. However,
the black share of the population was increasing at roughly the same rate,
and the increase was largely due to that fact.

What stands out is that women, black and white, were catching up
with and indeed passing men in most of these categories. In 1976–1977,

Table 6   Trends and Gender Differences in Post–High School Education

	PERCENTAGES OF DEGREES AWARDED TO AFRICAN AMERICANS [a]		NUMBER OF FEMALE/MALE RECIPIENTS	
Degrees awarded	*Men*	*Women*	*Black*	*White*
1976–1977 ACADEMIC YEAR				
Associates	7.3	9.1	1.16	0.92
Bachelor's	5.1	7.9	1.33	0.84
Master's	4.6	8.9	1.70	0.91
Ph.D.	3.1	6.0	0.63	0.34
Professional	3.4	6.5	0.44	0.22
1995–1996 ACADEMIC YEAR				
Associates	8.2	10.1	1.89	1.51
Bachelor's	6.3	9.1	1.77	1.21
Master's	4.7	7.7	2.05	1.38
Ph.D.	2.7	5.1	1.24	0.83
Professional	4.7	9.1	1.38	0.66

NOTE: According to the CPS, African American men represented 10.9 and 13.0 percent of all men aged 24 years in 1976 and 1995, respectively; African American women represented 12.3 and 15.1 present of all women in the two respective years.

[a] Numbers refer to percentages within gender.

black women were already earning more associate, bachelor's, and master's degrees than were black males. By 1995–1996, they were far ahead of them in every category, earning 77 percent more bachelor's, for example, and more than twice as many master's degrees. This obviously is a major reason why African American females have made such impressive wage gains. It is also striking that white females are now collecting 51 percent more associate degrees, 21 percent more bachelor's degrees, and 38 percent more master's than are their male counterparts. Again, this is clearly reflected in the higher paychecks they have been collecting.

Table 7 provides evidence on changes in fields of concentration for black students in higher education between 1981 and 1996, the earliest and most recent years for which such data are available. It also shows the growth between 1981 and 1996 in the number of degrees collected by African Americans in these fields. The most striking change evident here is the shift

Table 7   Changes in Fields of Concentration Among African American College and Professional Degree Recipients

	MEN		WOMEN	
Major field	Percent of 1981 graduates	Ratio 1996/ 1981 graduates	Percent of 1981 graduates	Ratio 1996/ 1981 graduates
Bachelor's degree				
Business	26.5	1.19	19.1	1.81
Education	10.6	0.72	19.1	0.77
Engineering	8.2	1.51	1.2	3.15
Master's degree				
Business	25.2	1.68	7.3	3.90
Education	33.5	0.97	60.0	1.00
Engineering	3.6	2.38	0.3	6.26
First professional degree				
Medicine (M.D.)	25.1	0.87	28.0	1.85
Law (L.L.B. or J.D.)	51.1	1.28	57.9	2.50

NOTE: According to the CPS, the number of African American men aged 24 increased by 37 percent between 1981 and 1996, while the number of women increased by 35 percent.

of black students out of education into more remunerative fields. The biggest gains, again, were made by African American women.

More detail on this shift out of education is supplied in Table 8. In the period 1967–1971, almost a quarter of all black male college graduates were employed as elementary or secondary school teachers, and a stunning six out of ten black females with a college education. The proportions have plunged since then, dropping to just 6.7 percent for black men and 19.6 percent for black women.

Perhaps the most outstanding indication of expanding opportunities is the reduction in the proportion of black women employed in occupations that the Census Bureau classifies as devoted to "personal service." In the 1967–1971 period, 24.1 percent of all hours worked by African American women were in personal service (17.0 percent in private households). By 1992–1996, the concentration of black women in personal service work had plunged by three-quarters, to a mere 5.6 percent.

Although there was no similar concentration of black men in one sector of employment in the 1960s, the three decades since have seen a parallel story of occupational movement on their part away from traditionally low-paying jobs (agriculture, personal services, service stations) into jobs more representative of the distribution of jobs for all men.

Table 8   K–12 School Teachers as a Percentage of Total Employment of College Graduates

	MEN		WOMEN	
Years	White	Black	White	Black
1967–71	9.8	23.1	48.2	59.0
1972–76	9.0	20.1	42.7	50.4
1977–81	7.3	10.2	31.3	37.1
1982–86	6.0	11.1	25.5	31.2
1987–91	5.3	8.7	21.5	24.0
1992–96	5.0	6.7	20.9	19.6

NOTE: Percentages refer to fractions of aggregate annual hours reported by those college graduates whose occupation is teacher.

Half Full

Having gone to great lengths to illustrate the positive, and I absolutely believe it dominates, I close on a negative note. Table 9 indicates trends and levels of full-time equivalent employment rates for men and women aged 16–24 and 30–44. In the late 1960s, black males aged 16–24 and 30–44 were only a bit less likely than their white counterparts to have full-time jobs. In the three decades since then, a substantial gap has widened for both age groups. The percentage point difference among the younger group has grown from 2 to almost 14 points, and for the older group, from 6 to 12 points. One reason for this disturbing development is the continuing

Table 9   Full-Time Employment Rates, Ages 16–24 and 30–44

| | Percent employed full-time | | | |
| | MEN | | WOMEN | |
Years	White	Black	White	Black
	AGES 16–24			
1967–71	45.4	43.4	34.7	29.6
1972–76	48.2	38.4	36.7	26.3
1977–81	49.6	34.2	39.0	25.2
1982–86	45.0	29.9	37.8	23.3
1987–91	47.5	34.3	39.4	27.9
1992–96	45.3	31.6	36.9	27.0
	AGES 30–44			
1967–71	91.1	85.0	37.1	50.8
1972–76	89.1	79.7	40.7	51.2
1977–81	88.3	77.9	48.6	56.8
1982–86	85.8	72.9	54.8	60.1
1987–91	87.7	76.3	60.6	64.0
1992–96	87.2	75.2	61.6	62.9

NOTE: Numbers are simple averages of single-year-of-age-specific full-time-equivalent (FTE) employment rates. The individual FTE is weeks worked/52 for those who usually worked at least 35 hours. For those who usually worked less, weeks worked are each counted as one-half.

concentration of large numbers of African Americans in decaying inner-city neighborhoods from which businesses have fled. This is a serious problem for society.

Black women have not been affected nearly as much by this trend, perhaps because more of them have been staying at home and developing skills that are in demand. The employment rate for black females aged 16–24 has dropped only 2.6 points over the period, and for black women in their thirties and early forties it has climbed by a dozen points.

How much of the change described above can be attributed by affirmative action employment policies? I personally believe that Bound, Freeman, and others have placed too much weight on such policies, both in terms of the 1960s gains for African Americans and the mixed picture for black males since then. James P. Smith and I have written extensively on this subject. Though it is difficult to be precise, there are excellent reasons to believe that, aside from a short-run blip in the relative wages of young male college graduates in the early 1970s, affirmative action operated more to consolidate gains in the economic status of black Americans and to maintain long-established trends, trends firmly founded in cohort improvements in the quality and quantity of schooling, than to abruptly change underlying relations.

Where does this leave us? I suppose the first and most obvious point is that the progress we have seen in the relative economic status of black Americans was well under way before the modern antidiscrimination legislation and the various forms of enforcement were introduced.

School desegregation was prohibited with the *Brown v. Board of Education* Supreme Court decision of 1954. Even so, many desegregation plans were not introduced until the 1970s (Light and Welch 1987), and states like South Carolina and Mississippi regularly compiled and published "Statistics of Negro Schools" until well into the 1960s. It usually takes a long time for the effect of a court decision or of new legislation to percolate through the system.

Many of us believe that the primary effect of social legislation, including interpretations of earlier legislation by the courts, is to consolidate and tie up the loose ends of changes that have already been realized. The clearest example that I know is a study by Landes and Solmon (1972) of compulsory schooling legislation. This legislation took almost a full century to spread among the U.S. states, and the best predictor of the timing of adoption of a law that required attendance in school up to a given age was the date that voluntary attendance in the state reached 90 percent. In effect, the laws forced the relatively small trailing minority to adopt the behavior of the much larger majority.

I believe that a similar argument can be made for the school desegregation decision. It clearly did not take the ninety years from emancipation to the *Brown* decision for desegregation to be challenged. Why 1954 and not 1864? Actually, following the prohibition of slavery in 1863, there is some evidence of a trend toward improvement in the quality of the separate and unequal black schools. This trend ended, and the quality of Southern schools attended by America's black children reached a nadir over a couple of decades following the Supreme Court's "Slaughterhouse" decisions holding that the enforcement of civil rights was the purview of the individual states. Then, inexplicably except for the steady stream of litigation from the NAACP, things got better. As measured by such nominal characteristics as teacher salaries, students per teacher, the number of school days each year, attendance rates, expenditures per pupil, etc., segregated schools for blacks and whites were more equal in 1954 than at any earlier time in the twentieth century (Welch 1974).

Regarding the 1964 Civil Rights Act and Title VII of that Act, which prohibited discrimination by employers on the basis of race, national origin, and gender, similar observations hold for the relative economic status of African Americans (Smith 1984). We saw changes that, by historical standards, should be regarded as remarkable before the legislation could have had much effect. In fact, we now know that at the time Myrdal's dire warnings were written, black/white income ratios were rapidly increasing.

The ingredients of progress were partly the rural-to-urban migration that followed the growing divergence between labor productivity on- versus off-the-farm. There was also convergence in schooling levels. Over four decades, the gap among young men entering the job market fell from five to less than two years. The cause of the convergence seems to be convergence in the quality of schooling—the resources poured into the schools—that flowed through to the wage premium associated from added schooling. Even "free" schooling is expensive because there are alternative uses of time. We learned from the 1960 Census that, among those schooled in the 1920s and 1930s, an extra year of schooling was worth about 20 percent as much for a black man as for a white man (Welch 1976). By 1970, we saw that those entering the job market in the 1960s with newer and, presumably, more equal quality of schooling received approximately equal returns. Over a short time, added schooling became an important route to higher income, and the response, in terms of years in school, was dramatic.

At this point I should reveal a bias that I have had since I first began trying to understand the phenomena of racial discrimination and of race differences in income. It is trivial to understand how we can use the body politic to discriminate with publicly provided services. Anyone with a scintilla of concern who reads the historical record of the resources provided, including monitoring, to segregated schools cannot doubt that the instrument is blunt and effective. Discrimination in employment is harder to understand.

A dollar earned does not change its color depending on the color of the employees who assist in earning it.

This brings me back to the beginning of this section; the first and most obvious point is that the progress we have seen in the relative economic status of black Americans was well under way before the modern antidiscrimination legislation and the various forms of enforcement were introduced. Since the introduction of the new legislation, the trends have been more or less what had previously been established. On this basis, I believe that it is hard to argue for a major role of the legislation regarding employment discrimination. I am personally an advocate of such legislation, but I think its role has been more that of consolidation than a source of fundamental change. I should like to believe that the gains we have seen in the relative economic status of black Americans have resulted from positive responses to more equal opportunity.

Half empty? Of course! There is no shortage of problems to occupy all advocates of social justice. But, half full as well. All is not bleak; there is reason for pride. We are a diverse people, but differences between demographically distinct groups tend to erode over time.

Notes

1. Recall that the CPS data underlying these calculations are samples and are subject to luck-of-the-draw sampling noise. There is no reason of which I am aware to believe that the initial observation reflects a fundamental differential.

2. Wages are deflated by the Gross National Product deflation for consumer expenditures (all goods). See the Economic Report of the President, 1998.

3. Caution may be in order for the gender comparisons, however. The wage distributions for men refer to average weekly wages for men working full time. Men who work a greater number of weeks each year typically earn higher wages than do those who work fewer weeks, and I have used this fact to impute wages for men who either do not work or work part time (less than 35 hours per week). The distributions summarized in Table 4 include all men with observed wages for those working full time and estimated wages for others. It is less clear that women who work either part year or part time would earn less than their full-time/full-year peers. I restrict the observations of women's wages to those who were full time and full year (at least 40 weeks worked).

References

Bound, John, and Richard Freeman. "What Went Wrong?" *Quarterly Journal of Economics* 107, no. 1 (February 1992): 201–32.

Council of Economic Advisors, Economic Report of the President. Washington, D.C.: U.S. Government Printing Office, 1998.

Juhn, Chinhui, Kevin M. Murphy, and Brooks Pierce. "Accounting for the Slowdown in Black-White Wage Convergence." In Marvin Kosters, ed., *Workers and Their Wages* (Washington, D.C.: American Enterprise Institute Press, 1991).

Landes, William M., and Lewis C. Solmon. "Compulsory Schooling Legislation: An Economic Analysis of Law and Social Change in the Nineteenth Century." *Journal of Economic History* 32, no. 1 (March 1972): 54–91.

Light, Audrey, and Finis Welch. *New Evidence on School Desegregation.* Prepared for the

U.S. Commission on Civil Rights, Clearinghouse Publication 92. Washington, D.C.: U.S. Commission on Civil Rights, December 1987.

Smith, James P. "Race and Human Capital." *American Economic Review* 74, no. 4 (September 1984): 685–98.

Smith, James P., and Finis Welch. "Black Economic Progress After Myrdal." *Journal of Economic Literature* 27, no. 2 (June 1989): 519–64. Reprinted in Orley Ashenfelter and Kevin Hallock, eds., *Labor Economics* (London: Edward Elgar Publishing, 1994).

———. "Racial Discrimination: A Human Capital Perspective." In G. Mangum and P. Philips, eds., *Three Worlds of Labor Economics* (Armonk, N.Y.: M. E. Sharpe, 1988).

U.S. Department of Education, National Center for Education Statistics. *Digest of Education Statistics*, Washington, D.C., 1976–1998.

Welch, Finis. "Education and Racial Discrimination." In O. Ashenfelter and A. Rees, eds., *Discrimination in Labor Markets* (Princeton, N.J.: Princeton University Press, 1974).

———. "Employment Quotas for Minorities." *Journal of Political Economy* 84, no. 4 (August 1976): S105–S139.

Discrimination in Public Contracting

GEORGE R. LA NOUE

HOW MUCH DISCRIMINATION is there in contemporary public contracting in the United States? Because these contracts cover almost everything available in commercial markets and because virtually all governments need to make purchases and have the authority to do so, no definitive answer can be given to a question of such scope and complexity. Nevertheless, forming a reliable estimate is essential for at least two reasons.

First, public purchasing is one of government's most important functions. Its effective use or potential abuse can have a substantial impact on governmental efficiency, the income of particular companies and communities, and the financial burden on taxpayers. Current purchases by the federal government are about $180 billion a year, while state and local governments purchase about $465 billion more. It would be intolerable if governments used this formidable economic power to discriminate against businesses because of the race, ethnicity, or gender of their owners.

Second, in recent years public purchasing practices have undergone enormous scrutiny to determine whether or not discrimination exists.

There may be more publicly accessible information measuring discrimination in this area of public life than in any other. A multitude of studies about federal, state, and local public contracting have been completed that permit not only an assessment of their conclusions but also an evaluation of the political context of accusations and denials regarding discrimination.

The Development and Defense of MBE Programs

The source of the recent attention paid to discrimination in public contracting is the 1989 Supreme Court's decision in *City of Richmond v. Croson*.[1] In that case, the Court confronted one example of the hundreds of state and local minority business enterprise (MBE) programs that had been developed in the preceding decade. These programs sought to place firms that were certified as being owned by designated minorities (usually African American, Hispanic, Asian American, and Native American) in favored positions for public contracts. Some programs included women-owned businesses (WBEs) as well.

A variety of preferential techniques have been used. Certain contracts were set aside for MBE firms or were given price preferences in bidding against non-MBE firms. Often non-MBE prime contractors were required to hire a certain percentage of MBE subcontractors to meet a goal necessary for contract award.

In addition, since 1976, a number of federal MBE programs have been established.[2] The oldest is the Small Business Administration's 8(a) program, which sets aside about $4 billion of federal contracts a year for MBEs. There are also 10 percent MBE goal requirements in a wide variety of federal programs, including the $210 billion 1998 highway program. In October 1998, the Clinton administration also began a program of 10 percent price preferences for MBE bidders on contracts covering about 76 percent of all federal purchases.[3]

Sometimes these MBE programs were seen by their sponsors as economic development stimuli for minority communities, sometimes as remedies for general racial injustices, and sometimes as payoffs to emerging political power in minority communities. The policies usually reflected symbolic or redistributive politics and rarely were designed to respond to clearly identified problems. There was very little scholarly analysis of them, and bureaucratic reports covering them were often self-serving or incomplete. The consequences of altering conventional public purchasing programs by MBE programs were almost never evaluated. Which firms were helped, which were hurt, and how much these programs cost were questions almost never asked.

Croson, which covered state and local programs, and *Adarand v. Peña* in 1995, which applied the constitutional standard of strict scrutiny to federal MBE programs, changed all that.[4] In *Croson*, Justice Sandra Day O'Connor stated that before a local jurisdiction could use racial classifications it was necessary to make

> proper findings . . . to define the scope of the injury and the extent of the remedy necessary to cure its effects. Such findings also serve to assure all citizens that the deviation from the norm of equal treatment of all racial and ethnic groups is a temporary matter, a measure taken in the service of the goal of equality itself.[5]

Justice O'Connor further noted that the judiciary would have a responsibility to examine those findings:

> Absent searching judicial inquiry into the justification for such race-based measures, there is simply no way of determining what classifications are "benign" or "remedial" and what classifications are in fact motivated by illegitimate notions of racial inferiority or simple racial politics.[6]

Since the *Croson* decision, more than 145 state and local jurisdictions have commissioned so-called "disparity studies" to determine whether they had a sufficient evidentiary basis to initiate, maintain, or expand MBE programs. At least $65 million has been spent on this activity.[7]

Unfortunately, many of these studies do not meet federal court standards. For example, Judge James Graham of the Southern District of Ohio, Eastern Division, held:

A municipality which is considering the enactment of legislation which creates race-based and gender-based preferences in the award of public contracts must, in fairness to all of its citizens, fairly and fully investigate the issue of whether or not discrimination has actually occurred in the employment of minorities and females in the construction industry in its community and whether such discrimination has actually occurred in its award of contracts and in the award of subcontracts by the prime contractors it has employed. Only if a thorough and impartial investigation of the facts supports a finding that discrimination has occurred is the municipality justified in considering a scheme in which some of its citizens and firms are excluded from competing for a portion of its total contract dollars.[8]

Many disparity studies are neither "thorough" nor "impartial."

Flawed Conclusions

At first glance the disparity studies' consensus about discrimination in public contracting seems virtually unanimous and quite damning. The New York City study concluded: "In our view, the cumulative effects of discrimination by banks, bonding companies, general contractors, private companies, and public agencies is responsible for the gross underrepresentation of businesses operated by minorities and women in construction, services, and commodities."[9] But one might be a little suspicious about this sweeping conclusion because the identical language appears in at least two other studies completed by the same consultants regarding very different jurisdictions (San Antonio, Texas, and Hayward County, California.)[10]

The federal government has made similar conclusions. At the behest of the Justice Department, the Urban Institute analyzed 58 disparity studies and concluded that MBEs received only 57 cents for every public contracting dollar they were expected to receive.[11] When the United States Commerce Department analyzed federal procurement, they found DBEs underutilized in 51 of 74 Standard Industrial Codes.[12]

But on closer analysis, these statistical conclusions appear to be deeply flawed. Every time disparity studies have been challenged at trial, judges have found them unreliable, and a number of jurisdictions have settled cases rather than subject their studies to judicial scrutiny.[13]

In *Croson*, the Court provided guidelines for an appropriate statistical analysis by stating:

> Where there is a *significant* statistical disparity between the number of *qual-ified* minority contractors *willing and able to perform a particular service* and the number of such contractors actually engaged by the locality or the locality's prime contractors, an inference of discriminatory exclusion *could arise*.[14] (emphasis added)

In short, to infer discrimination, the statistical comparison must be between comparable contractors—an apples-to-apples comparison of qualified, willing, and able firms. Partly because of a substantial growth rate in recent years, MBEs are in general smaller and newer businesses. To assume that utilization in government contracts of MBEs and non-MBEs, which include large stockholder-owned corporations, should be the same may create a false inference of discrimination when statistical analysis based on headcounts of firms is carried out. Indeed, the Urban Institute acknowledged that probability in a private report to the Justice Department and then ignored its own conclusion in its public report.[15]

Anecdotal Research

In addition to statistics, most disparity studies collect anecdotes about discrimination. Properly done, anecdotes could be helpful in understanding the statistics and in pinpointing where, if at all, the discrimination exists. In practice, the anecdotal sections of most disparity studies reach conclusions of discrimination that are almost inevitable given the flawed methods used but that nevertheless serve to buttress MBE programs.

Generally two methods are used to gather anecdotal information: surveys and interviews. The disparity study surveys have been plagued with low response rates and poorly designed questions. Rarely have the surveys had a 20 percent response rate. When 80 percent of potential respondents throw the survey into the wastebasket, there is always the possibility that the tiny minority that does respond may be atypical. One federal court described the problem this way:

> First, whether discrimination has occurred is often complex and requires a knowledge of the perspectives of both parties involved in an incident as well as knowledge about how comparably placed persons of other races, ethnicities, and gender have been treated. Persons providing anecdotes rarely have such information. What looks like discrimination may involve nothing more than aggressive business behavior to overcome barriers faced by all new or small businesses.
>
> Second, when the respondent is made aware of the political purpose of questions or when questions are worded in such a way as to suggest the answers the inquirer wishes to receive, "interviewer bias" can occur. In addition, "response bias" may be a problem. The persons most likely to answer the survey are those who feel the most strongly about a problem, even though they may not be representative of the larger group.
>
> Third, individuals who have a vested interest in preserving a benefit or entitlement may be motivated to view events in a manner that justifies the policy. Consequently, it is important that both sides are heard and that there are other measures of the accuracy of the claims. Attempts to investigate and verify the anecdotal evidence should be made.[16]

The most important question is whether the anecdotes about discrimination are true. Some may be, while others are perhaps the consequence of honest misunderstanding or the result of purposeful exaggeration. Almost no disparity study has ever discussed whether the incidents it reported were factually correct, although they are usually described not just as feelings or perceptions but as facts that characterize the universe of business transactions in which discrimination is rampant. The DJ Miller company, which has completed scores of disparity studies, at least mentions that its anecdotes are "unsubstantiated" because "time did not permit a full investigation of these perceptions of discrimination during the study period time frame."[17] Asked whether the anecdotal information contained in the $600,000 Memphis–Shelby County study was true, the project manager testified that he didn't know that it was "untrue."[18] The chief architect of millions of dollars of disparity studies completed by the National Economic Research Associates was even more succinct. He testified:

> Q. Did NERA follow up the information in the surveys to determine if any of the allegations of discrimination in the survey are true?
> A. No.
> Q. Do you know if any of them are true?
> A. No.
> Q. Do you know if any of the anecdotes in any of the Denver-related studies are true?
> A. No.
> Q. Do you know if any of the anecdotes in any NERA study with which you have been connected is true?
> A. No.[19]

Some allegations of discrimination cannot be verified because they are "he said–she said" incidents. But when a company claims it was the low bidder on a public contract or could not get on a vendor list, that can be verified. Yet the disparity consultants do not check their facts, and the governments often cannot. Most studies regard the sources of anecdotal information as confidential and will not turn over transcripts or interview notes, even with names deleted, to the public sponsors that paid for the study. Therefore, cities or other governmental authorities involved usually know very little about the reputation of the person making the charge of discrimination or its context. Nevertheless, as sponsors of the disparity study, they will act as though all the complaints are true.

The use of anecdotal evidence is strange and alarming. On what other subject would governments consistently commission "research" that consists of rumors or is based on unverified sources? In what other area of public life would millions of dollars of tax funds be used to subsidize the gathering and publication of damaging allegations by one racial or ethnic group about another with so little concern for whether these complaints are factually accurate?

The willingness of governments and consultants to engage in this activity is a telling sign that most of these studies are results oriented—that is, they are designed to support a predetermined conclusion.[20] Finding discrimination is a prerequisite to maintaining or expanding an MBE program, and that is what many of these studies are designed to do. As the Eleventh Circuit found, after reviewing the context and conclusions of the Dade County disparity studies: "It is clear as window glass that the County gave not the slightest consideration to any alternative to a Hispanic affirmative action program. Awarding construction contracts is what the County wanted to do, and all it considered doing, insofar as Hispanics were concerned."[21]

Judges regularly assess the reliability of evidence, and fortunately they have been highly skeptical of the anecdotal information before them. In *AGC v. Columbus*, the federal district court established "Standards for the Collection of Anecdotal Evidence of Discrimination" and excoriated the consultants for bias in gathering anecdotes.[22] Similarly, in a Dade County case, the judge complained:

> Without corroboration, the Court cannot distinguish between allegations that in fact represent an objective assessment of the situation, and those that are fraught with heartfelt, but erroneous, interpretations of events and circumstances. The costs associated with the imposition of race, ethnicity, and gender preferences are simply too high to sustain a patently discriminatory program on such weak evidence.[23]

In a May 1998 decision, a court dismissed the anecdotes in the State of Florida's disparity study and stated:

> Individuals responding to FDOT's telephone survey have described their perceptions about barriers to FDOT's bidding procedures. But FDOT has presented no evidence to establish who, if anyone, in fact engaged in discriminatory acts against Black and Hispanic businesses. The record at best establishes nothing more than some ill-defined wrong caused by some unidentified wrongdoers; and under City of Richmond [*Croson*] that is not enough.[24]

The Future of MWBE Programs

The growth of minority- and women-owned businesses, propelled by basic demographic and economic factors, will continue regardless of the fate of MWBE programs. Between 1982 and 1992, according to the Census Bureau, the number of black-owned firms grew by 67 percent, Hispanic-owned firms by 189 percent, Asian-owned firms by 177 percent, women-owned firms by 162 percent, and non-MWBE firms by 24 percent. Perhaps MBE programs had an impact, but most firms market themselves in the private economy unaffected by public contracting programs.

Although firms owned by African Americans are the principal intended beneficiary of MWBE programs, those companies had the slowest growth rate of any MWBE group. There are now more than four times as many firms owned by Hispanics and Asian Americans and thirteen times as many owned by women than by blacks, which means that black firms will get decreasing shares of the benefits of MWBE programs in the future.

More time and money may have been spent in disparity studies investigating public contracting discrimination than in any other area of social research in our nation's history. And yet after this enormous public expenditure, the studies have documented no pattern of discrimination against MBEs by government purchasing procedures, by prime contractors against subcontractors, or by professional and trade organizations. Indeed, the studies have almost never identified any agency, procurement officer, or private firms where discrimination took place. This does not mean that such problems will not be found in the future or that we as a society are discrimination-free any more than we are crime-free or pollution-free. Nevertheless, the news about public contracting is basically good.[25] The procedures and ethics in the public procurement process are basically fair, in spite of sweeping politically motivated claims to the contrary.

The coalition politics that support MBE programs are not hard to understand, but what is not generally known is how few firms actually benefit from these policies.[26] Disparity studies do not discuss this issue. Nevertheless, some data exist. For example, in Cincinnati, of the 682 identified MWBEs in City vendor lists, thirteen firms received 62 percent of all the contracts and 83 percent of the dollars going to MWBEs.[27] Nationally there are over 2.2 million minority-owned businesses in the United States, but there are only about 6,000 8(a) certified firms—about 0.0025 percent of the total number of MBEs.[28] As administered by the SBA, the 8(a) program functions to give very well-established minority-owned firms privileged access to large amounts of federal contracts. In 1995, in a report to Senator Sam Nunn (D-Georgia), the General Accounting Office stated:

> As the value and number of 8(a) contracts continues to grow, the distribution of those contracts remains concentrated among a very small percentage of participating 8(a) firms, while a large percentage get no awards at all. This is a long-standing problem. For example, in fiscal year 1990, 50 firms representing fewer than 2 percent of all program participants obtained about 40 percent, or 1.5 billion, of the total of $4 billion awarded. Of additional concern is that, of the approximately 8,300 8(a) contracts awarded in fiscal 1990 and 1991 combined, 67 contracts were awarded competitively. In fiscal year 1994, the top 50 firms represented 1 percent of the program participants and obtained 25 percent or $1.1 billion, of the $4.37 billion awarded, while 56 percent of the firms got no awards.[29]

Further, in the 8(a) program, only a small percentage of these favored firms have ever graduated to be market competitive.

Even though litigation has exposed the statistical and anecdotal flaws in the disparity studies, the judicial process is arduous, expensive, and piecemeal. In the meantime, disparity studies with flaws equal to or greater than the ones found unreliable still serve as the basis for allocating billions of dollars in public contracts on the basis of the race and ethnicity of favored owners.

The problem with existing disparity studies is not just that most of them are technically defective. The more important issue is that they so often have made exaggerated claims of discrimination and failed to identify the forms of bias that might exist. They have supported preferential programs based on race and ethnicity and have rarely treated race-neutral solutions seriously. This is harmful to society in a number of ways.

The wounds caused by racial and ethnic conflict are very deep in

America. The healing process is difficult and uncertain but absolutely essential if we are to survive as a pluralistic society. Unfounded accusations of discrimination and thoughtless denials are both damaging.

Conclusions

Preference programs for MBEs have the potential to undermine the general safeguards built into the public purchasing process and to create a return to the era of contract patronage, this time built on racial connections. Politicians who believe that it is appropriate to set aside contracts for particular racial groups may be tempted to steer them to particular companies as well.

Assertions of generalized marketplace discrimination, "old boy networks," and other nebulous forms of bias may actually retard the formation of minority businesses, especially among African Americans. Who would want to make the investment of capital and labor that a new business requires if they were convinced that discrimination was so prevalent that success was highly unlikely?

Further, if discrimination is everywhere, committed by everyone, then it may seem futile to try to eradicate it. Indeed, this is the argument of many MBE program advocates, who believe the appropriate response to allegations of discrimination by whites is preferences for nonwhites rather than enforcement of antidiscrimination laws. Where do such assumptions and policy responses lead in the long run? Can our country endure built on a premise that there is such widespread discrimination by whites that it can only be countered by broad preferences for nonwhites?

Reckless allegations of discrimination tend to produce blanket denials by those accused. Most whites believe that the overt forms of discrimination that characterized American institutions in the past have disappeared. In their place, procedures based on subtle subjective decisions that sometimes reflect biased assumptions often coexist institutionally with affirmative action policies that clearly discriminate against nonfavored classes. Disparity studies generally have failed to document either overt or subtle forms of discrimination and have ignored the effects of MBE preferences. Unless our society is prepared to require the most careful documentation of where discrimination actually exists and to evaluate the effects of preferential programs, we cannot construct the interracial coalitions necessary to enforce antidiscrimination laws vigorously and improve access and overcome disadvantages in public contracting or anywhere else.

Viewed from this perspective, the Supreme Court in *Croson* sent the right message by emphasizing the dangers of racial politics and stereotyped assumptions and by insisting on analyzing the appropriate data and remedying identified discrimination. Unless that is done, as Justice O'Connor declared, "The dream of a Nation of equal citizens where race is irrelevant to personal opportunity and achievement would be lost in a mosaic of shifting preferences based on unmeasurable claims of past wrongs."[30] That is not an appropriate fate for public contracting or any other area of American life.

Notes

1. 488 U.S. 469 (1989).

2. Federal programs often define the beneficiaries as Disadvantaged Businesses (DBEs), but the definition of social disadvantage is based on identification with a particular racial and ethnic minority. All persons identified with the following groups are presumed to be disadvantaged: Black (a person having origins in any of the original racial groups of Africa; Hispanic (a person of Mexican American, Puerto Rican, Cuban, Central or South American, or other Spanish or Portuguese origin or culture, regardless of race); Native American (an American Indian, Eskimo, Aleut, or Native Hawaiian); Asian American, including Burma, Thailand, Malaysia, Indonesia, Singapore, Brunei, Japan, China, Taiwan, Laos, Cambodia (Kampuchea), Vietnam, Korea, the Philippines, U.S. Trust Territory of the Pacific Islands (Republic of Palau), Republic of the Marshall Islands, Federated States of Micronesia, the Commonwealth of the Northern Mariana Islands, Guam, Samoa, Macao, Hong Kong, Fiji, Tonga, Kiribati, Tuvalu, Nauru, India, Pakistan, Bangladesh, Sri Lanka, Bhutan, the Maldives Islands and Nepal. For a discussion of these presumptions, see George R. La Noue and John C. Sullivan, "Presumptions for Preferences: The Small Business Administration's Decisions on Groups Entitled to Affirmative Action," *Journal of Policy History* 6, no.4 (fall 1994).

Three federal district courts have found unconstitutional the concept of presuming that all members of particular racial and ethnic groups are disadvantaged or discriminated against for the purpose of awarding public contracts. Nevertheless, the concept is still at the heart of almost every MBE program. See *Adarand v. Peña*, 965 F. Supp. 1556, 1580 (D. Colo. 1997); *Houston Contractors Association v. Metro Transit Authority*, 954 F. Supp. 1013 (S.D. Tex. 1996); and *In re Sherbrooke*, 17 F. Supp. 2d 1026 (D. Minn. 1998). For a discussion of the issue of which group should receive preferences, see George R. La Noue and John C. Sullivan, "Gross Presumptions: Determining Group Eligibility for Federal Procurement Preferences," *Santa Clara Law Review* 41 (winter 2000).

3. John Sullivan and Roger Clegg, "More Preferences for Minority Businesses," *Wall Street Journal*, August 24, 1998, p. A13.

4. 515 U.S. 200 (1995).

5. *Croson*, 488 U.S. at 510.

6. Ibid., at 493.

7. See two works by George R. La Noue, *Local Officials Guide to Minority Business Programs and Disparity Studies* (National League of Cities, 1994), and "Social Sciences and Minority Set-Asides," *Public Interest*, Winter 1993.

8. *Associated General Contractors of America v. City of Columbus*, Order June 20, 1990, p. 10.

9. "The Utilization of Minority and Women-Owned Business Enterprises by the City of New York," NERA, 1994, p. 129.

10. "The Utilization of Minority and Woman-Owned Business Enterprises in Bexar County" (San Antonio), NERA, 1992, p. 155, and "The Utilization of Minority and Woman-Owned Business Enterprises by The City of Hayward (California)," NERA, 1993, p. 8-5.

11. "Do Minority-Owned Businesses Get a Fair Share of Government Contracts?" Urban Institute, October 1996.

12. Jeffrey L. Meyer, "Price Evaluations Adjustments and Benchmarking Methodology," U.S. Department of Commerce, June 23, 1998. Commerce has not released enough information for one to be certain how these calculations were completed, but apparently MBEs were counted as available whether or not they actually bid on federal contracts, while for non-MBEs only bidders were counted as available.

13. See, e.g., *Contractors Association of Eastern Pennsylvania v. Philadelphia*, 893 F. Supp. 419 (E.D. Pa. 1995), affirmed 91 F. 3d 586 (3d. Cir. 1996); *Associated General Contractors v. Columbus*, 936 F. Supp. 1363 (S.D. Ohio 1996); *Buddie v. Cleveland*, 1995 (settled); *Prior Tire Company v. Atlanta Public Schools* (No. 1-95-CV-825-JEC, 1997); *Houston Contractors Association v. Metro Transit Authority*, 954 F. Supp. 1013, 1018 (S.D. Tex. 1996); *Engineering Contractors Association of South Florida, Inc. v. Metropolitan Dade County*, 943 F. Supp. 1546 (S.D. Fla. 1996), affirmed 122 F.3d 922 (11th Cir. 1997); *Phillips and Jordan v. Watts*, 13 F. Supp. 1308, 1314 (N.D. Fla. 1998); *Ohio Contractors Association v. Cincinnati*, C-1-98-447, 1998; *Kossman v. TxDOT*, C.A. No. H-99-0637 (S.D. Tex. 2000); *Concrete Works v. City and County of Denver*, 86 F. Supp.

2d. 1042 (D. Colo. 2000); *Scott v. Jackson*, No. 3: 97CV719BN, affirmed 199 F.3d 206 (5th Cir. 2000); *Association for Fairness in Business v. New Jersey*, 82 F. Supp. 353 (D. N.J. 2000); *Webster v. Fulton County*, 82 F. Supp. 1375 (N.D. Ga. 2000); *Associated Utility Contractors of Maryland, Inc. v. The Mayor and City Council of Baltimore*, 83 F. Supp. 2d 613 (D. Md. 2000); *Associated General Contractors v. Drabik*, 50 F. Supp. 2d 741 (S.D. Ohio 1999), affirmed 6th Cir. 2000.

14. *Croson*, 488 U.S. at 509.

15. In "Evaluation of Disparity Study Methodology," pp. 3–4, the Urban Institute authors stated: "A study that uses a measure of availability that includes only firms that are ready, willing and able to perform government contract work is stronger than a study that includes all firms without trying to control for whether they are available or have the requisite ability. This is because including all M/WBEs may overstate the true availability of these firms, and bias results towards finding a disparity even when there is none."

16. *Engineering Contractors Association of South Florida, Inc. v. Metropolitan Dade County*, 943 F. Supp. 1546, 1579 (S.D. Fla. 1996).

17. A Disparity Study for Memphis–Shelby County Consortium, VII, p. 4.

18. Deposition of David J. Miller in *Associated General Contractors v. Shelby County*, May 27, 1988, p. 172.

19. Deposition of David Evans, July 30, 1998, in *Concrete Works v. Denver*, p. 66.

20. In *AGC v. Columbus*, the Court referred to the City's study as "examples of results-driven research" in which the outcome is politically predetermined (936 F. Supp. at 1431).

21. *Engineering Contractors Association of South Florida v. Metropolitan Dade County*, 122 F.3d 922, 936 (11th Cir. 1997).

22. 936 F. Supp. 1363, 1426 (S.D. Ohio 1996).

23. 943 F. Supp. 1546, 1584 (S.D. Fla. 1996).

24. *Phillips and Jordan v. Watts*, 13 F. Supp. 1308, 1314 (N.D. Fla. 1998).

25. As one of the most sophisticated and prolific authors of disparity studies has finally conceded: "First, it is virtually impossible for the type of discrimination described above to exist in construction prime contracting for government entities that follow normal public contracting procedures. City construction projects are publicly advertised. They are awarded to the lowest bidder. Almost by definition, construction contracts are awarded to the most qualified of the willing and able firms so there can be no discrimination under this extremely narrow view." Dr. David Evans, Rebuttal report, *Concrete Works v. City and County of Denver*, pp. 3–4.

26. The best description of local MBE politics and the few firms that benefit can be found in the chapters on Atlanta in Tamar Jacoby's *Someone Else's House* (New York: Free Press, 1998).

27. These data were produced for "City of Cincinnati Croson Study," Institute of Policy Research, 1992, but were not published.

28. 1992 Summary volume, *Survey of Women and Minority-Owned Businesses.*

29. General Accounting Office, "Small Business Administration—8(a) Is Vulnerable to Program and Contractor Abuse." Report to the Ranking Minority Member, Permanent Subcommittee on Investigations, Committee on Governmental Affairs, U.S. Senate, September 1995, pp. 3–4. See also, GAO "Small Business; Problems Continue with SBA's Minority Business Development Program" (GAO/RCED-93-145), September 17, 1993.

30. *Croson*, 488 U.S. at 505–6.

PART FOUR

EDUCATION

Desegregation and Resegregation in the Public Schools

DAVID J. ARMOR AND
CHRISTINE H. ROSSELL

WHEN THE SUPREME COURT declared the end of official (de jure) segregation in *Brown v. Board of Education* in 1954, the public schools became the center stage for the struggle to promote racial integration and equity in America. Most of us born by the beginning of World War II will never forget the graphic images of black children in Little Rock, Arkansas, being escorted into school buildings by soldiers, surrounded by crowds of jeering white adults. About a decade later, we saw similar crowds of white adults shouting epithets, throwing stones, and burning buses when school desegregation moved to the North in such cities as Pontiac, Michigan, and Boston, Massachusetts. Unlike other social policies, vehement public protests did little to deter the school desegregation movement because it was being advanced and enforced by the (almost) politically immune federal courts.

From the mid-1960s to the late 1970s a vast transformation took place in American public schools as federal courts and government agencies demanded race-conscious policies in every facet of school operations. The most controversial aspect of school desegregation during this period involved the rules for assigning students to schools, when racial balance quotas were adopted instead of neighborhood or other geographic rules.

In larger school districts these racial quotas required mandatory busing, whereby students were transported long distances from their former school to different schools across a city or county in order to attain racial balance.

But school desegregation court orders went far beyond student assignment, with requirements for racial quotas in hiring, racial balance in the assignment of faculty and staff, and racial equity in facilities (resources), transportation, and extracurricular activities. These six desegregation plan components—student assignment, faculty, staff, facilities, transportation, and extracurricular activities—became known as the *Green* factors. All school systems under court order had to show they had complied with each of them before they could be declared unitary (nondiscriminating) systems and released from court orders.[1]

There has been much debate about whether school desegregation should be judged a success or a failure, not just in the attainment of school racial balance but also with respect to other social and educational goals such as improved race relations and academic performance of minority children. So far as racial balance is concerned, initially the most important objective of desegregation plans, there is general agreement that substantial improvement occurred during the early 1970s. But some critics, especially Gary Orfield and his colleagues on the Harvard Project on School Desegregation, have asserted that resegregation began occurring in the late 1980s and worsened in the early 1990s, particularly as federal courts began declaring school districts unitary and ending court supervision.[2]

Although early Supreme Court school decisions did not address social and educational outcomes, there is little question that educators and civil rights activists viewed racial balance as merely a means to an end. According to these views, the ultimate goal of school desegregation was to reduce racial prejudice and improve the academic achievement of African American children; schools were to be the pathway to full economic and social parity with whites.

Assessing the extent to which school desegregation has achieved these broader goals, sometimes called extra-*Green* factors by the courts, is much more complicated than assessing compliance with the six *Green* factors. In particular, we have to assess a myriad of social and educational effects of desegregation, and to be complete we have to compare these effects with the costs of desegregation—monetary expenditures, political controversy, white "flight," and loss of local control. It is by no means obvious to the average citizen that school integration, and especially the more intrusive practice of mandatory busing, has any benefits at all, much less benefits that justify the costs. Indeed, many Americans believe that mandatory reassignment or "forced busing" has reduced the quality of education in school districts where it has been implemented.[3]

This essay will summarize the successes and failures of school desegregation with regard to these issues. First, we assess the impact of desegregation policies on actual racial balance in the public schools. The evidence indicates that school desegregation has created substantial racial balance in our public education systems. Second, we address the issue of resegregation to determine whether the racial balance established in the 1970s by school desegregation plans has been reversed by the unitary status findings of the 1980s and 1990s. We shall show that at least as late as 1995 racial balance trends are not reversing and that the changes in racial and ethnic isolation discussed by Orfield are in fact caused by long-term demographic trends of declining white and increasing minority enrollment, not the dismantling of desegregation plans.

Indeed, as James Coleman first found, the mandatory reassignment plans of the 1970s exacerbated these long-term demographic trends by accelerating the decline in white enrollment, thereby limiting the extent of actual integration in the school districts in which they were implemented.[4] This effect was greatest in our largest school districts. Finally, we evaluate evidence on the social and educational effects of desegregation, and especially academic achievement. We argue that in this area more than any other, school desegregation has failed to deliver on its promises, in spite of the early optimism of many social scientists and civil rights activists.

Racial Balance

Prior to *Brown*, most public schools in the South were one-race schools, either white or black. Ten years after Brown, one study estimated that 99 percent of black children in the South were in one-race schools. The first nationwide study of school segregation was ordered by the Civil Rights Act of 1964 and carried out by James Coleman and his colleagues during the 1965–66 school year.[5] The Coleman report estimated that nationally 65 percent of all black students attended schools that were over 90 percent black, while 80 percent of all white students attended schools that were over 90 percent white.

PRE-*SWANN* PROGRESS

The extent of racial isolation in the South was far greater than in the North, mainly because of de jure segregation in the South. Table 1 shows the percentage of elementary black and white students in schools over 90 percent black or white, respectively, for twenty-two of the largest Southern school districts in 1965 or 1968. Although it is fair to say that some racial integration had taken place in these Southern cities ten years after *Brown*, it was clearly nominal for black students, with the notable exceptions of Kansas City, Nashville, and Dallas. Indeed, it was precisely this token progress that led to the *Green* decision, which called for the elimination of segregated schools "root and branch."[6]

Racial imbalance also existed in Northern cities during the mid-1960s, but racial isolation was not nearly so extensive. Most Northern school segregation at that time was thought to be de facto, that is, brought about by the private decisions of citizens to live in different geographic areas. The highest levels of racial isolation existed in Chicago, Cleveland, Detroit, Indianapolis, Milwaukee, and Philadelphia where the black population swelled from post–World War II migration of Southern blacks looking for jobs in the large urban centers of the North. This migration overwhelmed the capacity of white neighborhoods to absorb blacks and still remain integrated, although none but Chicago approached school racial isolation rates of 90 percent. Other large cities with sizable, but in some cases smaller, black enrollments such as Boston, Cincinnati, Columbus (Ohio), Los Angeles, Newark, New York, and San Francisco had no more than half of their black students in predominately black schools.

Table 1   Percentage of Black and White Elementary Students in Schools
                 over 90 Percent Black or White, Southern Cities in 1965–1966
                 (except as noted)

School district	Blacks in black schools	Whites in white schools
Birmingham, Ala. [a]	99	99
Mobile, Ala.	100	100
Little Rock, Ark.	96	97
Miami-Dade, Fla.	91	95
Jacksonville-Duval, Fla. [a]	92	92
Tampa-Hillsboro, Fla. [a]	91	91
Atlanta, Ga.	97	95
East Baton Rouge Parish, La. [a]	95	95
New Orleans Parish, La.	96	84
Kansas City, Mo.	69	65
St. Louis, Mo.	91	66
Jackson, Miss. [a]	99	100
Charlotte-Mecklenberg, N.C.	96	95
Oklahoma City, Okla.	90	96
Tulsa, Okla.	91	99
Charleston County, S.C. [a]	99	99
Memphis, Tenn.	95	94
Nashville, Tenn.	82	91
Dallas, Tex.	83	90
Houston, Tex.	93	97
Norfolk, Va. [a]	90	90
Richmond, Va.	98	95

SOURCE: U.S. Commission on Civil Rights, *Racial Isolation in the Public Schools* (Washington, D.C.: U.S. Government Printing Office, 1967), pp. 4–5, except as noted.

[a] Computed by the authors from the 1968 Office for Civil Rights enrollment data.

POST-*SWANN* PROGRESS

The situation in the South changed dramatically in the 1970s. In the 1971 *Swann* decision for Charlotte-Mecklenburg, North Carolina, the Supreme Court endorsed strict racial balance quotas for all schools in a system and approved cross-district mandatory busing to attain complete racial balance.[7] In effect, the Supreme Court abandoned geographic school assignment (i.e., being assigned to the closest school) for Southern school systems unless it resulted in racially balanced schools, which was impossible in most larger school districts because of segregated housing patterns.

Court-ordered school desegregation moved to the North only two years later with the Supreme Court's *Keyes* decision for Denver, Colorado.[8] We shall not go into the complicated legal basis for Northern desegregation orders, almost none of which involved state-enforced segregation. Suffice it to say that despite de facto segregation in the North, systemwide racial balance remedies and mandatory busing plans were ordered for many Northern districts after *Keyes*. In addition, the Department of Health, Education, and Welfare (HEW) was active in pressuring school systems to implement desegregation plans, and several school systems adopted mandatory reassignment plans under this pressure.

As a result of local civil rights pressure, many other school systems adopted voluntary transfer plans that involved M to M (majority to minority) transfers where any student could transfer from a school in which his or her race was in a majority to a school in which his or her race was in a minority. Another common local initiative was to close some predominantly minority schools and reassign the students to predominantly white schools; this was carried out in such cities as Riverside, California, and Evanston, Illinois. Although these local measures did not involve mandatory busing of whites, they nonetheless accomplished some degree of school integration.

The first reliable data for assessing the impact of school desegregation on racial balance was collected in 1968 by the Office for Civil Rights in HEW (OCR).[9] The survey consisted of enrollment data by individual schools and by five racial-ethnic categories (white, black, Hispanic, Asian, and American Indian) in a sample of school districts. There was no survey in 1969, but from 1970 through 1974 OCR collected data annually. Beginning in 1974, the survey was conducted every other year and included all districts with court-ordered desegregation plans. The sampling scheme used by OCR varied from year to year, and thus after 1974 the OCR data do not constitute a representative sample of school districts. In fact, in some years important school districts are simply missing.

In 1990 the authors participated in a national survey of school desegregation and magnet schools sponsored by the U.S. Department of Education, for which a statistically representative sample of 600 school districts was drawn. The original sample included all 150 largest school districts in the country, those with enrollments over 27,000 students, and smaller percentages of the large, medium, and small districts in the U.S., selected randomly from their size category.[10] In this essay we use this national sample to assess racial balance trends, relying on OCR enrollment data from Fall 1968 through Fall 1987 and Common Core of Data (CCD) enrollments from Fall 1989 through Fall 1995.

The 1990 survey gathered information about whether school districts had adopted formal desegregation plans and what kinds of desegregation techniques were used. Table 2 shows the percentage of school districts that

Table 2   Prevalence of Formal School Desegregation Plans, 1990

Size of district	Percent with past or present desegregation plans	Percentage share of black/Hispanic students	Total districts in sample
Very large (N>27,000)	72	53	145
Large (N=10,000−27,000)	39	22	421
Medium (N=5,000−10,000)	34	13	770
Small (N<5,000)	11	12	4,012

SOURCE: David J. Armor, *Forced Justice: School Desegregation and the Law* (New York: Oxford University Press, 1995), table 4.1.

had past or current desegregation plans by size of district. The survey estimated from this random sample that nationally nearly 1,000 school districts had some type of formal desegregation plan, and the prevalence of formal plans increased with the size of the school district. Of the 145 "very large" school districts that responded to the survey, 102—more than 70 percent—had a formal desegregation plan at some point in time. We note that the largest districts enroll about half of all black and Hispanic students, while the smallest districts enroll only about one-tenth of these minority groups. Thus, black and Hispanic students are more likely to be found in larger districts, which are also more likely to have school deseg-regation plans.

Of the 28 percent of very large districts that did not adopt a formal desegregation plan, most were predominately white districts in the early 1970s, and indeed many remained predominately white until at least the early 1990s. Examples include Anoka County, Minnesota; Fairfax County, Virginia; Gwinnett County, Florida; and Spokane, Washington. These districts were over 90 percent white in 1972 and remained over 70 percent white until at least 1991. Obviously, there is less need for a formal deseg-regation plan when there are few minority students.

How effective have these plans been in achieving racial balance? To answer this question, we shall use an index that summarizes the degree of racial balance in a school system. Racial balance is defined as the degree to which each school's racial composition matches the districtwide racial composition for a given race. The index of racial imbalance, also called the dissimilarity index, ranges from 0 to 1, where 1 indicates total segregation (all schools are one race), and 0 means perfect racial balance (every school has exactly the same racial composition as the total district).[11] Intermediate values represent the proportion of students of one race who would have to be reassigned, if no students of another race were reassigned, in order to attain perfect racial balance.[12] The index can be computed for any two racial or ethnic groups; for example, whites and nonwhites, blacks and whites, or Hispanics and whites.

BLACK TRENDS

Figure 1 shows the trends in black-white racial imbalance from 1968 to 1995, separated by size of school district.[13] All three size categories show significant declines in black-white imbalance (or increased desegregation), with the sharpest drops from 1968 to 1972 corresponding to the widespread implementation of desegregation plans in the South. For very large districts, racial imbalance continues to decline until 1982 and remains stable thereafter; there is a slight upturn of just 1 point between 1991 and 1995. Medium-sized districts show slight improvements in racial balance until 1991. For the nation as a whole, then, contrary to Orfield's claims, there is no evidence of significant resegregation in terms of increasing racial imbalance as late as 1995.

There was, however, substantial variation by region in the timing and scope of desegregation plans, with Southern districts being the first to desegregate with comprehensive desegregation plans involving white reassignments. After *Swann*, most Southern districts that still had substantial racial imbalance were immediately back in court and typically ordered to adopt busing remedies along the lines of the Charlotte-Mecklenburg plan.

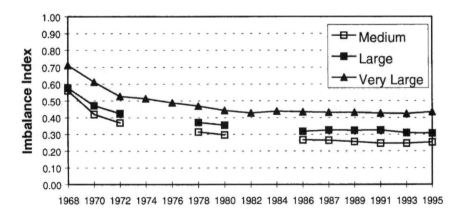

Fig. 1.   Trends in black-white school imbalance in medium, large, and very large districts.

As a result, comprehensive mandatory desegregation plans were in place for most Southern districts by 1972.

Northern mandatory busing remedies did not become commonplace until after the 1973 *Keyes* decision in Denver, Colorado. Therefore, implementation of comprehensive desegregation plans in the North tended to be distributed more evenly throughout the 1970s. In addition, while most Southern districts had to adopt formal desegregation plans, there were fewer formal plans in Northern districts primarily because there was no history of de jure segregation and ongoing litigation associated with dismantling it. Thus, fewer lawsuits were filed in the North, and occasionally a lawsuit was dismissed because the courts found only de facto segregation (e.g., Cincinnati). These different histories, not surprisingly, produced different patterns of racial balance trends.

Figure 2 shows the trends in black-white racial balance for very large districts—those that have received most of the attention by the courts and by school desegregation analysts—separated according to region and formal plan status. We do not show the small number of Southern districts that said they did not have formal plans.[14] The trends confirm the differences in desegregation timing in the North and South. As expected, the most dramatic improvements in racial balance occurred for Southern dis-

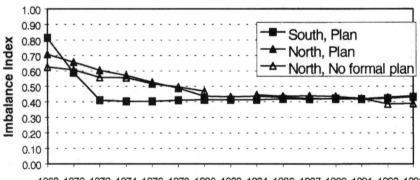

Fig. 2.   Trends in black-white imbalance by plan status, very large districts.

tricts as they rapidly implemented mandatory reassignment plans in the early 1970s. For Southern districts with plans, the index of racial imbalance dropped by 40 points in the four years 1968–1972, from an average of 0.81 to an average of 0.41.

The fact that the average index for Southern school districts was 0.81 in 1968 means that the dismantling of the de jure system of segregation had started before 1968; had it not, the index would have been 1.0. Free-dom-of-choice plans became popular following enactment of the U.S. Civil Rights Act of 1964, and they were the primary means of desegregation for many Southern school systems until the policy was ruled insufficient by the U.S. Supreme Court in the *Green* decision. Freedom-of-choice plans increased the number of black students attending former white schools, but not vice versa, and they are the major reason that the index was 0.80 in 1968 rather than 1.0.

The pattern for Northern school systems with plans is quite different from that of Southern systems with plans, in that the decline in imbalance is less rapid and is spread evenly throughout the 1970s. The index dropped 36 points during the decade, from 0.70 in 1968 to 0.44 in 1980, making them nearly as balanced as Southern districts. Interestingly, Northern dis-tricts without formal plans also experienced desegregation during this period, with the imbalance index declining from 0.62 to 0.47. This trend is explained by the fact that many school systems adopted desegregation practices during this time, such as closing older imbalanced schools, build-ing new schools in easier-to-integrate locations, and paying closer attention to attendance zone changes, but did not adopt a formal plan.

After 1980, racial balance trends level off for Southern districts but continue to improve slightly for Northern districts, and in 1991 all three groups show the same degree of racial imbalance (0.42). Most important, none of the categories of school districts shows any dramatic worsening of racial balance between 1991 and 1995, with gains of only 1 or 2 points in the imbalance index for Southern and Northern districts with plans, re-spectively. Once again, these data from the largest 145 school systems in the nation contradict Orfield's argument that school districts are resegregating as a result of the dismantling of desegregation plans.

In recent years the Orfield reports have expressed concern about the increasing segregation and isolation of Hispanic students. This problem did not exist in the era of de jure segregation because most early court decisions in the South did not identify Hispanic students as a minority group that was a victim of discrimination. Indeed, most Southern school districts classified students as black and nonblack, and Hispanic students were included in the nonblack category along with white students.

After the 1973 *Keyes* decision in Denver, however, where both black and Hispanic students were found to be victims of discrimination, it became commonplace to treat all minority (nonwhite) students as a group in student assignments to achieve racial balance. Interestingly, in a few school districts, such as Yonkers, New York, the federal court found that only black and Hispanic students were victims of discrimination, thereby combining Asian students with white students for the purposes of desegregation. The court agreed with plaintiffs' argument that Asian students were not a disadvantaged minority group, and therefore the Asian minority could be used to desegregate either black or Hispanic minority students! This same definition is being used in a recent desegregation plan in Rockford, Illinois. In the vast majority of school districts, however, Asians are classified as racial minorities and assigned accordingly.

Figure 3 shows the racial balance trends for Hispanic enrollment in relation to white enrollment.[15] Before 1970, Hispanics were clearly much less segregated than black students in all size categories, which may explain in part why Hispanics were not treated as victims of discrimination in early court decisions. In 1968 the index is only 0.55 for Hispanics in very large districts, compared with a value of 0.71 for black students. In large school districts the Hispanic-white imbalance is 10 points less than the black-white imbalance. The lower imbalance rates are explained by the greater

residential integration of Hispanics and whites during the 1960s, which is
due in part to their smaller population size.

After 1972, Hispanic-white imbalance declined steadily until trends
begin to level off in 1987, although there are still small declines as late as
1995. In very large districts, where most black and Hispanic students are
found, Hispanic imbalance is less than black imbalance during the entire
time period, and by 1995 Hispanic imbalance had fallen to 0.39, compared
with 0.43 for blacks. In large districts Hispanic students were more imbalanced than blacks between 1972 and 1980 but caught up with them by
1995. Hispanic imbalance has remained somewhat higher in medium-sized
districts during the 1990s, but we note that index levels of about 0.30 reflect
a relatively high degree of balance overall. That is, an index of 0.30 means
that in a district with half Hispanic and half white students only 15 percent
of Hispanics and 15 percent of whites would have to be reassigned to attain
perfect balance.

These data show quite clearly that Hispanic-white imbalance has not
been increasing from the mid-1980s to the present time; in fact, it has
continued to decrease slightly during the 1990s and remains lower than
black imbalance in very large districts. Thus, contrary to the claims of
Orfield, in our national representative sample of school systems there is no
evidence of increasing segregation of Hispanic students in terms of racial

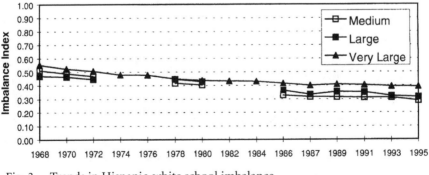

Fig. 3.   Trends in Hispanic-white school imbalance.

imbalance, the primary yardstick over the last four and a half decades for measuring the success of desegregation plans.

Segregation, Desegregation, and Resegregation

Having said that there is no evidence of resegregation in terms of racial balance, we must acknowledge that there are different ways of looking at this issue and different ways of defining these terms. The original legal meaning of segregation, as defined by the Supreme Court in 1954 in *Brown*, was the separation of the races by official state action (de jure segregation). At that time, *de*segregation was simply the abolition of state laws and government practices that enforced these laws. But the elimination of state laws requiring the separation of the races did not change segregated residential patterns, nor did it prevent a variety of other strategies adopted by some Southern states and school districts for avoiding meaningful integration.

The Supreme Court decision in *Green* (1968) put Southern school districts on notice that they must not merely stop discriminating but also must actually achieve desegregated schools. It was not until the *Swann* decision (1971), however, that a desegregated school was defined as one whose racial composition is roughly the same as the racial composition of the entire school system; that is, desegregation equals racial balance. This definition quickly became the standard throughout the nation for a desegregated school system, although the amount that a school could deviate from perfect balance varied from case to case.

Using this racial balance definition, there is no evidence of significant resegregation in our nationally representative sample of American public school systems. But the problem with a racial balance standard is that it ignores the total number or proportion of white students in a school system. A racial balance standard cares only that each school mirrors the school district's racial composition, not what the actual racial composition might be. A school system that is 90 percent black and 10 percent white would be perfectly balanced if every school had 10 percent white enrollment. Yet such a school system would not be considered desegregated by most interested parties. Many courts have defined a 90 percent black school as racially isolated, regardless of the systemwide composition.

Moreover, a desegregation plan can cause white flight and thus be the cause of a school system's being only 10 percent white. If a district starts out with a student enrollment that is half black and half white but becomes only 10 percent white several years later, most observers would not call the plan successful even if each school was highly balanced at or near 10 percent. Thus, a racial balance standard by itself gives us only a partial view of the amount of school desegregation that exists in a school system.

In order to overcome the limitation of racial balance definitions, James S. Coleman created a second definition of desegregation that takes into account the absolute proportion of white students in schools attended by black students (or any other minority group).[16] This definition is measured by a second summary statistic called the index of interracial exposure— that is, the percentage of white in the average black (or minority) child's school.[17] In this case a value of 0 means total black-white segregation, or no whites in schools attended by black students. The maximum value of this index is the proportion of students who are white in the school system. If every school's percentage of white exactly matches the school system's percentage of white, the index will be the same as the proportion (or percentage) of white in the school system.

For example, if a system is 30 percent white, then an index of 0.30 would mean that every school was 30 percent white (and therefore perfectly balanced), and an index of 0.25 would indicate substantial degree of desegregation relative to the available whites. But in absolute terms an index of 0.25 means that the average school is 75 percent black, which indicates a relatively low level of desegregation in absolute terms. Thus, the interracial exposure index reflects both the extent of racial balance in the school system and the absolute level of contact, that is, the percentage of white in the average black (or minority) child's school. When the exposure index is examined over time and is compared with the percentage of white in a system, one can obtain a more comprehensive picture of both the relative and absolute levels of desegregation.

Orfield's studies have used recent declines in the exposure index, rather than the imbalance index, to argue that resegregation is occurring, a phenomenon he attributes to the dismantling of desegregation plans. But there are two major causes for a declining exposure index, one of which is simply a decrease in the percentage of white in a school system. The decline in the percentage of white enrollment can be due to nondesegregation-related demographic changes that have nothing to do with racial balance, such as high black or Hispanic in-migration, declining white birthrates, or normal middle-class white suburbanization. It can also be caused by "white flight," where whites leave a school system to avoid mandatory busing. The other major cause of a declining exposure index, the one that concerns Orfield, is a reduction in the number of racially balanced schools, as might occur when a school district dismantles a desegregation plan and returns to neighborhood schools.

If the exposure index has been changing, is it due to declines in the percentage of white or is it due to the dismantling of desegregation plans? This question can only be answered by comparing the exposure index to trends in racial imbalance and also to trends in the percentage of white. We have already demonstrated in Figures 1–3 that racial imbalance has not changed significantly; it remains to examine trends in the exposure index and in the percentage of white.

Figure 4 shows the national trends in racial composition for very large school systems, including the average percentage of white that is the maximum for the exposure index. In 1968 very large public school districts averaged 71 percent white, 22 percent black, 6 percent Hispanic, and 1 percent Asian. For the next twenty-five years the percentage of white declined steadily, while the percentage of black, Hispanic, and Asian rose correspondingly, and by 1995 the percentage of white enrollment had fallen to only 48 percent—less than half for the first time. The decline in the percentage of white was somewhat steeper during the mid-1970s, undoubtedly influenced by white flight from desegregation. In the meantime, the percentage of black, Hispanic, and Asian in the public schools increased to 31, 16, and 5, respectively, as a result of demographic forces, including both in-migration and birthrates. Any interpretation of trends in school deseg-regation indexes, in particular trends in interracial exposure, must take into account these basic demographic patterns because they limit the amount of interracial exposure that can be achieved.

Figure 5 shows why the declining percentage of white cannot be ignored

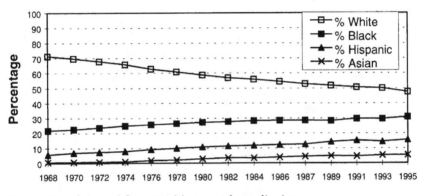

Fig. 4.   Trends in racial composition, very large districts.

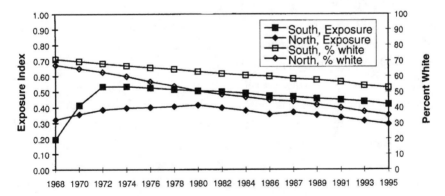

Fig. 5.   Black-white exposure in very large districts with formal desegregation plans.

in an analysis of interracial exposure. It shows the trends in black-white exposure by region for very large districts with formal desegregation plans, juxtaposed with the trend for percent of white enrollment. For Southern districts, the largest changes in interracial exposure (solid squares) occurred between 1968 and 1972, when the index rose from 0.20 to 0.53, an improvement of 33 points in the average percentage of white students in schools attended by blacks. After 1972, however, the index began a long, steady decline, falling to 0.42 by 1995. This reduction in the absolute exposure index is not caused by increases in racial imbalance, which remained nearly flat for the next twenty years (see Fig. 2), but rather the steady decline in the percentage of white enrollment (open squares), which dropped from 68 percent in 1972 to 53 percent in 1995. In fact, the exposure index for Southern districts fell at a slower rate than the percentage of white, indicating that interracial exposure was actually increasing slightly relative to the available white enrollment. The exposure index is 15 points from its maximum in 1972 (68 minus 53), and it is only 11 points from its maximum in 1995 (53 minus 42).

A similar pattern exists for very large Northern districts with plans. As was the case with racial balance, the exposure index (solid diamonds) increased over a longer period, improving from 0.32 in 1968 to 0.41 in 1980, a gain of 9 points in the average percentage of white in schools attended by blacks. The index does not even reach 0.50, however, before it begins a long, inexorable decline over the next fifteen years, falling to only 0.29 by 1995. As in the South, this decline is the result not of increasing racial imbalance, which is nearly flat during this time, but rather of a steeply falling percentage of white enrollment: this fell from 50 in 1980 to only 35 in 1995. Again, relative to the available whites, interracial exposure actually improves slightly; it is 9 percentage points from its maximum in 1980 and is only 6 points from its maximum in 1995.

Finally, Figure 6 shows the trends in the exposure index and the percentage of white for Hispanic students in very large districts with Hispanic enrollment greater than 1 percent.[18] As Orfield has noted, the exposure of Hispanics to white students has declined substantially from its high in 1972

(0.59) to its low in 1995 (0.45). But the decline is not due to increasing imbalance, because Figure 3 shows that Hispanic-white imbalance declined during this time for very large districts. Again, the decline is caused by the declining percent of white enrollment in these districts, which has fallen from 64 in 1972 to only 47 in 1995. Relative to the available whites, then, Hispanic-white exposure has actually increased, and in 1995 it is only 2 points from its maximum value. In other words, Hispanic students in very large districts are actually more desegregated than black students, both in absolute terms and relative to the available white enrollment.

By comparing the trends in racial composition with the trends in racial balance and interracial exposure, a much clearer picture emerges about how and why desegregation levels have changed in recent years. For the fifteen-year period between 1980 and 1995 (1972–1995 for Hispanics), three patterns emerge: the percentage of white has declined, racial balance has remained relatively constant, and interracial exposure has declined. Thus, the cause of declining interracial exposure is the overall decline in the percentage of white, rather than the dismantling of desegregation plans.

It may be appropriate to say that resegregation is occurring for both black and Hispanic students, in that they find themselves attending schools with a dwindling number of white students, particularly in larger Northern

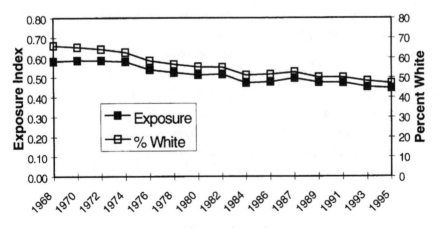

Fig. 6. Hispanic-white exposure for very large districts.

districts. But we must be clear about the cause of that resegregation: if ending desegregation plans were a significant factor, we would see significant increases in racial imbalance. Because this is not happening, and because the percentage of white enrollment is decreasing, we must conclude that the resegregation is due primarily to demographic change in the form of falling white enrollments and increasing minority enrollments.

Social and Educational Results

The existence of long-term national school enrollment data by race makes it a good deal easier to determine the effect of school desegregation plans on school racial balance and interracial exposure than to determine their effect on social and academic outcomes. Although there is a great amount of data on academic achievement, either from national efforts like the National Assessment of Educational Progress (NAEP) or from local school districts that administer standardized achievement tests, it is very difficult to sort out the impact of desegregation from the effects of many other factors that influence academic achievement, especially family socioeconomic characteristics, because there are so few data on these other factors. This has led to substantial disagreement among researchers about the academic effects of desegregation.

It is even more difficult to assess the effect of school desegregation on social and psychological outcomes such as race relations, racial prejudice, and self-esteem because we lack standardized measures for these variables. Consequently, with the exception of opinion polls on racial issues, there are few national data on social outcomes, and there is no way to relate that data to desegregated schools. Accordingly, we must rely on case studies carried out in individual school districts to assess the effect of desegregation on such outcomes as student interracial attitudes and behaviors. Fortunately, there are reviews of this research literature that are helpful.

ACADEMIC ACHIEVEMENT

The debate over desegregation and achievement has continued unabated since the early 1970s, when the first evidence appeared that desegregation was not improving black achievement.[19] In spite of the claims and expectations of many supporters of desegregation during the 1960s, and in spite of the existence of comprehensive and well-funded desegregation plans in many school districts throughout the nation, there is not a single example in the published literature of a comprehensive racial balance plan that has improved black achievement or that has reduced the black-white achievement gap significantly.

Significantly, the most recent social science study of school desegregation—Orfield and Eaton's attack on the courts for "dismantling desegregation"—cited only a single comprehensive desegregation plan that has led to significant minority achievement gains or a reduction of the achievement gap.[20] Indeed, out of seven major desegregation plans analyzed as case studies in this book, the authors did not even discuss minority achievement in three widely discussed cases—Charlotte-Mecklenburg, Detroit, and Little Rock.

Further, they were largely skeptical of local school staff reports claiming significant achievement gains in three other case studies—Kansas City, Missouri, and two Maryland counties, Montgomery and Prince Georges—but they did not conduct any original analyses to support their argument. Finally, the only case they cite where desegregation allegedly improved black achievement was Norfolk, Virginia, where the data they used were from a study by David Armor that concluded just the opposite![21] We shall remedy these omissions by presenting new and independent analysis of achievement results for Charlotte, Kansas City, and Prince Georges County.

There are a number of major reviews of the research literature on this question, and though they do not agree precisely on what the research says, a general picture does emerge. If there is any effect of desegregation on academic achievement, it is highly variable (sometimes it occurs and sometimes it does not), the effects are modest at best, and positive effects occur for reading but not for math. These are the conclusions of three major reviews of research, including one by Nancy St. John in 1975, one by Thomas Cook et al. in 1984, and one by Janet Schofield in 1994.[22]

The Cook review, synthesizing the separate reviews of a panel of six experts convened by the National Institute of Education, captured the essence of this equivocal state of affairs: "On the average, desegregation did not cause an increase in achievement in mathematics. Desegregation increased [black] mean reading levels . . . between two and six weeks. . . . Little confidence should be placed in any of the mean results presented earlier . . . [because] I find the variability in effect sizes more striking and less well understood than any measure of central tendency."[23]

Moreover, we now have massive amounts of national achievement data from the NAEP project, which also includes information on student background and school characteristics. How do the NAEP data inform us about the performance of minority students in desegregated versus segregated schools? What have we learned about the academic achievement of minority students who have spent most of their education in desegregated schools? Interestingly, official NAEP reports do not address these important questions. Indeed, it is remarkable, given all the national data, the controversy, and local experience, that there are few published studies that have tried to answer these questions using NAEP or case study data.

At the outset of this discussion, it is important to distinguish two different types of processes that would cause desegregation plans to have an effect on achievement. The first, and the one assumed by most studies of desegregation and achievement, is that the major causal mechanism is the change in the racial composition of schools; that is, by the improved racial balance that occurs with desegregation. Under this causal assumption, racial isolation is harmful because it deprives minority students of contact with more middle-class and (usually) higher-achieving white students, who help set the pace of study and the standards of achievement. Racial isolation might also lead to a concentration of less effective teachers in minority schools, if more effective teachers gravitate to more integrated or predominately white schools.

The second possible causal mechanism by which school desegregation might have an effect on achievement is when a school board makes significant changes in the types and distribution of programs and resources among schools as part of the desegregation plan. These effects might be most pronounced during the early years of desegregation, if a district maintained inferior programs and resources in predominantly black schools at the time of desegregation (a circumstance not generally found by the 1965 Coleman study of equal opportunity).[24] In this case improvement in minority achievement should take place regardless of racial balance. A corollary to this second effect is a condition where desegregation improves programs and resources for all schools, in which case we might see improvement for all students regardless of race or racial balance.

If the first effect is true, minority achievement should be higher or the gap narrower whenever racial composition improves, regardless of programs and resources, and there should be no achievement gains for segregated minority students or for white students. If the second effect is true, minority achievement could improve in desegregated or segregated schools, and white achievement might also improve. Of course, factors other than desegregation and program changes can improve academic achievement; the leading nonschool factor would be improved socioeconomic status. The impact of socioeconomic status on academic achievement is well documented in social science research, and therefore this possibility must be considered whenever achievement differences or achievement gains are studied.

NAEP STUDIES

The NAEP program has documented a significant improvement in black achievement (but not white achievement) and therefore a closing of the achievement gap between 1970 and 1990. In 1970 the gap in reading was just over one standard deviation for three different age groups, and by 1990 it had declined to between 0.7 and 0.8 standard deviations.[25] Similar patterns were observed for math achievement. Because this improvement corresponds to a period of extensive desegregation, some have suggested that desegregation was the primary cause.

In 1998 a Rand team carried out one of the few studies to use NAEP data to examine the possible effect of desegregation on black achievement gains. They concluded that desegregation might explain part of the improvement.[26] Unfortunately, their complicated methodology utilized aggregate data on several regions of the country, and they did not analyze achievement trends for black students who actually attended segregated or desegregated schools. Therefore, from their methodology it is impossible to determine whether potential effects are due to improved racial balance or to changes in programs that affected all minority students, regardless of their racial balance status.

The only published study to date that compares NAEP achievement trends for black students according to school racial composition found that black achievement gains were approximately the same in majority nonwhite and majority white schools.[27] Although this finding could reflect program improvements due to desegregation and implemented in all schools, the study suggested that improvement in parents' education (as documented in the NAEP data) was a major contributor.

A more direct way to determine the relationship between academic achievement and desegregation is to show how students are performing on NAEP tests according to their school racial composition. Because students who attend predominately white schools are more likely to have higher socioeconomic (SES) levels than those who attend predominately minority schools, such as higher parent education, more two-parent families, and more educational materials at home, we have to adjust the test scores of students to take these SES characteristics into account. This is done using a statistical technique (multiple regression) that removes the effect of SES on student achievement.[28] This statistical analysis enables us to adjust students' test scores for SES and in that way to make clear comparisons of students of the same social class in schools of varying racial composition.

Figure 7 shows the results of an original analysis of the national reading scores for thirteen-year-olds in 1992, adjusted for individual SES characteristics. Across the first four categories of racial composition, ranging from predominately black to 80 percent white, there are no significant differences or trends in black achievement or in the black-white gap. These schools enroll more than 97 percent of the national black sample. There is a significant improvement for a small group of black students in predominately white schools (only 45 out of 1,329 in the black sample), most of whom are in 90 percent–plus white schools. Even assuming this is a reliable result, it is not likely due to racial composition itself, given the lack of a trend in the other categories; more likely, it is a self-selection effect or an effect of unmeasured family characteristics that cannot be evaluated.

Figure 8 shows an analysis of math achievement for the same group of students. The pattern here is quite different; both black and white students score higher in schools that are over 40 percent white, and therefore the achievement gap remains relatively constant across the first four categories of school (it narrows significantly only for the small group of black students who are in highly white schools). Because the improvement occurs for both groups, it is probably not due to racial balance; rather, it is more likely to be due to programmatic differences among the schools or unmeasured SES factors. Whatever the cause, attending a racially integrated school does not

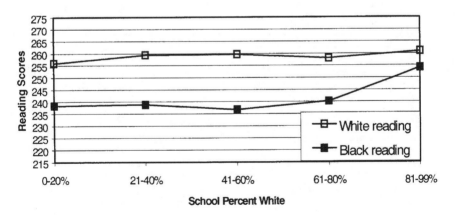

Fig. 7.   School percent white and reading achievement, 1992 NAEP, age 13, adjusted for individual SES.

reduce the math achievement gap between black and white students in this national sample.

Similar results were obtained for the seventeen-year-old age groups as well as for Hispanic students. Therefore, the NAEP data do not support the thesis that desegregated schools significantly benefit black or Hispanic reading achievement, nor do they reduce the black-white or Hispanic-white achievement gap in mathematics.

CASE STUDIES

The NAEP data have the advantage of being national in scope, but they have some serious drawbacks as well. For example, the NAEP data do not include information on the existence, scope, or duration of desegregation plans within a district. Although the data include the racial composition of the student's school, they do not explain why the racial composition exists or how long it has been that way. For this reason it is useful to look at a number of case studies of the effects of comprehensive desegregation plans on achievement.

Several recently published case studies include Pasadena, California; Norfolk, Virginia; and Charleston, South Carolina.[29] In 1970, three years before the *Keyes* decision, Pasadena became one of the first Northern school

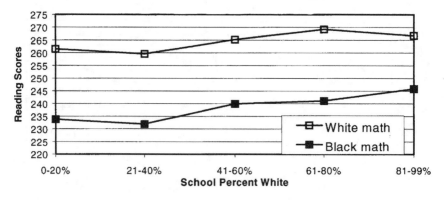

Fig. 8.   School percent white and math achievement, 1992 NAEP, age 13, adjusted for individual SES.

districts to implement a districtwide racial balance plan, having been ordered to do so by a federal district court. From 1970 to 1973 there was no improvement in the reading scores of a first-grade cohort of black students in fully desegregated schools.

Norfolk, Virginia, was fully desegregated and racially balanced by 1970. Fourth-grade test scores were available from 1965 to 1982. Both black and white test scores actually fell dramatically after desegregation. The black-white gap narrowed somewhat between 1970 and 1973 but only because white achievement fell more than black achievement. Between 1973 and 1980 achievement scores improved for both races, but they did not reach their predesegregation levels until 1978; the gap remained constant during this time. A special compensatory program that was initiated in 1978 may have produced the gains in 1979 and 1980. But in 1981, when a new test form was introduced, scores fell again. There was also some evidence that improper coaching and teaching before the test may have accounted for some of these increases. Even so, one can certainly conclude that racial balance had no positive impact on black or white fourth-grade achievement between 1970 and 1978.

Similar results were found in Charleston, South Carolina, where the court-approved desegregation plan did not produce racial balance in every school. Charleston was a countywide district with subdistricts that governed student and teacher assignment, hence racial balance was required only within subdistricts. The case study compared reading achievement for black third- and fourth-graders in schools with varying degrees of racial composition across subdistricts and found no significant difference in test scores, or change in test scores, among predominately black schools, predominately white schools, and racially balanced schools.

Some additional case studies (unpublished to date) are of special interest because of the nature of their desegregation plans. Three of these case studies present original data analyses from school districts discussed by Orfield and Eaton: Kansas City, Missouri; Prince Georges County, Maryland; and Charlotte-Mecklenburg County, North Carolina. Another is from the Wilmington–New Castle County district, which had a unique court-ordered desegregation plan.

In 1978 a federal court ordered the merger of predominately black Wilmington, Delaware, with ten predominately white New Castle County districts to form a single metropolitan school district, and a countywide desegregation plan was implemented. It is one of the few metropolitan consolidation and busing plans to be ordered by a court and ultimately adopted. The case is of special interest because, unlike many central city plans, black students attend most of their school years in majority white suburban schools whose student bodies have remained relatively middle class (in some cases, affluent) since the start of the plan. As late as 1993 the New Castle County districts (the single district was divided into four districts in 1981) were among the most racially balanced districts in the country. Not only did the vast majority of schools range from 65 to 75 percent white, but also every school was at least majority white.

Figure 9 shows trends in sixth-grade reading scores for students in all four New Castle County districts.[30] In 1985, when sixth-graders would have attended racially balanced schools since kindergarten, we see a black-white gap of 15 points, or about three-fourths of a national standard deviation. Moreover, there is no improvement in black sixth-grade test scores, nor is there a reduction in the achievement gap over the nine years shown. In 1993 the black-white gap is 17 points (on a different test), or about eight-tenths of a standard deviation, similar to the 1992 achievement gaps for

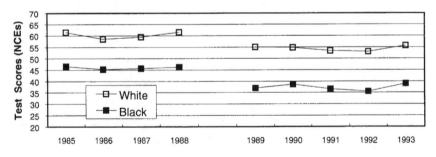

Fig. 9.   Trends in New Castle County, Delaware, 6th-grade reading.

the NAEP reading tests. In spite of these stable, desegregated, and majority white schools located in middle-class neighborhoods, the presumed ideal environments for raising black achievement, there are neither significant black gains nor reductions in the black-white gap. Clearly, the Wilmington case does not support the thesis that racial balance will reduce the achievement gap.

Nor is it a question of money. In 1986 a federal court ordered Kansas City, Missouri, to implement what may well be the most expensive remedial plan in history. Kansas City had been operating a desegregation plan since the late 1970s. But in 1986 the court ordered an expanded plan involving extensive construction, renovation, and the addition of magnet programs to most of the elementary and all the secondary schools, whose purpose was to attract suburban whites into this 70 percent minority school system. With a unique court-ordered tax levy and court-ordered funding from the state, total school expenditures reached $10,000 per pupil by 1990, with total funding exceeding $1.5 billion over approximately an eight-year period. Unfortunately, not enough white students came to the city from the suburbs to lower the minority percentage significantly.

As the achievement trends in Figure 10 reveal, this extraordinary degree

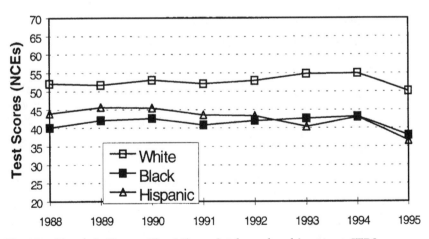

Fig. 10. Trends in Kansas City, Missouri, 5th-grade achievement, ITBS composite scores.

of expenditures for one of the largest magnet programs in the nation apparently did nothing to raise the achievement levels of black students, which remained substantially below white achievement from 1988 to 1995. In fact, when a new test form was implemented in 1995, scores of all students fell significantly, raising the possibility that some coaching or teaching of test content may have taken place during preceding years. Although the black-white achievement gap is somewhat narrower than in Wilmington or in the NAEP, this appears to be due to low white scores rather than to high black scores (Kansas City has a relatively high proportion of white students in the free lunch program). Thus, spending an extraordinary amount of money on a school desegregation plan and on magnet schools does not seem to improve minority achievement significantly or decrease the minority-white achievement gap.

The Prince Georges County case is noteworthy because of a different approach taken in its second school desegregation plan. A predominantly white suburban county outside Washington, D.C., Prince Georges adopted a comprehensive pairing and busing plan in 1973. This was followed by extensive white flight and black in-migration from the District of Columbia, and the county schools became majority black in the early 1980s. Recognizing that not all schools could achieve meaningful racial balance, a modified desegregation plan was adopted in 1985 that provided for several types of schools: desegregated magnet schools, desegregated regular schools, and "Milliken II" schools, which were predominantly black and received additional resources and funding. Later, as white enrollment losses continued, some of the magnet schools and some of the regular schools became predominately black; they also added a category of "Model" schools, which were predominately black and received extra resources but not as much as Milliken schools.

These different types of programs and desegregation levels offer a unique opportunity to sort out the potential effects of racial balance from the effects of special compensatory programs and extra funding. Figure 11 shows third-grade test scores (from a Maryland statewide test) for black students in six types of schools, after adjusting scores for student background characteristics. Though the scores vary somewhat across the different types of schools, there is no apparent benefit from attending a desegregated school, most of which are approximately half black and half white. After controlling for SES and initial ability, black students attending desegregated magnet and desegregated regular schools score no higher than black students at predominately black regular schools (which average around 90 percent black), and they score somewhat lower than black students in the enriched but predominately black Milliken and Model schools (which exceed 90 percent black). It is not clear why black students score lowest at the predominately black magnet schools and highest at the predominately black Model schools, but whatever the reason it is not because of their racial composition, which is identical.

The final case study to be presented is Charlotte-Mecklenburg, North Carolina, which is especially important historically because of the famous U.S. Supreme Court decision in this case. The *Swann* decision upheld a lower court order to adopt a comprehensive, countywide mandatory busing program to attain racial balance in all schools, thereby creating a standard for desegregation that was applied throughout the nation for many years. Because Charlotte was a large county district with a relatively low black enrollment in 1970, it was able to sustain very extensive racial balance for

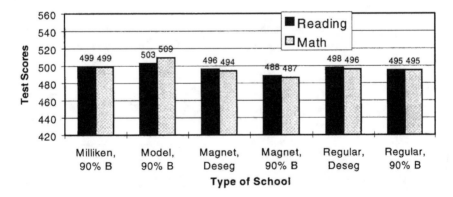

Fig. 11.   Prince Georges County, Maryland, black test scores by school type, 1996, grade 3.

the next twenty years while at the same time preserving a majority white school system. It has been described in the Orfield and Eaton book as one of the most successful desegregation plans in the country, with unprecedented local support from educators, civil rights leaders, and the business community.

Figure 12 shows the long-term achievement trends for third and sixth graders from 1978 to 1997. In 1978 black elementary students had been in well-desegregated schools from kindergarten on, yet they scored only at the 20th percentile in both reading and math compared with national norms. Test scores began increasing dramatically for both black and white students, reaching maximums in about 1983, when black students scored at the national norm of 50. The reason for the increase is not clear, but it is not likely due to desegregation, which had been in place for eight years before 1978. Some of the increases may have been due to coaching or teaching test content because scores for both races dropped significantly when a new test form was adopted in 1986. Though the black-white gap had diminished somewhat by 1983, it returned to its original magnitude in 1986 (about one standard deviation) and remained relatively constant until the last CAT test was administered in 1992. A sizable test score gap

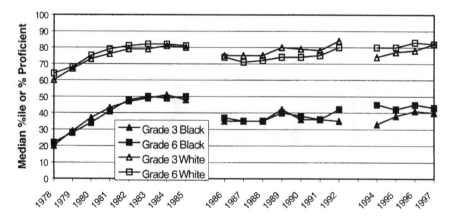

Fig. 12.   Achievement trends in Charlotte-Mecklenburg, North Carolina, grades 3 and 6.

also existed between 1994 and 1997, but it cannot be compared directly with the CAT gap because it comes from a different statewide test that uses a different metric. Thus, one of the most successful desegregation plans in the country did not reduce the black-white achievement gap significantly.

These case studies bolster the NAEP results shown in Figures 7 and 8, that racial composition by itself has little effect on raising the achievement of minority students or on reducing the minority-white achievement gap. Some studies show that there is no relationship at all between black achievement and racial composition (controlling for student SES), and other studies show that there is no relationship between the black-white achievement gap and racial composition. In either case, though there is some evidence here that achievement can be affected by programmatic changes, there is no evidence that it responds to improved racial balance by itself.

RACE RELATIONS AND ATTITUDES

Studies of the effect of desegregation on racial attitudes and race relations were fairly common during the 1970s, when the desegregation movement was at its peak. There seems to be less interest in these issues now, perhaps because the early studies offered little support for the notion that desegregation would bolster self-esteem, lower racial prejudice, and improve race relations.

The first major review of the effect of desegregation on race relations and attitudes was by St. John, whose study was published in 1975.[31] She evaluated 35 studies conducted between 1966 and 1973 of changes in white attitudes or behaviors after desegregation. She found 11 studies in which white prejudice worsened, 11 where it improved, and 13 where there was no change or mixed results. She also evaluated 28 studies of changes in black prejudice after desegregation, finding 10 where black prejudice worsened, 6 where it improved, and 12 where there was no change or results were mixed. Her review also evaluated the effect of desegregation on the self-esteem of black children, one of the key concerns of the Supreme Court in *Brown*. Out of 35 studies, she found 14 where black self-esteem was higher in segregated than desegregated schools, 5 where it was higher in desegregated schools, and 16 where there was no significant difference.

Walter G. Stephan conducted a similar type of review about ten years later.[32] Although he reviewed a smaller number of studies, his 28 studies covered a longer time span (1963–1981) and included only those with a reasonably sound methodology. His findings were remarkably similar to those of St. John. Out of 24 studies of change in white attitudes or behavior, he found 11 where desegregation increased white prejudice, 4 where it decreased, and 9 where there was no change. Of the 17 studies of black attitudes and behaviors, he found 5 showing that desegregation worsened black prejudice, 4 where it improved, and 8 where there was no difference. In his review of black self-esteem in 28 studies, he found 7 where desegregation lowered black self-esteem, 1 where it was improved, and 19 where there was no change. It is interesting that the majority of studies during this period found that black self-esteem was generally higher than white self-esteem, thus calling into question the Supreme Court's psychological harm thesis.[33]

The evidence on the benefit of school desegregation for race relations is probably the weakest of all. Indeed, there are more studies showing harmful effects than studies showing positive effects. This led to another and more recent reviewer of the race relations literature to conclude, somewhat generously: "In general, the reviews of desegregation and intergroup relations were unable to come to any conclusion about what the probable effects of desegregation were. . . . Virtually all of the reviewers determined that few, if any, firm conclusions about the impact of desegregation on intergroup relations could be drawn."[34]

The reluctance of reviewers to draw conclusions about the benefits of school desegregation for race relations or self-esteem only reinforces our conclusion that the psychological harm theory of de facto segregation and the social benefit theory of desegregation are clearly wrong, at least when applied to desegregation as a racial balance policy. Of course, the original psychological harm theory presumed official segregation sanctioned by laws, which was pretty much gone by the mid-1960s and before the time when most of the studies above were conducted. But supporters of the harm and benefit thesis have applied it far more broadly, to cover any type of racial imbalance or racial disparity arising from any cause, and even today it forms the ideological basis for desegregation and affirmative action policies. It is this broader formulation that fails under scrutiny of the research evidence.

Conclusions

What can we say about the success and failures of the school desegregation movement? If we evaluate school desegregation policy within the constitutional framework established by the Supreme Court on the matter of race in *Brown*, which is much narrower than the goals of many civil rights advocates, there are indeed successes. The failures come, for the most part, from attempts to extend this original framework to see school desegregation as a means of resolving a whole host of racial issues never contemplated by *Brown*.

First, we must not diminish the fact that *Brown* forever changed the fundamental way in which America deals with race, not only in schools but also throughout society. In particular, it forbade all official actions that segregated students or staff by race, or that sanctioned discriminatory distribution of resources, facilities, and activities. Second, after the Court allowed consideration of race in fashioning desegregation plans, what followed was an unprecedented change in the way students and staff were assigned to schools, eventually creating extensive racial balance in schools to an extent never attained in any other sector of society.

That racial balance has largely continued to the present time, with or without court orders. Although the Supreme Court has returned to its original conception of race, permitting school systems to be declared "unitary," after which race cannot be used for student assignment (whether for racial balance or imbalance), there has been no rush to dismantle desegregation plans and return to strict neighborhood school policies. The reason is that racial balance and racial diversity have become desired goals, especially within the educational establishment. True, a number of unitary school systems, like Norfolk, Oklahoma City, Cleveland, and Prince Georges County, now have some neighborhood schools, but most of these districts have retained such politically palatable desegregation policies as magnet programs, voluntary transfers, and minimal integrative geographic zoning. Indeed, that is why the racial balance indexes have remained so stable for the past fifteen years.

The biggest threat to desegregation is not the dismantling of plans but rather the inexorable demographic changes that have left the majority of larger school systems predominately minority. No type of permissible plan will result in substantial desegregation in New York, Los Angeles, Chicago, Cleveland, Detroit, Atlanta, Dallas, and dozens of other large cities.[35] The declining measures of interracial exposure for both black and Hispanic students are caused not by dismantling desegregation plans but rather by the falling percentage of white students in all but the smallest public school districts. Though these demographic trends do effect the success of deseg-regation plans, they do not reflect failures of the courts or of public policy in general.

It is only when we turn to educational and social benefits that we find the most significant failures of desegregation policy. Of course, these are not failures of Supreme Court doctrines or federal law, which never con-templated such benefits; rather, they are a failing of the benefit theory as embraced by many civil rights advocates, some lower courts, and even a few Supreme Court Justices. Desegregation and racial balance have not brought the gains in minority achievement and a closing of the achievement gap envisioned by so many believers in this thesis because the thesis is invalid.

There is some evidence that special programs have benefited achieve-ment slightly—even when not accompanied by racial balance—but the benefit has not been sufficient to close the black-white or the Hispanic-white gaps. In all the case studies discussed here, and in many others not discussed, the achievement gaps in well-desegregated school systems re-main very close to the national achievement gap, and this gap is only slightly smaller than the gap that existed when major desegregation plans began in 1970. If desegregation is responsible for this modest reduction in the gap, it is most likely due to programmatic and resource changes, not racial balance policies.

There is even less evidence that school desegregation has reduced racial prejudice, improved race relations, or benefited self-esteem. Here the expectations of benefits were based either on inadequate social theory or on misinterpretations of the widely accepted contact theory of Gordon Allport.[36] Given the very large differences in academic achievement between black and white students, and the fact that desegregation did not eliminate these differences, it may have been naïve to expect that integrated schools would improve black self-esteem, when blacks were plunged into an academic environment where the competition was far more rigorous than in segregated schools. The unequal achievement and resulting unequal grades in desegregated schools also violated one of the contact theory's requirements for positive race relations—that there would be equal status contact.

This is not to say there are no social benefits of school desegregation. First, school desegregation has brought each race greater personal knowledge about other races living in their community, albeit without guaranteeing positive race relations in all cases. Second, knowledge, proper instruction, and tolerant staff can help schools become places where children learn how to treat and respect persons of other races, which helps prepare them for the later realities of living in a multiracial society. Finally, many individual students do find meaningful interracial experiences and friendships, which they value and want to have, even though this outcome may not apply to the majority of students. This is one of the reasons we have always supported voluntary desegregation plans, which let individual students and families decide whether or not to attend an integrated school, for whatever reasons are important to them.

It is this last set of social benefits that leads us to support desegregation policies for unitary school systems, though these are more restricted than the original types of plans. Desegregation should be strictly voluntary, as with magnet schools or open enrollment options, and it should be available across district lines as part of choice programs that include private schools. Race cannot be used explicitly as a criteria for school assignment in a unitary system, even in the case of voluntary options. Poverty (i.e., free lunch status) is, however, a permissible criteria for government decisions. By offering voluntary transfer options to all students, with some financial incentive (such as transportation) for free lunch students, we can expand the opportunities for desegregation for those families that desire it most, across district lines and between public and private sectors, and without the unintended negative consequences that have plagued the massive mandatory busing schemes of the past.

Notes

1. The criteria for a unitary or nondiscriminatory school system were first formulated in a brief footnote in a Supreme Court decision, *Green v. New Kent County (Va.)*, 430 U.S. 391 (1968). There was no discussion or explanation of the meaning of these factors or the level of compliance that would be required.

2. Gary Orfield and Susan E. Eaton, *Dismantling Desegregation* (New York: New Press, 1996), p. 53.

3. Alexander M. Bickel, "Untangling the Busing Snarl," *New Republic*, September 23 and 30, 1972.

4. James S. Coleman, Sara D. Kelly, and John A. Moore, *Trends in School Integration* (Washington, D.C.: Urban Institute, 1975).

5. James S. Coleman et al., *Equality of Educational Opportunity* (Washington, D.C.: U.S. Government Printing Office, 1966).

6. *Green v. New Kent County* at 437.

7. *Swann v. Charlotte-Mecklenburg Board of Education*, 402 U.S. 1 (1971).

8. *Keyes v. School District No. 1, Denver*, 413 U.S. 189 (1973).

9. HEW, Office of Elementary and Secondary Education, did a school census in 1967 and published a book with enrollment by school and three ethnic groups, white, black, and other, in several thousand school districts. The data was not kept in machine-readable format.

10. For a more detailed description of the original national study, see Christine H. Rossell and David J. Armor, "The Effectiveness of School Desegregation Plans," *American Politics Quarterly* 24 (1996): 267–302.

11. The formula is $D = 1/2 \Sigma \mid (Wi/W) - (Bi/B) \mid$ where Wi is the white enrollment in each school, W is the white enrollment in the school system, Bi is the black enrollment

in each school, and B is the black enrollment in the whole school system. The absolute sum of the difference between whites and blacks is calculated for each school, then summed down the schools, and the total divided by two.

12. It also equals the sum of the proportion of students of one race and the proportion of students of the other race that would have to be reassigned to attain perfect balance. In a school system exactly half white and half black, the percentage of each group to be assigned could be derived by dividing the index by two.

13. The number of cases for small districts was insufficient to provide stable estimates.

14. All Southern districts with both black and white students had to have some type of plan if they had practiced segregation in 1954; some districts may have eliminated segregation by geographic zoning, which they did not view as being a formal plan. Only ten districts fell into this category.

15. The index of dissimilarity measures the imbalance of only two groups at a time. In calculating Hispanic-white imbalance, black and other enrollment is ignored. Similarly, in the calculation of black-white imbalance, Hispanic and other minority enrollment is ignored.

16. See Coleman, Kelly, and Moore, 1975.

17. The formula is $E = (\Sigma_i nb_i pw_i) \div \Sigma nb_i$ where nb_i is the number of black students in school i, and pw_i is the proportion of white in the same school. The number of black students is multiplied by the proportion of white in each school, and this is then summed across schools. That total is divided by the number of blacks in the school system.

18. It is necessary to exclude districts with very small numbers of Hispanic students, because they tend to inflate the exposure index with very high values.

19. David J. Armor, "The Evidence on Busing," *Public Interest* 28 (1972): 90–126.

20. Orfield and Eaton, *Dismantling Desegregation.*

21. See Armor, *Forced Justice: School Desegregation and the Law* (New York: Oxford University Press, 1995), pp. 79–81. Black and white scores in Norfolk actually fell after desegregation in 1970, and neither group returned to its predesegregation achievement levels until 1978. The black-white gap narrowed somewhat between 1970 and 1973, but only because white achievement fell more than black achievement. Achievement improved for both groups between 1973 and 1980, but the gap remained constant during this time; scores fell again in 1981 when a new test form was introduced.

22. Nancy St. John, *School Desegregation* (New York: Wiley & Sons, 1975); Thomas Cook et al., *School Desegregation and Black Achievement* (Washington, D.C.: National Institute of Education, U.S. Department of Education, 1984); Janet Ward Schofield, in Banks and Banks, *Handbook of Research in Multicultural Education* (New York: Macmillan, 1994).

23. Cook et al., pp. 40–41.

24. Coleman et al., *Equality of Educational Opportunity*.

25. It fell to 0.5 sd's for thirteen-year-olds in 1988 and 1990, but by 1992 this age group was back to 0.71.

26. David Grissmer, Ann Flanagan, and Stephanie Williamson, "Why Did the Black-White Score Gap Narrow in the 1970s and 1980s?" in Christopher Jencks and Meridith Phillips, eds., *The Black-White Test Score Gap* (Washington, D.C.: Brookings Institution, 1998).

27. Armor, *Forced Justice*, p. 95.

28. The adjustment uses multiple regression analysis to predict student scores solely according to their parents' education, family structure, household reading items, and gender.

29. Armor, *Forced Justice*, pp. 77–83.

30. The break in the trend line denotes the change in 1989 from the California Achievement Test (CAT) to the Stanford Achievement Test (SAT).

31. St. John, *School Desegregation*.

32. Walter G. Stephan, "The Effects of School Desegregation: An Evaluation 30 Years After *Brown*," in M. Saks and L. Saxe, eds., *Advances in Applied Social Psychology* (Hillsdale, N.J.: Erlebaum, 1986).

33. In fairness to the Supreme Court, they were simply referring to the testimony of social scientists at that time, who may have misinterpreted the famous doll studies of Kenneth and Mamie Clark. See Armor, *Forced Justice*, pp. 99–101.

34. Janet Ward Schofield, "School Desegregation and Intergroup Relations: A Review of the Literature," in *Review of Research in Education* 17: 335–412, ed. Gerald Grant (Washington, D.C.: American Educational Research Association, 1991), p. 356.

35. The Supreme Court established in 1974 in *Milliken v. Bradley* that there can be no cross-district remedy without a cross-district violation (i.e., collusion between city and suburban government officials to segregate the city and suburban school districts). Proving a cross-district violation is almost impossible, and there have been only a handful of cross-district remedies since 1974.

36. Gordon Allport, *The Nature of Prejudice* (Reading, Mass.: Addison-Wesley, 1979).

The Racial Gap in Academic Achievement

ABIGAIL THERNSTROM

As early as second or third grade, [African American students] generally have much lower grades and test scores than Asians and Whites—patterns that persist over the course of their school careers.
> —The College Board, "Reaching the Top: A Report of the National Task Force on Minority High Achievement"

You have to demand more of your students while providing them with the structure to meet those demands. The more difficult the curriculum, the greater the likelihood your students will be successful.
> —Gregory Hodge, principal, Frederick Douglass Academy in central Harlem, New York City

IN 1903, W. E. B. Du Bois, the preeminent black intellectual of his time, described "the problem of the color line [as] the problem of the twentieth century." And four decades later he peered sixty years down the road and saw a new century in which—for blacks—there would be nothing new.

We have, of course, arrived at that new century, and much has changed. But in certain respects, not nearly enough. Although almost half of blacks are today in the middle class, racial inequality remains a fundamental fact about American life. And much of that inequality can be traced to one source: the underachievement of black students in school. The racial gap in cognitive skills is the nation's most serious educational problem, and its most critical race-related issue.

Most discussions of the racial gap in academic achievement contrast the scores of blacks and Hispanics to those of Asians and whites. But the Hispanic and black stories are not the same. Hispanics are a classic immigrant group. With the passage of time, their academic profile (already less worrisome than that of blacks) is likely to change. African Americans are the real concern.

Skills Matter

Educational reform is sweeping the nation. Every state, except Iowa, has developed specific learning standards, and all but three are committed to statewide tests to determine compliance with those standards in at least one core subject. Thirty-eight states have aligned their standards, curricula, and assessments in all four major subjects—English, math, science, and history. More than half the states are making high school graduation conditional upon a passing grade on a state test. The standards are often rock-bottom, but even clearly defined minimal expectations are a sharp break from the past.[1]

Teachers, too, are facing tougher tests for certification, and many states have the power to assume control of a failing school, or even an entire district. Charter schools are bursting out all over; thirty-six states and the District of Columbia now have some sort of charter law. There are other reforms connected to high standards and accountability: early intervention programs, some of which target both parents and children; an end to social promotion; summer school, after-school, and Saturday programs; a variety of incentives (including free college tuition) designed to promote high achievement; summer workshops in content areas for teachers; the addition of more reading and writing to the curriculum; and much else.

Educational improvement means, above all, raising the performance of urban students, and particularly those who are black. The academic performance of black youngsters on standardized tests is worse than that of any other group; if educational reforms do not raise black test scores, they will have failed. And if current efforts fail, a substantial percentage of African American families will remain below the poverty line. Blacks and whites today have equal high school graduation rates and nearly equal college attendance rates. Over 85 percent of both groups finish four years of high school (although not necessarily by age eighteen), and among those who obtain a high school diploma, 60 percent of blacks (versus 68 percent of whites) go directly into college. But blacks and whites do not leave the twelfth grade equally well educated, and thus they do not have the same college graduation rates or the same earnings down the road.

Blacks are more likely to earn a college diploma than whites with the same twelfth-grade test scores.[2] And blacks earn no less than whites when they are equally academically prepared. There is much talk in the media and elsewhere about the rich getting richer and the poor becoming poorer. In fact, it is those with skills who are doing well economically. In recent decades, earnings for low-skilled work have declined, while those for jobs that require a good command of language and numbers, as well as the ability to analyze complicated problems, have risen dramatically.[3]

Thus, it is actual knowledge—not years spent in school warming a seat—that makes the difference in an individual's income. What often looks like discrimination is better described as rewarding workers with relatively strong cognitive skills. One study of men twenty-six to thirty-three years old who held full-time jobs in 1991 found that when education was measured in the traditional way (years of school completed), blacks earned 19 percent less than comparably educated whites. But when the yardstick was how well they performed on basic tests of vocabulary, paragraph comprehension, arithmetical reasoning, and mathematical knowledge, the results were reversed. Black men earned 9 percent more than white men with the same education—as defined by skill.[4]

Other studies contain similar findings. Among men thirty-one to thirty-six years old whose cognitive skills put them above the 50th percentile on the well-respected Armed Services Vocational Aptitude Battery test, the difference between black and white earnings is a mere 4 percentage points, Christopher Jencks and Meredith Phillips report in a Brookings Institution volume on *The Black-White Test Score Gap.*[5] A 1999 College Board report came to much the same conclusion: "Differences in job performance ratings and wages among people with similar educational credentials are related in part to differences in academic achievement and skills levels, as measured by standardized test scores, class rank in college, and even high school grades or test scores." Other factors do come into play—"motivation, perserverance," even "plain old luck," it went on. White racism, however, was not on the list.[6]

Scary Numbers

Test scores matter, and those for blacks and whites, on average, are not the same. For a while the rate of progress was heartening. During the 1970s and the better part of the 1980s, black school children were making more rapid gains than whites on the standardized tests administered periodically to a representative sample of students by the National Assessment of Educational Progress (NAEP). NAEP results are often called the nation's report card on education, and in 1971, when the tests were first given, the average African American seventeen-year-old could read no better than the typical white eleven-year-old. By 1988, the gap had been narrowed to just 2.5 years, still too large but less than half of what it had been sixteen years before. Math and reading tests are given in different years, but the data are similar. In 1973, black students were 4.3 years behind their white peers; in 1990, the difference was down to just 2.5 years.

Toward the end of the 1980s, however, black progress came to a halt. Scores began to go down. By 1996, the racial gap in math of 2.5 years in 1990 had grown to 3.4 years. The average African American high school senior thus had math skills precisely on a par with those of the typical white student in the middle of ninth grade—a huge disparity in a world in which numeracy is becoming at least as important as literacy.

The reading scores are even more dismaying. Although the black-white gap closed by a remarkable 3.5 years between 1980 and 1988, it widened by more than a year and a half in the following decade, erasing half of the previous gain. As a result, in 1998 the average seventeen-year-old African American could only read as well as the typical white child who had not yet reached age thirteen. In 1992, just 18 percent of black students in twelfth grade were rated "proficient" or "advanced" in reading, as compared with 47 percent of whites. As of 1998, those numbers were unchanged.

Backsliding is evident in both science and writing as well. In the decade following 1986, the science gap widened by a half a year, and between 1988 and 1996, the difference between white and black scores on the writing assessment increased by 1.2 years. The most recent data thus show black students in twelfth grade dealing with scientific problems at the level of whites in the sixth grade and writing about as well as whites in the eighth grade.

The Middle-Class Puzzle

The racial gap in academic skills is a problem that starts before kindergarten and affects black youngsters from every social class. Thus, the median scores of black and white five- and six-year-olds who took the Peabody Picture Vocabulary Test in the years 1986–1992 were quite different.[7] In an essay in *The Black-White Test Score Gap*, Meredith Phillips and colleagues estimate that about half the difference between white and black twelfth-grade students is explained by the gap that is already evident in first grade.[8] Could that gap be eliminated by better schooling? No one knows for sure. But schools scattered across the landscape are beating the demographic odds—educating children from whom regular public schools expect less.

More discouraging, because it's more bewildering, is the poor academic performance of middle-class black students. Shaker Heights is a tony Cleveland suburb; its black residents are well-to-do. And its schools, as of 1998, were pouring nearly $10,000 a year into educating every child. It has had a rich program aimed at raising the level of black achievement. Successful black students mentor those doing poorly in the earlier grades;

tutors work with small groups of kindergarten children who need help reading; after-school, weekend, and summer academies are open to those who want to attend; special high school classes are available for those who do not keep up; a high school counselor works with youngsters whose grades do not reflect their potential; and so forth. The results have the school administators totally baffled. About half the students in the Shaker Heights school system are black, but blacks are 7 percent of those in the top fifth of their class, and 90 percent of those in the bottom fifth.[9]

"At virtually all socioeconomic levels," black students do not perform as well as those who are white or Asian, the College Board's recent task force report acknowledged. In fact, the racial gap in academic achievement is widest among middle-class students from educated families; the NAEP scores of black and white youngsters whose parents lack even a high school degree are more alike.[10] The SATs, too, paint a dismal picture. In 1995, black students from families in the top income bracket—$70,000 and up— were a shade behind whites from families earning less than $10,000 on the verbal assessment and significantly behind them in math.[11]

Trash the Tests

Many educators, policy makers, and others argue, of course, that staring at these numbers is a fundamentally misguided way of looking at the question of black academic achievement. Test scores tell us little, they say, and should never be used to decide who moves up a grade, attends summer school, or graduates. Their disparate racial impact "should be cause for further inquiry and examination," the U.S. Department of Education's Office of Civil Rights (OCR) contends. In draft guidelines issued in December 1999, it warned states and local school districts that they must be prepared to defend their "high stakes" tests in federal court. Low scores may reflect limited educational opportunities; if so, decisions that rely upon test performance are "problematic"—that is, discriminatory. Numerical cut-off scores on a statewide test as a condition of graduation are particularly suspect.[12]

OCR's views square with those of many who identify themselves as members of the civil rights community. Christoper Edley Jr. was President Clinton's main advisor on race for a number of years; the guidelines, he said, protect students from "harsh high-stakes sanctions."[13] In a resolution approved on November 19, 1999, the NAACP came out against the use of SAT and ACT exams for purposes of college admission on the grounds that they are racially biased and a poor indicator of success in college.[14] In doing so, it ignored much evidence that, in fact, the SAT overpredicts black college grades; black students tend to do worse than their test scores suggest they should. The tests are indeed biased—in favor of black students.[15]

In 1999, the Educational Testing Service, too, took a swipe at the SATs for which it is ultimately responsible. When kids are from disadvantaged households—as measured by a host of possible criteria—SAT scores should be adjusted to reflect the hurdles they must overcome, ETS tentatively suggested in September 1999. A score of 1,000 should be read as 1,200 if the student is black, for example, and has thus outperformed the black average.[16] The arguments of both the NAACP and ETS logically apply to all tests at every grade level. If standardized assessments are biased and therefore misleading, then grades should be adjusted. On an eighth-grade math test, a Hispanic's "B" is really an "A." Scores are not scores. They are numbers to be read within a demographic context. And the uniformly high academic expectations that are integral to standards-based educational reform are a grave mistake.

That is certainly what Jonathan Kozol, a well-known writer on education, believes. The increasingly popular statewide tests, he has declared, evoke memories of "another social order not so long ago that regimented all its children . . . to march with pedagogic uniformity, efficiency, and every competence one can conceive—except for independent will—right into Poland, Austria, and France, and World War II."[17] Deborah Meier, the much-celebrated founder of the Central Park East schools in New York City, condemns standardized tests as failing to "measure the only important qualities of a well-educated person." "Life scores [not math scores] based on living" should be the educator's concern, she has written.[18] Theodore

Sizer, former dean of the Harvard Graduate School of Education, is also opposed to the entire standards-based educational package. "The myriad, detailed and mandatory state 'curriculum frameworks,' of whatever scholarly brilliance, are attacks on intellectual freedom," he says. "High stakes tests arising from these curricula compound the felony."[19]

Kozol, Meier, Sizer, and their allies have many fans, including most members of the faculty at the leading graduate schools of education. U.S. Senator Paul Wellstone has introduced legislation to ban standardized tests from being used as the sole criterion for grade promotion and high school graduation.[20] But they seem to be fighting a losing war. Powerful currents are pushing education in a different direction. Asked in a 1999 poll whether they had "respect and confidence" in public schools, only 36 percent of Americans said they had a "great deal/quite a lot of confidence." A year earlier 59 percent had listed low academic standards as a "very serious concern," with another 29 percent choosing "somewhat serious." Moreover, polling by the nonpartisan Public Agenda in the winter of 1997–98 revealed that 78 percent of black parents agreed that testing "calls attention to a problem that needs to be solved."[21]

Peter Sacks, the suthor of a recent book on testing, dismisses those who support testing as part of a "conservative backlash advocating advancement by 'merit,'" but important advocates for black and Hispanic children have joined the standards crusade.[22] Ramon C. Cortines, formerly the interim superintendent of schools in Los Angeles, recently called the attack on assessments "insidious racism" on the part of those who "want the status quo."[23] To ignore the information that tests provide, in other words, is to perpetuate a system that has been historically indifferent to the fate of black and Hispanic students. The Education Trust is a Washington, D.C., organization devoted to promoting academic achievement among blacks, Hispanics, and low-income children. "Traditionally, of course, most advocates for such children have shied away from high standards and high stakes," Kati Haycock, the director, has written.[24] But she in unequivocal in her demand for no-nonsense standards with uncompromising consequences for those who fail to meet them. "Backing off from testing would just kick the problem of low student achievement under the rug again," she has said.[25]

Peter Sacks talks about the "stigma of poor performance on mental tests."[26] But Kati Haycock and those behind the drive for state educational reform are more fearful of the consequences of letting schools ignore the racial gap in academic achievement. That fear has prompted New York, Texas, and California to consider racial and ethnic data in ranking public schools. In New York, for instance, beginning with 2001, the performance of black and Hispanic students in each school will be reported, and schools with a large racial gap in academic performance won't earn a good grade. Thus, an affluent suburb in which the average score on the statewide tests is high will be penalized if that average masks group differences.[27]

New York and other states are rejecting the notion of racial double standards—lower academic expenctations for non-Asian minorities. The job of educators is to close the racial gap, they say; the tests tell a story that America ignores at its peril. The scores cannot be fudged with formulas that adjust for "disadvantage" and suggest that black children cannot keep up with their Asian peers.

An Unsolved Mystery

Why do so few black students graduate from high school with strong academic skills? Black poverty, racial segregation, and inadequate funding for predominantly black schools are standard items on the list of explanations. None withstands close scrutiny. Income inequality, for instance, appears to play only a very small role in black test performance. The rise in scores after 1970 came at a time when the poverty rate was not changing significantly.[28] And when that educational progress halted, black poverty was not on the increase. In fact, Jencks and Phillips conclude, eliminating black-white income disparities would make almost no difference in the score of young black children on a basic vocabulary test. (They focus exclusively on black-white differences, ignoring the roughly similar gap between blacks and Asians.)

The huge rise in out-of-wedlock births, precipitating the steep and steady decline in the proportion of black children growing up with two parents, might seem important in explaining educational performance of African American children. Children raised in single-parent families do less well in school than others, even when all other variables, including income, are controlled.[29] But marriage, per se, appears to make little difference. "Once we control a mother's family background, test scores, and years of schooling," Jencks and Phillips conclude, "whether she is married has even less effect on her children's test scores than whether she is poor."[30] Moreover, the disintegration of the black nuclear family, noted by Daniel Patrick Moynihan as early as 1965, was occurring rapidly in the period in which black scores were rising.

Do urban schools—which a majority of black youngsters attend—lack the resources needed to educate children properly? Spending on education has risen dramatically in recent decades, and those new dollars have gone disproportionately to schools with high concentrations of economically disadvantaged children.[31] Contrary to widespread popular belief, there is little difference in average expenditures per pupil in central cities and suburbs.[32]

Nor does a school's racial mix matter after the sixth grade; it seems to affect reading scores only in the early years and math scores not at all. Scores went up from the early 1970s to the late 1980s when courts were instituting busing plans, but black students who remained in predominantly African American schools showed as much improvement as those attending integrated schools.[33] Moreover, the slide in black scores beginning in 1988 does not coincide with increasing racial isolation.[34]

The number of teachers per student, their credentials, and pay are also unaffected by the racial identity of the children in a district, Jencks and Phillips show. Schools that are mostly black, however, have teachers with lower test scores—in part because black schools have more black teachers, they forthrightly acknowledge. In addition, to the extent that schools substitute "critical thinking" for factual knowledge, those who come to school from homes that impart very little in the way of academic skills are likely to be further disadvantaged, a problem that is further compounded when, in the name of racial sensitivity, little is expected of black children.[35] Moreover, disorder in the classroom is a sure recipe for little learning.[36]

Good Schools Get Good Results

Many will argue, of course, that politicians, state boards of education, and often the public are asking too much of schools. And solid scholars like Jencks and Phillips make a strong case that "cognitive disparities between black and white preschool children are currently so large that it is hard to imagine how schools alone could eliminate them." Those skills will improve when we change the way black parents "deal with their children."[37] They suggest that social scientists take a close look at: "the way family members and friends interact with one another and the outside world"; "how much parents talk to their children, deal with their children's questions, how they react when their child learns or fails to learn something"; "cultural and psychological differences."[38]

Pessimism is seductive, but good schools with impressive results scattered across the nation suggest that educational mediocrity is the central problem. All the students at the KIPP Academy, a South Bronx public school for grades 5 through 8, are from very low-income black or Hispanic families. As the school's literature acknowledges, in the neighborhood in which these youngsters live "illiteracy, drug abuse, broken homes, gangs, and juvenile crime" are rampant. But KIPP has the highest reading and math scores of any middle school in the entire Bronx—despite the fact that two-thirds arrive in fifth grade unable to read. In math, last year, it ranked fifth in all of New York. Its daily attendance record of 96 percent is one of the highest in the whole state.[39]

KIPP's success is no mystery. All great schools have fabulous leadership, and KIPP is the brainchild of David Levin, the director, who started out as the partner of Michael Feinberg, running a sister school in Houston. The school day runs from 7:30 A.M. to 5:00 P.M., with four hours of classes on Saturdays and three weeks of mandatory attendance in the summer. (The package adds up to 67 percent more time in the classroom than the national average.) Those who chronically do not finish their homework stay even later. Teachers are available on a toll-free cell phone number from the moment they leave the school until they arrive the next morning, and many receive ten to fifteen calls a night.

KIPP aims both to prepare students for college and to change peer culture. As the school counselor put it, "We nurture feeling good about being a nerd; we tell the students, you can play basketball and read books too." Levin adds: "We train kids to look at people and talk to them. Every moment in class, teachers are role models, treating kids with respect. They dress properly. Everything about the school is designed to teach. I never walk by a student without saying hello." He knows the name of every student, speaks Spanish, and thus can talk directly to Hispanic parents with limited English.

KIPP parents sign a contract that commits them to getting their kids to school on time, helping their children to the best of their ability, and so forth. Parents know how their kids are doing through a system of student "paychecks" that also reward the students directly. Checks (in KIPP dollars) are issued weekly on the basis of teacher evaluations in ten specific areas of performance—including dress. Once a parent has endorsed the check, it can be redeemed at the school store for books, supplies, and even CDs.

Performance is linked to awards in other ways as well. Students who get 100 on a test see their names up on the classroom bulletin board. Students of the month are listed. "You can't have students feeling good about nothing," Levin says. "We make kids feel successful over little things . . . writing a complete sentence."

Not a minute of the KIPP day is wasted. When students arrive in the morning, they pick up worksheets with problems to solve while teachers are correcting homework or are otherwise occupied. If they have five minutes, they do five minutes of work. Every class is structured, and the walls are plastered with posters that, for instance, walk students through the process of writing. (Think about what you want to say, organize your thoughts, write a draft, revise, proofread.) Other posters go through the definition of an independent clause and other rules of grammar. At every grade level, students write and write and write.

The messages the school delivers on its walls and through its teachers are integral to its success. The guidance counselor talks about the dangerous culture of the streets. Everywhere there are encouraging signs: "There Are No Shortcuts"; "No Excuses"; "Be Nice!!! Work Hard!!!"; "All of Us Will Learn"; and "True Champions Always Work Hard." Other celebrated schools tell children they are loved; KIPP says something more important: self-discipline and civility will get you where you want to go.

The KIPP students I spoke to all described their previous schools as places to which they would never want to return. As one young boy put it: "We have a closer relationship with our teachers here. We all get along. There is no fighting. We learn more. In my other school, the teachers didn't care that much." A girl added: "In my old school . . . there were three fights every day. Here you would get in trouble for fighting. Why would a college want someone who doesn't behave?"

KIPP's demand that parents sign a contract of cooperation means the school, to some extent, chooses its students. And that choice is probably integral to its success. The many parochial schools that have a track record of success with black and Hispanic children also have students whose parents want them to be there.[40] But most of these same youngsters in a different educational setting would not be flourishing academically, it seems safe to say. Schools do make a difference, but they need a minimal level of parental cooperation. Michael Feinberg at Houston's KIPP believes nine out of ten low-income parents in the community with which he works would sign the contract.[41]

The American Project

"The moral pulse" beats more strongly in America than in Europe, the great Swedish economist Gunnar Myrdal noted in 1941.[42] It was a theme he often returned to. The country is "continuously struggling for its soul," he wrote in his classic 1944 work, *An American Dilemma*.[43]

Myrdal did Americans the honor of taking seriously their commitment to liberty, equality, justice, and fair opportunity. "The Negro problem," in his view, was a moral issue over which even ordinary Americans brooded in their thoughtful moments. It may not have been true then, more than half a century ago, but it is true now. Myrdal's was a prescient voice. Today, most Americans care about racial equality. In a land of plenty, they do not want African Americans left out—second-class citizens, a deprived nation within our nation. Racial equality is a moral commitment from which few dissent.

But until the day on which blacks and whites are equally well educated, that equality will remain a dream. The good news is that most eyes are now on K–12 schooling. Can we fix the schools? If KIPP and other such schools (woefully few in number) provide ground for hope, they also deliver a sobering message: most public school systems are an obstacle course that only the most extraordinary principals can negotiate. Closing the racial gap in academic achievement will require radical educational reform against which there will be much resistance. But if racial equality is the persistent American dilemma, it is also the American project. And thus, down a long road, schools will be forced to change.

Notes

1. This information on the number of states instituting reform, etc., is taken from the American Federation of Teachers' most recent annual report, *Making Standards Matter, 1999*, available only on the AFT Web site (http://www.aft.org). The report notes that "historically, states and districts haven't organized curriculum around a clearly defined set of expectations, nor have they developed assessment systems that measure whether students are meeting rigorous, publicly available standards." The AFT's 1999

report lists twenty-two states as meeting the organization's criteria for standards that are academically solid, a sharp rise from only three the year before.

2. Christopher Jencks and Meredith Phillips, eds., *The Black-White Test Score Gap* (Washington, D.C.: Brookings Institution, 1998), pp. 7, 8, figs. 1–4.

3. See Richard J. Murnane and Frank Levy, *Teaching the New Basic Skills: Principles for Educating Children to Thrive in a Changing Economy* (New York: Free Press, 1996). A more detailed technical version of their analysis is available in Richard Murnane, John Willett, and Frank Levy, "The Growing Importance of Cognitive Skills in Wage Determination," *Review of Economics and Statistics* 77 (1995): 251–66.

4. George Farkas and Keven Vicknair, "Appropriate Tests of Racial Wage Discrimination Require Controls for Cognitive Skills: Comment on Cancio, Evans, and Maume," *American Sociological Review* 61 (August 1996): 557–60. This is a critique of A. Silvia Cancio, T. David Evans, and David J. Maume, "Reconsidering the Declining Significance of Race: Racial Differences in Early Career Wages," in the same issue of the *American Sociological Review*, pp. 541–56, which had measured education crudely by levels of schooling completed. The authors' rejoinder to this critique (ibid., pp. 561–64) argues that it is inappropriate to control for education by using tests of cognitive skills because those tests are biased and really only test "exposure to the values and experiences of the White middle class" (p. 561). Employers are apparently guilty of class and racial bias if they want employees to be able to read a training manual or to calculate how many bags of grass seed and fertilizer the customer will need to make a lawn that is 60 feet long or 40 feet wide.

5. Jencks and Phillips, p. 6.

6. "Reaching the Top: A Report of the National Task Force on Minority High Achievement," College Board, 1999, p. 4.

7. Meredith Phillips et al., "Family Background, Parenting Practices, and the Black-White Test Score Gap," in Jencks and Phillips, eds., *Black-White Test Score Gap*, chap. 4. The entire chapter is an analysis of the PPVT and other data bearing on the relation between young children's cognitive skills and family background.

8. Meredith Phillips, James Crouse, and John Ralph, "Does the Black-White Test Score Gap Widen After Children Enter School," in ibid., p. 232.

9. Michael A. Fletcher, "A Good-School, Bad-School Mystery: Educators Striving to Close Racial Gap in Affluent Ohio Suburb," *Washington Post*, October 23, 1998, p. A01.

10. The College Board's contrast is actually between white and Asians on the one hand, blacks, Hispanics, and Native Americans on the other. But the performance of Hispanics (and Native Americans) is a topic for another essay.

11. College Entrance Examination Board, *1995 National Ethnic/Sex Data*, unpaginated.

12. The OCR draft guidelines, entitled "Nondiscrimination in High-Stakes Testing: A Resource Guide," were first issued on May 17, 1999. They came close to equating

disparate impact and discrimination, intimating that high-stakes tests of any sort could be used only if the consequences of getting a low score would not be the same for blacks and Hispanics as for whites and Asians. In mid-December a revised and softened version was leaked to the *Chronicle of Higher Education* (Patrick Healy, "Education Department Softens Its Tone in Latest Draft of Guide to Using Test Scores in Admissions," Dec. 13, 1999); as this essay is being written, the full text is not available.

13. Patrick Healy, "Affirmative Action Defenders Push Colleges to Back Draft Guidelines on Testing," *Chronicle of Higher Education*, June 25, 1999, p. A42. Edley's ringing defense of the guidelines referred to the harsher version issued in May.

14. Julie Blair, "NAACP Criticizes Colleges' Use of SAT, ACT," *Education Week*, December 1, 1999, p. 10.

15. William G. Bowen and Derek Bok, *The Shape of the River: Long-Term Consequences of Considering Race in College and University Admissions* (Princeton, N.J.: Princeton University Press, 1998), is a brief on behalf of racial preferences and thus argues for the admission of black and Hispanic students with academic credentials weaker than those of their Asian and white peers accepted to highly competitive schools. Nevertheless, the authors acknowledge the underperformance of black college students relative to their SAT scores: "The average rank in class for black students is appreciably lower than the average rank in class for white students *within each SAT interval. . . .* It is one strong indication of a troubling phenomenon often called 'underperformance.' Black students with the same SAT scores as whites tend to earn lower grades"; p. 77, italics theirs.

16. News of what ETS called its "Strivers" program surfaced in the *Wall Street Journal* on August 31, 1999, and was subsequently picked up by other publications. It was an unfinished project, although ETS was willing on the record to discuss the central idea. For more detail, see "The End of Meritocracy: A Debate on Affirmative Action, the S.A.T., and the Future of American Excellence" between Nathan Glazer and Abigail Thernstrom, *New Republic*, September 27, 1999, pp. 26–29.

17. Deborah Meier, *Will Standards Save Public Education?* (Boston: Beacon Press, 2000), foreword by Jonathan Kozol, p. xi.

18. Meier, ibid., p. 85.

19. Theodore Sizer, "A Sense of Place," responding to Meier, ibid., p. 72.

20. Rob Hotakainen, "Calling Graduation Tests Harsh, Wellstone Offers Alternative Plan," Minneapolis *Star Tribune*, April 4, 2000, p. 1A.

21. The "respect and confidence" question was asked in a 1999 Gallup poll; the judgment about "low academic standards" was made in response to a Peter D. Hart Research Associates 1988 survey; Public Agenda polled employers in 1988. The poll of black parents is reported in Steve Farkas and Jean Johnson, "Time to Move On: African-Americans and White Parents Set an Agenda for Public Schools," A Report from Public Agenda, 1998, p. 17.

22. Peter Sacks, *Standardized Minds: The High Price of America's Testing Culture and What We Can Do About It* (Cambridge, Mass.: Perseus, 2000), p. 6.

23. Todd S. Purdum, "A 'Pied Piper' Is Shaking Up the Schools in Los Angeles," *New York Times*, April 15, 2000, p. A7.

24. "Ticket to Nowhere: The Gap Between Leaving High School and Entering College and High-Performance Jobs," in *Thinking K–16* (a publication of the Education Trust) 3, no. 2 (fall 1999): 2.

25. Letter to the *New York Times*, April 16, 2000, sect. 4, p. 14.

26. *Standardized Minds*, p. 5.

27. Kate Zernike, "Regents Vote to Rank Schools, Weighing Performance of Minority Students," *New York Times*, May 5, 2000, p. A23.

28. U.S. Bureau of the Census, Current Population Reports, pp. 60–189, *Income, Poverty, and Valuation of Noncash Benefits: 1994* (Washington, D.C.: U.S. Government Printing Office, 1996), table B-6.

29. See Sara McLanahan and Gary Sandefur, *Growing Up with a Single Parent: What Hurts, What Helps* (Cambridge, Mass.: Harvard University Press, 1994).

30. Jencks and Phillips, *Black-White Test Score Gap*, p. 10 and chap. 4.

31. Between the 1969–70 school year and 1995–96, nationwide expenditures per pupil (in constant '95–'96 dollars) rose from $3,337 to $6,146, a gain of 84 percent. In the same period, per capita income (in constant dollars) rose by only 46 percent; *1998 Digest of Educational Statistics*, p. 183; *1998 Statistical Abstract of the United States*, p. 476. Since the passage of the Elementary and Secondary Education Act (ESEA) in 1965, the federal government has spent $118 billion on making sure poverty ceased to be "a bar to learning"—although with results no one celebrates. For an excellent discussion of Title I of the ESEA, see George Farkas, "Can Title I Attain Its Goal?" paper prepared for presentation at a Brookings Institution conference, May 17, 1999.

32. National Center for Education Statistics, *Disparities in Public School District Spending, 1989–1990*, NCES 95-300 (Washington, D.C.: U.S. Government Printing Office, 1995), p. 15. William N. Evans has also tabulated census data for 1972, 1982, and 1992 and concluded that the average black student and average white student both live in districts that spend just under $5,400 per pupil. Evans, Sheila Murray, and Robert Schwab, "School Houses, Court Houses, and State Houses After *Serrano*," *Journal of Policy Analysis and Management*, January 1997, pp. 10–31.

33. David J. Armor, *Forced Justice: School Desegregation and the Law* (New York: Oxford University Press, 1995), pp. 92–98.

34. On the stability of de facto segregation, see *America in Black and White*, chap. 12.

35. E. D. Hirsch Jr., *The Schools We Need and Why We Don't Have Them* (New York: Doubleday, 1996), pp. 43, 54. Shelby Steele has made the point with particular eloquence about low expectations packaged as racial sensitivity. Even minimal academic

demands, he argues, are often stymied by a deep and painful sense of "racial vulnerability" that whites and blacks share. The vulnerability of whites is to the charge of racism, that of blacks is to the claim of inferiority. In different ways both are wracked by powerful doubts about their own self-worth. See "The Race Not Run," *New Republic,* October 7, 1996, p. 23. *The Content of Our Character: A New Vision of Race in America* (New York: St. Martin's Press, 1990) makes the argument at much greater length.

36. On chaos and violence in the schools, see Abigail Thernstrom, "Courting Disorder in the Schools," *Public Interest* 136 (summer 1999): 18–34.

37. Jencks and Phillips, eds., pp. 24, 45, 46. The College Board task force also refers to the "cultural attributes of home, community, and school" and talks at length about the attitudes toward school and toward hard work that Asian parents transmit to their children. "Reaching the Top," pp. 14, 17–18.

38. Jencks and Phillips, eds., p. 43.

39. All the information on KIPP comes from the author's three visits to the school, from the literature the school provides, and from Samuel Casey Carter, *No Excuses: Lessons from 21 High-Performing High-Poverty Schools* (Washington, D.C.: Heritage Foundation, 2000).

40. Scholars have been looking closely at the record of Catholic schools for decades; there is solid research tracing the sources of their success with inner-city students. See, for instance, Anthony S. Bryk, Valerie E. Lee, and Paul B. Holland, *Catholic Schools and the Common Good* (Cambridge, Mass.: Harvard University Press, 1993); James S. Coleman and Thomas Hoffer, *Public and Private High Schools: The Impact of Communities* (New York: Basic Books, 1987). All the experimental voucher programs are being carefully watched as well. For a summary of the evidence on vouchers as of 1998, see the collection of essays in Paul E. Peterson and Bryan C. Hassel, eds., *Learning from School Choice* (Washington, D.C.: Brookings Institution, 1998).

41. Personal communication with Michael Feinberg.

42. Quoted in Walter A. Jackson, *Gunnar Myrdal and America's Conscience: Social Engineering & Racial Liberalism, 1938–1987* (Chapel Hill: University of North Carolina Press, 1990), p. 151. The quotation was from *Kontakt med Amerika,* a book co-authored with Myrdal's wife, Alva, but Jackson attributes the sections on race solely to Gunnar Myrdal.

43. Gunnar Myrdal, *An American Dilemma* (New York: McGraw-Hill paperback ed., 1964), p. 4.

Schools That Work
for Minority Students

CLINT BOLICK

HYSTERIA FOLLOWED the plummeting admission rates of blacks and Hispanics at elite public universities in California and Texas following the curtailment of race and ethnic preferences.[1] The concern was appropriate but overdue and misdirected. Critics claimed that the demise of race-based "affirmative action" meant the end of college opportunities for many blacks and Hispanics.[2]

In reality, the enrollment decline was a long-overdue wake-up call to a dire crisis that seemingly has escaped the attention of many public policy makers and the establishment civil rights groups: the appalling failure of the nation's public school system to deliver quality educational opportunities to a large portion of America's schoolchildren. Though concentrated primarily on economically disadvantaged youngsters in the inner cities, that failure manifests itself in disproportionately poor academic credentials for black and Hispanic students. In a nondiscriminatory college admissions process, that disparity leads to lower admissions rates for blacks and Hispanics; by contrast, in a system where blacks and Hispanics are leapfrogged over more qualified applicants into academic institutions for which they are not adequately prepared, it leads to disproportionately higher college dropout rates for the two groups.

No substitute exists for high standards and adequate academic preparation at the elementary and secondary school levels, and we are perpetuating a cruel hoax to assert otherwise. Race-based affirmative action in college admissions is a purely cosmetic response that allows underlying educational problems to fester and grow. An immigrant cabdriver recently distilled the policy dilemma: "They don't understand that the problem is not in college. The problem is in kindergarten." Removing the superficial tool of racial preferences from the policy-making arsenal means that policy makers must address at last the core problems that produce racial and ethnic disparities in higher education.

Traditional "civil rights" responses to educational inequality have focused on (1) racial balancing through forced busing or other mechanisms or (2) increased spending. Both approaches have failed utterly to close the gap in educational achievement.[3] Fortunately, promising alternatives are appearing on the horizon, focusing not on social engineering but on parental empowerment. By giving parents—who have the greatest stake in their children's success—greater power over education decisions and resources, it appears we finally can deliver on the sacred promise of equal educational opportunities for all of America's schoolchildren.[4]

Educational Crisis and Systemic Failure

It seems impossible that nearly forty-five years have passed since *Brown v. Board of Education*. During that time, much progress has been made toward erasing the color line from education. As Stephan and Abigail Thernstrom report in *America in Black and White*, high school graduation rates now are nearly the same for blacks and whites. Progress for blacks in this regard has been explosive: in 1980, only 51.2 percent of blacks over age 25 had graduated from high school; but by 1995, 73.8 percent of blacks over 25—and 86.5 percent of blacks between the ages of 25 and 29—were high school graduates; college attendance rates are up, too, from 21.9 percent of blacks in 1980 to 37.5 percent in 1995.[5] Those gains are important because education correlates closely with income. For instance, black women who have graduated from high school, attended some college, or graduated from college all make more money on average than their white female counterparts.[6]

But from there the news gets bad. Although black high school students steadily were closing the achievement gap with whites in the 1980s, that gap has widened substantially during the past decade. The typical black high school student graduates roughly four academic years behind typical white high school seniors.[7] The National Assessment of Educational Progress (NAEP) reported in 1995 that only 12 percent of black high school seniors (compared with 40 percent of whites) were proficient in reading.[8] The 1997 NAEP found that while 76 percent of white fourth-graders were proficient in basic mathematics skills, only 41 percent of Hispanic and 32 percent of black students demonstrated basic proficiency.[9]

The crisis is far more pronounced and debilitating among low-income minority children, who are consigned disproportionately to failing large urban school systems. Students often must pass through metal detectors and literally risk their lives on a daily basis for the chance to obtain a woefully substandard education. Two cities where I have litigated present the problem in especially graphic terms. In Cleveland, the numbers 1 in 14 are emblazoned permanently on my memory: children in the Cleveland Public Schools have a 1-in-14 chance of graduating on time from high school at senior-level proficiency—and an equivalent 1-in-14 chance each year of being a victim of crime in the schools. In the Milwaukee Public Schools (MPS), only 48 percent of the students graduate—a dropout rate more than seven times the statewide average—and only 15 percent of children from families on public assistance graduate. In eleven Milwaukee public high schools that enroll more than three-fourths of the city's black students, the median grade-point average is less than 1.5 on a four-point scale.

When poor and minority inner-city students have no greater chance of graduating with basic proficiency than of being a victim of crime in the schools, we know the system is failing. With statistics like these, what is surprising is not that minority schoolchildren are admitted to colleges and universities at rates lower than their proportionate share; what is surprising is that the numbers are not much, much worse.

Apologists for the status quo search frenetically for scapegoats: standardized tests are biased, the students are too poor to educate, their parents don't provide sufficient support, the schools are inadequately funded.[10] Yet students from identical socioeconomic circumstances do much better in private schools. A recent study by University of Chicago economist Derek Neal found that although Catholic schools produce negligible academic gains for suburban and white students, they strongly improve educational outcomes for urban minority children. Holding other factors constant, Neal found that the odds of high school graduation for urban black and Hispanic children increase from 66 percent to at least 88 percent in Catholic schools. In turn, he found that three times as many black students who attend Catholic high schools go on to graduate from college. Not surprisingly, those academic gains translate into substantially higher wages in the labor market. Neal concludes bluntly, "Urban minorities receive significant benefits from Catholic schooling because their public school alternatives are substantially worse than those of whites or other minorities who live in rural or suburban areas."[11]

Why do suburban public schools and urban private schools do a relatively good job in educating children, while urban public school systems as a whole are failures? That question was addressed in a pathbreaking Brookings Institution study by John E. Chubb and Terry M. Moe.[12] They found that although student ability and parental background are important factors in student achievement, school organization also plays a central role. The key differences between effective and ineffective schools are autonomy, parental involvement, and a sense of mission. Urban public schools, Chubb and Moe observed, are characterized by massive bureaucracies that make it difficult for teachers to teach, for parents to exert influence, or for reform to take hold. Moreover, because poor students usually have nowhere else to go, large urban school systems are unresponsive to consumer demands and instead try to satisfy special-interest groups and politicians who control the purse strings. Meanwhile, parents have little influence, particularly on an individual basis. Private and suburban public schools, by contrast, tend to have smaller bureaucracies and to be more responsive to parental concerns, in part because parents have the resources to take their children elsewhere. Chubb and Moe found that effective schools boost student achievement by one year for every four. They concluded that greater parental choice and control over resources are necessary for low-income parents to improve their children's education and to effectively prod public schools to improve.

The Catalyst: Parental Choice

Those were the goals State Representative Annette Polly Williams had in mind when she proposed the Milwaukee Parental Choice Program, the nation's first school choice program targeted to inner-city, low-income families. The program initially was modest in scope: only 1 percent of Milwaukee Public School students (roughly 1,000) were eligible to use their share of the state's education contribution as full payment of tuition in nine participating nonsectarian private schools. But the implementation of the program in the fall of 1990 set off an education revolution. For the first time ever, the program transferred control over public education funds from bureaucrats to parents and forced the public schools to compete for low-income youngsters and the resources they commanded.

Predictably, the program prompted litigation by the teachers' union and a blizzard of regulations designed to destroy the program by bureaucratic strangulation. Both counterattacks were beaten back.[13] So in the fall of 1990, nearly one thousand low-income youngsters were able to cross the threshold to a brighter educational future in a dozen or so nonsectarian community private schools.

The assessments by the state's designated researcher, John Witte, produced odd findings over the program's first four years: parental involvement was strong, satisfaction was high, but student achievement failed to

rise. Those results were seemingly contradictory, given that parental involvement and student achievement are closely linked. That conundrum
was magnified by Witte's refusal to release data to other researchers.[14]

The confusion dissipated when a team of researchers led by Harvard
University political scientist Paul E. Peterson finally obtained the data. For
the first time, they compared achievement of students who had gained
access to private schools through the random selection process with students who had not. The result: little academic change over the students'
first two years in the program, but significant progress in the third and
fourth years. Peterson found that over its first four years, the program
narrowed the gap between minority and nonminority test scores by between one-third and one-half—an absolutely momentous accomplishment.[15]

Zakiyah Courtney, director of Milwaukee's Parents for School Choice
and former principal of Urban Day School, testified:

> I was glad to see . . . a study that reflected what many of us who have been
> working directly with the families and the children all along knew. And that
> is that parental satisfaction does make a difference; and that oftentimes you
> may not see those high achievement scores in the beginning, but if you give
> those children the opportunity to stay and work in the program, that you
> do see those differences.[16]

But apart from its benefits for kids for whose parents now can choose
better schools, the program unquestionably has also had a positive impact
on the public schools, forcing them to pursue long-overdue systemic reforms. At an evidentiary hearing on the program in 1996, both former MPS
superintendent Dr. Howard L. Fuller, and his successor, Robert Jasna,
agreed that the program had created a prod for long-overdue systemic
reforms.[17] Fuller supported the program's expansion in 1995 to increase
the number of eligible children to 15,000 and to allow religious schools to
participate. Fuller explained:

> I think that what it will bring into play would be, in addition to the existing
> schools, there will be new schools out there that will come into being that

will find their niche to begin to teach kids that we are not currently reaching or that we're losing. I think it will begin to give poor parents some capacity to have leverage over this entire discussion. And the reason they will have leverage is because they will begin to have leverage over resources, the same type of control over resources that people with money have. . . . You begin to create a synergism for change that I think is key, if the system is going to be changed, so that we . . . save these kids that we're losing each and every day.[18]

The Milwaukee program's expansion was enjoined before it could go into operation in the fall of 1995 as a result of litigation brought by the teachers' union, the American Civil Liberties Union, the National Association for the Advancement of Colored People (NAACP), and others, who asserted that the program violated the prohibition of religious establishment in the state and federal constitutions. (Similar lawsuits are pending against school choice programs in Ohio, Vermont, Arizona, Maine, and Pennsylvania.) In June 1998, the program was upheld by the Wisconsin Supreme Court, setting up possible resolution of the constitutional issue by the U.S. Supreme Court.[19] In the fall of 1998, the expansion of the Milwaukee program finally commenced, with an estimated 6,000 low-income youngsters attending more than eighty private religious and non-sectarian schools.[20]

Meanwhile, a second school choice program championed by Governor George Voinovich and City Councilmember Fannie Lewis was created in 1996, providing $2,500 scholarships to approximately 3,000 economically disadvantaged children, allowing them to attend private secular and religious schools in Cleveland. Again, early results appear promising.[21] Similar promising results are also reported in privately funded scholarship programs serving low-income schoolchildren in dozens of other cities across the country.[22] As Paul Peterson has observed, "The choice movement is spreading in good part because its theoretical underpinnings seem more powerful than ever."[23]

Other forms of parental choice are blossoming. Arizona, which boasts the nation's most wide-ranging charter school system, approved a $500 state income tax credit for contributions to private scholarship funds, which was upheld by the Arizona Supreme Court.[24] In May 1999, a bipartisan majority of the Florida Legislature enacted Governor Jeb Bush's A+ public education reform program, within which parental choice is an important element. The program creates a grading system for all public schools in the state, provides financial rewards for excellent schools, gives extra help to students in failing schools, and allows families whose children are in failing schools to opt out into better public schools or private schools. In essence, the program offers the first money-back guarantee by creating both choice and competition that should improve public education for everyone. It emphasizes that the proper concern of public education is not *where* children are educated but *whether* they are educated. The threat of scholarships also is spurring spirited efforts among public school districts to improve schools that are receiving "F" grades.[25]

Still, a school choice program for the District of Columbia, approved in 1998 by bipartisan majorities in both houses of Congress, was vetoed by President Clinton, in spite of support from a large majority of residents, particularly blacks. Powerful special interest groups have combined to stifle parental choice all around the nation. The question is how long those defenders of the status quo can delay the day of reckoning with America's most urgent crisis—and how many children's lives and educational opportunities will be sacrificed in the process.

Parental Choice and Public Opinion

Public opinion is moving strongly and steadily in favor of parental choice. There are several possible explanations: (1) In spite of massive financial resources and constant excuses from the education establishment, the academic performance of public schools, even in affluent suburbs, is declining, particularly compared with schools in other industrialized nations. (2) The news about parental choice programs such as school vouchers and charter schools is generally promising; reality is debunking the fears raised by choice opponents. (3) Changing demographics are influencing public opinion: young people with children are used to making choices and are comfortable about selecting from an array of educational options.

Whatever the explanation, the trend is unmistakable. For the first time, the 1998 Phi Delta Kappa–Gallup poll found that a majority of Americans support parental choice. Asked whether they favor allowing parents to send their school-age children to any public, parochial, or private school of their choice with the government paying part or all of the tuition, 51 percent of all respondents support choice, while 45 percent are opposed. Only two years ago, the same idea was opposed by a margin of 54 to 43 percent. Among the groups who most strongly support parental options are non-whites (68 percent), people 18–29 years of age (63 percent), and, notably, public school parents (56 percent).[26]

Support for parental choice is even greater in Wisconsin, which has had eight years of experience with the Milwaukee program. A 1998 poll by Louis Harris & Associates found that Wisconsin residents support parental choice by a margin of 61 to 32 percent.[27] Parental choice draws majority support in all areas of the state and from whites, blacks, men, women, Republicans, Democrats, independents, conservatives, and liberals. The margin in Milwaukee is 65 to 29 percent, and residents back the Milwaukee Parental Choice Program specifically by an even greater 71 to 24 percent. The closer people reside to the program, the more likely they appear to support parental choice.

What is perhaps most remarkable, and disturbing, is the chasm between mainstream minority individuals and establishment civil rights organizations on issues over parental choice. Black Americans consider education the top national priority.[28] That concern is well placed. A 1997 survey by the Joint Center for Political and Economic Studies found that while 37.5 percent of white parents considered their schools "fair" or "poor," 64 percent of blacks and 61 percent of Hispanics gave their schools the same low grades. Not surprisingly, the poll found that while support for school choice was evenly split among whites, it was strong among both blacks (56 to 37.5 percent in favor) and Hispanics (65 to 29 percent in favor). Support for school choice was most intense among those in the age bracket most likely to have school-age children: 86.5 percent of blacks between ages 26–35 back school choice, with only 10 percent opposed.[29]

Similarly, a *Washington Post* poll found that a large majority of District of Columbia residents backed the low-income scholarship program passed by Congress but vetoed by President Clinton and opposed by liberal black politicians such as Delegate Eleanor Holmes Norton.[30] The residents supported the scholarship program by a margin of 56 to 36 percent. While whites and blacks with incomes over $50,000 split fairly evenly over the issue, lower-income blacks favored the legislation by a margin of 65 to 28 percent. "I would jump at the chance to send my son to private school," said Janice Johnson, who lives in one of the poorer sections of the city. Meanwhile, 1,001 low-income children from among more than 7,500 applicants received support from the Washington Scholarship Fund, which is financed by businessmen Theodore J. Forstmann and John Walton.[31]

In light of strong minority support for school choice, there is little wonder that establishment civil rights groups such as the NAACP are struggling for relevancy. The Milwaukee NAACP chapter joined the lawsuit against the Milwaukee Parental Choice Program in spite of overwhelming support for the program among black city residents. The national NAACP last year announced an unholy alliance against parental choice with People for the American Way. Parental Choice is "exploitative of the black community," contends Mary Jean Collins, PAW's national field director. "The philosophy of the right is always, 'Give my kid what he wants and to hell with the rest.' For that attitude to get into the black community would be shameful."[32]

Dissenters such as the Urban League of Greater Miami and former Atlanta mayor and U.N. ambassador Andrew Young reject such patronizing attitudes and support school choice as an essential component of civil rights. Former representative Floyd Flake, whose church in Queens, New York, operates a private school, says: "When a white person kills a black person, we all go out in the street to protest. But our children are being educationally killed every day in public schools and nobody says a thing."[33]

It is time for politicians to recognize the will of the people, to reject the entreaties of special-interest groups, and to make parental choice a reality.

The Broader Context of Education Reform

Never has the climate for reform been so vibrant—nor the need for reform so urgent. In addition to parental choice encompassing private schools, promising reforms include (1) charter schools, which are autonomous public schools often operated by private or nonprofit entities;[34] (2) contracting out public schools to private management firms such as the Edison Project;[35] and (3) tax deductions and credits that allow people to deduct their children's education costs or to contribute to privately funded scholarship funds.[36]

Meanwhile, private philanthropy is working to meet demand from low-income parents to secure better education for their children through programs like the Children's Scholarship Fund and CEO America. In April 1999, 1.25 million children applied for 40,000 CSF scholarships. Andrew Young likened the outpouring to Rosa Parks's refusal to give up her bus seat and to Martin Luther King Jr.'s letter from a Birmingham jail. Declared Young:

> If families were allowed to seek a quality education wherever it may be found, who would benefit? Simple: Those who aren't getting a quality education and those who can deliver it. Certainly, some will oppose competition—just as AT&T once fought the breakup of its monopoly. Others will reflexively resist the redistribution of power to poor families. Still others will wave their worn-out ideologies to defend a system of educational apartheid while demonizing anyone who promotes a parent's right to choose. . . .
>
> I predict that we will one day look back on the 1.25 million who applied for educational emancipation—for the chance to seek the light and oxygen of a nourishing education—not as victims, but as unwitting heroes with whom a great awakening was begun.[37]

Parental choice is a central facet of systemic education reform that places equal resources behind each child and allows the funds to follow children to whatever schools—public, private, or religious—their parents choose.[38] Child-centered education funding transforms the focus of public education from public schools as ends in themselves to publicly funded education in whatever schools parents deem best. If parents choose public schools, the funds stay in those schools under the control of the schools themselves, rather than filtering down through an education bureaucracy. Only through a system of choice, competition, and accountability where parents are sovereign will public schools in the inner cities begin to improve.

If we can do only one thing in public policy to improve prospects for minority individuals and economically disadvantaged people, there is nothing more tangible or important than making good on the promise of equal educational opportunities. As I have acknowledged before, if I were given the option, straight up or down, of abolishing racial preferences or adopting parental choice on a nationwide basis, in a heartbeat I would opt for the latter, for it would reduce the pressure for divisive race-based solutions. Unfortunately, no one is offering that choice: the same reactionary leaders who support racial preferences are blocking the schoolhouse doors for the very people whose interests they falsely claim to represent.

That won't last long. Nothing that Jesse Jackson, Kweisi Mfume, Bill Clinton, Al Gore, or others like them can say to inner-city parents will convince them not to pursue educational opportunities their children desperately need. Milwaukee parent Pilar Gonzalez makes that plain: "I will find a way to have my children attend private school even if it means less food on the table. A quality education for my children is that important."[39]

That is the primary civil rights goal of the millennium: making it possible at last for Pilar Gonzalez and millions of others like her to secure the best possible education for their children.

Notes

The author expresses appreciation to Daron Roberts, a University of Texas student who interned at the Institute for Justice in the summer of 1998, for research assistance.

1. The end of racial preferences in California was attributable first to a decision to curb preferential admissions policies by the Regents of the University of California, which subsequently was extended by the California Civil Rights Initiative (Proposition 209) to all public postsecondary schools. In Texas, the cessation of preferences was due to the decision striking down preferential admissions at the University of Texas School of Law in *Hopwood v. Texas*, 78 F.3d 932 (5th Cir.), *cert. denied*, 116 S.Ct. 2850 (1986).

2. In any event, that prediction has now definitively been discredited. See, e.g., James Traub, "The Class of Prop. 209," *New York Times Magazine*, May 2, 1999, p. 44.

3. For an examination of the effects of forced busing, see David J. Armor, *Forced Justice: School Desegregation and the Law* (New York: Oxford University Press, 1995). For a discussion of the lack of correlation between increased educational performance, particularly in the context of the lavish Kansas City desegregation decree, see Blake Hurst, "Runaway Judge," *American Enterprise*, May–June 1995, pp. 53–56.

4. In *Brown v. Board of Education*, 347 U.S. 483, 493 (1954), the U.S. Supreme Court declared that education, "where the state has undertaken to provide it, is a right which must be made available to all on equal terms."

5. Stephan Thernstrom and Abigail Thernstrom, *America in Black and White: One Nation, Indivisible* (New York: Simon & Schuster, 1997), pp. 190–91, 192.

6. Ibid., p. 445.

7. Ibid., p. 355.

8. See Dennis Kelly, "Kids' Scores for Reading 'In Trouble,'" *USA Today*, April 28–30, 1995, p. 1A.

9. See "U.S. Students Make Progress in Math," *Dallas Morning News*, February 28, 1997, p. 6A.

10. In fact, like many other large urban school districts, the Milwaukee and Cleveland districts spend more per pupil than the statewide averages.

11. Derek Neal, "The Effects of Catholic Secondary Schooling on Educational Achievement," *Journal of Labor Economics* 15: 100. Neal's findings echo similar studies from the 1980s. See James Coleman, Thomas Hoffer, and Sally Kilgore, *High School Achievement: Public, Catholic, and Private Schools Compared* (New York: Basic Books, 1982); and Andrew Greeley, *Catholic High Schools and Minority Students* (London: Transaction, 1982). Recent evidence indicates that Hispanic students, too, fare better in Catholic schools. See Anne-Marie O'Connor, "Many Latinos Fare Better in Catholic Schools," *Los Angeles Times*, August 3, 1998.

12. John E. Chubb and Terry M. Moe, *Politics, Markets, and America's Schools* (Washington, D.C.: Brookings Institution, 1990).

13. See *Davis v. Grover*, 480 N.W.2d 460 (Wisc. 1992).

14. Witte subsequently has concluded that the results of limited school choice are favorable. See John F. Witte, *The Market Approach to Education: An Analysis of America's First Voucher Program* (Princeton, N.J.: Princeton University Press, 2000).

15. Jay P. Green, Paul E. Peterson, and Jingtao Du, *The Effectiveness of School Choice in Milwaukee: A Secondary Analysis of Data from the Program's Evaluation* (Cambridge, Mass.: Harvard University John F. Kennedy School of Government, 1996).

16. Transcript of Evidentiary Hearing, *Jackson v. Benson*, No. 95-CV-1982 (Dane County, Wisc., Circuit Court, Aug. 15, 1996), p. 77.

17. Ibid., pp. 48, 165.

18. Ibid., p. 51.

19. *Jackson v. Benson*, 578 N.W.2d 602 (Wisc. 1998).

20. See Jon Jeter, "As Test of Vouchers, Milwaukee Parochial School Exceeds Expectations," *Washington Post*, August 31, 1998.

21. See Jay P. Greene, William G. Howell, and Paul E. Peterson, "Lessons from the Cleveland Scholarship Program," in Paul E. Peterson and Bryan J. Hassel, eds., *Learning from School Choice* (Washington, D.C.: Brookings Institution, 1998), p. 357.

22. See, e.g., R. Kenneth Godwin, Frank R. Kemerer, and Valerie J. Martinez, "Comparing Public Choice and Private Voucher Programs in San Antonio," in ibid., p. 275; and David J. Weinschrott and Sally B. Kilgore, "Evidence from the Indianapolis Voucher Program," in ibid., p. 307.

23. Paul E. Peterson, "School Choice: A Report Card," in ibid., p. 8.

24. *Kotterman v. Killian*, 972 P.2d 606 (Ariz. 1999).

25. Carol Innerst, *Competing to Win: How Florida's A+ Plan Has Triggered Public School Reform* (2000). (This report was copublished by five groups.)

26. *The 30th Annual Phi Delta Kappa–Gallup Poll of the Public's Attitudes Toward the Public Schools* (1998). The poll surveyed attitudes about a wide range of parental choice alternatives. The pollsters found that one proposal championed primarily by Republicans—tax credits for private school tuition—actually is supported by a higher percentage of Democrats (by 61 to 37 percent in favor) than by Republicans (57 to 42 percent in favor).

27. Louis S. Harris & Associates, Inc., "Wisconsin Residents Strongly Favor Voucher System and Choice," news release, August 17, 1998.

28. A survey conducted November 5–7, 1996, by the Polling Company found that a large plurality of blacks (42 percent) considered education the top national priority, compared with 25 percent of whites. Fighting crime and drugs was the second top priority for blacks (21 percent).

29. See David A. Bositis, *1997 National Opinion Poll: Children's Issues* (Washington, D.C.: Joint Center for Political and Economic Studies, 1997).

30. See Sari Horwitz, "Poll Finds Backing for D.C. School Vouchers," *Washington Post*, May 23, 1998, p. F1.

31. Debbi Wilgoren, "1,001 D.C. Students Win Scholarships," ibid., April 30, 1998, p. B1.

32. Quoted in Samuel G. Freedman, "The Education Divide," *Salon Magazine*, September 30, 1997.

33. Quoted in ibid.

34. Several dozen states permit charter schools, although some jurisdictions (such as Arizona, Michigan, and the District of Columbia) provide for far greater autonomy than others. See, e.g., Clint Bolick, *Transformation: The Promise and Politics of Empowerment* (Oakland, Calif.: Institute for Contemporary Studies, 1998), pp. 53–60; Bruno Manno, Chester E. Finn Jr., and Louann A. Bierlein, "Charter Schools as Seen by Students, Teachers, and Parents," in Peterson and Hassel, eds., p. 275; and Bryan J. Hassel, "Charter Schools: Politics and Practice in Four States," in Peterson and Hassel, p. 249.

35. See, e.g., John E. Chubb, "The Performance of Privately Managed Schools: An Early Look at the Edison Project," in Peterson and Hassel, eds., p. 213.

36. In addition to the Arizona state income tax credit for contributions to private scholarship funds, Minnesota provides tax deductions for school tuition, and both houses of the Illinois legislature passed a tax credit for tuition in 1999.

37. Andrew Young, "Let Parents Choose Their Kids' Schools," *Los Angeles Times*, April 29, 1999, p. 9.

38. The concept of child-centered education funding is championed most prominently by Arizona Superintendent of Public Instruction Lisa Graham Keegan. See, e.g., Clint Bolick, "Charter Reformer: Arizona's Superintendent of Schools Points the Way to an Education Revolution," *National Review*, April 6, 1998, pp. 42–44.

39. Quoted in Bolick, *Transformation*, p. 34. Ms. Gonzalez is one of the parents defending the constitutionality of the Milwaukee Parental Choice Program, and I am proud to represent her.

Preferential Admissions in Higher Education

MARTIN TROW

THE HISTORICAL and legal development of racial preferences in higher education, as well as their impact, have been extensively analyzed.[1] This essay approaches the issue from a somewhat different vantage point, exploring how race-based preferences operate as they are actually administered in a university setting. Universities are little affected by Supreme Court decisions, the state of race relations generally, or broad public opinion about "affirmative action" and the extent of discrimination in the larger society. On campus, the leading players are the presidents, chancellors, deans, department chairmen, and the affirmative action bureaucracy that has emerged in response to the need to implement various affirmative action laws and regulations. In describing the picture inside the academy, I draw chiefly on material gathered in the course of watching the dramatic events surrounding the public policies affecting university admissions in California since July 1995, when the University of California Board of Regents voted to prohibit the use of race or ethnicity in admissions and appointments.

It is important to note that the issue of racial preferences in admissions to universities and colleges arises only in those institutions that have more applicants than they can admit. This group includes no more than a hundred or so out of the 3,700 colleges and universities in the United States, but it consists of the leading research universities, both public and private, as well as a few dozen elite private liberal arts colleges that function as feeder institutions for graduate and professional schools. The private research universities—Yale, for example—and elite colleges like Amherst and Swarthmore typically choose their students for admission largely on the basis of academic performance and promise, although decisions are made on a case-by-case basis. To secure greater "diversity," they look with special favor on applicants from certain "underrepresented" racial and ethnic groups. By contrast, the big public research universities admit most undergraduates according to general criteria and formulas. In seeking to secure a racially and ethnically diverse student body, they must specify exactly how much weight is to be given to racial and ethnic considerations.

Admissions Procedures at the University of California

The baseline formula for admission to the University of California has been prescribed by the state's Master Plan for higher education, virtually unchanged since it was drawn up in the 1950s. It defines "eligibility" for admission to the university as ranking in the top 12.5 percent in academic achievement of graduates of California public high schools. The top 12.5 percent is identified by a formula that combines the student's high school grade point average and his or her combined math and verbal SAT scores. In addition, the Regents have allowed each of the eight campuses that make up the system to admit up to 6 percent of their entering classes without regard for the 12.5 percent standard. This arrangement for admission by "special action" permitted many athletes who were not top students to enter, as well as students with unusual forms of preparation or talent— for example, outstanding musicians and those who were educated at home or abroad. Before the statewide ban on racial preferences in admissions, many of these discretionary places were used to admit students from "underrepresented" racial and ethnic groups who failed to qualify under the regular requirements.

In the 1980s and early 1990s, a number of the UC's eight "general campuses" found that they had more, and in some cases many more, eligible applicants than they could admit. The solution was to allow each individual school to adopt a policy somewhat independent of the statewide criteria, out of which came explicitly preferential policies. The formulas differed on the several campuses. With the approval of the Regents, Berkeley decided to admit half the entering class on the basis of their scores on the combined SAT/GPA. In filling the other half, *all* eligible minority applicants were automatically admitted. But critics charged the school with having adopted a quota or "set-aside" for minority applicants, and in 1989 it abandoned the guarantee of admission for all eligible applicants from minority groups. Yet it continued to give a huge advantage to black and Hispanic applicants. The average black student admitted, for example, had SAT scores 250–300 points lower than his or her white and Asian classmates and a substantially weaker high school grade record as well.

These students were not necessarily "disadvantaged" by any nonracial criteria. Berkeley, for example, was especially attractive to the sons and daughters of the new black middle class; in 1995, 30 percent of black undergraduates came from families earning over $70,000. It was a troubling fact. Admissions decisions, especially in public institutions, must appear as legitimate to those not admitted to their campus of choice, the parents of future applicants, and the general public. The legitimacy of the institution, supported by taxpayer dollars, depends on criteria for entrance that are perceived as fair. And yet most Americans do not believe in judging citizens on the basis of the color of their skin.

Those convictions have prevailed in California. The Regents' vote to ban preferences in 1995 and the passage of Proposition 209 a year later brought a halt to all race-based admission procedures. Today, UC Berkeley is developing a selection policy based on a reading of all applicant files rather than a statistical formula, a more individualized system like those used by private universities.

Fair Criteria

Racial and ethnic preferences, where they are employed, rest on the assumption that color is the central feature of a person's identity—that character, intelligence, energy, initiative, socioeconomic circumstance, and other qualities are all less important. And thus in California both economically privileged and low-income black and Hispanic students were equally eligible for preferential treatment, whereas an Asian immigrant struggling with the language and trying to support indigent parents got no break for "disadvantage." Similarly, whereas a white youngster from a single-parent, low-income household was treated as a privileged Anglo, neither the son of a ruling family in a South American country nor the student whose remote ancestors came from Spain was asked to meet regular academic criteria. The whole Hispanic category as defining identity was particularly troubling. For inexplicable reasons, European Spaniards obviously count. But does the term also include Portuguese and Brazilians?

Hispanic was not the only troubling category. The term Asian covers a wide variety of groups with little in common: old and new Chinese immigrations, Japanese, Thai, Vietnamese of various kinds, Indonesians, Koreans, among others. Crudely lumped together they outnumber whites at UCLA and Berkeley—the most selective campuses—raising questions about their "overrepresentation." In April 1995, in Sacramento, President Clinton warned that "there are universities in California that could fill their entire freshman classes with nothing but Asian Americans."[2] The Asians had become yesterday's Jews: an allegedly too-ambitious group eligible for exclusion on the basis of their national origins. Ironically, some of the "Asians" who were kept out in order to make room in the university for more blacks and Hispanics were the grandsons and granddaughters of the Japanese Americans who were confined to relocation camps during World War II.

Preferential admissions policies have a powerful and inherent tendency to reduce people in all their variety and complexity to their racial or ethnic identity. And yet higher education is supposed to enhance our sense of individuality, to encourage and educate distinctive qualities of mind and character. Intelligence and creativity, if allowed, burst through the constraints of social origin; nurtured by our origins, we transcend them. In our private lives we may choose to honor and celebrate the culture of a group to which we feel we belong. Or we may reject that identification. People differ, and must be allowed to differ, but the choices they make should be matters of private, not public, policy.

Counting the "Disadvantaged"

The policy of group preferences forces impossible choices on the rapidly growing number of Americans from multiracial backgrounds. The university, in effect, says to students of mixed race, choose between your mother and your father. If you decide to identify yourself as a member of a preferred group, you increase your chances of being admitted and of receiving substantial financial support. If you identify yourself as Asian, even though your father is black, you are less likely to get in. If you choose to check the box labeled "other" or refuse to choose at all, we will simply treat you as if you were white. Which parent are you prepared to reject?

There is an additional problem: the whole process invites fraud—difficult to discern by large impersonal institutions like the University of California. One anecdote illustrates the form it takes. A university officer observed a student filling out his application form and checking the box labeled "Hispanic." "Oh, you're Hispanic," he said, trying to make friendly conversation. "No," came the reply. "Actually I'm Iranian, but my teacher told me to check Hispanic if I wanted to get into Berkeley."

Although no one knows how often such advice was given, such stories were frequently told with a cynical chuckle when the University of California was still giving preferences. They led to a general cynicism about the fairness of admissions procedures and to a broader sense that the whole enterprise was a racket. I once asked an admissions officer about the problem. "We are not in the business of enforcing Nuremberg Laws," he said indignantly. The university (rightly) was unwilling to decide whether a student one-eighth black was indeed "black" and who would determine, and by what means, just how large the fraction actually was. But without clear criteria and a settled process for determining fraud, no penalties for false representation could be imposed. And UC was certainly not prepared to set such criteria and procedures. But without the danger of identification or penalty, a "victimless crime" that carried substantial benefits was increasingly attractive, at least to high school teachers and counselors.

How Much Preference Is Enough? The Case of Boalt Hall

Racial preferences are ubiquitous in selective institutions of higher education, except where they have been banned, as in California, Texas, and the state of Washington. But no one ever defines precisely the point at which "diversity" has been reached. How large a preference should be given to reach what goal? Here again some evidence from the University of California may be enlightening, this time from a professional school.

Until the Regents acted to end race-driven admissions, the policies adopted by UC schools were said to be guided by the Supreme Court's 1978 decision in *University of California v. Bakke*, which outlawed quotas but permitted institutions to consider race as "one factor in admissions." What did this mean, exactly? Some schools read the Court's majority as having said, "other things being equal," race could be a basis for selection at the margin. Most, though, saw the decision as a license to achieve diversity by giving heavy weight to race and ethnicity.

Berkeley's Law School, Boalt Hall, was among those that interpreted *Bakke* permissively. Unlike most other graduate departments and professional schools, the admissions process used a formula that placed applicants into one of four "Ability Ranges," A through D, on the basis of undergraduate GPAs and LSAT scores. In 1996, only 855 students were admitted to

Boalt, out of 4,684 who applied, but the rate of acceptance for black and Hispanic students in every "Ability Range" below the top one A was much higher than that for whites and Asians.

For example, eighteen applicants from the preferred groups fell into the top two ranges, and all but one of them were accepted. Almost all applicants from all ethnic groups in the A range were admitted, but among those who fell in the B range, 69 percent of Asians, 62 percent of whites, and 94 percent of blacks and Hispanics were admitted. Looking at range C, only 19 percent of Asians and 17 percent of whites were admitted, while 77 percent of the blacks and Hispanics got in. In the lowest range, the disparities were even greater.

When we look at specific ethnic groups, the differences are even more striking. Of applicants in Ability Range C, ten were students of Japanese origin, and ten were black. All the blacks and none of the Japanese were accepted. In range D, a significant number of blacks but no students of Chinese origin were admitted.

These disparities were the consequence of highly race-conscious admissions processes, and when Boalt Hall's freedom to engage in race-based admissions was curtailed, the drop in blacks admitted was dramatic. Just one black student would be entering the first-year class in 1997, the media widely reported, and that student had deferred admission after having been accepted previously, when preferences were still permissible. The end of preferences, it was said despairingly, meant the virtual end of African American students at the University of California's top law school.

The figures for Boalt were reported before those for other professional and graduate programs had been made available, and the press presented them as the sign of things to come. In fact, Boalt Hall, together with other UC law and medical schools, was distinctive. The proportion of blacks and Hispanics entering Berkeley's graduate programs in general was little changed by the change in admissions policy—news that was basically ignored in the media.

Between 1996 and 1997—before and after preferences—the number of African Americans in UC graduate schools increased by 2 percent, while the "other" and "declined to state" categories increased by 25 percent, the Office of the President reported. (Those figures excluded the professional schools.) One might have imagined that the UC administration would be eager to spread the good news, but there were no press conferences or statements by senior administrative officers calling attention to these surprising figures. Instead, they gave the Boalt Hall story maximum publicity.

Boalt was different from most other graduate and professional programs in one important respect: it was competing for the most academically able black and Hispanic applicants with other leading law schools, especially those at the top private research universities. Unfortunately, however, it had never been very successful in that competition. Long before the Regents' vote and Proposition 209, Boalt had consistently lost all or almost all its best-qualified non-Asian minority applicants to Harvard, Yale, Stanford, and other law schools that were both more prestigious and could offer more financial support and more attractive job prospects upon graduation. But when no minority students enrolled in Boalt's 1997 entering class, public statements by administrators inside and outside the school blamed the results on the change in admissions criteria.

The end of race preferences at UC had dramatic effects on Boalt, in other words, because the school had gone very far down the road of racial double standards in an effort to compensate for a competitive disadvantage against more prestigious and affluent schools. But in 1997,[3] it could no longer take large numbers of poorly qualified minority students over white and Asian students with higher GPAs and LSATs. By contrast, most other graduate and professional programs within the university system had not had to change their admissions criteria and practice so drastically after preferences were abolished, and their black and Hispanic enrollment was almost unaffected.

In fact, the University of California has an advantage over most other universities in being a system of eight universities whose central office keeps records of their enrollments year by year and by the old ethnic-race categories. What those records show is that after the passage of 209 the non-Asian minority students who had applied but had not been admitted to Berkeley and other UC campuses that had been using race and ethnicity as criteria for admission tended to enroll in one of the other UC campuses, which were admitting all applicants who were academically qualified for admission to the university. The result of this process of "cascading" is that by 1999, only two years after the first class was admitted color blind, the University of California as a whole showed a decline of only 3 percent in the numbers of non-Asian minority freshmen enrollees. Even that figure overestimates the decline because it does not count the minority students who refused to give their race or ethnicity now that it no longer affected their admission to the university. But 3 percent is a far cry from the predictions of the effects of Proposition 209 on minority enrollments in the University of California. By 2000, the number of non-Asian minorities newly admitted to UC was already higher than in the last year that preferences were still in effect. The numbers admitted who refused to give their ethnicity had also risen.

Consensus and Coercion

Senior administrators in the academy are solidly behind racial preferences, and they are the seemingly united voice of almost every university. But in fact there is considerable division among members of the faculty. A 1995 Roper poll asked voting members of the University of California Academic Senate which they favored: granting preferences to women and certain racial and ethnic groups, or promoting equal opportunity without regard to an individual's race, sex, or ethnicity. A wide plurality (48 percent) chose the latter policy; only 31 percent supported preferences.[4] Another survey, of a national sample of college teachers, came up with much the same result.[5]

These findings are consistent with American public opinion in general, which has been deeply divided on the issue for three decades. What explains this curious combination of outward consensus and internal division in the academy? A mixture of principle and pragmatism—sincere belief coupled with a keen sense of who on or around campus can make trouble—explains the unanimity among university administrators. The officials who administered UC's large affirmative action bureaucracies were appointed on the understanding that they would support the preferential regime, and most of them probably did so genuinely. But they also know that those who are opposed to race-conscious admissions will seldom speak out and will never lead marches or sit-ins, whereas those who profit from preferences are combatants. In part, the silence on the part of opponents is a consequence of intimidation. Very few academics wish to offend both the senior administrators who govern their careers and budgets and the well-organized affirmative action pressure groups that will quickly stereotype faculty members as "racists" or, at very least, "right-wingers."

A distinguished federal judge who is familiar with academia has summarized the scene well:

> Groups holding considerable power in the university loathe speech with the wrong content about topics important to them, and . . . those who say the wrong things will have little peer or institutional protection. . . . Many ideas may not be expressed, many subjects may not be discussed, and any discussion on matters of political salience has to avoid defending groups powerful in the university.[6]

The problem at the University of California went beyond a lack of institutional protection for dissenting voices. Like other universities, UC over the years developed not only a strong climate but also an organizational structure in support of preferences from the president's office down. Every campus had administrative offices and academic senate committees to plan and enforce preferential policies; every department had an "affirmative action" officer to monitor its behavior. Needless to say, there was no equivalent organization of people and energy inside the university devoted to criticizing the preference policies or trying to reform them.

The pattern of consensual coercion brands dissenting points of view as illegitimate and deprives those who hold them of protection. Students and other faculty members need not read or listen to their arguments.

Already discredited, opponents of racial preferences are then demonized. They are not merely mistaken; they are evil—and fair game for late-night calls and hate mail. But coercion does not need to reach the point of anonymous name-calling to be effective. The administrative unanimity behind the policy can itself have a chilling effect that is enough to stifle debate.

What Proposition 209 Hath Wrought

The Regents' actions and Proposition 209 are slowly liberating UC campuses from the atmosphere of coercion. Although the president and the chancellors and their senior staffs may not have changed their views, it is now possible, indeed even necessary, for people to talk about how to admit students in ways that might preserve and enhance diversity without allowing race and ethnicity to drive admissions decisions.

California voters and the Regents have forced important reforms. The university has had to abandon its categorical formulas and admit students by inspecting their folders rather than simply their scores and race. Some students have always been admitted on the basis of their individual qualities and promise, but the process has now been extended more broadly.

In implementing race-neutral policies, admissions officers need not be blind to inequalities in American society and their impact on academic performance and life prospects. California admissions officers can still give a break to students who, though their scores are a bit low, seem highly motivated and come from mediocre high schools. And they can pay special attention to the high school senior who shows academic promise, although he or she has been struggling with English as a second language. Weighing such disadvantages is quite different from racial and ethnic preferences. The process requires schools to look at individual qualities; they cannot make stereotypical assumptions about group characteristics. And, as a result, all students admitted to the University of California today know they have earned a place in their class under uniform standards. None needs to feel like a second-class citizen, brought in to keep the "diversity" numbers up. Preference's burden of guilt and resentment has been lifted from UC students; one can feel it in a classroom.

But Proposition 209's greatest contribution has been its indirect impact on the lives of students before they apply to college. With racial preferences abolished, California residents can no longer ignore the problem of too few blacks and Hispanics academically prepared for seats in highly selective schools. Racial and ethnic preferences in higher education simply masked the inadequacies of California schools; elementary and secondary education must change, the university finally understands. In fact, with the help of a recent grant of $40 million from the state legislature, each UC campus now has an opportunity to create a program for improving the quality of K–12 schooling. With better primary and secondary education, the number of black and Hispanic youth who are prepared and motivated to continue their education in colleges and universities should expand. And they will be going to colleges that have looked at their talents and aspirations, not at their skin color or national origin, in admitting them. By many criteria the abolition of preferences for admission to the University of California has been a success.[7] The nature and extent of that success deserve to be studied and made more widely known in other parts of the country. We no longer have to merely speculate about the effects of ending racial preferences in higher education. Some results are in.

Notes

1. Portions of this essay are drawn from the author's "California After Racial Preferences," *Public Interest*, Spring 1999, pp. 64–85. For varying perspectives on racial preferences in higher education, see Stephan Thernstrom and Abigail Thernstrom, *America in Black and White: One Nation, Indivisible* (New York: Simon & Schuster, 1997), chap. 14; Shelby Steele, *A Dream Deferred* (New York: HarperCollins, 1998); William G. Bowen and Derek Bok, *The Shape of the River: Long-Term Consequences of Considering Race in College and University Admissions* (Princeton, N.J.: Princeton University Press, 1998). Although proponents of preferential policies have hailed the Bowen-Bok work as definitive, it has been subjected to serious methodological and substantive criticism. The fullest critiques are the author's "California After Racial

Preferences" and Stephan Thernstrom and Abigail Thernstrom, "Reflections on *The Shape of the River*," *UCLA Law Review*, June 1999.

2. Quoted by Leo Rennert, *Sacramento Bee* Washington bureau chief, under the headline "President Embraces Minority Programs," *Sacramento Bee* (Metro Final), April 7, 1995, p. A1. One might have imagined that the university would protest publicly that there was no such danger and, moreover, that that kind of invoking of the Yellow Peril was deplorable. Similar remarks from a Pat Buchanan, say, would likely have produced a flood of criticism. But no objection was forthcoming from university officials because the remarks were made by someone on their side of the preference issue.

3. The ban on preferences took effect in graduate and professional schools in 1997; undergraduate admissions were not affected until 1998.

4. The Roper Center Survey of Faculty Opinion About Affirmative Action at the University of California, October 1996, sponsored by the California Association of Scholars, at http://www.calscholars.org/roper.html.

5. This was an October 1996 survey of academics in colleges and universities all over the country. It found even higher proportions of respondents opposed to race-ethnic preferences in admissions and appointments than was found in the UC survey. See http://www.nas.org/roper/exsum.htm. A recent survey of undergraduates by Zogby International found that 79 percent said lowering the entrance requirements for some students, regardless of the reason, was unfair to other applicants. And 77 percent said it was not right to give preferential treatment to minority students if it meant denying admission to other students. Ben Gose, "Most Students Oppose Racial Preferences in Admissions, Survey Finds," *Chronicle of Higher Education*, May 5, 2000, p. A52.

6. Andrew J. Kleinfeld, Circuit Judge on the United States Court of Appeals for the Ninth Circuit, in an essay, "Politicization: From the Law Schools to the Courts," *Academic Questions*, Winter 1993–94, p. 17.

7. See Pamela Burdman, "After Affirmative Action," *Crosstalk* 8, no. 1 (winter 2000): 7–8.

PART FIVE

LAW

Racial and Ethnic Classifications in American Law

EUGENE VOLOKH

WHEN DOES THE U.S. CONSTITUTION allow government officials to discriminate based on race? This question has occupied the American judiciary for at least 130 years, and to this day it remains in considerable measure unanswered.

At least since the 1940s, courts have said that governmental race classifications—policies that sort people by racial categories—are presumptively impermissible, though acceptable if the government gives a very good justification for them. The legal rule is the so-called "strict scrutiny" test: to pass constitutional master, a race-based policy (whether it benefits whites or nonwhites) must be "narrowly tailored to a compelling governmental interest." The U.S. Supreme Court enunciated this test as to state laws in the *City of Richmond v. J. A. Croson Co.* case (1989) and as to federal laws in *Adarand Constructors v. Peña* (1995).[1] But this principle was endorsed only by a five-to-four majority and is thus somewhat precarious.

"Narrow tailoring" and "compelling government interest," moreover, are such vague phrases that creative judges could use them to uphold or strike down virtually any race-based program they wish. The test's substantive meaning must therefore come not from its words but from the decisions—again, usually ones made by narrow majorities—that apply the test and therefore implicitly elaborate it.

In determining the constitutional legitimacy of a race-conscious government policy, then, a court must answer three questions. First, does it indeed involve a racial classification? Second, is the government's justification one that the courts have recognized as "compelling"? And, third, is the race-conscious government action "narrowly tailored," carefully designed to target the specific problem that is said to justify the race-based policy?

When is something considered a racial classification? Courts have been close to unanimous in concluding that any different treatment based on race, whether it amounts to a quota, a "plus factor" favoring a particular racial group, or any other race-based decision making, triggers strict scrutiny. (Rigid quotas are considered especially constitutionally suspect because they are less likely to be "narrowly tailored" to whatever interest they seek to serve, though even quotas have sometimes been upheld.)[2] Policies that set "goals" and "timetables" are treated like all other preference programs and must likewise face strict scrutiny.[3]

It is harder to tell whether racially targeted "outreach" programs will be treated as race classifications. Consider, for instance, an advertising program targeted solely at blacks and aimed at increasing the number of black applicants and therefore of black employees. On the one hand, such a program does not involve actual discriminatory treatment of any individual, which is why these programs are often popular even among those who generally oppose race preferences. On the other hand, the advertising campaign does aim to provide a certain valuable benefit (information) to people of a particular group, which is why antidiscrimination statutes have generally been read as applying to such targeted recruitment the same way that they apply to more tangible forms of discrimination.[4] Few cases have addressed this question, so no consensus has emerged.

A facially race-neutral program does not become a race classification simply because it has an unintentionally different impact on one racial group than on another.[5] Thus, for instance, a preference for police officers who speak Spanish is itself perfectly acceptable, unless it is proved to be a mere pretext for preferring people who are ethnically Hispanic.[6] Intent, not impact, is the question. Of course, it is often hard to determine the precise intentions behind a particular rule; because of this, courts are generally reluctant to infer that a facially race-neutral rule is intended to discriminate based on race, unless there is strong evidence of such an intention.

Once a court concludes that a government program involves a racial classification, it asks whether it is narrowly tailored to a compelling government interest. Here is what the precedents tell us about what this means.

1. The desire to remedy societal discrimination cannot justify a governmental race classification; that was the Supreme Court's holding in the *Croson* case.[7] Thus, for instance, the University of Michigan cannot defend its race preference system by saying, "Blacks have gotten a raw deal for many generations, and are still getting it today, and our preference for blacks and discrimination against whites is a rough payback."

2. A government agency's desire to remedy its own identified past discrimination, or to counteract others' identified present discrimination, does justify race-based programs that are carefully designed to compensate for this wrong. Thus, for instance, a government employer that finds it has discriminated against blacks in the recent past may set up a preference system that aims to increase black representation to roughly the level of black participation in the qualified labor pool. It doesn't matter that this compensates black applicants against whom the employer has not discriminated at the expense of white applicants who have not benefited from discrimination at the employer's hands—the preference for a race can indeed be justified by past discrimination against that race.[8] Similarly, a government agency that shows, using statistically valid "disparity studies," that there is discrimination by contractors against minority subcontractors may set up a preference program for contractors that use minority subs.[9] On the other hand, the University of Texas cannot just say, "We discriminated against black applicants until the late 1960s, so we have to discrim-

inate in favor of blacks today"—too much time has passed to assume that the past discrimination by the University of Texas has direct consequences for admissions now.[10]

For an agency to implement a preference program under this rubric, it need not have been found guilty of discrimination in court: the agency may act based on a "strong basis in evidence" that this discrimination had taken place.[11] As one might guess, it is not entirely clear exactly what evidence suffices to show this.

3. The desire to have a particular racial balance for its own sake—for instance, wanting to have a university that "looks like America"—does not justify race classifications.[12]

4. What if a public university (or a government employer) argues that it wants to have a certain racial mix not for its own sake but for the greater "intellectual diversity" of ideas, outlooks, and experiences that such a mix would supposedly yield? This is one of the big unresolved questions. Justice Lewis Powell endorsed this argument in *Regents of the University of California v. Bakke* (1978), but he was the only Justice to do so. The U.S. Court of Appeals for the Fifth Circuit rejected this argument in *Hopwood v. Texas* (1996), but since then the Nevada Supreme Court has accepted it as applied to university faculty hiring.[13]

5. A university is unlikely to win with an argument that admitting more medical or law students of a particular race is narrowly tailored to the interest in providing better medical and legal services to communities of that race. Though the Court has never ruled on this specific question, it is clear that race generally may not be used as a proxy for various attributes, even when it is a statistically accurate proxy. Instead of relying on stereotypical assumptions about the skills or education possessed by members of a certain group, for instance, employers and educators must measure the skills or education of the applicants directly.[14] Similarly, for future community service: schools may give preference to applicants who have track records of past community service or to people who commit themselves to engage in such service in the future, but they cannot assume that, say,

blacks are more likely to go back to serve poor black communities (even if that's a statistically sound prediction).

6. The government generally cannot justify race-based decisions by pointing to the public's race-conscious attitudes. Thus, for instance, the government may not refuse to integrate a park for fear of racist violence. The government may not refuse to hire black policemen on the theory that some whites will reject their authority. When deciding on child custody, a court may not take into account the possibility that placing a child with a parent who has remarried across races will lead to the child's being shunned or even attacked by his peers.[15]

What about similar arguments in support of preferences that help minorities? For instance, may the government prefer nonwhite teachers because nonwhite students will supposedly be more inspired by having them as role models? May the government prefer Hispanic policemen because Hispanic members of the public will trust the police more if they see more Hispanics on the force? May the government prefer black guards for a boot camp for juvenile offenders on the theory that the mostly black inmates may react better to the black guards than to white guards?

In these questions, the matter is less clear. The role model justification was rejected in *Croson*,[16] but the police and prison "operational needs" argument is more controversial. Even Judge Richard Posner, who is generally skeptical of race preferences,[17] wrote an opinion upholding the preference for black boot camp guards and suggesting that the same rationale might apply to police forces.[18]

7. Most judges—even including Justice Antonin Scalia, who would impose a close to total ban on governmental race classifications—have accepted that in certain very narrow circumstances the government may consider race in order to avoid imminent violence. This is especially true of violence by prisoners; the law may normally refuse to give effect to public prejudices, insisting instead that the public conform its behavior to the law's demands, but many prisoners have already shown their (often violent) unwillingness to comply with legal norms. Thus, courts have suggested that race-segregated lockdowns following prison riots may be constitu-

tional and have upheld some race-based cellmate selections for violently racist prisoners.[19]

8. The strict scrutiny framework leaves room for courts to recognize still other interests as "compelling." Thus, for instance, the U.S. Court of Appeals for the Ninth Circuit Court recently upheld a race-based admission policy at a UCLA-run experimental elementary school on the grounds that the policy was needed to have a more lifelike educational experiment.[20] One can question whether the government has a truly compelling interest in such experimentation and whether an artificially integrated school in any event particularly serves this interest, given that most schools are much more segregated; but these judges bought the argument, as judges applying strict scrutiny always can. Similarly, some courts have taken the view that preservation of a child's "cultural heritage," or more broadly "the child's best interests," are compelling enough interests to justify race-based adoption policies.[21]

Racial classifications are thus sometimes tolerated by the U.S. Constitution as currently interpreted. It is important to note, however, that they are not *required*: even those classifications that are not forbidden by the U.S. Constitution may be curtailed by Congress, by state legislatures, or by the voters directly through the initiative process.[22]

What broader practical or political conclusions can one draw from the above?

(a) The law is vague enough that die-hard race preference supporters can implement such policies while plausibly arguing that each policy is somehow narrowly tailored to a compelling interest. A court might, several years later, strike down such a policy, but the supporters can often try again with a slightly revised policy or with a supposedly fuller factual record. Only a per se ban on preferences, or a diminution in the zeal of the preference supporters, could prevent this. Nonetheless, strict scrutiny, as applied by the courts in recent years, seems a tough enough test that more pragmatic government officials who don't want to bother with the cost, hassle, and uncertainty of litigation may abandon their preference plans and shift to race-neutral solutions.

(b) The law's vagueness leaves lower court judges plenty of latitude to write opinions that go whichever way they like. A few justifications—for instance, remedying historical discrimination by society at large, maintaining racial proportionality for its own sake, and providing role models—will probably have to be rejected by any conscientious judge because the Supreme Court precedent on these issues is so clear. Still, there are enough permissible (or not clearly forbidden) justifications and enough wiggle-room in "narrow tailoring" that many programs may be upheld by judges who want to uphold them. Federal courts have struck down most of the preference programs that they have faced in recent years, but this has more to do with the skepticism of the judges who have applied the doctrine than with the innate force of the doctrine itself.

(c) The Supreme Court has usually been split five-to-four on preferences. Were, say, Chief Justice William Rehnquist or Justice Sandra Day O'Connor to step down and be replaced by a more propreference Justice, the antipreference rule might well be reversed or at least undermined. The composition of the lower courts is also vital; lower court judges who are ideologically inclined to support race-based policies can exploit the law's vagueness to uphold preferences.

(d) It is a mistake to say that the Court's decisions establish a per se rule of color blindness. These decisions hold that race preferences are disfavored by the Constitution, but not that preferences are always illegal. To take one example, the notion that a government agency may hire black applicant X over white applicant Y today because it discriminated against black applicant Z and in favor of white applicant W some years ago is far from a color-blind approach. The Court might be wrong and the antipreferences movement might be right, but the movement must recognize the limits to how much it can base its arguments on the Court's decisions.

(e) It is equally a mistake to argue that antipreferences initiatives are unnecessary because the Constitution already severely limits race preferences. Opponents of antipreferences initiatives (such as California's Prop. 209) often make this argument, but it is just not so.[23]

Some courts continue to accept the desire for intellectual diversity as a justification for race preferences, and many government agencies continue to urge this argument; the "remedying identified discrimination" rationale is potentially quite broad; and some other justifications for race-based policies remain possibly available. Given all this, and given the number of judges (federal and state) who sympathize with race preferences, race preferences are hardly limited to any narrow, uncontroversial area.

And just as important, the U.S. Supreme Court is closely split on this question and may easily reverse itself in years to come. It is therefore wise for voters who oppose race-based policies not to rely simply on the Justices but to make sure themselves that state statutes, state constitutions, and federal statutes mandate color blindness.

Notes

1. 488 U.S. 469 (1989); 515 U.S. 200 (1995).

2. See, e.g., *United States v. Paradise*, 480 U.S. 149 (1987) (upholding "a 50% promotional quota in the upper ranks" of the Alabama Department of Public Safety); *Davis v. City and County of San Francisco*, 890 F.2d 1438, 1447 (9th Cir. 1989) (upholding a Fire Department quota that mandated "the hiring of minorities and women in percentages equal to their representation in the labor market . . . and the promotion of minorities and women in percentages equal to their representation in the relevant labor market"); *Middleton v. City of Flint*, 810 F. Supp. 874 (E.D. Mich. 1993) (upholding "a 1:1 quota" in promotions); *Aiken v. City of Memphis*, 37 F.3d 1155 (6th Cir. 1995) (stating that a "20% promotion 'floor'" based on race was constitutional); *Quirin v. City of Pittsburgh*, 801 F. Supp. 1486, 1491 (W.D. Penn. 1992) (striking down a particular quota plan, but making clear that some quotas are constitutional); *North State Law Enforcement Officers Ass'n v. Charlotte-Mecklenburg Police Dep't*, 862 F. Supp. 1445, 1457 (W.D. N.C. 1994) (same); *Associated General Contractors v. City of New Haven*, 791 F. Supp. 941, 949 (D. Conn. 1992) (dictum) (same); *Mallory v. Harkness*, 895 F. Supp. 1556 (S.D. Fla. 1995) (same).

3. *Bras v. California Public Utilities Comm'n*, 59 F.3d 869, 874 (9th Cir. 1995); *Lutheran Church–Missouri Synod v. FCC*, 141 F.3d 344, 352–54 (D.C. Cir. 1998).

4. See, e.g., *Lutheran Church–Missouri Synod v. FCC*, 141 F.3d 344, 351 (D.C. Cir. 1998) (suggesting, but not deciding, that race-based outreach should be treated the same way as race-based hiring decisions); Eugene Volokh, "The California Civil Rights Initiative: An Interpretive Guide," *UCLA Law Review* 44 (1997): 1335, 1349–53 (discussing this point in more detail).

5. *Washington v. Davis*, 425 U.S. 229, 242 (1976).

6. See, e.g., *Hernandez v. New York*, 500 U.S. 352, 375 (1991) (criteria based on language skills are not per se criteria based on ethnicity).

7. *Croson*, 488 U.S. at 498.

8. See, e.g., *Billish v. City of Chicago*, 989 F.2d 890, 893 (7th Cir. 1993) (en banc).

9. *Croson*, 488 U.S. at 509.

10. See, e.g., *Hopwood v. Texas*, 78 F.3d 932 (5th Cir. 1996).

11. *Croson*, 488 U.S. at 500.

12. Ibid., at 507; *Regents v. Bakke*, 438 U.S. 265, 307 (1978) (Powell, J.).

13. *Regents v. Bakke*, 438 U.S. 265, 307 (1978) (Powell, J.); *Hopwood v. Texas*, 78 F.3d 932 (5th Cir. 1996); *University & Community College Sys. of Nevada v. Farmer*, 113 Nev. 90 (1997). See also *Wessmann v. Gittens*, 160 F.3d 790 (1st Cir. 1998) (taking a skeptical look at the diversity justification but not dismissing it entirely).

14. See, e.g., *Powers v. Ohio*, 499 U.S. 400, 410 (1991); *Croson*, 488 U.S. at 501.

15. *Watson v. Memphis*, 373 U.S. 526, 533 (1963) (park); *Baker v. City of St. Petersburg*, 400 F.2d 294, 301 (5th Cir. 1968) (police); *Palmore v. Sidoti*, 466 U.S. 429, 433 (1984) (child custody).

16. *Croson*, 488 U.S. at 497–98.

17. See Richard A. Posner, "The DeFunis Case and the Constitutionality of Preferential Treatment of Racial Minorities," *1974 Supreme Court Review*, p. 1.

18. *Wittmer v. Peters*, 87 F.3d 916, 919 (7th Cir. 1996); see also *Barhold v. Rodriguez*, 863 F.2d 233, 238 (2d Cir. 1988) (police officers); *Talbert v. City of Richmond*, 648 F.2d 925, 931–32 (4th Cir. 1981) (police officers), suggested to no longer be good law; *Hayes v. North State Law Enforcement Officers Ass'n*, 10 F.3d 207, 213 (4th Cir. 1993); *Detroit Police Officers' Ass'n v. Young*, 608 F.2d 671, 695–96 (6th Cir. 1979) (police officers), recognized as no longer being good law; *Michigan Road Builders Ass'n, Inc. v. Milliken*, 834 F.2d 583 (6th Cir. 1987); *Minnick v. California Dep't of Corrections*, 95 Cal. App. 3d 506 (1979) (prison guards), certiorari dismissed on procedural grounds, 452 U.S. 105 (1981). On the other side, see *Hayes v. North State Law Enforcement Officers Ass'n*, 10 F.3d 207, 213 (4th Cir. 1993), which explicitly says that the question whether operational needs may justify race classifications is not resolved; and *Croson*, 488 U.S. at 493, and *Hopwood*, 78 F.3d at 944, which suggest that race classifications may only be justified by the desire to remedy past discrimination.

19. *Croson*, 488 U.S. at 521 (Scalia, J., concurring in the judgment); *Lee v. Washington*, 390 U.S. 333, 334 (1968) (Black, Harlan, and Stewart, JJ., concurring); *Harris v. Greer*, 750 F.2d 617, 619 (7th Cir. 1984) (dictum); see also *Weathers v. Gasparini*, 1998 WL 8853, *4 (N.D. Ill. Jan. 8); *Waler v. Walker*, 654 So. 2d 1049, 1050 (Fla. App. 1995); *Abbott v. Smaller*, 1990 WL 131359, *3 n.2 (E.D. Pa. Sept. 5) (dictum).

20. *Hunter v. Brandt*, 1999 WL 694865 (9th Cir. Sept. 9), available at http://laws.findlaw.com/9th/9755920.html.

21. In re Adoption/Guardianship No. 2633, 646 A.2d 1036 (M.D. App. 1994); In

re Moorehead, 75 Ohio App. 3d. 711, 723, 600 N.E.2d 778, 785 (1991); Petition of D.I.S., 494 A.2d 1316 (D.C. 1985).

22. *Coalition for Economic Equity v. Wilson*, 110 F.3d 1431 (9th Cir. 1997).

23. See, e.g., Marci A. Hamilton, "The People: The Least Accountable Branch," *U. of Chicago Roundtable* 4 (1997) (arguing that Prop. 209 is unconstitutional in part because under the Supreme Court's precedents, "affirmative action may only be employed constitutionally to battle proven historical discrimination").

Illusions of Antidiscrimination Law

NELSON LUND

SLAVERY IS RESPONSIBLE for the most serious and intractable political problems the United States has faced. Along with the poisonous legacy of that thoroughly un-American institution, we must also face its intersection with the very American tendency to conduct political struggles in the form of legal controversies.

Opponents and proponents of racial preferences have alike fixed their hopes largely on the courts. Advocates of reform focus on a series of recent decisions that evince an increasingly firm commitment to the norm of color-blind laws.[1] Defenders of the pervasive and well-entrenched system of racial and ethnic preferences have for their part noted how narrowly divided the Supreme Court is and have desperately sought to delay further developments in the hope that new appointments will shift the balance in their favor.[2]

As a matter of tactics, both sides are probably right to view the Supreme Court as the decisive center of power. Although public opinion polls have for many years shown overwhelming opposition to racial preferences, Congress has done virtually nothing to curtail them. The legislature itself has created numerous preference programs, and there are no indications that this is likely to change soon.[3]

This has nothing to do with the merits of the issue but is entirely the result of interest group politics. In spite of the public sentiment opposing racial preferences, elected politicians have found that relatively few voters are so intensely repulsed that they will vote against candidates merely because they support these devices. Politicians also understand that a relatively small group of voters and activists, consisting largely of those who expect to benefit from preferences, will invest enormous resources in defense of the status quo. Just as with sugar quotas, racial quotas generate large economic bonuses for a narrow class of beneficiaries, who are therefore easily mobilized, while the corresponding economic losses are distributed, often invisibly, among a large and diffuse population. If sugar quotas cost each consumer a few cents a year, they can generate millions of dollars for a small group of sugar producers without generating meaningfully strong opposition from consumers; in those circumstances, elected politicians will naturally respond to the producers, who alone threaten to take political action in defense of their interests. The same calculations work against the reform of other special interest laws, including racial preferences.[4]

This public-choice analysis suggests two corollaries. First, that the courts (because of their relative insulation from interest group politics and their heightened commitment to reason and principle) are the right place to thresh out the issues of racial preferences and affirmative action. Second, that we have no alternative forum for the vindication of enduring principles because the Congress is a hopeless lackey of special interests. Although I accept the public-choice analysis, I do not believe the corollaries are necessarily valid. On the contrary, the history of antidiscrimination law shows that the Supreme Court has often been a more malignant and unprincipled practitioner of racial politics than Congress and that the Court's political activism in this area has had a corrupting influence on the Court's own capacity for adhering to reason and principle.

Though I believe that the moral and political arguments against racial preferences are overwhelming on the merits, I do not claim that principled disagreements are impossible. In any event, whatever one's views on the merit of racial preferences, one might expect that the political decisions about that issue reflected in the Constitution and in the statutes adopted by Congress ought to be adhered to until they are changed by constitutional amendment or by new congressional legislation. The Supreme Court has not accepted that proposition, choosing instead to replace the law with its members' personal views of sound policy virtually at will. This usurpation of power has made a mockery of the vigorous and impassioned debates that led up to our major civil rights laws. And the Court's history hangs like a slyly grinning specter over the current disputes about affirmative action. Whatever Congress may choose to do, is it likely to mean more than it has meant in the past?

A Very Short Sketch of the History of Antidiscrimination Law

The law affecting racial discrimination is by now so extensive and complex that no brief summary can offer more than a few illustrations, inadequately explained. The two main sources of genuine law, the Constitution and statutes, form the smallest portion of this body of law: they are far outweighed in bulk and importance by thousands of judicial decisions that provide what are taken as their authoritative interpretation. The development of this law has occurred primarily in three great phases: first during the antebellum period, then during and after Reconstruction, and finally during the modern civil rights era that began after World War II. For all their differences, the three periods have been remarkably similar in certain respects. First, Congress has in almost all the most important cases acted to reduce racial discrimination. Second, the Supreme Court has frequently ignored the Constitution and the statutes enacted by Congress, often preferring instead to protect and promote discrimination while indulging itself in an airy presumption of superior wisdom.

THE *DRED SCOTT* PHASE

The original Constitution ceded to the new federal government several important powers, but not the power to establish or abolish slavery in the states. The Constitution acknowledged the existence of slavery in three somewhat awkward locutions. First, it established an apportionment rule that treated "free Persons" differently from "all other Persons."[5] Second, it specified a twenty-year moratorium on congressional interference with state choices about which persons to admit through "Migration or Importation."[6] Third, the Constitution required each state to deliver up escapees who had been "held to Service or Labour" in another state.[7]

The most famous case construing the original Constitution's position on slavery is *Dred Scott*, which is familiar to everyone as a politically disastrous and morally offensive exercise of judicial power.[8] That was indeed atrociously shameful, though not exactly for the reasons commonly assumed. If Chief Justice Roger B. Taney could come back to defend the decision, he would have to argue that he should not be blamed, for he was merely enforcing the Constitution. If that is what he was doing, we should indeed blame those who adopted the Constitution (rather than Taney and his colleagues) for the decision in *Dred Scott*.

But this defense of Taney fails. Recall the case. Scott's master took him from the slave state of Missouri to the Upper Louisiana Territory (where slavery had been outlawed by the Missouri Compromise) and then back to Missouri. When Scott sued for his freedom, the Supreme Court turned him down, first because Congress had no power to forbid slavery in the territories, and second because a black person was in any case ineligible for American citizenship under the Constitution.

Taney's first conclusion was based on a theory that the right of property in slaves was "distinctly and expressly affirmed in the Constitution" and therefore protected by the Fifth Amendment's Due Process Clause.[9] This theory has multiple fatal errors. Taney provided no support for his counterintuitive claim that due process protects substantive (as opposed to procedural) rights. Even if it did, no right in slaves was distinctly or expressly affirmed in the Constitution, and even the slave states did not pretend that slavery had any basis outside state law. Taney's second, and even more outrageous, conclusion was based on the theory that blacks had not been considered eligible for citizenship when the Constitution was adopted. But this was factually incorrect, and Taney knew it: Justice Benjamin R. Curtis presented the evidence in his dissenting opinion, just as he demolished Taney's due process theory.[10] Taney was not interpreting the Constitution, or even misinterpreting it. He was simply lying.[11]

RECONSTRUCTION AND RETROGRESSION

Dred Scott's jurisprudence of the barefaced lie did not prove unique. That technique was to resurface in future Supreme Court opinions, along with noxious blends of legalistic sophistry and unsupported ex cathedra pronouncements.

Once the Union was restored, Congress sent constitutional amendments to the states abolishing slavery, forbidding the states to violate certain fundamental rights of equality and nondiscrimination and outlawing racial discrimination in connection with the right to vote.[12] Congress also passed several statutes to help safeguard these new constitutional guarantees, which were enforced fairly vigorously for a time.[13] In 1877, however, the Republicans agreed to stop protecting black rights in a corrupt political deal that settled a disputed presidential election.[14] The Jim Crow era was born.

The most famous of the Jim Crow cases is *Plessy v. Ferguson*, in which the Supreme Court considered the constitutionality of a Louisiana statute that required railroads to furnish "equal but separate accommodations" for white and black passengers and forbade breaches of the required separation.[15] Because the statute made it equally illegal for blacks to travel in "white" compartments and for whites to travel in "black" compartments, it was not entirely obvious whether the Constitution was violated by this formally equal treatment of the races.

The Court did not find the answer to this question because it never asked it. Justice Henry Billings Brown's majority opinion simply declared that the Fourteenth Amendment permits every regulation that is "reasonable."[16] Arguing that Louisiana's statute could not stamp blacks with a badge of inferiority unless they foolishly chose to read something into it, Brown found that the law was reasonable because "legislation is powerless to eradicate racial instincts or to abolish distinctions based upon physical differences, and the attempt to do so can only result in accentuating the difficulties of the present situation."[17] To emphasize the Court's total commitment to this utterly political judgment, Brown concluded that "if one race be inferior to the other socially, the Constitution of the United States cannot put them upon the same plane."[18] Brown's dishonest assertion about the degrading implications of the statute is matched only by his breathtaking insinuation that the Constitution is powerless to forbid regulations that the Supreme Court considers reasonable. Nor can the Court be defended by drawing a distinction between "social" inferiority (allegedly immune from legal controls) and "legal" inferiority (presumably curable by law). The statute at issue in the case forbade the *voluntary* mixing of the races on trains and was thus a *legal* effort to *promote* "social" inferiority.

Justice John Marshall Harlan wrote an eloquent dissent, which has come to be very highly regarded.[19] Unlike the majority, Harlan had no interest in lying about the statute's degrading intent, which he thought was likely to inflame racial animosity rather than keep the peace. But his legal analysis was little better than the majority's, for he declared that the Constitution forbids "discrimination by the General Government or the States against any citizen because of his race."[20] This is a lie of its own, in two ways. First, the Constitution contains no language forbidding racial discrimination by the federal government, except in the area of voting rights. Second, although the Fourteenth Amendment forbids the states from violating certain civil rights, the broad and somewhat mystifying description of those rights does not contain any explicit or self-evidently general ban on racial discrimination. Harlan may well have been right that the Louisiana statute violated the Constitution, but he did not give a single good reason for his conclusion.[21] Like the *Plessy* majority, Harlan simply assumed that

the Constitution reflected what he considered good policy without attending in the least to what the Constitution says.[22]

THE MODERN ERA BEGINS

Plessy established the terms for the modern era's constitutional debates
over race discrimination, which has consisted of an elaborate series of
decisions applying Justice Brown's "reasonableness" standard.[23] This process has been punctuated by occasional evocations of Justice Harlan's color-
blind constitutional vision, but the Supreme Court left the Constitution
itself aside so long ago that the document has become little more than a
curio in this field.

The Court's most revered decision on racial discrimination illustrates
the pattern. Without any analysis of the Constitution's text, *Brown v. Board
of Education* dismissed the legislative history of the Fourteenth Amendment
as "inconclusive" and unanimously declared separate educational facilities
for black and white children "inherently unequal."[24] This conclusion was
based entirely on a theory about childhood education: at least in the context
of public schools, separating children from others of similar age and qualifications solely because of their race "generates a feeling of inferiority as
to their status in the community that may affect their hearts and minds in
a way unlikely ever to be undone."[25]

Whatever its merits as pedagogical theory, this rationale proved to be
merely a cover story. *Brown* was followed by a series of decisions declaring
unconstitutional many disparate forms of segregation while refusing to
strike down laws dealing with the sensitive subject of miscegenation, and
all without any explanation whatsoever.[26] Because the rationale on which
Brown was ostensibly based applied only to primary and secondary education, the real basis unifying that decision with its immediate progeny
could hardly have been anything but political intuitions about what was
"reasonable" at the moment.[27] As in *Dred Scott* and *Plessy*, the Constitution
that was supposedly being interpreted was simply ignored. A few years

later, the Court took the logical next step by declaring its own opinion in *Brown* to be the "supreme law of the land."[28]

It would be easier to understand the reverence for *Brown* if the Court's contemptuous disregard for judicial obligations and limits had accomplished some great and salutary political effect that could not otherwise have been achieved. In fact, however, the Court could have arrived at the same result that *Brown* reached had it been willing to engage in standard legal research and standard legal reasoning, rather than in pedagogical theorizing and nonjudicial politicking.[29] Furthermore, *Brown* did not even begin the process of school desegregation in the Deep South, which began to occur only after Congress armed the federal government with real enforcement powers ten years later.[30]

The Civil Rights Act of 1964 and subsequent statutes deserve the principal credit for desegregating the schools and for the abolition of Jim Crow generally. In addition to provisions giving the federal government meaningful school-desegregation tools, the 1964 Act contained elaborate statutory provisions outlawing racial discrimination in public accommodations, by recipients of federal funding, and in private employment. The following year, Congress enacted strong provisions for enforcing the voting rights guaranteed by the Fifteenth Amendment, which had been notoriously flouted for many decades. In 1968, legislation aimed at reducing discrimination in the housing markets was enacted, and four years later Congress extended the ban on employment discrimination to the state and federal governments.

Although the principal provisions of these statutes were generally written with considerable clarity, the Supreme Court has frequently treated them with cavalier disregard, as it had previously treated the Constitution itself. Consider, for example, the statutory language banning employment discrimination:

It shall be an unlawful employment practice for an employer

(1) to fail or refuse to hire or to discharge any individual, or otherwise to discriminate against any individual with respect to his compensation, terms, conditions, or privileges of employment, because of such individual's race, color, religion, sex, or national origin; or

(2) to limit, segregate, or classify his employees or applicants for employment in any way which would deprive or tend to deprive any individual of employment opportunities or otherwise adversely affect his status as an employee, because of such individual's race, color, religion, sex, or national origin.[31]

To eliminate any doubt about the meaning of this straightforward language, Congress added:

Nothing contained in this [statute] shall be interpreted to require any employer . . . to grant preferential treatment to any individual or to any group because of the race, color, religion, sex, or national origin of such individual or group on account of an imbalance which may exist with respect to the total number or percentage of persons of any race, color, religion, sex, or national origin employed by any employer . . . in comparison with the total number or percentage of persons of such race, color, religion, sex, or national origin in any community, State, section, or other area, or in the available work force in any community, State, section, or other area.[32]

The Supreme Court quickly began turning this statute from a straightforward prohibition against discrimination into a device for promoting discrimination. In its unanimous 1971 *Griggs* decision, the Court relied on a series of factual misstatements, logical non sequiturs, and sophomoric philosophizing to write into law a wholly new and different statute.[33] Under the *Griggs* law, an employer who does *not* intentionally discriminate because of race can nevertheless be held liable if the failure to discriminate produces a workforce with too few minorities, unless the employer's selection criteria meet an undefined, judicially created standard of "business necessity."[34] This new law encourages nondiscriminating employers with numerically unbalanced workforces to avoid potentially ruinous litigation by hiring more of the underrepresented minorities. Taking that step will often require discriminating against whites (and/or other minorities), in violation of the law that Congress actually wrote.[35]

That dilemma for employers was ameliorated by the Court's 1979 *Weber* decision, which held that Congress's prohibition against discrimination actually permits employers to adopt intentional and overt racial quotas if they are "designed to break down old patterns of racial segregation and hierarchy" and do not "unnecessarily trammel the interests of the white employees."[36] Acknowledging that this conclusion is inconsistent with the "literal" language of the statute, Justice Brennan's majority opinion claimed to rely on the law's "spirit."[37] As Justice Rehnquist's dissent conclusively proved, however, the debates in Congress about the statute's meaning did not contain a shred of evidence for the existence of any such spirit. Those debates, moreover, included overwhelming evidence that the spirit of the statute was perfectly embodied in its "literal" language.[38]

Though the Supreme Court decisively rewrote the Civil Rights Act to permit and encourage racial discrimination, it has had more difficulty in deciding what standard of reasonableness it should implant in the Constitution. To this day, the Court has been unable to settle on the rules under which governments may and may not discriminate. The *Bakke* case, which involved a minority set-aside for seats in a state medical school, set the pattern. Four Justices concluded that the Civil Rights Act of 1964 forbade such discrimination, relying on the following provision: "No person in the United States shall, on the ground of race, color, or national origin, be excluded from participation in, be denied the benefits of, or be subjected to discrimination under any program or activity receiving Federal financial assistance."[39] Four other Justices broadly concluded that both the statute and the Constitution permit racial quotas to be used to overcome minority underrepresentation in the medical profession. Justice Powell concluded that the statute and the Constitution forbid blatant quotas but allow more subtle systems of discrimination.

Justice Powell's *Bakke* opinion (with which none of the other Justices agreed) came to be widely regarded as the law. Powell recommended the Harvard admissions approach: conceal your discrimination by treating race and ethnicity as one factor along with many others, thus making it difficult to prove which whites are being rejected because they are white and which are being rejected for other reasons. Because it is obviously meaningless to treat anything as a "factor" unless it will sometimes be the deciding factor, the Harvard-Powell approach is really just the application of a public relations gimmick.[40] Because constitutional law itself had long since become a game of legerdemain where race is concerned, there is poetic justice in Powell's solitary embrace of disguised discrimination being taken as if it were a holding of the Court.[41]

In the years since *Bakke*, the Court has sustained some constitutional challenges to racial preferences and rejected others, but without reaching agreement on the rationale for deciding such cases.[42] The most recent decision is in some ways the most peculiar. This case, known as *Adarand*, was brought by a white-owned construction company that submitted the low bid on a federal highway contract but lost out because of a federal minority preference program.[43] The company claimed that the preference violated the constitutional guarantee of "equal protection of the laws."

For someone familiar with the Constitution, the most obvious obstacle facing the white plaintiff might seem to be that the Equal Protection Clause applies only to the state governments, not to the federal government.[44] Many years ago, however, the Justices had decreed that the Constitution as written was in this respect "unthinkable" (by which they could only have meant "intolerable") and therefore invented a fictitious new provision correcting the Constitution's insufferable oversight.[45] Accordingly, the *Adarand* plurality opinion for four Justices set the Constitution aside and launched instead into an extended consideration of the Court's own precedents.[46]

From those hopelessly confusing and conflicting precedents, a new rule was distilled: federal racial classifications, like those of a state's, would henceforth be subject to strict scrutiny, which was said to mean that they must be narrowly tailored measures serving "compelling governmental interests."[47] This rule, however, is almost completely uninformative without a definition of "compelling" government interests. Not only did the Justices provide no such definition, they were incapable even of applying their rule to the very case before them. Rather than make a decision, they voted to send it back to the lower courts, which were expected to investigate whether the flagrant, racial spoils systems at issue serve a compelling government interest.[48] Because it is quite obvious that the Court would have had no such uncertainty in a case where the government used similar means to favor whites (or, for that matter, such minorities as Jews or Irish Americans), *Adarand* leaves unresolved the issue first raised in *Bakke.*[49]

In a particularly bizarre touch, Justice Scalia joined the plurality opinion (thereby making it a majority opinion) "except insofar as it may be inconsistent" with his own separate statement. That statement featured his declaration that "government can never have a 'compelling interest' in discriminating on the basis of race in order to 'make up' for past racial discrimination in the opposite direction."[50]

Justice Scalia was quite right that it is impossible to discern whether his declaration is consistent with the plurality opinion or not, which highlights the essential meaninglessness of the Court's decision in the case. What is even more interesting, however, is the basis for Scalia's own view. Citing four provisions of the Constitution that prohibit specific forms of discrimination *other than* racial discrimination by the federal government, Scalia seemed to make the illogical suggestion that they somehow provide grounds for finding in the Constitution a fifth prohibition that is not there. Undoubtedly aware that this would violate his whole approach to interpreting the law, and that he had previously commented on the "sound distinction" that the Constitution created between the state and federal governments on matters of race, this apostle of adherence to the Constitution's original meaning rested in the end on manifestly Harlanesque policy grounds: "To pursue the concept of racial entitlement (even for the most admirable and benign of purposes) is to reinforce and preserve for future mischief the way of thinking that produced race slavery, race privilege and race hatred. In the eyes of government, we are just one race here. It is American."[51]

This is a very good policy, and one that Congress has already enacted in a variety of contexts.[52] Unfortunately, the Supreme Court has stubbornly refused to accept that congressional decision in some of the most important areas, including employment discrimination and discrimination by recipients of federal funding (which include virtually all private colleges and universities, as well as all public schools). The statutes enacted by Congress remain on the books, and the only obstacle to their enforcement is the Court's continuing refusal to overrule its own willfully erroneous precedents. Although the Court seems incapable either of attending to the language of the Constitution or of saying what the Reasonableness Clause it invented means these days, it should not be impossible to apply at least the clearest of the color-blind statutory commands. And if a majority of the Justices decide that those commands are politically desirable, they no doubt will apply them.

Conclusion

The Supreme Court sometimes follows the Constitution and statutes when adjudicating matters involving racial discrimination. But the frequency and insouciance with which it has refused to do so makes it very difficult to believe that it ever follows them *because* they are the law. Rather, the Court has arrogated to itself the privilege of enforcing whatever policy it believes is best.

Does this mean that we should admit the irrelevance of Congress, except to the extent that the Senate might be persuaded to reject judicial nominees who have policy views with which we disagree? Perhaps not. First, *Adarand* bespeaks at least a temporary inability or unwillingness of the Court to choose a policy for the nation. While this lasts, the Court may be likely to accept an unambiguous congressional reaffirmation of the principles embodied in the 1964 Civil Rights Act. And such a reaffirmation is not completely unthinkable. It is true that Congress is notoriously inclined to respond with inaction (or with hopelessly ambiguous legislation) when faced with a conflict between popular and enduring principles like governmental color blindness and the pressure of politically powerful special interests.[53] But enduring principles are sometimes vindicated, as so conspicuously happened when the 1964 Act was adopted.

In one respect, it should be easier to overcome the resistance to principle today than it was thirty-five years ago. For all their obstinate resistance to change, the forces seeking to preserve racial preferences are not nearly so powerful as those that were arrayed in defense of Jim Crow, and they do not have nearly as much at stake. And yet the stubborn fact remains that our current regime of racial preferences is not as brutally inconsistent with American principles as Jim Crow, let alone chattel slavery. Although the revival of color-blind laws would certainly advance the principles to which the Declaration of Independence first committed our nation, it would be an exaggeration to claim an advance comparable to that entailed in the destruction of Jim Crow. Thus, with less at stake now than in 1964, it should come as no surprise if Congress continues to temporize in the hope that someone else will somehow make the whole issue go away.

The most likely candidate for this role, of course, is the Supreme Court. But whatever Congress does or fails to do, and whatever further steps the Court itself decides to take, we may already have lost the possibility of resolving the issue through law. As Justice Curtis presciently noted in his *Dred Scott* dissent:

> When a strict interpretation of the Constitution, according to the fixed rules which govern the interpretation of laws, is abandoned, and the theoretical opinions of individuals are allowed to control its meaning, we have no longer a Constitution; we are under the government of individual men, who *for the time being* have power to declare what the Constitution is, according to their own views of what it ought to mean.[54]

Notes

For helpful comments on a preliminary draft of this essay, the author is grateful to Roger Clegg, Neal Devins, Stephen G. Gilles, Mara S. Lund, and John O. McGinnis.

1. See, e.g., *Adarand Constructors, Inc. v. Peña*, 515 U.S. 200 (1995) (racial classifications by federal government are presumptively unconstitutional); *Miller v. Johnson*, 515 U.S. 900 (1995) (racial gerrymandering is presumptively unconstitutional); *City of Richmond v. Croson*, 488 U.S. 469 (1989) (municipal set-aside program for minority contractors violated Fourteenth Amendment); *Taxman v. Board of Education of Township of Piscataway*, 91 F.3d 1547 (3d Cir. 1996) (employer with a racially balanced

workforce violated Civil Rights Act of 1964 when it granted a nonremedial racial preference in order to promote "racial diversity"), cert. granted, 117 S. Ct. 2506 (1997), cert. dismissed, 118 S. Ct. 595 (1997); *Hopwood v. Texas*, 78 F.3d 932 (5th Cir. 1996) (preference program for minority applicants to state law school violated Fourteenth Amendment), cert. denied, 518 U.S. 1033 (1996); *Podberesky v. Kirwan*, 38 F.3d 147 (4th Cir. 1994) (state university scholarship program open only to black students violated Fourteenth Amendment), cert. denied, 514 U.S. 1128 (1995).

2. See, e.g., Steven A. Holmes, "A Dilemma Led to a Deal Over Hiring Tied to Race," *New York Times*, November 23, 1997, sec. 1, p. 37.

3. See, e.g., Congressional Research Service, *Compilation and Overview of Federal Laws and Regulations Establishing Affirmative Action Goals or Other Preferences Based on Race, Gender, or Ethnicity*, Feb. 17, 1995 (identifying some 160 preferential laws and regulations) (reprinted in 141 *Congressional Record* S3930-3938 (daily ed., March 15, 1995)). This study included preferences based on sex and ethnicity as well as race. This essay will not deal with sex discrimination, and it will seldom distinguish between race and ethnicity. Though some exceptions exist (especially in the area of voting rights), the law generally treats race and ethnicity alike.

4. Whereas sugar quotas impose a very small cost on everyone, racial quotas will tend to impose on everyone a small risk of suffering a large loss (such as a job or promotion denied). This difference between the two phenomena does not significantly affect the analysis presented in the text.

5. U.S. Const., art. 1, sec. 2, cl. 3: "Representatives and direct Taxes shall be apportioned among the several States which may be included within this Union, according to their respective Numbers, which shall be determined by adding to the whole Number of free Persons, including those bound to Service for a Term of Years, and excluding Indians not taxed, three fifths of all other Persons."

6. Ibid., sec. 9, cl. 1: "The Migration or Importation of such Persons as any of the States now existing shall think proper to admit, shall not be prohibited by the Congress prior to the Year one thousand eight hundred and eight, but a Tax or duty may be imposed on such Importation, not exceeding ten dollars for each Person."

7. Ibid., art. 4, sec. 2, cl. 2: "No Person held to Service or Labour in one State, under the Laws thereof, escaping into another, shall, in Consequence of any Law or Regulation therein, be discharged from such Service or Labour, but shall be delivered up on Claim of the Party to whom such Service or Labour may be due."

8. *Scott v. Sandford*, 60 U.S. (19 How.) 393 (1857).

9. Ibid., p. 451. The Fifth Amendment provides in relevant part that no person shall be "deprived of life, liberty, or property, without due process of law."

10. See *Dred Scott*, pp. 572–75, 626–27 (Curtis, J., dissenting).

11. For a somewhat more detailed summary of the issues in *Dred Scott*, see Nelson Lund, "The Constitution, the Supreme Court, and Racial Politics," *Georgia State University Law Review* 12 (1996): 1129, 1132–36.

12. Abolishing slavery: U.S. Const., amend. 13, providing in relevant part: "Neither slavery nor involuntary Servitude, except as a punishment for crime whereof the party shall have been duly convicted, shall exist within the United States, or any place subject to their jurisdiction."

Nondiscrimination: ibid., amend. 14, providing in relevant part: "No State shall make or enforce any law which shall abridge the privileges or immunities of citizens of the United States; nor shall any State deprive any person of life, liberty, or property, without due process of law; nor deny to any person within its jurisdiction the equal protection of the laws." Much of modern constitutional law purports to be based on the due process and equal protection provisions of the Fourteenth Amendment. Very little of this law, however, or of the constitutional scholarship that typically aims to influence the development of the law, is based on any coherent and defensible analysis of the constitutional text. For an important exception, see John Harrison, "Reconstructing the Privileges and Immunities Clause," *Yale Law Journal* 101 (1992): 1385.

Right to vote: ibid., amend. 15, providing in relevant part: "The right of citizens of the United States to vote shall not be denied or abridged by the United States or by any State on account of race, color, or previous condition of servitude."

13. Significant elements of the statutory matrix enacted during Reconstruction for the enforcement of these protections were held unconstitutional, in whole or in part, by the Supreme Court. The Civil Rights Act of 1875, for example, was struck down in the *Civil Rights Cases*, 109 U.S. 3 (1883). Among the most important enactments that survived judicial review were the Civil Rights Act of 1866 (codified as amended at 18 U.S.C. sec. 242; 42 U.S.C. secs. 1981–83); the Enforcement Act of 1870 (codified as amended at 18 U.S.C. sec. 241); and the Ku Klux Klan Act of 1871 (codified as amended at 42 U.S.C. secs. 1983, 1985(c)). Eventually, the Supreme Court swung in the opposite direction and began broadening the reach of the surviving statutes in highly questionable ways. See, e.g., *Jones v. Alfred H. Mayer Co.*, 392 U.S. 409 (1968); *Runyon v. McCrary*, 427 U.S. 160 (1976); *Monell v. Dept. of Social Serv. of the City of New York*, 436 U.S. 658 (1978).

On early enforcement practices, see: Frank J. Scaturro, *President Grant Reconsidered* (Lanham, Md.: University Press of America, 1998), pp. 63–100; Robert J. Kaczorowski, "Federal Enforcement of Civil Rights During the First Reconstruction," *Fordham Urban Law Journal* 23 (1995): 155.

14. C. Vann Woodward, *Reunion and Reaction: The Compromise of 1877 and the End of Reconstruction*, 2d rev. ed. (Garden City, N.Y.: Doubleday, 1956); Michael W. McConnell, "The Forgotten Constitutional Moment," *Constitutional Commentary* 11 (1994): 115, 123–40.

15. 163 U.S. 537 (1896).

16. Ibid., p. 550.

17. Ibid., p. 551.

18. Ibid., p. 552.

19. See, e.g., Nathaniel R. Jones, "The Harlan Dissent: The Road Not Taken—An American Tragedy," *Georgia State University Law Review* 12 (1996): 951.

20. 163 U.S. at 556 (quoting *Gibson v. Mississippi*, 162 U.S. 565 (1896)). To similar effect, see 163 U.S. at 554, 563.

21. A central purpose of the Fourteenth Amendment's Privileges or Immunities Clause was apparently to outlaw state restrictions of basic civil rights—like the right to contract—on the basis of race. See Harrison, "Reconstructing the Privileges and Immunities Clause." Like antimiscegenation laws, the statute at issue in *Plessy* imposed just such a restriction, and the fact that it imposed symmetrical racial restrictions on whites and blacks alike would seem merely to have rendered it unconstitutional in its application to both classes of citizens. See ibid., pp. 1459–60, 1462.

22. For further analysis of *Plessy*, see Lund, "The Constitution, the Supreme Court, and Racial Politics," pp. 1141–48.

23. See Andrew Kull, *The Color-Blind Constitution* (Cambridge, Mass.: Harvard University Press, 1992), p. 118: "Racial classifications, announced Justice Brown (in *Plessy*), are like every other sort of classification, and those racial classifications will be constitutional that a majority of the Supreme Court considers to be 'reasonable.' That rule of constitutional law, and no other, will explain every Supreme Court decision in the area of racial discrimination from 1896 to the present."

24. 347 U.S. 483, 489, 495 (1954).

25. Ibid., p. 494.

26. *Mayor of Baltimore v. Dawson*, 350 U.S. 877 (1955) (per curiam) (desegregating public beaches and bathhouses); *Holmes v. City of Atlanta*, 350 U.S. 879 (1955) (per curiam) (desegregating public golf courses); *Gayle v. Browder*, 352 U.S. 903 (1956) (per curiam) (desegregating public buses); *New Orleans City Park Improvement Ass'n. v. Detiege*, 358 U.S. 54 (1958) (per curiam) (desegregating public parks); *Turner v. City of Memphis*, 369 U.S. 350 (1962) (per curiam) (desegregating municipal airport restaurant); *Naim v. Naim*, 350 U.S. 891 (1955) (per curiam), 350 U.S. 985 (1956) (per curiam) (refusing to accept mandatory appellate jurisdiction over state supreme court decision upholding antimiscegenation statute).

27. Eventually, the Court got the feeling that the time was right to invalidate antimiscegenation laws. See *Loving v. Virginia*, 388 U.S. 1 (1967).

28. See *Cooper v. Aaron*, 358 U.S. 1, 18 (1958): "The interpretation of the Fourteenth Amendment enunciated by this Court in the *Brown* case is the supreme law of the land." The Constitution, by way of contrast, provides: "This Constitution, and the Laws of the United States which shall be made in Pursuance thereof; and all Treaties made, or which shall be made, under the authority of the United States, shall be the supreme Law of the Land." U.S. Const., art. 6, cl. 2.

29. For a powerful and detailed presentation of legal arguments (too complicated to summarize here) that support the result in *Brown*, see Michael W. McConnell, "Originalism and the Desegregation Decisions," *Virginia Law Review* (1995): 947. Had

the Court adopted an argument along the lines of Professor McConnell's, *Brown* would have been an ordinary and respectable (if not unchallengeable) act of constitutional interpretation. The Court might have had to wait until someone developed an argument like McConnell's, but it is hard to believe—in light of the extraordinary industry and resourcefulness that the modern civil rights bar has displayed—that it would have had to wait forty years. In any event, the Supreme Court was unwilling to wait for such an argument and perhaps had already created an intellectual climate that discouraged the kind of research and analysis set forth in McConnell's work.

30. There is a controversy about the exact nature of *Brown*'s ultimate and indirect effects. Compare, e.g., Gerald N. Rosenberg, *The Hollow Hope: Can Courts Bring About Social Change?* (Chicago: University of Chicago Press, 1991), pp. 39–174 (emphasizing evidence suggesting that *Brown* contributed little to the modern civil rights revolution), with Neal Devins, "Judicial Matters," *California Law Review* 80 (1992): 1027, 1039–46 (accusing Rosenberg of exaggeration and arguing that *Brown* both helped energize the civil rights movement and produced important direct effects beginning in 1964). Although it is probably impossible to eliminate all doubt about the nature of *Brown*'s indirect effects, or to know for sure what would and would not have happened without that decision, it is agreed that no significant desegregation took place until after the Civil Rights Act of 1964. In addition to the sources cited above, see Gary Orfield, *The Reconstruction of Southern Education: The Schools and the 1964 Civil Rights Act* (New York: Wiley-Interscience, 1969), pp. 356–57; Neal Devins and James Stedman, "New Federalism in Education: The Meaning of the Chicago School Desegregation Cases," *Notre Dame Law Review* 59 (1984): 1243, 1245–51.

31. 42 U.S.C. sec. 2000e-2(a). The statute contains certain exceptions to this general rule against discrimination, the most important of which is an exemption for small, private employers. See ibid., sec. 2000e(b). Only one of the other exceptions arguably authorizes racial discrimination, and that is limited to preferences for American Indians living on or near Indian reservations. See ibid., sec. 2000e-2(i). One other exception appears to authorize certain forms of discrimination based on national origin (but not race); this rarely litigated exception has been construed narrowly. See ibid., sec. 2000e-2(e); *Avigliano v. Sumitomo Shoji America, Inc.*, 638 F.2d 552, 559 (2d Cir. 1981) ("'bona fide occupational qualification' ('bfoq') exception of Title VII is to be construed narrowly in the normal context" (citing *Dothard v. Rawlinson*, 433 U.S. 321, 334 (1977)), vacated on other grounds, 457 U.S. 176 (1982).

As applied to the state and federal governments, the prohibition of employment discrimination is unquestionably constitutional. The Supreme Court's broad reading of Congress's power under the Commerce Clause has been assumed to eliminate any doubt about the constitutionality of prohibiting discrimination by private employers. See, e.g., *EEOC v. Ratliff*, 906 F.2d 1314, 1315–16 (9th Cir. 1990).

32. 42 U.S.C. sec. 2000e-2(j).

33. *Griggs v. Duke Power Co.*, 401 U.S. 424 (1971).

34. For a detailed discussion of the *Griggs* opinion, see Nelson Lund, "The Law of

Affirmative Action in and After the Civil Rights Act of 1991: Congress Invites Judicial Reform," *George Mason Law Review* 6 (1997): 87, 91–101.

35. The *Griggs* opinion was in several respects highly confused and ambiguous, and it left considerable uncertainty about the *extent* to which employers with "too few" minorities were thereby exposed to legal liability. In a series of later decisions, culminating in *Wards Cove Packing Co. v. Atonio*, 490 U.S. 642 (1989), the Supreme Court eventually interpreted *Griggs* in a manner that seemed to insulate employers from liability in most cases involving normal business practices that are not intentionally discriminatory. In 1991, Congress codified a version of the *Griggs–Wards Cove* theory of liability, apparently preserving most of the employer protections established in *Wards Cove* but using language that was highly ambiguous in several important respects. See Nelson Lund, "Retroactivity, Institutional Incentives, and the Politics of Civil Rights," *Public Interest Law Review* (1995): 87, 109–10; Lund, "The Law of Affirmative Action in and After the Civil Rights Act of 1991," p. 116 and n. 149. The Supreme Court has not yet interpreted these provisions of the 1991 statute, but some lower courts have adopted highly questionable interpretations of the law, which seem likely to create new incentives for quotas. See, e.g., *Lanning v. SEPTA*, 181 F.3d 478 (3d Cir. 1999); *Bradley v. Pizzaco of Nebraska, Inc.*, 7 F.3d 795 (8th Cir. 1993).

36. *United Steelworkers v. Weber*, 443 U.S. 193, 208 (1979).

37. Ibid., p. 201.

38. For a brief discussion of the legal arguments in *Weber*, see Lund, "The Law of Affirmative Action in and After the Civil Rights Act of 1991," pp. 101–6.

39. 42 U.S.C. sec. 2000d. Justice Stevens's opinion, which was joined by Chief Justice Burger and by Justices Stewart and Rehnquist, included a detailed demonstration of the congruence between this language, which Stevens correctly described as "crystal clear," and the congressional intent reflected in the debates leading up to passage of the 1964 Act.

40. Justice Powell implicitly recognized the gimmickry when he explained that the advantage of the Harvard approach was that applicants are not "foreclosed from *all* consideration" because of their race or ethnicity (438 U.S. at 318, emphasis added). He nonetheless assured would-be discriminators that the gimmick would work because "a court would not assume that a university, professing to employ a facially nondiscriminatory admissions policy, would operate it as a cover for the functional equivalent of a quota system."

41. Justice Stevens pointed out that the only issue before the Court was the validity of the set-aside program challenged in the *Bakke* litigation. See 438 U.S. at 408–11 (Stevens, J., dissenting). Five Justices having voted to hold that program invalid under the 1964 Act, the remarks of Justice Powell about the validity of materially different affirmative action programs should not properly be considered part of the Court's holding. See, e.g., Alan J. Meese, "Reinventing *Bakke*," 1 *Green Bag 2d* 381 (1998).

42. The Court has issued one majority opinion, in *Metro Broadcasting, Inc. v. FCC*,

497 U.S. 547 (1990), a decision that was later overruled by *Adarand Constructors, Inc. v. Peña*, 515 U.S. 200, 225–27 (1995).

43. *Adarand Constructors, Inc. v. Peña*, 515 U.S. 200 (1995).

44. See U.S. Const., amend. 14.

45. *Bolling v. Sharpe*, 347 U.S. 497, 500 (1954).

46. One subsection of the opinion, which dealt with the doctrine of *stare decisis*, expressed the views of only two Justices. Four Justices concurred in the remainder of the opinion, which (as explained below) was also joined to some indeterminate extent by a fifth Justice.

47. 515 U.S. at 227.

48. *Adarand* expressly refused to overrule *Fullilove v. Klutznick*, 448 U.S. 448 (1980), which had upheld a minority preference program almost identical to the one at issue in *Adarand*. As the chief congressional sponsor of the *Fullilove* program had explained, its purpose was to make sure that "minority businesses get a fair share of the action." 123 *Congressional Record* 5327 (1977) (remarks of Rep. Parren Mitchell).

49. Although the plurality opinion declared that the Constitution required the courts to treat all races "consistently" when applying equal protection analysis (515 U.S. at 224), it nevertheless concluded that the constitutionality of a law might well depend on which race it disfavored: "The principle of consistency simply means that whenever the government treats any person unequally because of his or her race, that person has suffered an injury that falls squarely within the language and spirit of the Constitution's guarantee of equal protection. It says nothing about the ultimate validity of any particular law; that determination is the job of the court applying strict scrutiny. The principle of consistency explains the circumstances in which the injury requiring strict scrutiny occurs. The application of strict scrutiny, in turn, determines whether a compelling governmental interest justifies the infliction of that injury" (ibid., pp. 229–30). Thus does the Supreme Court render consistency and inconsistency consistent. For a detailed discussion of *Adarand*'s place in the Court's lengthy exercise in issue avoidance, see Neal Devins, "*Adarand Constructors, Inc. v. Peña* and the Continuing Irrelevance of Supreme Court Affirmative Action Decisions," *William and Mary Law Review* 37 (1996): 673.

50. 515 U.S. at 239 (Scalia, J., concurring in part and concurring in the judgment).

51. *Adarand*, 515 U.S. at 239 (Scalia, J., concurring in part and concurring in the judgment). This passage was clearly inspired by Harlans words: "In view of the Constitution, in the eye of the law, there is in this country no superior, dominant, ruling class of citizens. There is no caste here. Our Constitution is color-blind, and neither knows nor tolerates classes among citizens. . . . The humblest is the peer of the most powerful. The law regards man as man, and takes no account of his surroundings or of his color when his civil rights as guaranteed by the supreme law of the land are involved. . . . State enactments, regulating the enjoyment of civil rights, upon the basis of race, and cunningly devised to defeat legitimate results of the war, under the pretense

of recognizing equality of rights, can have no other result than to render permanent peace impossible, and to keep alive a conflict of races, the continuance of which must do harm to all concerned." *Plessy v. Ferguson*, 163 U.S. at 559–61 (Harlan, J, dissenting). On the "sound distinction" between the state and federal governments, see *City of Richmond v. J. A. Croson Co.*, 488 U.S. 469, 521–24 (1989) (Scalia, J., concurring in the judgment).

52. See the summary, earlier in this essay, of the main provisions of the Civil Rights Act of 1964. Congress's departures from the policy of governmental color blindness have occurred mostly in the discrete and relatively limited context of set-aside programs like the one at issue in *Adarand*.

53. Examples of particularly excruciating ambiguity can be found in the Civil Rights Act of 1991 and the Voting Rights Act amendments of 1982. For a thorough discussion of the 1982 amendments, see Abigail N. Thernstrom, *Whose Votes Count? Affirmative Action and Minority Voting Rights* (Cambridge, Mass.: Harvard University Press, 1987).

54. 60 U.S. (19 How.) at 620–21; emphasis added.

PART SIX

POLITICS

Race, Ethnicity, and Politics in American History

MICHAEL BARONE

THE ROLE OF RACE in American politics cannot be understood except as an example of the role of ethnicity in American politics. In spite of the long-standing elite opinion that ethnicity should not play any role in politics, that voters and politicians should act without regard to ethnic factors, in fact ethnicity has always played an important part in our politics. This is what we should expect in a country that has always had forms of racial and ethnic discrimination, and in which civic and university and corporate elites, for all their tut-tutting about ethnic politics, have often been more hearty practitioners than ordinary people of ethnic discrimination—of anti-Jewish discrimination up through the 1960s and of racial quotas and preferences since the 1970s.

Over the long course of our history politics has more often divided Americans along cultural than along economic lines—along lines of region, race, ethnicity, religion, and personal values. This is natural in a country that has almost always been economically successful and culturally multivarious, in which economic upward mobility has been the common experience and in which cultural and ethnic identities have often been lasting and tenacious. It has been observed by none less than our current vice president that we are moving into a new and unprecedented era in American history in which our people are being transformed from one to many. But Mr. Gore in doing so not only mistranslated the national motto *E pluribus unum*—a mistake that would have been met with ridicule if made by his predecessor—but also ignored the long history of American political divides along racial and ethnic lines. We are not in a totally new place; we have been here before, and we can learn from our history—and our motto.

The common pattern seems to be this: there is an inrush into the electorate of a new ethnic or racial group, with a strong preference for one political party, and politics seems to be structured around this division. Attempts are made to limit the new group's strength in the electorate, sometimes successfully, more often not. Then there are inrushes of other groups, with checkerboarded political preferences, depending more on local circumstances and issues than on any single national pattern. Politicians and parties compete for the support of these groups, with generally benign results. Eventually, there is regression to mean: the issues and identities that once led a group to favor one party heavily are replaced by other issues and identities that tend to divide them pretty much along the lines of the electorate generally. But this is a process that can take a long time, and in which the original identities and issues continue to play an important role in politics for many years.

Such inrushes occurred even in colonial times. Puritans in Massachusetts were alarmed by inrushes of Anabaptists; the response was expulsion and the establishment of the Rhode Island colony. Benjamin Franklin was alarmed by the growing numbers of Germans in the interior of Pennsylvania; the response was gerrymandering to maintain the primacy of the Delaware River valley counties settled by Quakers and others from the North Midlands of Britain. Coastal North Carolinians were alarmed by the inrush of Scots-Irish to the Piedmont; the response was Loyalism in the Revolution. Interestingly, these divisions are still discernible in the election returns: Massachusetts and Rhode Island remain separate; the

Pennsylvania Dutch counties are the most heavily Republican territory in the Northeast; the North Carolina lowlands are much more Democratic than the Piedmont.

The first great inrush of newcomers to the electorate of the young Republic, of Irish Catholics, began in large numbers after the potato famine of 1846. But even in the 1830s the Whig mayor of New York, Philip Hone, noted with disapproval how Irish immigrants were being marched from the docks to the polls by Democratic precinct politicians; in those days noncitizens could vote. The Whig governor of New York, William Seward, elected in 1838, sought the Irish votes by promising state support for Catholic schools.

But by overwhelming numbers the Irish became Democrats. The party of Andrew Jackson, following the example of Thomas Jefferson, was more friendly to religious dissenters than its rivals; Whig Connecticut in the 1830s still had an established Protestant church. The Democracy (as it was called) was a laissez-faire party, in economics and also in culture. The Whigs favored federal road-building, and Upstate New York, settled mostly by New England Yankees and heavily Whig, was seething with agitation for abolition of slavery, temperance and prohibition, new Protestant sects— busybody activism abhorrent to the Irish. The Irish were greeted by discrimination; my Irish American grandmother, born in 1881, explained her support of the Civil Rights Act of 1964 by recalling the "No Irish Need Apply" signs of the late nineteenth and early twentieth centuries. There was a racial element here: the Irish, with low rates of intermarriage and usually of distinctive appearance, were widely regarded as not "white."

Their Democratic preference remained solid for more than a century. Irish votes were what made New York, the largest and by far the most politically prominent state, a key marginal state in most elections rather than heavily Whig and then Republican. In New England, politics was divided on Catholic-Protestant lines up through 1960s as much as politics is divided on black-white lines in Mississippi today. The Irish propensity for large families made Yankee Republicans proponents of birth control (President George Bush's mother supported Planned Parenthood even as she had five children herself) in an effort to prevent being outnumbered by Catholics. But it was in vain. In 1918 Henry Cabot Lodge defeated John F. Fitzgerald in a Senate race divided on Catholic-Protestant lines; by 1952 the numbers had changed enough that Fitzgerald's grandson defeated Lodge's grandson for reelection.

The strong Irish preference for Democrats continued up through 1960, when Fitzgerald's grandson was elected president. In that election, 78 percent of Catholics voted for John Kennedy, while 63 percent of white Protestants voted for the Scots-Irish Protestant Richard Nixon. Four years later, even as Lyndon Johnson was elected by a landslide, the Catholic Democratic percentage declined slightly to 76 percent; it has never remotely approached those levels since. You can only elect the first Irish Catholic president once. The election of Kennedy, his high job approval, the pomp and ceremony of his funeral—all established conclusively that Catholics were fully American. At the same time, with the Vatican II reforms, a sudden decline in the number of large Catholic families and in vocations for the priesthood, and the end of the Latin mass and meatless Fridays, Catholics were becoming less distinctive. Today Irish Catholics vote pretty much like the electorate as a whole.

Following the inrush of Irish Catholics was a second stream of new voters, Germans who arrived in large numbers after the failed revolutions of 1848 and up through the 1880s. Unlike the Irish, they did not all head for the major cities—many became farmers—and they were not monolithically Democratic. German Protestants tended to be Whigs and then Republicans; German Catholics were more Democratic; Germans in heavily German Milwaukee in time elected a Socialist mayor and congressman (the latter was a secular Jew but seems to have been regarded by himself and by voters as an ethnic German). In some places the Germans voted against Protestant Republicans; in others they voted against Irish Democrats. Germans were wooed by both political parties. One reason Abraham Lincoln was nominated by the Republicans in 1860 was that he had always opposed the nativism of the American (Know-Nothing) party, many of whose supporters had become Republicans: the Republican kingmakers wanted a candidate who could win German votes in New York, Pennsylvania, Ohio, and Indiana. Republicans promoted to the Cabinet Carl Schurz, a German immigrant with a political base in St. Louis's German community.

German ethnicity survived as a political factor until well into the twentieth century. Many German Americans opposed American entry into World War I and were understandably resentful of the heavy-handed, even authoritarian way in which Woodrow Wilson's administration suppressed German culture. In 1940 German Americans, though few were sympathetic to the Nazis, and Scandinavian Americans turned sharply against Franklin Roosevelt, fearful that he would produce war with Germany; this was the "isolationist" vote. But there were other German traditions as well. New York's Senator Robert Wagner, born in Germany and a frequent visitor there, was an admirer of Germany's social democratic tradition. He was one of the few Democratic officeholders in the early 1930s who supported welfare state measures (most others were progressive Republicans like Robert LaFollette Jr., from heavily German Wisconsin). Wagner was the lead sponsor of the Social Security Act and the National Labor Relations Act, which made possible the rise of the industrial unions.

The next great inrush of an ethnic group into the electorate resulted from the enfranchisement of the former slaves after the Civil War. Suddenly, with federal troops enforcing their rights, blacks were a majority of voters in South Carolina and Mississippi and large minorities in several other southern states. (There were few blacks in northern states, some of which had prohibited the settlement of free blacks; in 1870, 91 percent of blacks lived in the South.) Not surprisingly, they were overwhelmingly Republican, voting 90 percent or more for the party of the man who signed the Emancipation Proclamation. This black preference for the Republicans continued up through the 1930s; most blacks voted for Herbert Hoover over Franklin Roosevelt in 1932. But blacks switched to the Democratic party in the 1930s in thanks for New Deal programs and the pro–civil rights stance of some New Dealers—interestingly, the most prominent, Eleanor Roosevelt, Harold Ickes, and Henry Wallace, were all former Republicans themselves. It should be noted that Democratic percentages among blacks were not nearly as high in the 1940s and 1950s as they became starting in the 1964 election. John Kennedy won 63 percent of black votes, far below his 78 percent among Catholics, and such prominent blacks as Martin Luther King Sr. and Jackie Robinson supported Richard Nixon.

But of course for many years most Americans of African descent were not allowed to vote. The inrush of blacks into the southern electorate in the 1860s and early 1870s was followed by moves by white Democrats to bar them from voting. Often these took the form of physical intimidation that might well be called terrorism; this persisted until the 1960s. Legal means were used as well: grandfather clauses, poll taxes, all-white Democratic primaries, literacy requirements administered discriminatorily.

In some southern cities—Memphis, New Orleans—blacks were allowed to vote on the understanding that they would vote as directed by white political bosses. In other southern cities—Richmond, Louisville—a tradition of black Republican voting continued. But for nearly 100 years most Americans of African descent were disenfranchised. In the 1930s blacks made up perhaps 3 percent of the national electorate; Jews, with 4 percent, were a larger voting bloc. In 1948 the benign competition to be seen as supporters of civil rights among Harry Truman, Thomas Dewey, and Henry Wallace was aimed politically more at Jewish voters in New York and other large and politically marginal northern states than at the mostly disenfranchised blacks in the politically mostly safely Democratic states of the South.

Inrush and disenfranchisement: this was the pattern for blacks, but it was, to a lesser extent, the pattern among Irish and other immigrant groups as well. By the late nineteenth century, noncitizens were no longer allowed to vote. Voter registration requirements were passed, literacy requirements were passed, party printing of ballots was prohibited—all at least partly to reduce the huge numbers of immigrants and ethnics voting. Voter participation—the percentage of the potential electorate voting—peaked in the 1890s and declined rapidly up through the 1920s. Even the enfranchisement of women was motivated in part by the belief that immigrant and Catholic women would not vote while white Protestants would, and so it turned out: Republicans carried Illinois in 1916, when, thanks to its enfranchisement of women, it cast more votes than any other state, and the Nineteenth Amendment, passed in 1919 (but never ratified by New York) swelled Republican percentages in the 1920s.

These methods of partial disenfranchisement also reduced voter participation by the eastern and southern European immigrants who began arriving in large numbers around 1880—the most numerous were Italians, Jews, and Poles. Like the Irish and unlike the Germans, they flocked almost exclusively to the industrial cities of the northeast and the Great Lakes; like the Germans and unlike the Irish, these immigrants developed checkerboard patterns of political allegiance. It was almost an odd-even phenomenon: in any given metropolitan area, the native Protestants tended to vote Republican, the second group (almost always the Irish) Democratic, the next group Republican, the next Democratic, and so forth. Thus, Italians in New Haven tended to vote Republican, Italians in Cleveland Democratic. Poles in Buffalo were Republican, in Detroit Democratic. In Philadelphia, which developed a strong Republican machine, almost every group tended to vote Republican; in New York, with its strong Democratic machine, most groups tended to vote Democratic.

The Jews were an exception, voting often for Socialists and other leftist candidates. In New York, repelled by the heavily Irish Tammany Hall, they voted for Social Democratic Fusion candidates, of whom the most prominent was Fiorello LaGuardia, a half-Italian, half-Jewish Episcopalian who was elected to Congress in the 1920s on the Republican and Socialist tickets and mayor in 1933, 1937, and 1941 on the Republican and American Labor party lines. In often marginal and fiercely contested New York, the Jews often held the key votes. This had national consequences, for if the Jews on the party spectrum stood between Upstate Protestants and New York City Catholics, on the issues spectrum they were well to the left of both groups—social democratic on economic issues, pro–civil rights and civil liberties on cultural issues. This helps to explain the leftish leanings of nationally important Democrats like Al Smith, Robert Wagner, and Franklin Roosevelt and Republicans like Thomas Dewey and Nelson Rockefeller.

The New Deal changed the checkerboard voting patterns of these ethnic groups. Local loyalties were overshadowed by national issues, and all the groups became heavily Democratic by the late 1930s. Jews, poised between the two parties in the 1920s, became heavily Democratic by the 1940s, giving Roosevelt more than 80 percent of their votes; they remain heavily Democratic today, though a smaller proportion of the electorate (2 percent versus 4 percent). In time, ethnic groups like the Italians and Poles tended to regress to mean; after the elections of 1960 and 1964 they became much less heavily Democratic, like the Irish. This was part of a process of assimilation. Immigration was reduced to negligible levels by the immigration act of 1924, and there was no inrush of immigrant groups until after the law was revised in 1965.

At the time of Pearl Harbor, America seemed to have reached a pause in its racial and ethnic politics. But only a pause. For in the second half of the century, new groups entered the electorate, the groups that are now officially recognized as "minorities"—blacks, Hispanics, and Asians. On the surface this seems to have produced an altogether new "multicultural" politics, as predicted by Al Gore among others; some analysts proclaim with relish that white non-Hispanics will some time in the next century cease to be a majority and that "people of color" will control American politics. But on closer examination these new inrushes of voters have produced an ethnic politics closely, almost eerily, resembling the ethnic politics of 100 years ago. And the results are likely to be similar: one constituency remaining solidly Democratic for years, others the subject of benign competition between the parties, and ultimately regression to mean.

First came the inrush of blacks into the electorate between 1940 and 1970. It was caused first by the huge migration of blacks from the rural South to the cities of the North and then by the end of the disenfranchisement of blacks in the South after passage of the Voting Rights Act of 1965. Before 1940 there was relatively little migration of blacks to the North. In

1900, 90 percent of blacks still lived in the South; in 1940, in spite of some migration in World War I and the emergence of the visible black ghettoes of Harlem and South Side Chicago, 77 percent of blacks still lived in the South. But the war industries of the 1940s and the booming auto and steel factories of the 1950s and 1960s, whose unions strongly opposed racial discrimination, brought blacks north: the percentage of blacks living in the North rose from 23 percent in 1940 to 32 percent in 1950, 40 percent in 1960, and 47 percent in 1970. At that point, migration leveled off; as many blacks moved south as north, and the percentage in the North was still 47 percent in 1990. But for three decades the black move northward was one of the great migrations of American history.

These northward-moving blacks became the most heavily Democratic constituency in the nation—perhaps even more Democratic than the Irish at their most monopartisan. In some states their votes were actively sought by Republicans, notably Nelson Rockefeller in New York. But where civil rights was strongly championed by Democrats, like Governor Mennen Williams and UAW President Walter Reuther in Michigan, blacks were voting 90 percent or more Democratic in the 1950s. (Interestingly, Williams came from a Republican and Reuther from a Social Democratic family; neither had any connection with the laissez-faire Democratic party, which refused to interfere with either segregation or the saloon.) The Democratic percentage among blacks everywhere rose to around 90 percent when President Kennedy backed the civil rights bill in 1963 and when the Republican party's presidential nominee, Barry Goldwater, voted against it in 1964 (and in spite of the fact that a higher proportion of congressional Republicans than of Democrats voted for it). Since then, blacks have enthusiastically supported the national Democrats' antipoverty and big government programs. They have strongly supported race quotas and preferences, which were originated in the Nixon administration but have been supported enthusiastically by Democratic and opposed by some Republican politicians. They gave overwhelming percentages to Jimmy Carter, Walter Mondale, Michael Dukakis, and Bill Clinton and almost unanimously supported Clinton against charges of scandal in 1998. For the last third of the twentieth century, they have been the solid core of the Democratic party.

Then the passage of the Voting Rights Act of 1965 suddenly swept away all barriers against blacks voting in the South. Blacks rose from about 6 percent of the electorate in 1964 to 10 percent in 1968. But this did not have entirely positive effects for the Democrats, for in the same years, white Catholic voters were moving toward the Republicans. In part this was a natural regression to mean: the first Catholic president had been elected, and they were free to decide on other issues. But in part it was a reaction to the urban riots of 1964–1968, to the attacks by black politicians on mostly white police forces, to the school busing ordered by some federal judges in the North, to the antipoverty programs, which were closely associated with blacks.

In the meantime, southern white voters were moving rapidly away from the Democratic party. In part this was also a regression to mean: it was 100 years since Sherman marched through Georgia (John Kennedy's number two state in 1960). But it was also in part a response to issues. Only a negligible number of southern whites wanted to restore segregation: the integration of public accommodations and workplaces ordered by the 1964 Civil Rights Act was accepted much more readily than almost anyone expected. But most southern whites did oppose the antipoverty programs at home and the national Democrats' increasingly dovish policies abroad. This did not mean that black-backed candidates always lost in the South: Andrew Young was elected to Congress by a white-majority district in Atlanta as early as 1972. But just as Yankee Protestants united in voting against Irish-backed Democrats in Massachusetts in the early 1900s, so did white Southerners unite in voting against black-backed national Democrats in Mississippi in the 1970s.

The Voting Rights Act was not the only 1965 law that changed the shape of the American electorate. So did the 1965 immigration act, in ways that were almost entirely unforeseen. Many members voting for it may have expected a resumption of the European immigration so sharply cut off in 1924. But postwar Europe was prosperous and sent few immigrants.

Instead they mostly came from Latin America and from Asia. Latin America accounted for 40 percent of immigrants in 1971–1980 and 39 percent in 1981–1993, Asia (including the Middle East) for 36 percent in 1971–1980 and 27 percent in 1981–1993.

Like the immigrant groups that followed the Irish from the 1850s to the 1920s, these new Hispanic and Asian groups did not flock almost unanimously as "people of color" to the Democratic party but produced a checkerboard pattern of political allegiances. Hispanics and Asians have not necessarily seen discrimination as their greatest problem and have not seen big government as their greatest friend; for them America has been not an oppressor but a haven. And some liberal policies have arguably worked against their interests. Poor public education and bilingual education programs that prevent children from learning how to speak, read, and write English well have arguably hurt Hispanics; racial quotas and preferences have clearly hurt Asians, just as they hurt Jews from the 1920s to the 1960s. It simply does not make sense to see today's Hispanics and Asians as the counterparts of blacks during the civil rights revolution. Certainly, their political behavior is different. Blacks remain heavily Democratic, but the picture is quite different among Hispanics and Asians. Hispanics on balance currently lean Democratic, but not everywhere, and by differing margins and for different reasons in different places. Asians have actually been trending Republican: they were the only group in exit polls to register a higher percentage for George Bush in 1992 than in 1988, and they voted by a narrow margin for Bob Dole over Bill Clinton in 1996.

Today's blacks, like the Irish of 100 years ago, have a history that gives them reason to doubt the legitimacy of the demands of the larger society— slavery and segregation in one case, anti-Catholic laws in the other. Like the Irish of 1900, the blacks of 2000 are concentrated heavily in ghettoized neighborhoods of big cities; even in the South, heavily black rural communities have continued to lose population, and an increasing percentage of southern blacks live in the region's burgeoning metropolitan areas. To be sure, significant numbers of blacks have moved to suburbs—some to heavily black neighborhoods, others to mostly white areas—just as many Irish were moving out from Boston in 1900. But they are still more highly concentrated than any other identifiable ethnic group.

This has been reflected in political representation. In the 1990s redistricting the Voting Rights Act was interpreted as requiring the maximization of the number of majority-black districts, resulting in many convoluted district lines and a sharp increase in the number of black congressmen and state legislators. However, such districting also reduced the number of blacks in adjacent districts, and so arguably reduced the number of congressmen with an incentive to pay heed to black voters' opinions. It also meant that most successful black politicians fell on the far left of the Democratic party, a comfortable place in majority-black constituencies but not a good position from which to seek statewide or national office; it is significant that the first black to lead in presidential polls was not Jesse Jackson, who rose through protest politics, but Colin Powell, who rose through the most integrated segment of American society, the United States Army.

The blacks of 2000, like the Irish of 1900, have had high rates of crime and substance abuse; they have also produced large numbers of police officers and an influential clergy. They have produced many great athletes and entertainers and a cultural style that most Americans find attractive. They have tended not to perform well in economic markets, but they have shown an affinity for rising in hierarchies, particularly the public sector and in electoral politics. California, which is only 7 percent black, has over the past twenty years produced a black lieutenant governor and a black Assembly speaker, black mayors of Los Angeles and San Francisco, and came within 1 percent of electing a black governor in 1982. And of course blacks in 2000, like the Irish in 1900, are one of the main core constituencies of the Democratic party, although blacks are still awaiting, as the Irish were a century ago, their Al Smith and John F. Kennedy.

The blacks of 2000, like the Irish of 1900, show no sign of abandoning their overwhelming allegiance to the Democratic party. Republican percentages among blacks have risen in the last two decades, but only very slightly except for a few unusual elections in a few states. Indeed, allegiance to liberal Democratic ideas seems stronger among more educated and affluent blacks than among others; yet the cultural conservatism of many higher religious blacks has not translated into support for Republican candidates to any substantial extent. Regression to mean still seems a long time ahead in the future.

Today's Hispanics, like the Italians of 1900, come from societies with traditions of ineffective centralism, in which neither public nor private institutions can be trusted to act fairly or impartially; southern Italians and Latin Americans were all subjects of the Emperor Charles V. Like the Italians, the Hispanics have migrated vast distances geographically and psychologically, moving from isolated and backward farming villages to particular city neighborhoods pioneered by relatives and neighbors from home. The Hispanics of 2000, like the Italians of 1900, tend to be concentrated in only a few states (even today, half of all Italian Americans live within 100 miles of New York City): more than three-quarters of Hispanics live in California, Texas, New York, Florida, and Illinois.

Here they often maintain contact with their old homes, sending back remittances and in many cases returning; their commitment to remaining in the United States is in many cases not total. They often have strong religious faith, but they tend to mistrust most institutions, including government and businesses. They work exceedingly hard, and often with great pride in craftsmanship, but often do not seek to rise economically and tend to drop out of school early. They depend on family and hard work to make their way.

Politically, the Hispanics of 2000, like the Italians of 1900, tend to vote for different parties in different cities. Cubans in Miami are heavily Republican, Puerto Ricans in New York heavily Democratic. There are rivalries as well between different Hispanic groups: in New York Dominicans may overtake Puerto Ricans as the leading Hispanic group, while in Chicago the North Side Puerto Ricans currently have an edge over the South Side Mexicans.

Most important are the sharp differences between the politics of Latinos in the two largest states, Texas and California. Mexican Americans in Texas, some of whom have deep roots in local communities and churches, elect Republican and conservative Democratic congressmen and legislators as often as liberal Democrats and in 1998 polls were shown casting majorities for Republican Governor George W. Bush. The pro-Bush feeling can be attributed to his fluent Spanish, his frequent visits to Hispanic communities, his policy of close ties with Mexico, his emphasis on family and hard work—his showing that he understands and appreciates the Latinos' strengths. It also may rest on the fact that relations between Anglos and Latinos in Texas, for all its past history, have been relatively close and friendly: almost nobody doubts that Latinos are truly Texans.

In contrast, Mexican Americans in California often seem to live in a nation apart and are met with a certain hostility by Anglo elites, from the leftish Jews of Los Angeles's Westside to the rightish whites living in gated communities in the outer edges of metro Los Angeles, to San Diego surfers worried about the discharges of Tijuana's sewage on their beaches. California's Latinos tend to live in enormous swaths of metro L.A. that until very recently had few Latinos, in atomized local communities where politics is waged by direct mail financed by rich liberals. The candidates they elect tend to come from a small group of politically connected Latino Left Democrats.

In addition, California Latinos were repelled by the 1994 campaign of Republican Governor Pete Wilson and his support of Proposition 187, barring aid to illegal immigrants. What bothered them was less the substance of the issue (some 30 percent of Latinos voted for it) but the implication they saw in Wilson's ads that immigrants were coming to California only to get on the welfare rolls. "He's saying we're lazy," as one Latino businessman put it, although in fact Hispanic men have the highest workforce participation rate of any measured group. Wilson's failure to appreciate the genuine strengths of California's Latinos and, until 1998, at least, California Republicans' apparent lack of interest in them have produced higher Democratic percentages among Latinos there in the late 1990s than in the middle 1980s—an ominous sign for national Republicans because

Latino turnout has been rising sharply, and without a sizable share of Latino votes a Republican presidential ticket will have trouble carrying California.

Latino voters could turn out to be the focus of the 2000 presidential race. If the Republicans nominate Bush, they would have a good chance of turning around the Mexican American vote in California, in consolidating Cuban American support in Florida (where his brother Jeb Bush was elected governor in 1998), and in making inroads among Latinos in other large states. The Democrats may counter that by nominating for vice president Energy Secretary Bill Richardson, former New Mexico congressman and ambassador to the United Nations, who, despite his name, is Hispanic. There is a historic precedent, the focus by both Democratic and Republican strategists on Jewish voters in 1948.

Finally, the Asian Americans of 2000 in many ways resemble the Jews of 1900. The Asians, like the Jews, come from places with ancient traditions of great learning and sophistication but with little experience with an independent civil society or a reliable rule of law. Like the Jews, many Asians in this century—overseas Chinese, Vietnamese, Koreans, Moslems and Hindus in India and Pakistan—have been subject to persecution and have had to make their way in the world amid grave dangers. They tend to excel at academic studies and have quickly earned many places at universities—and have been greeted by quotas that bar them in spite of their achievements. They have had great economic success and perform well in economic markets. Like the Jews, they tend to be concentrated in a few places—in the great metropolitan areas of California, in New York City, around Washington, D.C., Chicago, and Houston. (The Japanese Americans of Hawaii are mostly descended from immigrants who arrived in the late nineteenth and early twentieth centuries.)

Politically, the Asians have been taking a different route from the Jews. Few, aside from some campus activists, have been attracted to left-wing causes; some but not very many (the Japanese Americans in Hawaii) have been staunch organization Democrats. Asians with a history of anticommunism have voted mostly Republican: Koreans, Vietnamese, Taiwanese. Filipinos, mostly in low-income jobs and subject to discrimination by

Americans for a century, have been heavily Democratic. The Asian trend toward Republican in the 1990s has not been much studied and is a bit mysterious. Contributing to it may be the Los Angeles riots (in which the Los Angeles elite tended to portray the rioters as victims and the shop owners of Koreatown as oppressors) and the racial quotas and preferences that bar so many Asians from places in universities. The Jews, after all, reacted against the quotas of a Republican Protestant elite by voting Democratic ever after; the Asians may be reacting against the quotas of a Democratic liberal elite by voting Republican for many years. Similarly, the Jews, understandably on the alert for possible persecutors, believed they would come mostly from the political right wing; Asians may see their threat coming from big city rioters and murderers who are not held responsible by local juries for their crimes.

The experience of the immigrants of 100 years ago should give us at least cautious optimism about the future course of the minorities of today. The high rates of crime and substance abuse among the Irish receded after some time; crime rates and welfare dependency among blacks have experienced a sudden and sharp decline in the 1990s. The aversion to education and economic advancement of Italian Americans waned in time, and in spite of the civic poverty of their homeland and the dire predictions of elites earlier in this century the Italians have blended in well to American life; there is good reason to think the same will happen to today's Latinos. The Jews, early in scaling the economic and academic heights, have seen discrimination and anti-Semitism diminish down toward nothing; the Asians may find the barriers they face receding as well. Politically, all these new Americans have the advantage of living in a society where there is a tremendous political penalty for shows of intolerance and ethnic discrimination, and in which both political parties have an incentive to seek their support. There will be times when ethnic conflicts in politics will be wrenching, but American history also teaches us that ethnic competition in politics can very often be benign and in any case is as American as apple pie (or pizza or tacos).

The Politics of
Racial Preferences

DAVID BRADY

IN THEIR SUCCESSFUL drive to eliminate racial preferences in the public sector, opponents of race-based policies in California and the state of Washington turned not to the legislature but directly to the voters. That is, they organized a ballot initiative and, by that mechanism, altered state constitutions. But such referenda have their detractors. Critics argue that both California's Proposition 209 and Washington's Initiative 200 gave voters a crude up-or-down choice.[1] "The State shall not discriminate against, or grant preferential treatment to, any individual or group, on the basis of race, sex, color, ethnicity, or national origin in the operation of public employment, public education, or public contracting," the initiatives read. Agree or disagree? voters were asked. In contrast to a referendum, the argument runs, legislatures are arenas for negotiation and compromise—for lawmaking with greater subtlety.

The point has seeming plausibility. But faced with politically tricky issues—like that of racial preferences—a legislator's natural tendency is to go with the status quo. Legislatures are risk-adverse. Thus, without the referendum process, citizens would be severely limited in their ability to

express themselves on critical and controversial questions such as affirmative action.

From one perspective, opposition to racial and gender preferences
would seem politically safe. Most Americans don't like them. And yet a
close look at survey data reveals a more complicated landscape. The response of those polled depends on precisely how the question is worded.
The term "quotas," for instance, elicits a very different reaction from the
phrase "affirmative action." In general, questions involving race tap into
considerable ambivalence. Most Americans, that is, understand the history
of black oppression and are sensitive to the need to acknowledge grave
wrongs; they do not think African Americans have attained full equality.
But most also believe in a meritocracy that awards individual initiative and
hard work. They believe in equal treatment but not race-based preferences.[2]

With respect to race-related public policy, most Americans are thus
torn. And as legislators outside California and Washington know, the antipreference initiatives in those states did not pass by large margins. Proposition 209, on the California ballot in November 1996, got only 54 percent
of the vote. It is no surprise, then, that in 1998, when Senator Mitch
McConnell (R-Kentucky) introduced an amendment that would have
eliminated the 10 percent racial and gender set-aside embedded in a massive
highway bill, he met with defeat.[3] Even though the Supreme Court, in 1995,
had ruled that financial incentives to hire minority subcontractors for
federal highway construction projects were unconstitutional, the Senate
voted 58 to 37 against the McConnell proposal.[4] Moreover, 15 Republicans
joined 43 Democrats in voting to kill the amendment. The view of those
15 was that of John McCain. "Unfortunately," the Arizona senator said,
"the danger exists that our aspirations and intentions will be misperceived
. . . harming our party."[5]

Members of Congress don't like bills that potentially harm their party.
Their skittishness involves issues other than race, of course. On technical
issues like the omnibus Communications Act of 1995 or legislation to set
standards for high-density television, members delegate crucial decisions
to bureaucracies; if something goes wrong, they can hold hearings and

blame the administrators. The question of high-density television (HDTV) is instructive because there were only three transmission standards to choose from: American, European, and Japanese. Because Europeans and the Japanese don't vote in American elections, it might seem obvious that the American standard was preferable—but not necessarily. In the case of VCRs, the Japanese manufacturers had beaten all other competition; if the same thing happened with HDTVs, a decision in Congress to adopt American technology could have been politically costly. The result: a legislative decision to pass the buck. The market could sort the problem out.

Legislators understand policies, but they cannot gauge with certainty the impact of a particular policy on their reelection prospects. In the debate over the Clinton health care plan in 1993 and 1994, members of Congress could not accurately predict, for instance, how managed care would affect the freedom of patients to choose a doctor. As two Democrats on the House commerce committee said at the time, "If two or three years from now, Mr. and Mrs. Smith don't have their doctor, you can bet I'll have an opponent in the primary or [the] general [election] blaming me for it."[6] Neither congressman supported the Clinton or Cooper bills.

Race is potentially an even more explosive issue. Support for legislation that abolishes racial and gender preferences—if the statutory language is framed in the wrong way—can be depicted as racially insensitive, if not positively mean-spirited. But opposing such a bill is also politically risky: supporting preferences over merit may invite opposition in the next election. Members of Congress do not want to appear as "against" civil rights, but neither are they eager to seem to be "for quotas."

Politicians are in fact doubly vulnerable. The strange American phenomenon of democracy within a party (primary elections as the vehicle for party nominations) means that incumbents can face opposition in both primaries and general elections. There is another danger as well. The majority of voters in a district may favor an antipreference statute. But if the district is, say, 10 to 20 percent black, white Democrats who support such legislation not only risk an opponent in the primary, but they also court depressed minority turnout in the general election. They may get their party nomination, only to find themselves stripped of needed black support. Moreover, Republicans, too, can pay a political price for supporting a legislative move to abolish set-asides and other race-based programs. Whatever position they take will invite opposition. For candidates of either party, the problem is especially acute in competitive districts; thus, the narrower the incumbent's margin of victory, the more risk-adverse he (or she) is likely to be. The politically vulnerable do not want to vote on controversial legislation.

Politicians like secure seats, and obviously don't like to cast votes for bills on issues—like that of race—that inevitably generate controversy. Racial preferences are thus an unlikely subject for legislative action; the initiative process appears to be the only means by which they can be attacked. That means, of course, that federal affirmative action statutes are safe because the Constitution does not provide for national referenda on questions of policy. A good thing, too, critics of state referenda will say. They argue that legislatures can deal with complex issues and the multiple interests that surround them. A process that simplifies the question makes for bad policy. Without a referendum process, however, politically charged policies opposed by the majority of voters, or policies about which voters are ambivalent, will remain in place—unless, of course, a court steps in, as the U.S. District Court of Appeals of the Fifth Circuit did, when it abolished racial preferences in institutions of higher education in Texas.

The story of I-200 in the state of Washington is instructive. In March 1997, state representative Scott Smith and a small business owner, Tim Eyman, filed the initiative with the legislature, which meant that if they collected enough signatures, the lawmakers would have to approve the bill or put it on the ballot in November 1998. The bill prohibited preferences based on race or gender in state employment, in the awarding of state contracts, and in the admission of students to public institutions of higher education. Indeed, the language was identical to that of Proposition 209, which had amended the California state constitution. By early January 1998, over 280,000 signatures had been submitted to the secretary of state (only 179,248 were actually needed), but, although voter approval was running two to one in favor of the measure, the Republican-controlled legislature declined to take a stand on the issue.

Perhaps legislators knew that extraordinary support for such initiatives in the early months is a bit deceptive. In California, four months before the election (in July 1996), 59 percent of voters backed Proposition 209; in July 1998, 65 percent of the Washington electorate liked I-200. In both cases, however, as the elections drew near, the numbers went down (see Table 1). In Washington, political leadership may have been a factor; the governor and the mayor of Seattle were strong opponents. But enthusiasm also waned in California where Governor Pete Wilson campaigned for the proposition.

Women were an unknown political element, and that uncertainty could have made legislators nervous. If white and minority women came together against the measure, it would go down. As it happened, the opposition was unable to mobilize the female vote. As Table 2 shows, in California, prior to the election, 58 percent of whites and 54 percent of women favored Proposition 209; in Washington, the numbers were 55 and 59, respectively. By November, support by women had slipped somewhat but was still unexpectedly high.

I-200 opponents had argued that gender inequality was real and that

Table 1   Support for P-209 and I-200 over Time (in percents)

P-209 (Calif.)	*7/96*	*9/16/96*	*11/4/96*
For	59	60	52
Against	29	25	38
Undecided	12	15	10
I-200 (Wash.)	*7/13/98*	*9/14/98*	*10/9/98*
For	64	53	55
Against	25	34	35
Undecided	11	13	10

SOURCE: Based on data from polls conducted by the *Los Angeles Times* in California and by the *Seattle Times* in Washington state over the course of the campaigns.

preferences were in their interest. "The biggest beneficiaries of affirmative action in Washington State are white women, and women know that discrimination still exists. The problem is that people still don't know what this deceptive initiative is about," Kelly Evans, the manager of the NO! 200 Campaign said a month before the election.[7] And perhaps there was indeed some confusion. A month earlier, a survey indicated that half the voters in the state favored affirmative action, while almost 60 percent intended to vote for I-200. Those were simply incompatible positions, as the pollster who conducted the poll stated: "It's clear that some voters don't know exactly what this initiative is going to do."[8]

When the actual wording of I-200 was read to respondents, 53 percent supported the initiative, 34 percent were opposed, and the rest were undecided. When asked in a separate question how they felt about affirmative action, 50 percent said they were in favor. Given the ambivalence of most Americans on issues related to race, the precise wording of the question matters. About half the electorate in that survey registered support for some sort of special consideration for disadvantaged groups, but more than half disagreed with the notion of granting preferences. Race is still the American dilemma—acknowledged as such—but there is no agreement over what the political response should be. Legislative action thus remains politically risky.

At the end of the day, however, the initiatives won comfortably in both

Table 2   Preelection Racial and Gender Gaps on P-209 and I-200
               (in percents)

Category	P-209 (CALIF.)		I-200 (WASH.)	
	For	*Against/DK*	*For*	*Against/DK*
White	58	42	55	45
Nonwhite	29	71	37	63
Male	67	33	70	30
Female	54	46	59	41

SOURCE: Based on data from polls conducted by the *Los Angeles Times* and the *Seattle Times*.

states, with 54 percent of the vote in California and a 58 percent majority in Washington. The victory in Washington was especially striking: the political and media establishment was opposed, and the proponents were outspent three to one. Nevertheless, exit polls showed that 66 percent of men and 80 percent of Republicans supported the initiative. Surprisingly, 62 percent of the Independents and 54 percent of union members also voted yes. Women divided evenly on the issue, while over 40 percent of Democrats cast their ballots in favor.[9] In California, as Table 3 shows, support for the measure came from whites (63 percent), political moderates (52 percent), conservatives (77 percent), and males (61 percent). Less than half of women (48 percent) and about a quarter of the liberals (27 percent) voted for it. As expected, blacks, Latinos, and Asians, in decreasing magnitude, were also opposed, although their support did not drop below 25 percent in either state. Their opposition had more impact in California (where minorities make up half the population) than in Washington (84 percent white).

The leadership in the initiative drives interpreted the final tally as an

Table 3   The Vote for Proposition 209 (in percents)

	Yes on 209	No on 209	% of all voters
All voters	54	46	100
Race			
White	63	37	74
Black	26	74	7
Latino	24	76	10
Asian	39	61	5
Ideology			
Liberal	27	73	21
Moderate	52	48	47
Conservative	77	23	32
Gender			
Male	61	39	47
Female	48	52	53

SOURCE: Based on polls conducted in California by the *Los Angeles Times*.

antipreferences vote. Thus, Ward Connerly, who led the movement in California and played a very important role in Washington, saw the American people as "beginning to rethink the whole question of race and affirmative action." He went on, "The three main rationales for affirmative action—compensation for the discrimination of the past, current discrimination, and diversity—aren't acceptable to people any more."[10] Opponents, on the other hand, blamed the allegedly misleading and confusing language of the two initiatives for their defeat. Washington's governor, Gary Locke, described opponents' effort as "always an uphill battle because the ballot title was motherhood and apple pie." People asked themselves, "How can I disagree with that?" and thought, "I very much support an end to discrimination." Sue Tupper, the chief consultant for NO! 200, said, "We really had to work day and night to clarify what kinds of programs would go away if this initiative passed."[11]

Which side was right? Did voters know what they were doing—declaring their opposition to racial and gender preferences—or were they confused by "motherhood and apple pie" rhetoric? Perhaps the question should be put slightly differently: Did supporters understand that signing on a measure that prohibited discriminatory policies of every sort (including those that distributed benefits on the basis of race or gender) would mean an end to "affirmative action," as commonly practiced? The rhetoric was appealing because it did indeed embrace basic American values, as I-200 opponents lamented. Did the majority of voters mean to reaffirm those values?

Yes, postelection surveys suggest. The two main reasons voters gave for supporting I-200 were a belief that it would end preferential treatment and that it would ensure fairness and equality in the way government and public universities operate. They wanted a change in existing programs. At the same time, however, they seemed to believe that the revised law would allow some form of affirmative action. Thus, among I-200 backers, two-thirds thought the measure would not ban all minority-targeted programs. As one voter put it, "Minority goals in employment and student admissions can still be achieved under I-200. The secret is recruitment, training, and accomplishment." In other words: help, yes; preferences, no. Only a small minority of the electorate seemed totally confused about what they voted for. Seven percent of the initiative's supporters said they wanted affirmative action programs *un*changed, while 10 percent of those opposed to prohibiting preferences said that in fact they wanted them eliminated.[12]

Identical initiatives have passed in two states, and the decision of the majority of voters will not be overturned, it appears. In California, a federal district court issued a preliminary injunction blocking implementation of the initiative, a decision that was subsequently reversed by the U.S. Court of Appeals for the Ninth Circuit. The U.S. Supreme Court declined to take the case. Student protests appear to have fallen flat. In the 1998 gubernatorial race, neither Dan Lundgren, a conservative Republican, nor Gray Davis, a former aide to the very liberal Jerry Brown, focused on the issue. Although Davis reminded congregants at black churches just prior to the election that he opposed 209 and promised that appointments to state jobs in his administration would reflect the diversity of the state, he did not say he would try to circumvent the law. "One thing I've learned in my years, of service," he said, "is when the people speak—at least on Earth—they are the final word."[13] And on 209, the people had spoken.

On the other hand, the University of California system—in keeping with the desire of most voters—is looking for alternative ways to create "diversity."

Notes

1. The best and most influential work arguing against referenda is Peter Shrag, *Paradise Lost* (New York: New Press, 1998).

2. On the public's complicated views on issues involving race, see Paul M. Sniderman and Thomas Piazza, *The Scar of Race* (Cambridge, Mass.: Harvard University Press, 1993).

3. The McConnell amendment would have eliminated the Disadvantaged Business Enterprise (DBE) program from the bill that renewed funding for the Intermodal Surface Transportation Efficiency Act, otherwise known as ISTEA (pronounced "ice-tea"). The DBE provision required that no less than 10 percent of federal highway and transportation money go to firms owned by minorities and women. Congress voted

on the ISTEA amendment eight months before the referendum in Washington on I-200, but the voters' rejection of preferences, once again, probably would not have made any difference.

4. The decision was *Adarand Constructors, Inc. v. Peña*, 515 U.S. 200 (1995).

5. Helen Dewar, "Minority Set-Asides Survives in Senate," *Washington Post*, March 7, 1998, p. 1.

6. Personal interview with author.

7. "Initiative 200 Favored in Poll; Affirmative Action Ban in State Has 55 Percent Support," *Seattle Post-Intelligencer*, October 9, 1998, p. A1.

8. "Most in Poll Support I-200; But Half Defend Affirmative Action," ibid., September 14, 1998, p. A1.

9. Tom Brune, "Poll: I-200 Passage Was Call for Reform," *Seattle Times*, November 4, 1998, p. A1.

10. "Affirmative Action Rules Tossed Out by State Voters," *Seattle Post-Intelligencer*, November 4, 1998, p. A1.

11. Ibid.

12. Brune, "Poll: I-200 Passage Was Call for Reform."

13. Dan Smith and Amy Chance, "Davis Smells Victory; Lungren Sees Rebound," *Sacramento Bee*, October 26, 1998, p. A3.

From Protest to Politics: Still an Issue for Black Leadership

TAMAR JACOBY

IN POLITICS, as in many other aspects of civic life, America has come a long way since the civil rights era. In the years since the 1965 Voting Rights Act, the number of black elected officials has grown from under 100 to nearly 9,000, while black voter registration has soared, particularly in the South. (Even in the southern states that began with the best numbers, registration has doubled and, in some places, multiplied by a factor of ten.)[1] Yet, for all the increase in participation and political sophistication, the nation's black leadership is still in a state of transition from "outsider" to "insider" politics—still caught between the appeal of expressive, symbolic protest tactics and the challenges of effective, problem-solving governance.

Nothing captures the uncertain moment better than the election in 1998 of Anthony A. Williams as mayor of the District of Columbia. The reserved, Harvard-educated former city financial officer was hailed even before he was elected as one of a "new breed" of black mayors: low-profile, nonideological, "technocratic" city executives who eschew racial politics for managerial savvy. Like Detroit's Dennis Archer, Cleveland's Michael

White, and Denver's Wellington Webb, among others, Williams campaigned on a promise of efficient government and fiscal solvency. Before and after the election, in front of both blacks and whites, he emphasized the need "to bring everybody in our city together."[2] Unlike his confrontational predecessor, Marion Barry, he avoided color-coded power plays, and his low-keyed, fiscally minded campaign paid off handsomely in support from middle-class white voters. To many, in the city and further afield, Williams's election seemed a triumph for black politics—a victory, finally, for responsibility over theatrics and for sober-minded government over empty millennial promises.

The only problem was that many poor, black Washingtonians were at best indifferent, if not hostile, to their new mayor. In the Democratic primary, tantamount to the election in the overwhelming Democratic District, 70 percent of the majority-black electorate stayed home. Worse still, though Williams dominated in better-off white enclaves, winning by a factor of four to one, he managed only to split the vote in middle-class black areas, as he lost outright in the poorest black neighborhoods east of the Anacostia River.[3] In the wake of his victory, several black newspaper columnists assailed the outcome. "The eastern sections of town are downright disillusioned," one critic wrote bitterly, denouncing Williams as a traitor and a tool of the white establishment whose budgetary restraint could only be bad for black people.[4] (Williams did little better among poor blacks in the general election, once again eliciting a heavy turnout in affluent, white neighborhoods, while only one in four voters from across the Anacostia bothered to come out to vote for him.)

It was a small pocket of dissent, seemingly inconsequential in the short run—Williams was elected by a healthy margin—but potentially ominous for the longer-term future. For years now, well-meaning whites and a handful of black intellectuals have bemoaned the state of the nation's black leadership, elected and otherwise. In the wake of the civil rights era, this conventional wisdom held; no one had emerged to guide the later, more difficult stage of the black struggle for inclusion. Instead, angry and often corrupt, race-baiting demagogues had taken over and misled impressionable followers, ushering in an era of urban decline, stalled race relations, and divisive identity politics, among other ills. Disturbing as it was, in its way, this was a hopeful diagnosis because it meant that change at the top could ease many of the black community's remaining problems. But the experience of the new mayors, Williams included, tells a more complicated story. Whatever the flaws of the older generation of angry, color-conscious spokesmen, they have an enduring appeal for a certain segment of the black population, and as long as their brand of divisive racial politics plays in the inner city and elsewhere, the transition from outside to inside leadership will never be complete.

Thirty-five years after the passage of the great civil rights laws, the old-style "outside" leadership is no longer as explicitly radical as it once was. Except for an occasional, high-profile demonstration, by now the movement has come in off the streets, and few black spokesmen still talk about overturning or seceding from the system. But black protest politics haven't disappeared; they've just gone under cover. The new breed of black mayors is still the exception, not the rule. Most black members of Congress and most executives of the NAACP, the National Urban League, and Jesse Jackson's Rainbow/PUSH Coalition still view the world in color-coded terms and, even when they have chosen to work within the system, still see their jobs as essentially protest by another means. Their methods, as often as not, are confrontational; their stock-in-trade is racial grievance and racial remedies. Like many insurrectionary or protest movements, they brook little dissent within their ranks. (Those with differing views, like Supreme Court Justice Clarence Thomas and California businessman Ward Connerly, are castigated as race traitors.) And whatever their success in delivering for their people, they still command respect as racial champions willing to stand up to power.

Yet, popular as the old-style leadership may be, a number of signs suggest that it is no longer truly in step with the people it claims to represent. On educational issues, all-important to black advancement, one recent survey found that 84 percent of rank-and-file blacks believed parents should be able to send their children to a school of their choosing, whether public or parochial.[5] But most national black leaders—in Congress and the major civil rights organizations—vigorously oppose school choice of any kind. On crime, another survey found 73 percent of black respondents in favor of "three strikes and you're out" laws that sentence thrice-convicted violent criminals to life imprisonment.[6] Yet when this issue came up for a vote on Capitol Hill in 1993, the Congressional Black Caucus voted over-whelmingly against the sterner penalties. On welfare, 91 percent of blacks are in favor of requiring able-bodied recipients to work for their benefits.[7] But when welfare reform came to the floor in Congress, in 1996, only three out of nearly forty black Democrats voted for it.

This gap is at least two decades old, and, if anything, it is getting wider. It is often seen, in ideological terms, as a gap between liberal leaders and a more conservative community, and there is something to that: the black population also differs from most of its spokesmen on questions of abortion and school prayer and, indeed, how one labels oneself politically. (Though the black rank and file almost never votes Republican, in ideological ori-entation, by its own account, it is evenly divided—32 percent conservative, 32 percent liberal, 32 percent moderate[8]—while virtually no one in the civil rights establishment would use the C-word to describe themselves.) But to see the divide in purely partisan terms is to miss its deeper philosophical significance: a critical, growing difference in assumptions about what ex-actly ails the black community and what can most usefully be done to fix it.

Perhaps the most striking aspect of the leadership gap was first un-earthed in 1985 when an American Enterprise Institute poll found that 66 percent of rank-and-file black respondents felt that blacks as a group were "making progress" in America, whereas 61 percent of their spokesmen said that as a whole the group was "going backwards."[9] The same division appeared again a year later when a survey by two national news organiza-tions asked ordinary blacks how much discrimination they faced in their daily lives, and sizable majorities answered, in effect, "relatively little." (Seventy-five percent experienced no discrimination in "getting a quality education," 73 percent experienced no discrimination in "getting decent housing," 60 percent experienced no discrimination in "getting a job," and 57 percent experienced no discrimination in "getting equal wages" for their work.)[10] In contrast, if one listens to the national black leadership, one would believe that discrimination and enduring "institutional racism" dominate the lives of every black American.

The difference is critical, not so much as a gauge of bigotry but because of what it says about most blacks' hopes and expectations for their own lives. Though few black politicians explicitly discourage followers from taking advantage of opportunity, if the leadership's dire picture is correct, then there is little point for blacks in making much personal effort: no matter how hard one tries at school or work, no matter how talented you are, in the end, "the system" is always going to hold you back and limit your possibilities for achievement. But apparently most of the black rank and file harbor some doubts about this demoralizing vision of America. Whatever skepticism or anger they feel, and whatever discrimination they have faced in their lives, the polls suggest that ultimately they are far more optimistic than their leadership—an optimism reflected in their gradually shifting personal and political strategies.

As their responses to questions about education, crime, and welfare show, more and more ordinary blacks feel that the road ahead runs through personal responsibility and what in another context is called "development"—schooling, work, community-building, and a stake in the status quo. Though much black leadership remains committed to a strategy of agitation from outside to change the system—protest, legal challenges, economic boycotts, and the like—ordinary blacks seem increasingly committed to making their way from within, using the system to their own advantage and sharing in its fruits.

This shift has drawn little attention, and it is far from complete, but it is already producing a measure of ferment across black America. There is a growing sense among black scholars on both the right and the left that the civil rights establishment is not serving the interests of ordinary blacks. Political scientists as ideologically diverse as Harvard's Martin Kilson, Columbia's Manning Marable, and San Francisco State's Robert C. Smith have all voiced bitter criticism of their community's alleged spokesmen. Kilson denounces not just the "lawbreaking and norm-flouting" of many black elected officials, but also what he sees as a kind of nationalist "immaturity on the part of the black leadership . . . an ethnographic solidarity [that] is both misplaced in a pluralistic democracy and politically counterproductive." Smith, whose book on the subject is entitled bluntly, *We Have No Leaders*, complains that the political class is so committed to "symbolic" gestures and "the politics of personality" that it is largely "irrelevant in post-civil rights era national politics." These and other black critics differ over whether their leadership is too radical or too conservative, too preoccupied with defending affirmative action or not attentive enough, too concerned with their own power and prerogatives or too enthralled with identity politics. But all agree that the real needs of the black poor—whether for better schools or jobs or police protection—are being sorely neglected.[11]

Meanwhile, like all Americans, black voters are showing less and less interest in electoral politics. Black turnout is notoriously volatile, dependent on spikes of enthusiasm—and distaste—for individual candidates. But even when black participation runs high, as it did in 1998, it remains slightly lower than national turnout figures, which were lower in 1998 than they had been any year since 1942.[12] Queried by journalists, many blacks express dissatisfaction with the relentlessly color-coded concerns of their elected officials: "Most issues should not be defined as black or white," Atlanta realtor Terry Tate, among others, told a *Wall Street Journal* reporter surveying national sentiment. "We *all* need jobs, we *all* need safety, we *all* need to be rid of the scourge of drugs."[13] And in many cities, rather than rallying to politicians, the black rank and file is now turning instead to urban ministers like Rev. Eugene Rivers of Boston and Rev. Floyd Flake of New York (a retired U.S. congressman) who use their church coffers and bully pulpits to promote an agenda of self-help and community development.

What's complicated is that, like any group undergoing a major change, many blacks are still ambivalent and uncertain, confused about what exactly their people need and what they want from their leaders. The men who attended Rev. Louis Farrakhan's 1995 Million Man March brought this uncertainty home for all America to see. As much as anything, it was clear, the ideology that drove these men was about self-help: the issues of personal responsibility and accomplishment and community-building that Farrakhan evoked when he talked about "atonement." The irony is that all these themes have been staple fare among black conservatives for more than two decades now. But unlike Farrakhan, virtually no conservative black spokesmen could produce enough followers to hold a rally—in large part because their prescriptions come without the angry edge that Farrakhan specializes in. In the long run, that hate-filled, race-baiting rhetoric is antithetical to a real push for self-help and development. (The more you blame "the system" for holding you back, the less likely you will be to take full responsibility for your own life.) Yet the men who traveled to Washington for the Million Man March didn't want to have to choose between protest and self-help. They thrilled to Farrakhan's angry outsider's politics—and wanted to work the system, too. Uncertain which way to go, they held fast to both antithetical options.

Theirs isn't an uncommon ambivalence. However much the black rank and file may differ from its leaders on important questions like education, crime, and welfare reform, they reelect members of the Congressional Black Caucus by overwhelming margins. (Once they've won a place in Congress, half of all caucus members run unopposed in either the next primary or general election, and their average margin of victory falls in the 80 percent range.) Technocratic "crossover" mayors like Anthony Williams have been running and winning elections for more than a decade now, but they almost never inspire a large, enthusiastic black turnout either in middle-class neighborhoods or in poorer parts of town, and many find it hard to win a second term or to rally black voters when they try for higher office. Meanwhile, at the other end of the spectrum, flamboyant race-baiting street leaders like New York's Rev. Al Sharpton and Khalid Abdul Muhammad command only a very small following. In spite of repeated tries for office— for U.S. senator and mayor—Sharpton has never garnered more than 130,000 votes in all of New York City or New York state, and Muhammad's so-called "million youth marches" in Harlem in 1998 and 1999 drew no more than a few thousand followers. But, except in the rarest of circumstances, neither rank-and-file blacks nor more respectable black elected officials dare to denounce demagogic race men like Sharpton and Farrakhan. To do so would be implicitly to repudiate the anger they trade in— an anger that still galvanizes blacks of all classes.

Which trend is stronger—the commitment to self-help and development or the angry alienation? It's hard to say, and it would be a grave mistake to underestimate black estrangement. Every TV viewer remembers the black reaction to the O. J. Simpson verdict. Millions of black Americans, poor and better-off alike, still believe that "white society" has a "plan" to destroy them. According to one 1990 poll, 29 percent think it is or "might be" true that "the virus which causes AIDS was deliberately created in a laboratory in order to infect black people"; 58 percent think it's true or likely that "the government deliberately makes sure that drugs are easily available in poor black neighborhoods in order to harm black people"; and 77 percent believe it's possible that "the government deliberately singles out and investigates black elected officials in order to discredit them in a way it doesn't do with white officials."[14] Surprisingly enough, educated, middle-class blacks are even more likely than the poor to harbor these paranoid fantasies. And both the poor and the better-off are often suspicious of plans for the economic revival of black neighborhoods. Though it would bring jobs and stores and opportunity where now there are none, many residents of places like Harlem and the majority-black city of Detroit fear that development will inevitably mean economic exploitation of blacks by whites—and, if so, they would rather forego the prosperity. Indeed, much of the black opposition to technocratic mayors like Anthony Williams and Detroit's Dennis Archer turns on just this sort of economic nationalism: because he advocates fiscal solvency and color-neutral economic growth, Williams is denounced by both poor and better-off blacks as a "bandit" whose policies will usher in an era of "occupation."[15]

Still, in the long run, the appeal of the technocratic mayors lies in their pragmatism, and, for all the alienation of better-off blacks, it is an appeal that should only grow as more and more of the black population make the transition into the middle class. The new crop of managerial executives benefits from the experience of earlier pioneers going back a generation: Los Angeles's Tom Bradley, Atlanta's Andrew Young, and Baltimore's Kurt Schmoke, among others, who tried with varying degrees of success to move beyond old-style racial leadership and govern more effectively for all constituents. Like them, the new guard generally steers clear of ideology. They avoid open repudiations of their predecessors, no matter how demagogic. They never explicitly abandon the civil rights tradition and rarely dismantle the racial remedies they inherit—including, in many cities, extensive municipal set-asides. They are not immune to racial pressures, as Anthony Williams proved disappointingly less than a month into his mayoralty, when he allowed public opinion to force out a key city official for no other reason than that he had used the word "niggardly" at a meeting. But even when they can't rise above racial politics, what's important about the new mayors is their focus on the bottom line: not, after all these years, the realization of a millennial civil rights vision but "merely" fiscal solvency and a city that works—for both blacks and whites.

But the truth is that, even more than the middle class, it is the black poor who need leaders with a more pragmatic, bottom-line approach. Whatever the appeal for poor people of an angry, outside protest leadership, they more than any are the ones who suffer when their politicians don't deliver. The experience of the city of Detroit makes the case as vividly as any. "Mayor for Life" Coleman Young, who governed from 1973 to 1993, was an old-style leader in the classic mold. He came into office promising Black Power in one city, then made a career out of gratuitous race-baiting and thumbing his nose at the white suburbs. Detroit voters thrilled to his racial grandstanding and hardly seemed to notice as businesses fled and city services deteriorated—everything from schools to garbage pickup to, most disastrously, the police. By the early 1990s, the auto industry had all but abandoned Detroit for the suburbs. One in three residents lived below the poverty line, and, in some neighborhoods, more than half were unemployed. Two decades of ill-disguised contempt by the mayor had disastrously undermined the police force, allowing crack and the crime that came with it to devastate huge swatches of the city. Teenage pregnancy was more the norm than the exception, and by the time they got to high school, 70 percent of the city's young men had already had some involvement with the criminal justice system, often for major offenses.[16] Young's successor, Dennis Archer, makes no appeals to solidarity, but he has devoted himself to restoring services, markedly improving the quality of life for both poor and more comfortable Detroiters.

Like all the "technocratic" black mayors, Archer has waged a multifront war. Like Cleveland's Michael White and a number of the others, he has moved aggressively to reduce crime in the city by restoring confidence in the police department. Also like many of his fellow pragmatic urban executives, he has pushed to restore the city's school system. (The mayors' methods vary from city to city. In Cleveland, for example, White is moving toward a voucher system; in Detroit, with Michigan governor John Engler's support, Archer has replaced the old elected school board with a more directly accountable "reform board" of his own choosing.) Like many of the other new mayors, Washington's Anthony Williams included, Archer is nudging the city toward a more balanced budget. But perhaps most important, in Detroit, as in Cleveland and other places governed by the new breed, Archer has made it a top priority to bring business back into the center of town. Some of Detroit's new enterprises are big, revenue-generating behemoths: a $220 million casino, a new GM headquarters expected to employ hundreds of people. More significant in the long run, some are smaller, start-up companies that will restore jobs and create a business culture in poorer neighborhoods. ("The secret to revival," one Detroit city planner said recently, explaining the mayor's success, "is connecting the dots" of big, downtown commercial projects with an urban fabric of restaurants, shops, and other small enterprises.[17]) The one thing Archer does not particularly care about is whether the new business is white- or black-owned. This fiscally minded color blindness has infuriated many of the city's middle-class black residents, who complain among themselves that the mayor isn't "black enough."[18] But over time, it is hard to imagine that the all too tangible, day-to-day benefits of Archer's approach—the lowered crime and better-paying jobs and new housing development—won't eventually wean both the city's poor and its better-off blacks from their yen for confrontational, outside leadership.

An old cliché left over from the heyday of the civil rights movement captures the uncertainty ahead in Detroit and other cities. "There is a little bit of Malcolm X," the old phrase went, "and a little bit of Martin Luther King in every black man"—a little bit, that is, of angry, alienated outsider but also a measure of hope about eventually belonging and feeling at home in America. Just which of these two sides prevailed has depended over the years on several things, including which tendency the reigning black leadership encouraged and how open the system proved to black advancement. Today, the hope is that the new-style leadership can make a difference, reinforcing and fortifying the side of people that wants to let go of the past and take advantage of new opportunities. The difficulty, as the experience of the managerial mayors shows, is that leaders can do only so much to change hearts and minds. At long last, a better leadership is emerging in black America. The question for the future is whether its followers are ready.

Notes

1. Figures are from David A. Bositis, the Joint Center for Political and Economic Studies.

2. *USA Today*, September 16, 1998.

3. *Washington Post*, September 17, 1998.

4. *Washington Times*, September 18, 1998.

5. *Investor's Business Daily*, April 1, 1998; poll conducted in 1997 by the Washington-based Center for Education Reform.

6. *Ethnic News Watch*, January 4, 1997; poll conducted in 1996 by the Joint Center for Political and Economic Studies.

7. *Investor's Business Daily*, April 1, 1998; poll conducted in 1993 by Fabrizion, McLaughlin & Associates.

8. David A. Bositis, "The Joint Center for Political and Economic Studies 1997 National Opinion Poll—Politics."

9. Cited in Martin Kilson, "Problems in Black Politics," *Dissent*, Fall 1989.

10. Ibid. The poll was conducted in 1986 by ABC News and the *Washington Post*.

11. See Kilson, "Problems in Black Politics"; Robert C. Smith, *We Have No Leaders: African Americans in the Post-Civil Rights Era* (Albany: SUNY Press, 1996); Manning Marable, *Black Leadership* (New York: Columbia University Press, 1998).

12. *New York Times*, November 6 and 8, 1998; *Wall Street Journal*, November 5, 1998.

13. *Wall Street Journal*, October 13, 1992.

14. *New York Times*, October 29, 1990.

15. *Washington Times*, September 18, 1998.

16. Tamar Jacoby, *Someone Else's House: America's Unfinished Struggle for Integration* (New York: Free Press, 1998).

17. *Wall Street Journal*, September 13, 1999.

18. *U.S. News and World Report*, March 15, 1999.

PART SEVEN

ONE NATION, INDIVISIBLE

The New Politics of
Hispanic Assimilation

LINDA CHAVEZ

HISPANICS HAVE ALWAYS been an afterthought in the American debate on race. At the beginning of the modern civil rights movement, Hispanics were too few in number, too disorganized, and too far removed from the locus of news stories about civil rights marches, church bombings, and bus boycotts to attract much attention or concern. Of the approximately 4 million Hispanics who lived in the United States in 1960, 85 percent were Mexican Americans who lived primarily in five southwestern states: California, Texas, New Mexico, Arizona, and Colorado. Today, more than 30 million Hispanics live from California to New York, from Chicago to Atlanta, and they will soon become the largest minority group in the country, surpassing blacks within ten years. Still, Hispanics rarely generate the soul-searching anxiety routinely aroused whenever the subject of race comes up. In large measure, this indifference is testament to the tremendous social and economic progress Hispanics have made in the last forty years, but it may also reflect how unaware many Americans are that the paradigm of race and ethnicity has shifted dramatically in the last quarter century.

Hispanics do not constitute a single racial group. There are black Hispanics, like Chicago Cubs outfielder Sammy Sosa; white Hispanics, like pop singers Gloria Estefan and Ricky Martin; Indian or Mestizo Hispanics, like actor Edward James Olmos; even Asian Hispanics, like Peruvian President Alberto Fujimori. Hispanics hail from twenty-four Latin American countries, as well as the United States itself. Some can trace their lineage in the U.S. for generations, others are new immigrants. Indeed, about half of all adult Hispanics in the U.S. today are foreign born. It is this divide, whether we are talking about U.S.-born Hispanics or immigrant, that is the key to understanding what has happened to the Hispanic population in the U.S. over the last few decades and predicting whether Hispanics will remain a permanent minority or become just another of America's many ethnic groups.

At the time of the civil rights movement of the 1950s and 1960s, most Mexican Americans faced obstacles similar to those of blacks living outside the Deep South. Although Mexican Americans did not have to contend with de jure segregation, prejudice and discrimination were nonetheless common, impeding Mexican Americans' full integration into American society. Many Mexican Americans lived in appalling conditions, especially in south Texas and other border areas, residing in dilapidated shanties in towns with unpaved streets and poor or nonexistent sewage facilities. Mexican American children attended crowded, ill-equipped schools staffed by overworked, undercredentialed teachers. Most dropped out before they ever reached high school. Mexican American poverty was endemic in some regions, and the median income of Mexican Americans was 57 percent of non-Hispanic whites. In spite of their low socioeconomic status, Mexican Americans did participate in the political process, however. Mexican Americans served in Congress throughout the twentieth century, initially only from New Mexico, where until 1940 they constituted a majority of the population, and by the 1960s from Texas and California as well.

The advent of the civil rights laws, which outlawed discrimination on the basis of national origin and ethnicity as well as race and color, no doubt played a crucial role in the rapid upward mobility of Mexican Americans in the last several decades, but so did the general expansion of educational opportunity and the movement of the Mexican American population from small towns and rural areas to cities. But while Mexican Americans were quickly climbing the educational and economic ladder into the mainstream of American society, another important change was taking place within the Hispanic population. Mexican Americans, though still the dominant Hispanic group even today, were being joined every year by hundreds of thousands of new immigrants from Mexico, Guatemala, El Salvador, Nicaragua, and elsewhere in Latin America. Some 8 million Mexican and more than 4 million Central and South American immigrants make up the second largest group of Hispanics now living in the United States. Puerto Ricans, once the second largest group, number only about 3 million in the U.S., and Cuban refugees and their American-born children another 1.1 million.

Nevertheless, even with the tremendous demographic shift taking place within the Hispanic population, many observers failed to recognize that Hispanics could no longer be considered a single group, with a common history, experience, and interests. Many Hispanic leaders continued to make the case that Hispanics had been left behind in the quest for equal opportunity. At the very time that many Mexican Americans were closing the gap with their Anglo peers in terms of education and earnings, Representative Edward Roybal (D-California) bemoaned, "We are no better off today than in 1949." His sentiments were echoed countless times. As the head of the National Council of La Raza, one of the oldest and most respected Hispanic advocacy groups, said in 1990: "Each decade offered us hope, but our hopes evaporated into smoke. We became the poorest of the poor, the most segregated minority in schools, the lowest paid group in America and the least educated group in this nation." And to casual observers, these statements rang true, at least with respect to the aggregate achievement of all Hispanics living in the United States at the time.

What these commentators failed to note, however, was that the population they were describing no longer consisted largely of Mexican Americans who had lived in the United States for generations but instead included millions of recent immigrants, most of whom had resided here for less than a decade or two. What's more, few of these immigrants spoke any English when they arrived, and they had had little formal schooling, so they could hardly be expected to earn wages equal to native-born Americans—Anglo or Hispanic—who had benefited from the tremendous opportunities that opened up in the wake of the civil rights movement. Thus, aggregate statistics that purported to represent the social and economic achievement of Hispanics concealed more than they revealed, minimizing the great progress made by native-born Hispanics in closing the gap with their fellow Americans while at the same time underestimating the great challenge posed by recent immigrants whose skills and education lagged far behind those of others in this society.

So how are the children and grandchildren of those civil rights–era Mexican Americans faring today? By and large, well. One of the best recent studies of Hispanic progress, an analysis of Hispanics living in five Southern California counties by Pepperdine University research fellow Gregory Rodriguez, shows that a majority of U.S.-born Hispanics are middle class, as defined by household earnings and home ownership. American-born Hispanics have not fully caught up with non-Hispanic whites—about 10 percent fewer Hispanics than whites had middle-class household incomes in 1990 or owned their own homes in the Rodriguez study—and U.S. Hispanics are far less likely to attend or complete college. Fewer than one in ten Hispanics holds a four-year college degree or higher, compared with more than one-quarter of non-Hispanic whites. Even among the youngest cohorts, only 11.5 percent of Hispanics have earned a bachelor's or advanced degree, compared with nearly one-third of young non-Hispanic whites. These differences are not primarily the result of discrimination but are due to more subtle factors, including culture. In many respects, Hispanics in the U.S. have followed a pattern of social and economic progress not unlike that of certain previous ethnic groups, such as Italians and Poles, both of which took longer to catch up with other Americans in education, for example.

The real question today is whether this slow but steady movement of

Hispanics up the economic ladder and into the social mainstream will continue in the face of unprecedented Latin immigration, which brings millions of poorly educated, non-English-speaking immigrants each decade. There are two problems that this phenomenon poses. First, the immigrants themselves differ in important respects from previous immigrants, even those who came in greater numbers (in relation to population) at the beginning of the century. Second, our expectations of what to demand from these immigrants have changed, as has our public policy for dealing with them.

Latin immigrants, unlike the waves who came from southern and eastern Europe from 1900 to 1924, speak a single language, and most come a relatively short distance, made shorter still by air travel, which allows them to return home frequently to renew their cultural ties to their homeland. More importantly, however, Americans no longer seem to expect newcomers to abandon their language and culture when they arrive—or so it appears, judging from the myriad of public policies in place to promote "multiculturalism" and separate ethnic identities. Where once immigrant children were expected to learn English immediately upon entering public schools and to adopt American civic values, cultural norms, even habits of dress, manners, and hygiene, today the public schools proclaim as their mission "diversity" in all its forms.

Bilingual education and multicultural curricula have worked to undermine commitment to a common civic identity that was once a mainstay of public education. Mexican children newly arrived in American public schools now frequently find themselves in classrooms where they are taught part of the day in Spanish, where they learn more about the achievements of Mayans and Aztecs than about the Puritans, where they are taught to revere Miguel Hidalgo and Emiliano Zapata on the same plane as George Washington or Thomas Jefferson, and to celebrate Cinco de Mayo with more fanfare than the Fourth of July. Although such efforts are aimed at boosting the self-esteem of children whose backgrounds were not white Anglo-Saxon Protestant, the clear consequence has been to promote a separate identity among some ethnic and racial groups. The goal is no longer assimilation. The intent of such policies is not to help the many become part of the one but to perpetuate separate racial and ethnic identities for generations to come. Nor do these multicultural policies affect only the schools. Whether in providing Spanish-language ballots, creating majority Hispanic voting districts, or giving preferences in jobs, government contracts, or admission to college on the basis of race and ethnicity, public policies that encourage groups to divide themselves by color or ancestry discourage them from forging a common, American identity.

Whether these policies will have a long-term effect on the assimilation of Hispanics and their full social and economic integration into the mainstream of American society remains to be seen. Evidence abounds on both sides of the debate. On the one hand, Hispanic immigrants seem somewhat slower to learn English or to become U.S. citizens than previous immigrants or even other contemporary immigrants from non-Latin countries. Three-quarters of Mexican immigrants who arrived in the 1980s do not speak English well a decade or more later. Moreover, only about 15 percent of Latin immigrants now living in the U.S. have become citizens, a rate that reflects not only lower naturalization but also the higher proportion of Latinos who are very recent immigrants or are here illegally and therefore ineligible to become citizens.

On the other hand, some immigrant parents and other Hispanics are beginning to balk at programs like bilingual education. In California, some 40 percent of Hispanic voters joined the more than 60 percent of other Californians who voted to abolish bilingual education in a statewide referendum in 1998. Test scores from the first year under the new program suggest that the shift in state education policy, which now emphasizes special English immersion programs for non-English-speaking youngsters, has been a modest success, with double-digit gains by students in most districts that have adopted the new methods. Moreover, perhaps in the ultimate test of full assimilation, Hispanics are intermarrying at faster rates than many members of other immigrant ethnic groups traditionally have, with about one-third of third-generation Hispanic females now marrying non-Hispanic whites. Still, if our public policies continue to treat the offspring of such unions as somehow different from other Americans—and entitled to special benefits and consideration because of their ethnicity—we should not be surprised if Hispanics fail to follow in the footsteps of previous ethnics who have become virtually indistinguishable from the American mainstream. Unless we recommit ourselves as a nation to put aside race and ethnicity, to abandon all foreign allegiances, as our oath of citizenship still requires, America's national motto—*E pluribus unum*, one out of many—will become mere hollow words in the twenty-first century.

In Defense of
Indian Rights

WILLIAM J. LAWRENCE

WHAT SHOULD AMERICA's policies toward American Indi-
ans be as we enter the new millennium? Should Indian tribes be viewed as
"sovereign nations," "domestic dependent nations," wards of the federal
government, or membership organizations similar to culturally based nonprofit corporations? Should Indians be viewed as full Americans with the
same rights and responsibilities as every other American? Or should Indians
and tribes attempt to maintain a "separate but equal" status in American
life, and should a separate status continue indefinitely?

In fact, today, Indian people are *citizens* of the United States, *citizens*
of the state in which they reside, and, in some cases, *members* of a tribe
representing some aspect of their genealogical heritage. Tribal membership
should not affect the citizenship rights of Indian people, but it often does.
And the status of tribal governments, in some cases, even affects the citizenship rights of non-Indian citizens who come in contact with a tribal
government.

As of the 1990 U.S. census, there were 1,959,234 people who identified
themselves as Indian, 60 percent of whom are enrolled members of one of

the 557 federally recognized tribes, bands, or communities.[1] But many, if not most, people who identify themselves as "Indian" are actually only one-quarter or less Indian, with the balance of their family lineage being of some other racial combination. In fact, many people who consider themselves Indians are of a primarily non-Indian heritage and ethnicity.

The percentage of Indian people living on reservations has been in continuous decline in recent decades. Currently, less than 20 percent (437,431) of the Indian population live on reservations. And 46 percent (370,738) of the total number of people living on reservations are non-Indians.[2] On the nine most populous Indian reservations in the country other than the Navajo, less than 20 percent of the population is Indian. Most Indian reservations are populated primarily by non-Indian families, many of whom were invited to homestead on reservation land in the late 1800s during the "allotment era," when the federal intent was to abolish the system of Indian reservations and merge Indian people and land into surrounding communities. And many reservation families include both Indian and non-Indian family members, resulting in children who have some Indian genealogy but may not have a blood-quantum high enough to qualify for tribal membership, generally considered to be one-quarter.

In light of these facts, what should current and future policies be regarding Indian people, tribes, and reservations? At some point, the federal government must reassess its policy of maintaining so-called "Indian reservations" and treating Americans who have an Indian heritage or identity as a separate class of citizens. Should that occur when Indians are 10 percent, 5 percent, or 2 percent of the reservation population? How long should the federal government maintain a Bureau of Indian Affairs (BIA), Indian Health Service, and other programs solely for citizens with some Indian genealogy? This nation is rapidly approaching a time when there will hardly be any Indians left on reservations, and those Indians who remain there will hardly be Indian.

History: Where We've Been

In the U.S. Constitution, no governmental powers are set aside for, granted to, or recognized as existing for Indian tribes. In fact, no plan was laid out in the Constitution for how to deal with Indian tribes at all, although the United States considered tribes to be under its dominion. Nowhere in the U.S. Constitution, or in any treaty or in any federal statute, are Indian tribes recognized as sovereign. The Supreme Court confirmed this in 1886 when it stated: "Indians are within the geographical limits of the United States. The soil and the people within these limits are under the political control of the Government of the United States or of the States of the Union. There exist within the broad domain of sovereignty but these two."[3]

The first American treaty with Indians was signed in 1778 with the Delaware Indians. The last was signed with the Nez Perce in 1868. Over a span of approximately 100 years, nearly 400 treaties were negotiated between dozens of Indian tribes and the U.S. government, most during the westward expansion of the mid-1800s. Nearly a third were treaties of peace. The rest were treaties ceding Indian land to the U.S. government and establishing reservations.[4] During this period, the United States paid more than $800 million for the lands it purchased from tribes.[5]

Treaties were *not* solemn promises to preserve in perpetuity historic tribal lifestyles, lands, or cultures, as is often claimed today. In fact, plans for assimilating Indian people into mainstream American life were spelled out in most treaties, often requiring that treaty payments be used for construction of schools, homes, programs to train Indian adults in agriculture, and promises to aid the transition from a subsistence lifestyle to active citizenship. Rather than being an indication that tribes were sovereign, many treaties specifically noted the lack of tribal sovereignty, and through treaties, many individual Indians and even entire tribes became U.S. citizens.[6] In 1871, Congress ended all treaty making with tribes and stated that the federal government would instead govern Indians by federal policy, acts of Congress, and presidential orders.

Great Indian leaders in history, such as Chief Joseph of the Nez Perce, Sitting Bull and Crazy Horse of the Sioux, Geronimo of the Apache, and many others, are remembered for their steadfast resistance to being placed on Indian reservations and becoming wards of the federal government. Chief Joseph expressed a common view of his time when he said in 1879:

> Treat all men alike. Give them all the same law. Give them all an even chance to live and grow. All men were made by the same Great Spirit Chief. They are all brothers. The mother Earth is the Mother of all people, and people should have equal rights upon it. We only ask an even chance to live as other men live.[7]

In 1887, the federal government too decided that attempting to keep Indian tribes separate from the rest of American civilization was not a good idea. The Board of Indian Commissioners wrote in its recommendations to Congress:

> No good reason can be given for not placing . . . [Indians] under the same government as other people of the States . . . where they live. No distinction ought to be made between Indians and other races with respect to rights or duties. No peculiar and expensive machinery of justice is needed. The provisions of law in the several States . . . are ample both for civil and criminal procedure, and the places of punishment for offenses are as good for Indians as for white men.[8]

These words resonate even more today, 135 years after the Civil War resulted in the end of black slavery and 35 years after the civil rights movement ended a separate status for black Americans. Yet America still maintains race-based tribal courts, tribal laws, tribal sovereign immunity, and a policy of tribal "self-governance," cutting off reservation Indians and non-Indians from equal justice under law.

In 1887, Congress passed the Dawes Act, also called the General Allotment Act, with the idea that Indians would fare better living as full citizens and individual members of society rather than as members of tribes. Under the Dawes Act, reservation lands held by the federal government were divided into parcels for individual Indian families after they were deemed "competent" to handle their own affairs. The stated intent was to merge Indians into American society and to give them the means, through land ownership, of being self-sufficient members of the larger community. When all reservation land had been allotted or sold, the plan was then to abolish the BIA and thus eliminate federal bureaucratic control over Indian life.[9]

The "allotment era" lasted approximately fifty years, during which time tribal land holdings fell from 138 million acres in 1887 to 48 million acres in 1934.[10] Many Indians lost title to their property because their land was arid or untillable or because they were for other reasons unable to make a living for themselves or pay taxes. But allotment also allowed many individual Indians to own land, support themselves through farming, become U.S. citizens, and be active members of the larger community instead of relying on federal handouts for survival.

In 1924, the Indian Citizenship Act extended national and state citizenship to all Indians born within the territorial limits of the United States who were not already citizens and granted them the right to vote. This Act should have made Indians equal to all other citizens of the United States, with the same Constitutional protections, rights, and responsibilities. But the federal government has continued to treat Indians separately from other citizens, especially if they live on reservations.

In 1933, John Collier became commissioner of the BIA under President Franklin D. Roosevelt. Collier initiated a new federal Indian policy called the "Indian New Deal," which became law as the 1934 Wheeler-Howard Act, also known as the Indian Reorganization Act. Collier admired Chinese communism, which he saw as a model for society. He wanted to implement these communist ideals on American Indian reservations, including communal ownership of property and central control of economic, political, and cultural activities.[11] Many of these key aspects of the Indian Reorganization Act are still in effect on reservations today.

The Indian Reorganization Act moved away from assimilation, again made Indians wards of the federal government, and provided for placing previously allotted land back into federal trust, with the federal government, not Indian people, holding the title. The law also provided a means through which tribes that did not have a reservation could gain federal recognition and reestablish reservation lands. Under the Indian Reorganization Act, reservations expanded an estimated 7.6 million acres between 1933 and 1950,[12] and BIA authority, programs, and staff were also expanded. Today, there are approximately 53 million acres of land in federal trust status for Indian tribes.[13]

After World War II, President Dwight D. Eisenhower established a "termination policy" in which the "trust responsibility" of the federal government to maintain Indian tribes would be terminated. The resolution that put this policy into effect stated: "It is the policy of Congress as rapidly as possible, to make the Indians within the territorial limits of the United States subject to the same laws and entitled to the same privileges and responsibilities as are applicable to other citizens of the United States, to end their status as wards of the United States."[14] Full integration was once again the stated federal policy toward Indians.

Under the termination policy, tribes could continue to exist as they chose, but federal supervision of Indian lands, resources, and tribal affairs would end, and the BIA and Indian reservations would eventually cease to exist.[15] In 1953, there were 179 federally recognized tribes.[16] By 1970, when the termination policy unofficially ended, almost 100 tribes, with an approximate total tribal membership of only 13,000 (less than 2 percent of the total Indian population), had their relationship to the federal government terminated.[17] Few tribal members were actually affected by the termination policy, owing largely to resistance in Congress to implement it.

The federal Indian Claims Commission, which existed from 1946 to 1977, paid $880 million to a number of tribes as compensation for instances in which tribes had not received fair compensation for lands they sold to the United States in the nineteenth century. Tribes made over 500 claims before the Indian Claims Commission and won awards in 60 percent of them. Most were property rights claims.[18]

Modern Times: Lack of Accountability in Tribal Governments

The idea that Indian tribes should "govern themselves" as they wish has romantic appeal, but, in practice, tribal sovereignty and self-governance have created many problems.

"The accumulation of all powers—legislative, executive, and judiciary—in the same hands, may justly be pronounced the very definition of tyranny," wrote James Madison, a founding father of the U.S. Constitution.[19] Today, the biggest exploiters and abusers of Indian people are tribal governments, in part because there is no guaranteed or enforceable separation of powers in tribal governments. Many of the largest and best-known American Indian tribes have rampant, continuous, and on-going problems with corruption, abuse, violence, or discord. There is a lack of oversight and controls in tribal governments. Most tribes do not give their members audited financial statements of tribal funds or casino funds, which on many reservations may represent tens or even hundreds of thousands of dollars per tribal member. It is literally impossible for tribal members to find out where all the money is going.

The underlying problem is that true democracy does not exist on Indian reservations. Tribal elections are often not free and fair elections, and typically they are not monitored by any third party. And true democracy includes more than just the presence of an election process. Democracy is also defined by limiting the power of the government by such things as the rule of law, separation of powers, checks on the power of each branch of government, equality under the law, impartial courts, *due process*, and protection of the basic liberties of speech, assembly, press, and property.[20] None of these exist on most Indian reservations.

Tribal chief executives and tribal councils possess near-dictatorial control over tribal members. Not only do they control the tribal court, police, and flow of money, but they also control which tribal members get homes, jobs, and health care services, and under the Indian Child Welfare Act, they can claim more control over children who are enrolled members than the children's own family, especially non-Indian family members. If they live on a reservation, Indian people who speak up run the risk of losing their homes, jobs, health care, and other services, making internal government reform even more difficult.

Some try to justify tribal government abuses and denial of civil rights by arguing that tribal members "consent" to being governed by the tribe and therefore willingly give up some of their inherent rights of citizenship. But if asked, the vast majority of tribal members never consented to any such thing.

Unfortunately, many Indian people who remain on the reservation either do not see themselves as having much choice, owing to personal addictions, depression, poverty, and despair, or because they are themselves benefiting from the unaccountable tribal system. Most of those who are in between these two extremes have left the reservation.

With many tribes claiming expanded jurisdiction and regulatory authority, including zoning, licensing, and taxing authority within long-extinguished former reservation boundaries, many non-Indians, too, are finding themselves subject to unaccountable tribal governments, without their consent and without a right to vote in tribal government elections.

The issue of consent might be relevant if tribes were simply membership organizations like any other religious, cultural, or community group, in which it can be assumed that if you don't want to be part of the group, you don't join. But the federal policy of the past thirty years, as described by the American Indian Policy Review Commission, has been to expand tribes from being membership organizations to being literal governments sanctioned by the United States, with actual legal authority over people who may or may not have given their consent to being governed. This expanding authority of tribal governments is dangerous to the rights and freedoms of Indian people.

Congressman Lloyd Meeds (D-Washington), wrote in his dissent attached to the American Indian Policy Review Commission's Final Report in 1977:

> The blunt fact of the matter is that American Indian tribes are not a third set of governments in the American federal system. They are not sovereigns. . . . It is clear that nothing in the United States Constitution guarantees to Indian tribes sovereignty or prerogatives of any sort. . . . To the extent tribal Indians exercise powers of self-government in these United States, they do so because Congress permits it. . . . American Indian tribal governments have only those powers granted them by the Congress.[21]

In spite of the American Indian Policy Review Commission's Final Report in 1977 laying out increased tribal "self-determination," "sovereignty," and "self-governance" as solutions to problems plaguing Indian reservations, in spite of the 1988 National Indian Gaming Regulatory Act, and in spite of the thirty-year push for increased tribal governmental power, the statistics show that life is getting worse for Indian people on reservations. Many news stories of late have documented shocking rates of murder, suicide, and violent assault, exceeding even that of the nation's core cities.[22] Claims of tribal sovereign immunity present additional problems. There are numerous cases of tribal casino patrons being injured or abused, businesses contracting with tribal casinos not getting paid for their services, and tribal casino workers being harassed and threatened, with no legal recourse. Any other business can be held accountable for such misdeeds in a state or federal court. But by claiming tribal sovereign immunity, tribal casinos have become the only businesses in the entire world that can totally avoid legal responsibility and liability within the United States.[23]

Many articles describe in detail the problems of trying to get anything resembling a fair hearing in tribal courts, which are not guaranteed to be separate from the tribal administration, where judges may not know anything about the law, where decisions are likely not documented, where *due process* is typically nonexistent, and where cases frequently don't even get a hearing because of claims of tribal sovereign immunity.[24] Yet many well-intentioned advocates for Indian causes mistakenly believe that increased tribal government rights is the same as protecting the rights of Indian people. Nothing could be further from the truth. Past civil rights movements provide lessons for the present. The late Hubert H. Humphrey, former U.S. senator, vice president, and presidential candidate, said in his famous civil rights speech fifty years ago at the 1948 Democratic National Convention: "There are those who say this issue of civil rights is an infringement on states rights. The time has arrived for the Democratic Party to get out of the shadow of state's rights and walk forthrightly into the bright sunshine of human rights."[25] Replace the word *state* with the word *tribe*, and you get a statement many Indians and non-Indians wish they would hear from their leaders today: "There are those who say this issue of civil rights is an infringement of *tribal* rights. The time has arrived to get out of the shadow of *tribal* rights and walk forthrightly into the bright sunshine of human rights."

The U.S. Supreme Court has in recent years expressed concern about the lack of controls on tribal sovereign immunity, including in May 1998 in its ruling in *Kiowa Tribe of Oklahoma v. Manufacturing Technologies*. Even as they upheld tribal sovereign immunity, the majority wrote:

> Though the doctrine of tribal [sovereign] immunity is settled law and controls this case, we note that it developed almost by accident. . . . [The 1919 precedent-setting case of] *Turner* . . . is but a slender reed for supporting the principle of tribal sovereign immunity. . . . Later cases, albeit with little analysis, reiterated the doctrine. . . . There are reasons to doubt the wisdom of perpetuating the doctrine. [W]e defer to the role Congress may wish to exercise in this important judgment.[26]

In this 6-3 decision, the minority was adamant about the need for limiting tribal sovereign immunity:

> Why should an Indian tribe enjoy broader immunity than the States, the Federal Government, and foreign nations? [The Court] . . . does not even arguably present a legitimate basis for concluding that the Indian tribes retained or, indeed, ever had any sovereign immunity for off-reservation commercial conduct. . . . [This] rule is unjust. . . . Governments, like individuals, should pay their debts and should be held accountable for their unlawful, injurious conduct.[27]

Through *Kiowa*, the U.S. Supreme Court has in effect sent an open letter to Congress asking them to correct the legal quagmire, confusion, and rank injustice of tribal sovereign immunity.

Minnesota Appeals Court Judge R. A. (Jim) Randall, in his eloquent and thoughtful dissent in *Sylvia Cohen v. Little Six, Inc. (Mystic Lake Casino)*, outlined the way Indian people are being wronged by current federal Indian policies and Indian laws, which give power to tribal governments at the expense of Indian people:

> Why here, are we tolerating segregating out the American Indians by race and allowing them to maintain a parallel court system and further, subjecting non-Indians to it? . . . The American Indian will never be fully integrated into this state, nor into this country, until we recognize this dual citizenship for what it really is, a pancake makeup coverup of *Plessy* which allowed separate but equal treatment. [*Plessy*, 163 U.S. at 551, 16 S. Ct at 1143 (holding that "equal but separate accommodations for the white and colored races" for railroad passengers was constitutional).] . . .
>
> We should have learned by now that this duality in America is so intrinsically evil, so intrinsically wrong, so intrinsically doomed for failure, that we must grit our teeth and work through it. . . .
>
> All bona fide residents of Minnesota, of all races and colors, enjoy identical opportunities for self-determination and self-governance. . . . Why is there this need to single out a class of people by race and give them a double dose of self-determination, and self-governance? . . . Are American Indians entitled to more self-determination than Minnesota gives to its other residents? . . . How can a state give more than it possesses? If this is deemed a federal issue, how does the federal government give more than it possesses? . . . Does that make Indians separate but equal? I suggest that *Brown v. Board of Education* will tell us this is a bad idea, a vicious and humiliating idea. Do we label Indians separate but more equal? . . . Do we label Indians separate but less equal? . . .
>
> [T]his issue, is about the future of the United States, and the future of the American Indian. This case is about whether we accept the American Indian as a full U.S. citizen, as a real American, or whether we will continue to sanctify tiny enclaves within a state and tell the individual Indian that if he or she stays there and does not come out and live with the rest of us, we will bless them with the gift of "sovereignty." . . .
>
> For some reason, we continue to insist that American Indians can be the

last holdout, a race that is not entitled to be brought into the fold, can be left to shift for themselves as long as, from time to time, we pat them on the head like little children and call them sovereign. Sovereignty is just one more indignity, one more outright lie, that we continue to foist on American citizens, the American Indian.[28]

Conclusion: Preserving
Our Cultural Past and Future

The nineteenth century view of "assimilation" envisioned that people would be accepted into mainstream American life only if they looked and acted like white Christians. That is quite different from the modern view of "integration," in which people are allowed into mainstream culture even as they maintain their own cultural traditions and identity within racial, ethnic, or religious groups.

The U.S. Constitution provides the greatest opportunity in the world for groups of people to preserve their cultures, religions, and identities, through its protections of speech, assembly, press, and religion. Ironically, the only place Indian people are *not* guaranteed these rights is on an Indian reservation. By denying Indian citizens basic civil rights, tribal governments' claims to sovereign immunity have done more to destroy tribal culture than to preserve it.

Preserving and living one's culture is one's own business. There are many unique groups within the United States, all preserving their own beliefs and cultures as they wish, and our government bends over backwards to protect their right to be different, whether it's the Amish, Mormons, Italians, Moonies, Pagans, Irish, Baptists, Roman Catholics, Greeks, Hassidic Jews, Nation of Islam, Swedes, or any manner of extremist, fundamentalist, traditionalist, or nonconformist. As Americans, we have the right to identify with a group and maintain a unique culture, to greater or lesser degrees, as we wish. Why would Indians and tribes be entitled to anything different?

As Judge Randall wrote in his dissent in *Cohen*:

There is nothing that Indian people are entitled to as human beings that cannot be afforded them through the normal process of accepting them as brother and sister citizens. . . .

The truly important goals of protecting Indian culture, Indian spirituality, self-determination, their freedom, and their way of life can be done within the same framework and the same system, by which we treat all other Minnesotans of all colors. The real issue is, do we have the will?"[29]

It is time to end the Noble Savage Mentality that keeps tribes in the ambiguous, inconsistent, and untenable position of being simultaneously wards of the federal government, domestic dependent nations, and supposedly sovereign nations. Indian people, whether tribal members or not, should be recognized as full U.S. citizens with all the rights, responsibilities, and protections thereof, nothing more and nothing less.

Notes

Julie Shortridge, managing editor of the *Native American Press/Ojibwe News*, contributed to this essay.

1. Bureau of the Census, U.S. Dept. of Commerce, *American Indian and Alaska Native Areas: 1990* (1991).

2. Ibid.

3. U.S. Supreme Court, *U.S. v. Kagama*, 118 U.S., at 375 (1886).

4. Vine Deloria Jr., *Custer Died for Your Sins* (New York: Macmillan, 1969), p. 32.

5. Francis P. Prucha, *American Indian Treaties: A History of a Political Anomaly* (Los Angeles: University of California Press, 1994), p. 153.

6. Charles Kappler, ed., *Indian Treaties 1778–1883* (New York: Interland Publishing, 1972), Wyandot Treaty of 1855, art. 1, p. 677.

7. Helen Addison Howard and Dan L. McGrath, *War Chief Joseph* (Lincoln: University of Nebraska Press, 1941), pp. 298–99.

8. *Board of Indian Commissioners: Annual Report*, 1887.

9. *Commission of Indian Affairs: Annual Report*, 1890.

10. *Editorial Research Reports*, April 15, 1977.

11. John Collier, *From Every Zenith* (Denver: Sage Books, 1963).

12. J. P. Kinney, *A Continent Lost—A Civilization Won: Indian Land Tenure in America* (Baltimore: Johns Hopkins Press, 1937), p. 351.

13. "Federal Lands: Information on the Acreage, Management, and Use of Federal and Other Lands," *Letter Report* (GAO-RCED-96-104, 1996).

14. Ruth Packwood Scofield, *Americans Behind the Buckskin Curtain* (New York: Carlton Press, 1992), House Concurrent Resolution 108, p. 93.

15. Theodore W. Taylor, *American Indian Policy* (Mt. Airy, Md.: Lomond Publications, 1983), p.106.

16. John R. Wunder, *Retained by the People: A History of American Indians and the Bill of Rights* (New York: Oxford University Press, 1994), p. 100.

17. Congress of the United States, *American Indian Policy Review Commission: Final Report* (Washington, D.C.: U.S. Government Printing Office, 1977), p. 451.

18. Congress of the United States, *Indian Claims Commission: Final Report* (Washington, D.C.: U.S. Government Printing Office, 1977), p. 21.

19. Michael Loyd Chadwick, ed., *The Federalist* (Washington, D.C.: Global Affairs, 1987), p. 260; James Madison, paper no. 47, "Separation of Power Essential for the Preservation of Liberty."

20. Fareed Zakaria, "The Rise of Illiberal Democracy," *Foreign Affairs*, November–December, 1997.

21. Lloyd Meeds, dissent, Congress of the United States, *American Indian Policy Review Commission: Final Report*. Meeds was vice chairman of the commission.

22. Debra Weyermann, "And Then There Were None," *Harper's*, April 1998.

23. Craig Greenberg, oral testimony, U.S. Senate, Indian Affairs Committee, April 7, 1998.

24. See, e.g., Pat Doyle, "Sovereign and Immune, Tribes Often Can't be Touched in Court," *Minneapolis Star Tribune*, July 24, 1995; Alice Sherren Brommer, "Should You Become Tribally Licensed?" *Minnesota Lawyer*, November 1, 1999; Bill Lawrence, "Tribal Injustice: The Red Lake Court of Indian Offenses," *North Dakota Law Review* 48, no. 4 (summer 1972): 639–59.

25. Hubert H. Humphrey, speech on civil rights at the 1948 Democratic Convention, as reprinted in the *St. Paul Pioneer Press*, June 14, 1998.

26. U.S. Supreme Court, *Kiowa Tribe of Oklahoma v. Manufacturing Technologies, Inc.*, majority opinion, May 26, 1998.

27. Ibid., minority opinion, May 26, 1998.

28. Minnesota Court of Appeals, *Sylvia Cohen v. Little Six, Inc., d/b/a/ Mystic Lake Casino*, file no. C9501701, February 13, 1995, pp. D47–D62.

29. Ibid., pp. D42–D62.

The Battle for
Color-Blind Public Policy

C. ROBERT ZELNICK

IN NO STATE was the liberal Democratic tide more evident on November 2, 1998, than in Washington. There, Senator Patty Murray, widely believed to be in jeopardy in her race against Representative Linda Smith, a conservative Republican, sailed to reelection with 58 percent of the vote. Democrats unseated Republicans in two of the state's congressional districts, bringing their total to six of Washington's nine House seats. A bid by "Right to Life" advocates to ban so-called "partial-birth" abortions was voted down handily.

That makes all the more remarkable the victory of Initiative 200, the move to end race preferences in public education, employment, and contracting. The measure, patterned after California's Proposition 209—adopted by that state's voters in 1996—captured 59 percent of the vote. Only in Houston's 1997 referendum did voters reject a ban on race preferences, and here opponents of the measure, led by Mayor Bob Lanier, so distorted the language on the ballot that the result was thrown out in court and a new vote ordered. The result in Washington is thus further evidence that when voters are presented with a clearly defined, up or down decision on race preferences, they will vote "no."

Further, the effort in Washington faced obstacles far more formidable than those that confronted backers of the California proposition. For one thing, in California the political and economic resources of the two sides were relatively equal. Governor Pete Wilson supported the measure and was able to pressure many big corporate opponents to keep their mouths and their wallets out of the fight. And though opposition groups still mounted an impressive campaign, the state Republican establishment, looking for some activity more rewarding than attempting to elect Bob Dole, campaigned actively for passage of the proposition.

In Washington, Democratic Governor Gary Locke was a fervent opponent of the antipreference measure and, as the *Seattle Times* reported, "implored corporate leaders to fight I-200 with their clout and the checkbooks." Among those making major contributions to the anti-I-200 campaign were Boeing, Microsoft, Hewlett-Packard, Costico, and Starbucks. According to the *Seattle Times*, in late July, "Eddie Bauer President and CEO Rick Fersch invited dozens of executives from the technology, communications, manufacturing and retail fields to his Redmond headquarters to discuss ways to defeat I-200." The group was treated to a guest lecture by Andrew Young, Jimmy Carter's U.N. ambassador and a long-time player in Georgia politics. In the end, opponents of I-200 outspent supporters by roughly four to one.

Yet opponents of race preferences can take only limited solace from the Washington vote. The very fact that Initiative 200 was able to prevail in spite of strong political currents moving from right to left makes it clear that many who supported it aligned themselves with liberal Democrats in other contests. This would suggest a lack of intensity to the opposition to preferences, an unwillingness on the part of many voters to withhold support from candidates simply because they disagree with them on the preference question. A similar assessment flows from the California vote, where the same electorate that adopted Proposition 209 overwhelmingly supported Bill Clinton and Al Gore Jr. over Bob Dole and Jack Kemp. Two years later California Democrats recaptured control of the governor's mansion and both houses of the legislature.

To this extent, opposition to race preferences is atypical. Social issues are often the defining issues of political campaigns, often disrupting traditional patterns of party allegiance. The same voter who will cast one vote against race preferences and another for a candidate endorsing them probably would have been far less likely during the 1970s or 1980s to engage in similar "ticket splitting" with respect to such issues as abortion, crime control, school busing, and welfare reform. These issues created millions of "Reagan Democrats" two decades ago. Race preferences are doing nothing remotely similar today.

Indeed, further analysis of the two votes might well suggest that the presence of antipreference initiatives on the ballots brings large numbers of voters to the polls who not only support preferences but also regard the issue as a litmus test for other candidates on the ballot. If so, this would call into question the efficacy of "Prop 209" type initiatives as a political strategy. To win on the referendum but lose valuable executive or legislative offices would be a trade-off even many opponents of race preferences might be unwilling to make. The frosty reception accorded advocates of a new antipreference initiative by Republican Governor Jeb Bush of Florida underscores this sentiment.

Another sign that elected officials in much of the country feel that defying majority sentiment on race preferences carries no political price came earlier in 1998. In March, the U.S. Senate approved a 10 percent minority set-aside in federal contracts under the Interstate Transportation Emergency Act (ISTEA), in spite of a growing body of judicial precedent holding such targets unconstitutional. The Departments of Justice and Transportation blandly assured the Congress that new regulations implementing the set-asides were designed to comply with the judicial concerns expressed in earlier cases.

In May, the House weighed in, rejecting by a hefty 249–171 vote the "Riggs Amendment," which would have effectively banned race preferences in admissions to state universities. The two votes were instructive. Not only will Congress refuse to undo racial preference programs already on the books, but it will also endorse efforts to reshape programs to skirt judicial holdings of unconstitutionality—all this in the face of polling data that show opposition to such preferences by a clear majority. To repeat: senators and representatives plainly have concluded that they can defy majority public sentiment on this issue and still keep their seats.

Consider, too, the position on the issue of Vice President Al Gore. Gore is far less circumspect in his support for race preferences than President Clinton, and far less reticent about seeking to demonize those who disagree with him. Clinton has long voiced caution about the wisdom and effects of preferences, saying early in his presidency that they produced few results and were difficult to justify. When he finally embraced the "mend it, don't end it" approach to affirmative action in 1995, preempting a primary challenge by Jesse Jackson appears to have been his chief aim. Former Clinton strategist George Stephanopoulos explained at Harvard during the Kennedy School's postmortem on the 1996 campaign that the administration felt Jackson would have entered the race had Clinton not moved on the issue as he did.

Clinton has been unerringly civil in discussing his support for affirmative action and most tolerant of those who have reached contrary positions. Gore has been substantially less so. Nowhere was the contrast between the two more evident than at a December 1997 White House meeting with a distinguished group of opponents of race preferences, including Ward Connerly, Abigail and Stephan Thernstrom, Linda Chavez, and Representative Charles Canady. Clinton again stated his philosophical difficulties with the race preferences and noted that they tend to benefit those "who are at least in a position for it to work." Moments later, he added, "A lot of the people that I care most about are totally unaffected by it one way or another."

Gore first chose to lecture the group on how inherent group antagonisms that are evident around the world justify protecting African Americans in the United States. He cited the ethnic hatred in Bosnia (where both sides are white), the "rape of Nanking" fifty years ago (committed by Asians against Asians), and the near-genocide in Rwanda of the Tutsis by the Hutus (where blacks slaughtered blacks). "I think that people are prone to be with people like themselves, to hire people who look like themselves, to live near people who look like themselves," he said. "And yet in our society we have this increasing diversity, we have community value, a national interest in helping to overcome this inherent vulnerability to prejudice."

That formulation runs counter to repeated Supreme Court pronouncements that quotas and other preferences cannot be invoked as a remedy for general societal discrimination. It also invites the task of allocating benefits among dozens of potential ethnic and racial claimants, a task government is ill equipped to perform. Are the Hispanics who come to this country, legally and illegally, in search of economic opportunity entitled to their cut of the quota pie upon arrival? What about the children of Vietnamese boat people? Or descendants of Japanese interned during World War II? Or Chinese, treated as railroad-building coolies and denied the legitimacy of citizenship?

One month after that White House session, Gore spoke at a ceremony commemorating the birth of Martin Luther King Jr. at the Ebinezer Baptist Church in Atlanta where King once preached. No longer were opponents of racial preferences well-intentioned people with whom there was a difference of opinion. Now they were evildoers trying to deceive the nation. In the words of Mr. Gore:

> Yet now we hear voices in America arguing that Dr. King's struggle is over— that we've reached the Promised Land. . . . They use their color blind the way duck hunters use their duck blind. They hide behind the phrase and hope that we, like the ducks, won't be able to see through it. They're in favor of affirmative action if you can dunk a basketball or sink a three-point shot. But they're not in favor of it if you merely have the potential to be a leader of your community and bring people together, to teach people who are hungry for knowledge, to heal families who need medical care. So I say: we see through your color blind.
>
> Amazing Grace, also save me;
> Was color blind but now I see.

For the record, of course, no one associated with the battle against race preferences has, to the author's knowledge, ever disputed the wisdom of taking community leadership or service potential into consideration in the college admissions process. Nor do opponents of race preferences urge a sterile exclusive reliance on such static indicators of student success as SAT scores and high school grade point averages, although the combination of these two factors is a valid and unbiased predictor of college success. They do, however, urge that whatever the admissions standards, they be applied in a nondiscriminatory manner so far as race and ethnicity are concerned. Race is not a proxy for community leadership. Nor is race a proxy for the willingness "to teach people who are hungry for knowledge" or "to heal families who need medical care." On the contrary, the overwhelming evidence is that the best teaching and healing are done by those whose tests indicate a mastery of their subjects.

Other factors contributed to the resistance by legislators to tamper with race preferences. In California, implementation of Proposition 209 resulted in a sharp drop in the number of blacks and Hispanics at the state's elite public universities (and a corresponding increase at several less selective schools). An even more dramatic decline of blacks and Hispanics occurred at the University of Texas law and medical schools following federal court decisions outlawing the consideration of race or ethnicity in public university admissions.

In a painful reconsideration of positions long advocated, Nathan Glazer called for special treatment of black applicants to the nation's elite universities, suggesting that such access is the most certain path toward economic and social progress. His plea received curious support from the book *The Shape of the River* by educators William G. Bowen and Derek Bok—"curious" because the statistics assembled by Bowen and Bok can be read as lending support to the nub of the case against race preferences in admissions. Reviewing the experience at twenty-eight select colleges and universities, the book shows that both high school grade point average and SAT scores account for statistically significant differences in college performance through all four years and that black students at selective universities, most of whom were admitted with the help of race preferences, maintain a GPA in the 23rd percentile of their schools, a full 30 percentile places lower than whites. Moreover, they achieve significantly lower graduation rates, 75 percent versus 86 percent, again emphasizing the point that their initial admissions were based upon race rather than relative academic potential. True, a high percentage attend graduate schools, which themselves maintain race preferences in admissions, but the Bowen-Bok study fails to show any point at which minorities admitted with inferior academic credentials manage to close the performance gap vis-à-vis whites or Asians. If anything, the study documents the supreme injustice practiced against those students among the unfavored races or ethnic groups who are denied admission to make room for the preferred categories.

It is difficult to determine the legal theory under which Mr. Glazer or the authors of *The Shape of the River* would effectuate the preferences they endorse. In the 1978 *Bakke* opinion written by Justice Lewis F. Powell, the "swing" vote in the case, state universities were forbidden to establish racial quotas but could—under their historic First Amendment right to determine the composition of their student bodies—make race a "plus" factor or "tie breaker." Thus the "diversity" rationale. But the vast spread embraced by many of the most selective universities for purposes of admitting the desired number of blacks and Hispanics mocks the very notion of a "plus factor" or "tie breaker." For example, the *Wall Street Journal* reported that at the Berkeley campus of the University of California in one recent pre-209 academic year, the math SAT scores were 750 for Asians, 690 for whites, 560 for Hispanics, and 510 for blacks. At that school race was not a *plus* factor in the admission of many blacks, it was *the* factor.

Of course, neither Glazer nor Bowen and Bok offer any realistic guidance for limiting the application of such preferences once they are in place. Optimistically, Glazer would extend preferences only to blacks and only at undergraduate institutions. But group entitlements quickly become a way of life. Already they extend to ethnic groups lacking even the historic claims of blacks, and to law, medical, and other graduate schools, to employment, and to local, state, and federal contracts. Even law reviews at many of the most prestigious universities now accept black editorial board members whose competitive credentials in terms of grades and legal research ability fall short of whites turned down for the same honor. Medical schools routinely admit blacks and Hispanics whose academic credentials are significantly lower than those of whites and Asians denied admission to the same institutions. In the spring of 1998, the NAACP held a demonstration involving civil disobedience outside the Supreme Court itself because it claimed that the Justices were hiring too few black law clerks. Because these cherished positions unfailingly go on the basis of merit to the outstanding young scholars in the legal community, the NAACP move in effect demanded that the Court employ standards for its own positions that have been held unconstitutional—yet are widely practiced—elsewhere.

Perhaps the most revealing defense of race preferences was offered by Nicholas deB. Katzenbach and Burke Marshall, two Justice Department giants during the Kennedy-Johnson civil rights era. Throughout much of their article, which appeared in the February 22, 1998, *New York Times Magazine*, Katzenbach and Marshall recite pretty much the standard litany: race preferences in employment are really an effort to counter attitudinal or even subconscious discrimination; similar preferences in university admissions are grounded in the belief that "a diverse student body contributes to educational excellence and to the preparation of students to live in an integrated society." But in the end, the authors have too much intellectual integrity to maintain that an Equal Protection Clause of the Fourteenth Amendment applicable to whites could countenance the kind of race preferences they endorse. The Supreme Court has repeatedly held that under the Fourteenth Amendment racial classifications are subject to strict scrutiny. To pass muster, they must serve a compelling state interest—usually the need to remedy past discrimination against the covered individuals. And they must be narrowly tailored in terms of scope and duration to serve the compelling interest involved.

It has been by applying these standards toward the protection of whites as well as blacks that the Court in recent years has declared unconstitutional state and federal set-asides for minority government contractors and the racial gerrymandering of congressional districts to make the election of minority candidates all but certain.

Here, in the view of Katzenbach and Marshall, is where the Supreme Court has gone wrong. Whites, they maintain, are not entitled to equal protection under the Fourteenth Amendment because the historic purpose of the Amendment and its implementing legislation was to forbid "abuse of white political superiority that prejudiced other races or ethnic minorities." They write:

> Reading the Equal Protection Clause to protect whites as well as blacks from racial classification is to focus upon a situation that does not and never has existed in our society. Unfortunately, it casts doubt upon all forms of racial classification, however benign and however focused upon promoting integration. If such a reading is finally adopted by a majority of the Court, it would put a constitutional pall over all governmental affirmative action programs and even put similar private programs in danger of being labeled "discriminatory" against whites and therefore in violation of existing civil rights legislation—perhaps the ultimate stupidity.

Thus, the ultimate political question and the ultimate legal question are one. Simply stated but not oversimplified, it is whether whites and Asians in this democracy have the same constitutional rights as blacks, Hispanics, and other favored groups. That is the core issue in arguments over whether the Equal Protection Clause of the Fourteenth Amendment forbids federal, state, or local government from preferring one group or another on the basis of race or ethnicity. And it is what is meant by the argument over whether our government and our Constitution should be "color blind." A color-blind legal order is not one that naïvely denies the existence of different races with vastly different histories any more than the pronouncement in the Declaration of Independence that "all men are created equal" suggests that we are all born with similar physical strength, mental aptitude, and family wealth. Rather, a color-blind legal order is one in which the government allocates neither rights nor burdens on the basis of race or ethnicity save as a remedy for proven specific acts of official discrimination.

Nicholas deB. Katzenbach and Burke Marshall reject the notion of a color-blind society because they do not believe that the Equal Protection Clause of the Fourteenth Amendment can apply to white people or Asian Americans and still achieve the goal of uplifting blacks. Apparently, Al Gore adheres to a similar view. In his words, "I was color blind but now I see."

Here, then, is an issue worthy of national debate as well as articulation by the courts. The legislative route to erase racial preferences has, for the time being, failed. The referendum approach has produced some stunning victories, but it has not convinced voters to underline their convictions by electing representatives who share them. But the stated attempt to write whites out of the Fourteenth Amendment could concentrate the national political mind and, appropriately framed in the right case, engage the attention of the Supreme Court.

One Nation, Indivisible

WARD CONNERLY

ON JULY 20, 1995, the Regents of the University of California (UC) eliminated the consideration of race, gender, color, ethnicity, and national origin in the admissions, contracting, and employment activities of the University. Thus, UC became the first public institution in America to confront its system of preferential policies. With that action, the Regents began a new era of civil rights reform, a new way of looking at race in America, and, yet, a return to a well-established American ideal.

Coming on the heels of the UC Regents' action was the overwhelming (54 percent to 46 percent) passage of the California Civil Rights Initiative (Proposition 209) by the voters of California. Proposition 209, approved on November 5, 1996, provided that "the state shall not discriminate against, or grant preferential treatment to, any individual or group, on the basis of race, sex, color, ethnicity or national origin, in the operation of public employment, public education or public contracting."

On November 3, 1998, the electorate of the state of Washington, in an election that can only be described as remarkable, approved Initiative 200 (I-200), a clone of California's Proposition 209. I-200 was approved by a margin of 58 percent to 42 percent. What made the victory remarkable and, indeed, revealing about the matter of race in America was the number of obstacles that had to be overcome to achieve the result.

I-200 was opposed by the popular Democratic governor of Washington, the Washington Democratic Party, the largest employers in Washington—Boeing, Microsoft, U.S. Bank, Weyerhauser, Eddie Bauer Company—and those who lay claim to being civil rights champions, the Urban League, the NAACP, Jesse Jackson, Maxine Waters, and others. The initiative was also opposed by virtually every newspaper in Washington, particularly the *Seattle Times*, whose publisher donated full-page ads worth over $200,000 to defeat the measure. Vice President Al Gore made four trips to Washington to raise funds and speak out against I-200.

At this election, the voters reelected freshman Democrat Patty Murray to the U.S. Senate, ousted two-term Republican congressman Rick White, stripped control of both houses of the Washington state legislature from Republicans, defeated a measure that would have banned partial-birth abortions, and approved a measure dramatically increasing the minimum wage.

In the face of these events, I-200 received the nod from 80 percent of Republicans, 62 percent of independents, 41 percent of Democrats, 54 percent of labor, and the majority of women, in spite of a campaign barrage aimed at convincing women that the initiative would adversely affect their best interests.

The exit polls tell the story: the people of Washington had decided that the time had come to end race-based preferences. Less than 15 percent of the electorate believed that it was still appropriate to compensate black people for past wrongs. The overwhelming majority of the electorate concluded that all residents of the state should be treated equally: no discrimination and no preferences.

Why did the voters of Washington ignore the advice of politically correct big corporations, politicians, the media, and race advocates, who hid behind the moral fig leaf of "diversity" and "inclusion," and end the system of preferences and de facto quotas that have come to define affirmative action? The answer is simple. There is a deeply rooted culture of equality in America that transcends political correctness, partisanship, and ideology. We can trace this culture back to the Declaration of Independence: "We hold these truths to be self-evident, that all men are created equal."

This culture of equality was underscored by Abraham Lincoln: "Four score and seven years ago, our fathers brought forth on this continent a new nation conceived in liberty and dedicated to the proposition that all men are created equal." When Martin Luther King Jr. led the nation through the tumultuous civil rights era, beginning with the public bus boycott in Montgomery in 1955, he invoked that culture of equality in calling on America to "live out the true meaning of your creed."

The principle of equality has been embraced by liberal Democrats and conservative Republicans alike. President Lyndon Johnson said:

> Rarely are we met with a challenge, not to our growth or abundance, or our welfare or security, but rather to the values and the purpose and the meaning of our beloved nation. The issue of equal rights . . . is such an issue. And should we defeat every enemy, and should we double our wealth, and conquer the stars, and still be unequal to this issue, then we will have failed as a people and as a nation."[1]

And Ronald Reagan, in one of his last addresses to the American people, said: "We are all equal in the eyes of God. But, in America, that is not enough, we have to be equal in the eyes of each other."[2]

The debate about affirmative action preferences is fundamentally about the rights and responsibilities of American citizenship. It is about whether we will have a system of government and a social system in which we see each other as equals. Although often lost in the rhetorical clamor about its benefits, race-based affirmative action as a concept is, at its core, a challenge to the relationship between individuals and their government. It is a direct threat to the culture of equality that defines the character of the nation.

Those who support affirmative action programs contend that such programs are necessary to provide equal opportunity for women and minorities. The argument is routinely advanced that without affirmative action women and minorities will be subject to the vagaries of the "good old boys network" and will be denied the opportunity of full participation in American life. But when you strip away all the rhetoric about "leveling the playing field" and "building diversity," preferential policies reduce themselves to two essential questions.

First, are white males entitled to the same assertion of civil rights and equal treatment under the law as women and minorities? Second, how much longer is the nation going to maintain policies that presume that American-born black people are mentally inferior and incapable of competing head-to-head with other people, except in athletics and entertainment? We cannot resolve the issue of race in America without coming to terms with these two questions. And we certainly cannot reconcile the conflicts about affirmative action preferences without answering these questions. More than anything else, however, the debate about race-based preferences has focused the nation's attention on the politics of race.

The affirmative action debates in California and Washington should convince us that we cannot settle the matter of race in America without settling the issue of affirmative action. But when we resolve the issue of affirmative action, we will be laying the foundation for the kind of race relations that the nation needs in order to live out the true meaning of its creed: one nation, indivisible.

American society was conceived and has been nurtured through the years as a society of individuals. At the center of our society is the concept that we are all a minority of one. Obviously, policies that herd the American people into groups, or political enclaves, are in direct conflict with the spirit of individualism that characterizes the nation. The phrase "people of color" has come to describe the way in which race and ethnicity are being politicized in America. Implicit in this phrase is the coalescing of minorities into a coalition or political caucus, which, together with white women, constitutes a power base of sufficient magnitude to preserve race- and gender-based preferences and to achieve other political benefits for the coalition.

Every day, in every region and hamlet of America, we are witnessing the deterioration of American individualism and the ascension of political group thinking, of which preferential policies are the most visible manifestation. How does this form of identity politics play out in the broader societal context? We don't have to look far to find evidence of how individuals identify with their group as opposed to reacting to issues as individuals. The O. J. Simpson verdict illustrated the profound difference between black and white groups in their perception of the American criminal justice system. Welfare reform was another example of differences between black and white. According to some polls, over 70 percent of black people initially opposed welfare reform, while a similar percentage of white people favored reform.

The issue of the impeachment of President Clinton is yet another example of group thinking, and a vivid illustration of the difference between the perspectives of blacks and whites. For example, a January 22, 1999, Zogby poll found that nearly 67 percent of blacks thought the President's impeachment and trial should just end. Only 22 percent of whites thought this way. Nearly 30 percent of whites felt the President should be removed from office, and a mere 1 percent of blacks felt the same way. Finally, black people support affirmative action preferences by about the same percentage as white people oppose them (over 65 percent in most public opinion polls).

The result of the 1960s civil rights movement should have been the promise of equal treatment under the law for all Americans. Instead, the result has been a presumption that the very term "civil rights" is synonymous with the rights of black people. In America, we are engaged in an exciting adventure, an adventure that is unrivaled elsewhere in the world. Can we take people from around the globe, who come from different cultures, who have different religious beliefs, who embrace different political ideologies, and who are all colors of the rainbow, and assimilate their differences into a common culture and national identity?

When Thomas Jefferson and the other founders laid out this adventure, they gave their new nation a moral blueprint to make the adventure a success. The centerpiece of that blueprint is our system of moral principles. Moral principles do not change with the seasons. That is precisely why the founders proclaimed that certain truths are "self-evident" and "endowed by our Creator." They are not meant to change or to be bargained away. Our inalienable rights are the centerpiece of that moral system, and the principle of equality is central to our system of rights.

But what can the average citizen expect from such a morality-based society? The citizens of America present and future had (and have) a right to know what benefits would obtain from an adherence to fundamental moral principles. The founders did not disappoint. They envisioned a more perfect union with freedom, liberty, justice, and equality for all Americans.

So equality is directly linked to our freedoms and to our system of liberty and justice for all. Giving someone a preference, lower academic requirements, contract set-asides, or employment quotas betrays that system. Preferences based on race and ethnicity diminish the value of the individual in ways too numerous to mention and have consequences far beyond their effects on the nation's character and the harm that they do to those who are not the beneficiaries of such policies. Preferences unwittingly damage the perceived beneficiaries more than one can ever imagine, in spite of the denials of preference advocates. This occurs in two principal ways.

First, preferential policies, by their nature, require a paradigm of victims and oppressors. In a highly competitive society such as America, there is nothing more debilitating to an individual than to crush the competitive instinct. It is like taking a baby animal from its mother, domesticating it, and then turning it loose in the wilderness. The probability is high that the animal, its natural instincts to survive dulled by the process of domestication, will have a difficult time surviving in the wild. So it is with people, especially black people. Though their ancestors successfully struggled to overcome tremendous obstacles, many young blacks seem to be lacking in the area that matters most in a modern, global economy: a competitive desire and self-confidence in one's ability to compete in academic pursuits. Too many young, bright black men and women have no confidence in themselves and in the American system when the subject is education. A similar phenomenon is now occurring among Latinos. Telling them that they need affirmative action becomes a self-fulfilling prophecy.

Following a lecture at Florida State University where I had vigorously opposed preferences based on race and ethnicity, a black woman grabbed my hand and led me to a corner of the room. "I am listening to what you are saying," she said, "and you are making sense. But I have four boys, and I want to do what is best for them. What advice do I give them about race?" I said, "Tell them that they may encounter an element of racism and discrimination along life's journey, but for every act of racism, they will probably experience five acts of fairness and opportunity."

"Tell them to study, study, study to prepare themselves for the opportunities that will present themselves and build their careers around the good things that will happen. If racial obstacles confront them, go under, around, over, or blast through those obstacles. But don't let them believe that their futures are contingent upon anyone else's generosity. Make them believe in themselves and trust our system. The concept of self-reliance is the best and most enduring gift you can give them." She smiled broadly and said, "Thank you."

The major obstacle facing the average black person in America is not race; it is the attitude and approach of black people toward their role in American society. If we have any hope of moving America forward in its attitudes toward race, we must get black people to acknowledge and act upon their role in resolving this issue. This is not to suggest that black people alone can resolve the American race dilemma. Nor is it to suggest that white people have no obligation to come to terms with their role in resolving this dilemma. But too often the race dialogue centers around what "white America" must do and is totally neglectful of the role of black people.

The second effect is equally as consequential: preferences create their own "glass ceiling." I don't know why the defenders of such policies fail to acknowledge or admit the enormous effect that such policies have upon the attitudes of others. Does it ever occur to them that the reason black

people and other "minorities" are not considered for more upper management positions, even in corporations that pound their chests about "cele-
brating diversity," is that such corporations still consider "minorities" to
be inferior and noncompetitive for higher positions?

Giving people who are classified in a certain group a "leg up" stems
from the view that those individuals have limited capacity and cannot
succeed without someone else's generosity. It is easy to be "generous" when
hiring someone to be the affirmative action officer or the community
relations coordinator. That generosity ends, however, when a more responsible position becomes vacant. The person hired out of a need for
diversity or because one wants to provide affirmative action is rarely included when candidates are being considered for chief executive officer.
Too often, I have heard selection panels reply, "We have never viewed him
(or her) as suitable for that position." The reason is that affirmative action
marginalizes its beneficiaries.

The people of California and Washington have begun to grapple with
and resolve issues of race and ethnicity. It is of vital importance that the
people in the rest of the nation too begin to resolve these issues. Unless
this national reform proceeds apace, a long period of quiet turmoil in
America is likely to be the result. Ultimately, the turmoil may no longer be
quiet.

Throughout the debate about race preferences, opponents as well as
proponents summon the words of Dr. King to help make their case. Obviously, no one knows what position Dr. King would have taken on this
issue if he were alive today. There is one statement that he made, however,
that should go unchallenged, and it can serve us well in our time: "Sooner
or later all the peoples of the world, without regard to the political systems
under which they live, will have to discover a way to live together in peace."[3]

As a nation, America has got itself into one hell of a mess because of
affirmative action preferences. Some groups of people believe it is their
entitlement, whereas others are seething with anger about such programs.
If the words of Dr. King are to come true, we must end the existing system
of preferences that differentiate the American people on the basis of race,

ethnicity, and gender. Only by doing that can we rededicate our nation to the principle of equality and bring social peace and harmony to America.

Notes

1. President Johnson, Special Message to the U.S. Congress, March 15, 1965, "The American Promise."

2. Ronald Reagan, speech to the Republican National Committee, Republican Party Convention, August 17, 1992.

3. From Dr. King's Nobel Peace Prize acceptance speech, December 10, 1964 (minus the middle clause).

Index

"Ability Ranges," 298

Absentee fathers, 21, 121

Academic achievement: black poverty levels and, 261; black/white gap in, 246, 248, 259, 260, 272, 279; Charlotte-Mecklenburg plan, 239; Coleman definition, 233; expenditure per student and, 247; forced busing and, 268; math in integrated schools, 243; non-Asian minorities, 267; performance incentives, 270; racial balance and, 241, 245, 247, 254; school desegregation, 239–41, 254; SES levels and, 242

Acculturation, 45

Achievement. *See* Academic achievement

ACT, 265

Activism, political, 320

Adarand v. Peña (1995), 203, 309, 329, 331

Affirmative action, 3, 70: academic support for, 78; antipreference vote, 365–66; *Bakke* decision and, 298; bureaucracy to support, 302; college dropout rate, 278; demise of, 277; disparity studies and, 208; employment policies, 196; initiative/referendum process and, 362, 364; Latinos and, 421; medical school admission, 127; politics of race and, 418; public opinion and, 293; racial balance and, 253; racial dichotomy, 419; rationale for, 138–40, 417–18, 422; Reagan administration and, 74; Regents, UC and, 415; support by ethnic groups, 55. *See also* Initiative 200; Proposition 209

African Americans, 16, 53, 89: attitudes on discrimination, 57–58, 59; aversion to surgery, 136; changing status of, 86; college admissions, 277; decline in violent crimes, 118; fertility rates, 100, 102, 123; historical victimization and, 20–21; index of dissimilarity and, 84, 85; inrush and disenfranchisement, 348; integrated neighborhoods and, 86; migration to North, 83, 222–23, 235, 248, 350; motivation and poverty, 58; parochial schools and, 280; physician's ethnicity and, 141; poverty among, 5; as practicing physicians, 139; race relations